LEVINAS AND THE TRAUMA
OF RESPONSIBILITY

STUDIES IN CONTINENTAL THOUGHT

John Sallis, editor

CONSULTING EDITORS

Robert Bernasconi
John D. Caputo
David Carr
Edward S. Casey
David Farrell Krell
Lenore Langsdorf

James Risser
Dennis J. Schmidt
Calvin O. Schrag
Charles E. Scott
Daniela Vallega-Neu
David Wood

LEVINAS AND THE TRAUMA OF RESPONSIBILITY
The Ethical Significance of Time

Cynthia D. Coe

Indiana University Press

This book is a publication of

Indiana University Press
Office of Scholarly Publishing
Herman B Wells Library 350
1320 East 10th Street
Bloomington, Indiana 47405 USA

iupress.indiana.edu

© 2018 by Cynthia D. Coe

All rights reserved

No part of this book may be reproduced or utilized in any form or by any means, electronic or mechanical, including photocopying and recording, or by any information storage and retrieval system, without permission in writing from the publisher. The Association of American University Presses' Resolution on Permissions constitutes the only exception to this prohibition.

⊗ The paper used in this publication meets the minimum requirements of the American National Standard for Information Sciences—Permanence of Paper for Printed Library Materials, ANSI Z39.48-1992.

Manufactured in the United States of America

Cataloging information is available from the Library of Congress.

ISBN 978-0-253-03196-9 (cloth)
ISBN 978-0-253-03197-6 (pbk.)
ISBN 978-0-253-03198-3 (e-bk.)

1 2 3 4 5 23 22 21 20 19 18

Contents

	Acknowledgments	vii
	Introduction	ix
	Abbreviations	xxi
1	Deformalizing Time	1
2	The Traumatic Impact of Deformalized Time	19
3	The Method of An-Archeology	39
4	Between Theodicy and Despair	73
5	The Sobering Up of Oedipus	101
6	Anxieties of Incarnation	129
7	Rethinking Death on the Basis of Time	159
8	Animals and Creatures	187
	Conclusion: Inheriting the Thought of Diachrony	219
	Bibliography	233
	Index	245

Acknowledgments

AN EARLIER VERSION of chapter 5 was published as "The Sobering Up of Oedipus: Levinas and the Trauma of Responsibility" in *Angelaki: A Journal of Theoretical Humanities* 18, no. 4 (December 2013). An earlier version of chapter 6 was published as "Contesting the Human: Levinas, the Body, and Racism," in *Epoché: A Journal for the History of Philosophy* 11, no. 1 (Fall 2006). Many thanks for the editors' permission to publish revised versions here.

I also owe a debt of gratitude to: Matt Altman, whose encouragement, editing skills, fellow parenting, and good sense have made this book very much better than it might otherwise have been; Paul Davies, Arnold Davidson, and Cheyney Ryan, who each had a key role in introducing me to the work of Emmanuel Levinas; Central Washington University, for granting me a sabbatical during the 2014–15 academic year, to Graduate Studies for their support of my scholarship, and my colleagues in the Department of Philosophy and Religious Studies and the Women's and Gender Studies Program, for letting me focus only on writing while they did the hard work of teaching, advising, filling out curriculum forms, and so on; my students, especially those in two courses where some of the ideas for chapters 4 and 5 initially arose: an interdisciplinary honors seminar called Trauma: Memory, History, and Identity, and a philosophy seminar on The Problem of Evil. I appreciate their grappling with these somber ideas thoughtfully and (mostly) cheerfully; and my parents.

Introduction
Intrigues of Time

The image on the cover of this book is a photograph of plaster casts and masks made in the studio of sculptor Anna Coleman Ladd for French World War I veterans who had suffered facial wounds. Fred Albee, an American surgeon who treated soldiers in that war, noted that the way that the war was fought, including the relatively new military technology of machine guns, made soldiers more vulnerable to such wounds: "soldiers failed to understand the menace of the machine gun. They seemed to think they could pop their heads up over a trench and move quickly enough to dodge the hail of bullets."[1] After multiple surgeries, soldiers' faces would often be so disfigured that interacting with other people or catching sight of their own reflections would cause further psychological distress. In British hospitals that treated these patients, mirrors were banned, and benches outside the hospital were painted blue to warn passersby that it might be upsetting to look at anyone sitting there. Between 1917 and 1918, under the auspices of the Red Cross, Ladd and her staff sculpted almost two hundred masks, designed to allow veterans to go out in public (and, in at least one soldier's case, to return home to his mother) without provoking revulsion and fear. The sculptors at the Studio for Portrait Masks would talk with each soldier, study photographs of the soldiers' faces before their injuries, and ascertain their remaining range of facial expressions. A plaster cast was the basis for a copper mask, which would then be painted to match the man's skin (balanced between the tone on a sunny day and on a cloudy day) and to represent a typical expression. Sometimes a mustache would be attached, and a pair of glasses would hold the mask to the person's face. These masks are palimpsests of the face in its vulnerability and its ethical demand; they simultaneously mark and cover over a wounded face.

Emmanuel Levinas lived through World War I as a child, although his life in Lithuania and then the Ukraine was much more directly impacted by the Russian Revolution and its aftermath. However, Franz Rosenzweig, one of the major influences on his thought, wrote *The Star of Redemption* while serving in the German trenches during the last stages of the war and in an army hospital immediately following the end of the war. In that text, Rosenzweig vehemently rejects the idealist neglect of the human being as a finite and unique individual. Levinas repeatedly gestures to Rosenzweig's critique of Hegel in contrasting totality and infinity, where infinity is the transcendence of the singular other. Totality categorizes individuals in order to incorporate them into a larger system, whereas Levinas argues that ethics begins from attending to the singularity of the other person—her uncategorizability.[2] Levinas discusses this singularity with reference to the face, in all its sensitivity and exposure. But the face for Levinas is not a phenomenon that lends itself to representation, although portraits can be painted, photographs can be used for identification, and masks that reconstruct one's uninjured face can be sculpted. In its immediacy, the face imposes the command "Thou shalt not kill," and that command forbids both physical violence and the violence that assimilates the other into a mere idea, a set of characteristics that makes no particular claim on the observer. Levinas recognizes that such a command does not prevent violence—"murder . . . is a banal fact"—but in a moral sense the face resists it (EI 87; see "Abbreviations" for definitions of this and other terms). In an interview, Philippe Nemo notes that "it is difficult to kill someone who looks straight at you," and Levinas responds that "the face is meaning all by itself. . . . It is what cannot become a content, which your thought would embrace; it is uncontainable" (EI 86–87). The mask is a representation of a face, which hides its vulnerability, and a trace of wounds.

Levinas's project should be read with the same duality in mind, in the sense that he tries to indicate both the trauma of responsibility and the limits of that conceptualization. This is the "subtle ambiguity" that he notes between "the individual and the unique . . . the mask and the face" (OUJ 229). The obliqueness of his discourse attempts to do justice to that ambiguity. Levinas's insistence that the meaning of the face is not contained in its physical attributes runs counter to Ladd's careful attention to reconstructing the shape of an injured soldier's jaw or nose and to painting the mask with an expression that reflected the individuality of each person. His point is also that the face in general, not specifically a wounded face, disturbs our ordinary representation of the world. But the plaster casts and masks, at least one step removed from the immediacy of the face, and the photographic representation of those objects, one further step removed, still evoke the "ethical resistance" of the face (TI 199). It is difficult to look at them simply as historical artifacts of the war, as pieces of medical equipment, or as sculptures. The representations lead back to the exposure that Levinas argues we experience in the face of the other. We may try to "mask [the] poverty" and exposedness of the face "by putting on poses, by taking on a countenance," but such a facade gestures to the face itself (EI 86). To be addressed by the face, I cannot study it as a specimen or catalog its features or take aim at it across a battlefield, but the face is always susceptible to such reductions. Indeed, to engage in philosophical discourse about the face is to trade in representations of it. Levinas's challenge is how to sustain the ethical force of alterity even as he describes it.

In his later work, Levinas shifts from speaking of the other as the excessive presence of the face to using the language of the trace, by which the other escapes conceptualization by never being fully present but instead only leaving marks of its passing in the present. The face is never present as just one perception among others. It instead imposes an obligation on the subject, and Levinas uses temporal language to express the sense in which the subject cannot avoid that obligation. The demand arises out of an "immemorial past," a source that cannot be represented and thus subjected to scrutiny (OB 89). As a trace, the face addresses the subject as a remnant of something past, but it makes a claim on the subject precisely because of this temporal distance. The claim is made before I analyze the source of the claim and judge its legitimacy, and hence the other resists my powers of representation. Time in its passing takes on ethical significance in Levinas's thought, by exposing the subject to the other without the protection of understanding or anticipation. I can return to reflect on the moment at which I encounter another's face, or represent that face through various media, but for Levinas, this process can only ever indirectly reflect the binding quality of that exposure to the other. A trace is susceptible to being converted into a sign, which lends itself to the conceptualizing activity of consciousness, but the trace is also the disturbance of that activity.

Ladd's plaster casts and masks are traces of wounds sustained now a century ago, injuries that we as viewers of them (or photographs of them, which are all that remain) cannot possibly have inflicted. The events of the past century or the past hour cannot be affected by any choice that we could make in the present; in some sense those events no longer exist and have passed us by. What can these soldiers' wounds be to us, beyond medical curiosities or reminders of the general brutality of war? But responsibility in Levinas's sense of that term allows us no such detachment or indifference. His fundamental project is the undoing of the presupposition that the ego is concerned only with itself and finds significance only in what it can represent. It is also the undoing of the wide-ranging implications of that presupposition in modern Western cultures. Instead, he argues that the claim of the other weighs on us before we have time to assert our innocence. What it means to be a subject is to be for-the-other, exposed to the other prior to any intention or action. Responsibility is the "prehistory" of the self-possessed, self-absorbed ego (OB 117). The face confronts the subject with that immemorial, incomprehensible, and incontrovertible bond.

In this book, I trace the role that time plays in Levinas's understanding of responsibility, with particular attention to how his account of time ultimately contests the ideal of autonomy, as it has been understood in modern European thought. At first glance, time seems to have little connection to the questions of normativity that preoccupy Levinas, but he argues that time has ethical significance in its impact on consciousness. This book begins from the question of what it means to claim that time has ethical significance and examines the radical implications of that claim for how we conceive of subjectivity. Responsibility as

Levinas describes it is the encounter with that which refuses representation, and thus challenges the ability of consciousness to convert all that it experiences into a present object to be comprehended: "It may be that we have to unravel other intrigues of time than that of a simple succession of presents" (OB 10). Time may seem to be a simple succession of presents, whose foreignness to consciousness can be overcome through representation, but Levinas suggests that there *may be* "other intrigues of time" (*autres intrigues du temps*) that resist representation altogether. Intrigues are intricacies, complexities, and riddles that establish a level of hidden activity or meaning, but they are also entanglements in which we may find ourselves. As Levinas uses this term, we are not the conspirators who generate intrigues but instead are subjected to them. In this sense, intrigues of time are not only a resistance to consciousness but the dismantling of the subject's power. In *Otherwise than Being*, a book that cumulatively describes the intensity and unavoidability of responsibility, Levinas begins by merely raising the possibility that such a register of time exists, without presuming to bring it easily within our gaze.

The movement of time may always be reduced down into the recuperable, linear succession of present moments, but Levinas's analyses of responsibility evoke how time in its ethical significance escapes this narrative comprehension. On the one hand, time functions as the framework within which consciousness makes sense of experience and can represent it to itself, and on the other, there is a lapse of time that resists such synchronization. He refers to this second, interruptive dimension of time as "diachrony," the passing of time that resists "the recuperation of all divergencies" and the assimilation of alterity into something present to consciousness (OB 9). If comprehension comes too late to sidestep responsibility for the other, if I am already responding to the other before understanding the content of the demand or articulating its authority, this movement of time arrests the activity by which consciousness makes all events into cognitive representations that can be arrayed before the mind.

In his late writings, Levinas refers to responsibility as traumatic, an event that in its unpredictability resists representation and demonstrates the vulnerability of the subject to what lies outside of it—although even the language of internality and externality presupposes a well-bounded subject. Responsibility ultimately refers to an exposure to the other that is part of the very constitution of subjectivity. Trauma is a peculiar characterization of the opening of the ethical, given the traditional assumption that responsibility is the domain of an autonomous subject—a distinctly untraumatized subject. But Levinas refers to trauma without pursuing the rich and interdisciplinary meanings of this concept, which converge with and amplify his claims in interesting ways.

World War I is the historical event that precipitated the study of trauma as a significant medical disorder, due to large numbers of soldiers suffering from what was called shell shock or war neurosis. It is around this period that the term "trauma" begins to be used not only for physical injuries but for psychological disorders that arose in the wake of train accidents or interpersonal violence. What is now categorized as post-traumatic stress disorder is caused by experiencing or witnessing sudden and fear-inducing events, particularly those that pose a threat of severe injury, sexual violence, or death.[3] Given their characteristic symptoms of flashbacks, nightmares, and hypervigilance, traumatic events tend to unsettle a person's sense of an orderly, predictable, and meaningful world and impede the ability to tell a coherent narrative of one's life.

In light of these ideas, I use the concept of trauma to explore the connection between responsibility and time in Levinas's thought, the vulnerability of the subject and the complex temporality that structures that vulnerability. This concept also functions as a lens that puts into relief Levinas's reaction against core assumptions in the history of Western philosophy, and in particular how responsibility destabilizes a person's comfortable self-possession. From this starting point, we can map out how radically he revises what subjectivity means in dominant strains of modern Western thought—our status as moral agents, knowers, and citizens. Levinas highlights the unanticipated nature of responsibility, the way in which encountering the other makes a claim against which the self cannot protect herself. The effect of this obligation is expressed in the language of psychological wounding—trauma, persecution, obsession, the self gnawing away at herself. The temporal structure of trauma, how the suddenness of an event breaks in on an unprepared consciousness, is the core of the ego's encounter with alterity. We are wounded in the sense of being exposed to the other, and that wound precedes our ability to identify the source of that claim on us or evaluate its legitimacy. That vulnerability is unsettling, as Levinas's dramatic rhetoric makes clear, but it threatens us particularly due to a historically mediated conception of ourselves as self-possessed beings. The modern identification of subjectivity with individual autonomy needs to be supplemented and troubled by an alternative understanding of the subject, in which responsibility for the other precedes our powers of comprehension, deliberation, and free commitment.

Whatever philosophical unraveling Levinas can accomplish with regard to intrigues of time can only ever be partial and temporary. In his account, philosophical reflection can represent in conceptual terms the trace of alterity and its traumatic impact on the subject, but it also must record the limitations of those attempts. Using the concept of trauma as an interpretive focus for Levinas's work, then, offers a rich understanding of his challenge to autonomous subjectivity, but it broadens out into issues of methodology and his responses to the history of philosophy. This radical rethinking of the subject then has further implications for how we think about mortality, gender, race, and animality—dimensions of subjectivity that have traditionally functioned to mark off the boundary between autonomy and heteronomy, or personhood or objecthood.

As an analysis of the ethical significance of time in Levinas's thought, this book follows a relatively linear structure. The first five chapters interpret Levinas's discussion of time and its implications for his understanding of subjectivity, with particular attention to how the concept of trauma links his emphasis on diachrony to responsibility. The following three chapters draw out the implications of this reconception of subjectivity to more specific clusters of issues: embodiment, mortality, and the relation between human and nonhuman animals. In examining the repercussions of his challenge to the autonomous subject, I discuss some of the unresolved tensions within Levinas's own work—including where he fails to explore all of the tangled ways in which autonomy and its attendant anxieties have shaped the Western moral imaginary. Despite this general progression from an exposition of the role that time plays in Levinas's account of the subject to an application and extension of those ideas, the central concepts resonate in diverse contexts throughout his work and so return in various chapters.

Chapter 1 examines Levinas's project of "deformalizing time," placing his understanding of time in the context of both those philosophers whom he associates with formal time, principally Aristotle and Kant, and those whom he identifies as moving beyond, at least partially, such conceptions—Rosenzweig, Bergson, Husserl, and Heidegger. Formal conceptions of time describe a neutral structure within which human experiences occur, whether that structure is understood metaphysically, as part of the order of the universe, or transcendentally, as the condition for the possibility of experience. By contrast, deformalized time begins from the subjective experience of time, in which the predictable order of "public time" is derived from our prior immersion in a world of becoming. In that mode, present, past, and future bear on each other in the unfolding of experience, rather than conforming to a linear series of present moments. This approach means that time—far from a neutral framework—imposes a certain meaning on human existence.

Chapter 2 continues this analysis by arguing that the traumatic impact of diachrony is the content or meaning of deformalized time. Levinas departs from his phenomenological predecessors in identifying the significance of time as responsibility, an exposure to the other that calls into question the fundamental attitude of the *conatus essendi*, the "striving to persist" that prioritizes above all else the preservation of one's own being. In *Otherwise than Being* and other late writings, Levinas characterizes this interruption of the *conatus* as traumatic, without thoroughly elaborating the significance of this term. I draw connections between Levinas's use of the concept and classic psychoanalytic approaches and more contemporary descriptions of post-traumatic stress disorder. The central claim of this chapter is that in all of these discussions the temporal features of trauma contribute to the disruption of the subject's ordinary sense of self-possession and ability to represent experience.

Chapter 3 focuses on Levinas's methodology in the light of the ethical significance of diachrony: how does philosophical reflection change if significant elements of our experience cannot be represented in any simple way? How can we discuss the trauma of responsibility intelligibly without distorting its traumatic qualities? Levinas's late writing incorporates these concerns about the work of philosophy and the kind of subject that it presupposes. His method then enacts what he calls the process of "saying and unsaying," which includes making claims—often with highly dramatic, emotionally charged rhetoric—and then raising paradoxes about the legitimacy of any such assertions, introducing ideas through questions or suggestions, or remaining silent on certain issues on which readers might expect him to elaborate (such as an articulation of normative principles that follow from the event of responsibility). One prominent element of his later discursive style is his hostility to narration. Memory and history position the subject as an observer-narrator who is capable of negating diachrony through representation, rather than a subject whose obligation to the other is "immemorial." Levinas refuses to tell a single developmental story about the origins of subjectivity, how subjects encounter alterity, and how they might fulfill the goal of justice, and this refusal reflects his claims about the traumatic, anarchic quality of responsibility.

Given Levinas's resistance to narrative, chapter 4 examines his concern about the ethical dangers of writing history, dangers that are crystallized in Hegel's philosophy of history. Levinas largely agrees with Hegel that human consciousness gravitates toward secular or religious theodicies that allow us to find a moral order within what first appears to be a chaotic and destructive series of historical events. But historical representation more generally counters the threat that time poses to human agency, by producing a narrative that represents an intelligible structure within the movement of time and thus reaffirming the reflective power and freedom of thought. Levinas's worry is that such representation normalizes the self-possessed subject as narrator, but also frames the suffering of others as sacrifices made for a greater good. This reduction of the singular to an element of the totality deflects the ethical exposure of the subject.

The traumatic quality of responsibility contests the desire for cohesive narratives—narratives that presuppose a subject capable of standing outside the movement of diachrony. In chapter 5, I discuss Levinas's work as an insistent challenge to the ideal of the sovereign ego as the foundation for ethics, an idea that dominates modern philosophical and legal accounts of responsibility, in which the agent's intentions largely define his culpability. Although Levinas attributes this orientation to the Greek philosophical tradition, in *Oedipus Tyrannos,* Sophocles also complicates this association between responsibility and deliberate choice. In the course of the play, Oedipus undergoes a fundamentally Levinasian arc of "sobering up," by moving from self-assured sovereignty, based on his ability to comprehend the world, to an awareness of responsibility that outstrips his intentions. In keeping with his repudiation of narration, however, Levinasian trauma can never be converted into the structure and reflective distance provided by the tragic representation of Oedipus's ruin.

The last three chapters collectively examine the wider implications of diachrony for the subject whose status rests on a disavowal of all that is associated with heteronomy: principally, the raced, gendered, mortal, animal body. In this sense Levinas's somewhat abstract discussion of time in its ethical significance opens up into more politically tangible issues of how personhood has been constituted and delimited. Chapter 6 considers how Levinas's account of the heteronomous subject contests dominant interpretations of the body. Through a reading that begins from Levinas's 1934 essay "Some Thoughts on the Philosophy of Hitlerism," I consider the implications of his treatment of embodiment for issues around race. In this early essay Levinas identifies two major movements within his contemporary culture: liberalism and Hitlerism, which each propose an ideal conception of the subject and a correlative understanding of the effect of time on subjectivity. At one level, these two movements are in strict opposition, but in its glorification of the sovereign subject, liberalism is haunted by anxiety about embodiment, in its mortality and apparently determined status. I argue that a highly traditional dualism underlies both liberalism and Hitlerism, as Levinas describes them, in the identification of spirit with freedom and of the body with inert matter, and that the attendant anxieties of dualism are expressed as racism in both systems. Levinas's reconception of the body as ethically significant overcomes this dualism, and thus offers resources for undoing contemporary manifestations of racism, despite his refusal to consider the particularity of bodies in their historical contexts.

Chapter 7 extends the analysis of embodiment to investigate the association between maternity and mortality in order to examine the devaluation of femininity in modern philosophy and Western culture more generally. To the extent that women have been defined by their reproductive capacities, they have been both sentimentalized and stigmatized: sentimentalized as nurturing, supportive, selfless beings, and stigmatized for creating merely physical and therefore mortal children. The logic of the *conatus essendi*, the concern with the perseverance of the self, undergirds both cultural constructions of femininity, by framing women as a kind of refuge from the aggressive rivalry of self-interested individuals and by expressing anxiety about the mortality of those individuals—an anxiety that fundamentally concerns the effect of the passage of time on human existence. Levinas's treatment of the mortal body as ethically significant challenges this governing attitude of the *conatus* and the kind of subject affirmed by it. His repudiation of dualism helps to dismantle the privileging of a sovereign subject who is culturally marked as masculine. Levinas's thought can thus contribute to the larger feminist project of overturning a patriarchal vision of subjectivity, one which depends upon the disavowal of embodiment, relationships of dependence, and other forms of vulnerability—and the projection of those traits onto others.

The intertwining themes of embodiment, vulnerability, and time raise the issue of what Levinas means by "creatureliness," a term he uses in conjunction with diachrony to express the exposure of the subject to the other. His discussion of the face and responsibility is unapologetically anthropocentric, and he has been roundly criticized for reinforcing this traditional stance within Western philosophy. The last chapter elaborates the tensions between what Levinas has to say about nonhuman animals, the subject as creature, and the anarchic nature of responsibility. I use the work of Cora Diamond and Jacques Derrida to broaden Levinas's intuitions about the source of responsibility, or the claim that is exerted on the subject by the other. The domain of moral considerability cannot be established definitively, in a way that would generate principles about who or what might make such a claim, according to Levinas's own discussion of the trauma of responsibility. Through this radical understanding of responsibility, Levinas's work can deepen dominant contemporary debates around animal ethics, which have centered on questions about the traits of nonhuman animals and the moral significance of those traits. As in the previous chapter on maternity and mortality, Levinas's disruption of the dominant ideal of the sovereign subject has wider repercussions than he himself developed—or in this case, than he himself would affirm. The repudiation of embodiment and vulnerability that results in the marginalization of femininity also naturalizes the devaluation of animality. But these anxieties lose their hold within a Levinasian understanding of subjectivity, in which the self is fundamentally embodied, mortal, and heteronomous.

In the conclusion I argue that creatureliness has two dimensions, one that Levinas emphasizes and one that he addresses only indirectly. The former kind of creatureliness is the subject's inescapable responsibility to the other, which arises out of a past that cannot be represented. The second kind of creatureliness results from our immersion in a particular history that we have not chosen but which structures our beliefs, norms, and habits. Levinas's lack of explicit attention to this second form of creatureliness means that he seems to be asserting universal, ahistorical claims about human nature. But in fact his work responds specifically, if often in a veiled way, to the moral imaginary structured by the presuppositions of modern philosophy. Throughout this book I emphasize how Levinas inherits central concepts from the Western philosophical tradition—sometimes by challenging those ideas (as in the case of the privileging of synchrony over diachrony), sometimes by preserving distinct pieces of those ideas but revising their significance (as he does in accepting the human tendency toward theodicy), and sometimes by uncritically repeating its well-entrenched prejudices, even when those prejudices are profoundly entangled with the ideal of autonomous subjectivity that he does so much to critique (its anthropocentrism and Eurocentrism, for example). His thought should be read as a response to moral intuitions and conceptions of subjectivity that continue to dominate contemporary philosophy and contemporary Western cultures more generally, and the radicality of his ethics as a reaction against that legacy. Levinas describes the ways in which we are beholden to an immemorial past, but he also shows how we are conditioned by a memorial, determinate, and contingent set of ideas and institutions. This book is intended to contribute to that ongoing work of identifying the moral presumptions that we have inherited, evaluating their legitimacy, and opening up alternative conceptions of normativity, responsibility, and subjectivity.

One note about the range of texts that I have referenced in this interpretation of Levinas's work: as readers of Levinas know, he was careful to distinguish his philosophical writings from his Talmudic interpretations, to the point of using different publishers for the two registers of his thought. But the boundary between the two is permeable, as recent scholars have argued, particularly in the sense that the same central concerns animate all of his thought—the problem of how one human being responds to another, how that meaning imposes itself in our experience, and how the relation of responsibility gets distorted and forgotten. Even the separation between Jewish and Greek forms of discourse—one tending toward dialogic plurality and the other toward unified comprehension—cannot be rigorously maintained.[4] With the interpretive assumption that the two bodies of work are in implicit conversation with one another, I have focused primarily on his philosophical writings but occasionally draw on the confessional texts where those analyses illuminate the ideas at the core of this project.

In examining the significance of Levinas's account of subjectivity and the role that time plays in that account, we engage in the impossible but urgent work of studying what resists detached reflection without distorting the character of that resistance. In this way we are following Levinas's own understanding of the practice of philosophy, even as we identify the shortcomings, silences, and tensions within his thought. Levinas's discussion of responsibility invites the question of how we should make use of these ideas, an issue that Levinas rarely addresses explicitly but enacts everywhere in his writing. The obscurity of his style shelters a profound attention to the least abstract question of all: how we should live. Philosophical reflection on what responsibility means is part of the process of dismantling normalized violence against the other, anxiety about the vulnerability of embodiment and mortality, and cultivated indifference to the stranger, the neighbor, the widow, and the orphan, whoever they might be.

However, for Levinas, the question of how we should live, pursued to its limits, leads to a much broader challenge to the ideal of the autonomous subject, to our understanding of time, and to the idea that we could possess moral knowledge that would adequately answer that question. Any particular normative claim, and the moral complacency that might accompany it, will be repeatedly unsettled by the traumatic rupture that is responsibility. We grapple instead with masks that invoke faces that undo any definitive representation, whose significance demands interpretation and reinterpretation, responses and still other responses. Time in its ethical significance leaves us with a subject who does not possess herself but is instead caught in intrigues that resist any final unraveling.

Notes

1. Quoted in Alexander, "Faces of War," 72.
2. Assigning gendered pronouns to the other violates Levinas's emphasis on the singularity of the other, who resists categorization as a particular phenomenon. Neither French nor English grammar supports speaking of the singular other in a gender-neutral way, for surely reference to an objectified "it" is inappropriate. Throughout this book, I have therefore alternated gendered pronouns when referring to the other or to a singular subject.
3. American Psychiatric Association, "Posttraumatic Stress Disorder."
4. See Ajzenstat, "Levinas versus Levinas: Hebrew, Greek, and Linguistic Justice," and Gibbs, *Correlations in Rosenzweig and Levinas*, 154–75.

Abbreviations

References to Levinas's writings are cited in the text, using the following abbreviations. All emphases are in the original text, unless otherwise noted.

BC "The Bad Conscience and the Inexorable." In *Of God Who Comes to Mind*, translated by Bettina Bergo, 172–77. Stanford: Stanford University Press, 1998.

BFO "Being-for-the-Other," translated by Jill Robbins. In *Is It Righteous to Be? Interviews with Emmanuel Levinas*, edited by Jill Robbins, 114–20. Stanford: Stanford University Press, 2001.

BM "Beyond Memory." In *In the Time of the Nations*, translated by Michael B. Smith. 64–79. London: Continuum, 2004.

BTD "Being-Toward-Death and 'Thou Shalt Not Kill,'" translated by Andrew Schmitz. In *Is It Righteous to Be? Interviews with Emmanuel Levinas*, edited by Jill Robbins, 130–39. Stanford: Stanford University Press, 2001.

DB "On Death in Bloch's Thought." In *Of God Who Comes to Mind*, translated by Bettina Bergo, 33–42. Stanford: Stanford University Press, 1998.

DEL "Dialogue with Emmanuel Levinas," translated by Richard Kearney. In *Face to Face with Levinas*, edited by Richard A. Cohen, 13–34. Albany: State University of New York Press, 1986.

DFT "Discussion Following 'Transcendence and Intelligibility,'" translated by Jill Robbins. In *Is It Righteous to Be? Interviews with Emmanuel Levinas*, edited by Jill Robbins, 268–86. Stanford: Stanford University Press, 2001.

DR "Diachrony and Representation." In *Entre Nous: Thinking-of-the-Other*, translated by Michael B. Smith and Barbara Harshav, 159–77. New York: Columbia University Press, 1998.

DYF "Dying For . . ." In *Entre Nous: Thinking-of-the-Other*, translated by Michael B. Smith and Barbara Harshav, 207–17. New York: Columbia University Press, 1998.

EE *Existence and Existents*. Translated by Alphonso Lingis. Pittsburgh: Duquesne University Press, 2001.

EI	*Ethics and Infinity: Conversations with Philippe Nemo.* Translated by Richard A. Cohen. Pittsburgh: Duquesne University Press, 1985.
EN	*Entre Nous: Thinking-of-the-Other.* Translated by Michael B. Smith and Barbara Harshav. New York: Columbia University Press, 1998.
EoI	"Ethics of the Infinite." In *Dialogues with Contemporary Continental Thinkers*, edited by Richard Kearney, 49–69. Manchester: Manchester University Press, 1984.
EP	"Enigma and Phenomena," translated by Alphonso Lingis, Robert Bernasconi, and Simon Critchley. In *Basic Philosophical Writings*, edited by Adriaan T. Peperzak, Simon Critchley, and Robert Bernasconi, 65–77. Bloomington: Indiana University Press, 1996.
FCW	"From Consciousness to Wakefulness: Starting from Husserl." In *Of God Who Comes to Mind*, translated by Bettina Bergo, 15–32. Stanford: Stanford University Press, 1998.
FO	"From the One to the Other: Transcendence and Time." In *Entre Nous: Thinking-of-the-Other*, translated by Michael B. Smith and Barbara Harshav, 133–53. New York: Columbia University Press, 1998.
GCM	*Of God Who Comes to Mind.* Translated by Bettina Bergo. Stanford: Stanford University Press, 1998.
GDT	*God, Death, and Time.* Translated by Bettina Bergo. Stanford: Stanford University Press, 2000.
GP	"God and Philosophy." In *Of God Who Comes to Mind*, translated by Bettina Bergo, 55–78. Stanford: Stanford University Press, 1998.
HA	"Humanity and An-archy." In *Humanism of the Other*, translated by Nidra Poller, 45–57. Urbana: University of Illinois Press, 2003.
HB	"Hommage à Bergson." In *Carnets de Captivité: Écrits sur la Capitivité Notes Philosophique Diverses*, 217–19. Paris: Éditions Grasset & Fasquelle, 2009.
HIB	"Humanity Is Biblical." In *Questioning Judaism: Interviews by Elisabeth Weber*, 77–86. Stanford: Stanford University Press, 2004.
IEL	"Interview with Emmanuel Levinas." In *Crossover Queries: Dwelling with Negatives, Embodying Philosophy's Others*, by Edith Wyschogrod, 283–97. New York: Fordham University Press, 2006.
IEO	"Intention, Event, and the Other," translated by Andrew Schmitz. In *Is It Righteous to Be? Interviews with Emmanuel Levinas*, edited by Jill Robbins, 140–57. Stanford: Stanford University Press, 2001.

IFP	"Interview with François Poirié," translated by Jill Robbins, Marcus Coelen, and Thomas Loebel. In *Is It Righteous to Be? Interviews with Emmanuel Levinas*, edited by Jill Robbins, 23–83. Stanford: Stanford University Press, 2001.
INO	"In the Name of the Other," translated by Maureen V. Gedney. In *Is It Righteous to Be? Interviews with Emmanuel Levinas*, edited by Jill Robbins, 188–99. Stanford: Stanford University Press, 2001.
IOF	"Is Ontology Fundamental?" In *Entre Nous: Thinking-of-the-Other*, translated by Michael B. Smith and Barbara Harshav, 1–11. New York: Columbia University Press, 1998.
IRM	Untitled interview with Raoul Mortley. In *French Philosophers in Conversation: Levinas, Schneider, Serres, Irigaray, Le Doeuff, Derrida*, edited by Raoul Mortley, 11–23. London: Routledge, 1991.
IT	"The I and the Totality." In *Entre Nous: Thinking-of-the-Other*, translated by Michael B. Smith and Barbara Harshav, 13–38. New York: Columbia University Press, 1998.
LP	"Language and Proximity." In *Collected Philosophical Papers*, translated by Alphonso Lingis, 109–26. Pittsburgh: Duquesne University Press, 1987.
MoS	"Manner of Speaking." In *Of God Who Comes to Mind*, translated by Bettina Bergo, 178–80. Stanford: Stanford University Press, 1998.
MS	"Meaning and Sense," translated by Alphonso Lingis, Simon Critchley, and Adriaan Peperzak. In *Basic Philosophical Writings*, edited by Adriaan T. Peperzak, Simon Critchley, and Robert Bernasconi, 33–64. Bloomington: Indiana University Press, 1996.
MT	"Messianic Texts." In *Difficult Freedom: Essays on Judaism*, translated by Seán Hand, 59–97. Baltimore: The Johns Hopkins University Press, 1990.
NC	"Nonintentional Consciousness." In *Entre Nous: Thinking-of-the-Other*, translated by Michael B. Smith and Barbara Harshav, 123–32. New York: Columbia University Press, 1998.
ND	"The Name of a Dog, or Natural Rights." In *Difficult Freedom: Essays on Judaism*, translated by Seán Hand, 151–53. Baltimore: The Johns Hopkins University Press, 1990.
NI	"No Identity." In *Collected Philosophical Papers*, translated by Alphonso Lingis, 141–51. Pittsburgh: Duquesne University Press, 1987.
NM	"Notes on Meaning." In *Of God Who Comes to Mind*, translated by Bettina Bergo, 152–71. Stanford: Stanford University Press, 1998.

OB   *Otherwise than Being, or Beyond Essence*. Translated by Alphonso Lingis. Pittsburgh: Duquesne University Press, 1981.

ON   "The Old and the New." In *Time and the Other*, translated by Richard A. Cohen, 121–38. Pittsburgh: Duquesne University Press, 1987.

OUJ   "The Other, Utopia, and Justice." In *Entre Nous: Thinking-of-the-Other*, translated by Michael B. Smith and Barbara Harshav, 223–33. New York: Columbia University Press, 1998.

PA   "Philosophy and Awakening." In *Entre Nous: Thinking-of-the-Other*, translated by Michael B. Smith and Barbara Harshav, 77–90. New York: Columbia University Press, 1998.

PD   "The Philosopher and Death," translated by Bettina Bergo. In *Is It Righteous to Be? Interviews with Emmanuel Levinas*, edited by Jill Robbins, 121–29. Stanford: Stanford University Press, 2001.

PDIC "The Philosophical Determination of the Idea of Culture." In *Entre Nous: Thinking-of-the-Other*, translated by Michael B. Smith and Barbara Harshav, 179–87. New York: Columbia University Press, 1998.

PFR   "The Philosophy of Franz Rosenzweig." In *In the Time of the Nations*, translated by Michael B. Smith, 135–44. London: Continuum, 2004.

PH   "Some Thoughts on the Philosophy of Hitlerism." In *Unforeseen History*, translated by Nidra Poller, 13–21. Urbana: University of Illinois Press, 2004.

PII   "Philosophy and the Idea of Infinity." In *Collected Philosophical Papers*, translated by Alphonso Lingis, 47–59. Pittsburgh: Duquesne University Press, 1987.

PJL   "Philosophy, Justice, and Love." In *Entre Nous: Thinking-of-the-Other*, translated by Michael B. Smith and Barbara Harshav, 103–21. New York: Columbia University Press, 1998.

PM   "The Paradox of Morality: An Interview with Emmanuel Levinas," translated by Andrew Benjamin and Tamra Wright. In *The Provocation of Levinas: Rethinking the Other*, edited by Robert Bernasconi and David Wood, 168–80. London: Oxford University Press, 1988.

PO   "The Proximity of the Other." In *Alterity and Transcendence*, translated by Michael B. Smith, 97–109. New York: Columbia University Press, 1999.

PP   "Peace and Proximity," translated by Peter Atterton and Simon Critchley. In *Basic Philosophical Writings*, edited by Adriaan T. Peperzak, Simon Critchley, and Robert Bernasconi, 161–69. Bloomington: Indiana University Press, 1996.

PPH	Prefatory Note to "Reflections on the Philosophy of Hitlerism." *Critical Inquiry* 17, no. 1 (Autumn 1990): 63.
PT	"Philosophy and Transcendence." In *Alterity and Transcendence*, translated by Michael B. Smith, 3–37. New York: Columbia University Press, 1999.
QA	"Questions and Answers." In *Of God Who Comes to Mind*, translated by Bettina Bergo, 79–99. Stanford: Stanford University Press, 1998.
QDE	"Que dirait Eurydice? What Would Eurydice Say?" In *Emmanuel Levinas en/in conversation avec/with Bracha Lichtenberg-Ettinger*, edited by Bracha Lichtenberg-Ettinger, 136–50. Paris: BCE Atelier, 1977.
RA	"A Religion for Adults." In *Difficult Freedom: Essays on Judaism*, translated by Seán Hand, 11–23. Baltimore: The Johns Hopkins University Press, 1990.
S	"Substitution," translated by Peter Atterton, Simon Critchley, and Graham Noctor. In *Basic Philosophical Writings*, edited by Adriaan T. Peperzak, Simon Critchley, and Robert Bernasconi, 79–95. Bloomington: Indiana University Press, 1996.
SC	"The Struthof Case." In *Difficult Freedom: Essays on Judaism*, translated by Seán Hand, 149–50. Baltimore: The Johns Hopkins University Press, 1990.
SH	"Secularization and Hunger," translated by Bettina Bergo. *Graduate Faculty Philosophy Journal* 20/21, no. 1–2 (1998): 3–12.
SI	"The State of Israel and the Religion of Israel." In *Difficult Freedom: Essays on Judaism*, translated by Seán Hand, 216–20. Baltimore: The Johns Hopkins University Press, 1990.
STI	"Secularism and the Thought of Israel." In *Unforeseen History*, translated by Nidra Poller, 113–24. Urbana: University of Illinois Press, 2004.
TaI	"Transcendence and Intelligibility," translated by Simon Critchley and Tamra Wright. In *Basic Philosophical Writings*, edited by Adriaan T. Peperzak, Simon Critchley, and Robert Bernasconi, 149–59. Bloomington: Indiana University Press, 1996.
TE	"Transcendence and Evil." In *Collected Philosophical Papers*, translated by Alphonso Lingis, 175–86. Pittsburgh: Duquesne University Press, 1987.
TH	"Transcendence and Height," translated by Tina Chanter, Simon Critchley, Nicholas Walker, and Adriaan Peperzak. In *Basic Philosophical Writings*, edited by Adriaan T. Peperzak, Simon Critchley, and Robert Bernasconi, 11–31. Bloomington: Indiana University Press, 1996.

TI   *Totality and Infinity: An Essay on Exteriority.* Translated by Alphonso Lingis. Pittsburgh: Duquesne University Press, 1969.

TO   *Time and the Other.* Translated by Richard A. Cohen. Pittsburgh: Duquesne University Press, 1987.

TOT   "The Temptation of Temptation." In *Nine Talmudic Readings*, translated by Annette Aronowicz, 30–50. Bloomington: Indiana University Press, 1990.

TRO   "Trace of the Other," translated by Alphonso Lingis. In *Deconstruction in Context*, edited by Mark Taylor, 345–59. Chicago: University of Chicago Press, 1986.

TT   "Totality and Totalization." In *Alterity and Transcendence*, translated by Michael B. Smith, 39–51. New York: Columbia University Press, 1999.

US   "Useless Suffering." In *Entre Nous: Thinking-of-the-Other*, translated by Michael B. Smith and Barbara Harshav, 91–101. New York: Columbia University Press, 1998.

VF   "Violence of the Face." In *Alterity and Transcendence*, translated by Michael B. Smith, 169–82. New York: Columbia University Press, 1999.

WH   "The Work of Edmund Husserl." In *Discovering Existence with Husserl*, translated by Richard A. Cohen and Michael B. Smith, 47–89. Evanston, IL: Northwestern University Press, 1998.

LEVINAS AND THE TRAUMA OF RESPONSIBILITY

1   Deformalizing Time

In a 1988 interview, Levinas claims that the "essential theme of my research is the deformalization of the notion of time" (OUJ 232). At first glance, this identification of time as his "essential theme" seems counterintuitive, given his steadfast focus on the nature of responsibility and the subject's relation to alterity. However, how we understand time shapes how we understand the self, and Levinas argues that a formal conception of time supports the modern ideal of autonomous subjectivity. Time can be seen as either enabling or disrupting the position of the subject as a detached knower and willful agent in the world. In the first case, time is the linear framework within which we can make sense of experience and act on the basis of that knowledge, but in the latter, the subject is caught up in the movement of time in ways that cannot be overcome.

This chapter will examine what Levinas means by this phrase, the "deformalization of the notion of time," as a way of tracing the enduring significance of time in Levinas's understanding of subjectivity and alterity. In that 1988 statement, he clearly means the "deformalization of time" in the objective genitive—that our conception of time should be deformalized, or revised to recognize time in its ethical significance, rather than merely as a structure of experience. But that revision results in the deformalization of time in the sense of the subjective genitive: that diachronous time has the effect of deforming the fundamental activity of intentionality.

The first section of this chapter discusses the formal conceptions of time that Levinas rejects, specifically in the work of Aristotle and Kant, where time functions as a neutral order within which experience unfolds. In these models, time has no particular significance for the subject but is merely the structure for the content of our experience. In contesting these accounts of time, Levinas builds on the work of Bergson, Husserl, Heidegger, and Rosenzweig, who in their various approaches retrieve the lived significance of time in its becoming.[1] But Levinas takes a more radical approach by arguing that the meaning of time is not the possibility of free will outside of a spatialized, mechanistic world; the intentional integration of past, present, and future; my own being-toward-death; or the disclosure of a spiritual order of creation, revelation, and redemption. Instead, time has an ethical significance that dismantles my ability to comprehend the other. In arising out of an "immemorial past," responsibility cannot be made fully present to consciousness. Its hold on the self therefore emerges unexpectedly, introducing a traumatic demand on the self that challenges the logic of knowing and even deliberating and willing. In this way, time has a destabilizing effect on "the unity of the *I think*" that characterizes the autonomous subject (DR 176).

Aristotle: Cosmological Time

In a move that recurs in various writings, Levinas juxtaposes two ways of understanding time: synchrony and diachrony.[2] Synchronous time is the linear order that allows events in the past, present, and future to be gathered into the present moment by consciousness. As Augustine notes in the *Confessions*, the mind works in three tenses: "the present of past things, the present of present things, and the present of future things."[3] All that we can experience can be represented, regardless of that event's chronological location. Synchronous time positions the self as an observing subject, with every object, including other people, at least potentially accessible to it. The object is present in two related ways. In direct perception but also in memory and anticipation, the object lies in front of the knowing subject, at least in a metaphorical sense. Temporally it is "at hand," and Levinas often hyphenates the French word for "now"—*main-tenance*—to draw out how the mind grasps an experience, as if consciousness were a hand—*la main* (PT 3). Second, the object is presented or given for comprehension. In this way, intelligibility requires "the gathering of all alterity into presence" (DR 161). This picture of intelligibility assumes a formal conception of time, in which time functions as a backdrop against which such presentation or representation can occur. Understood as synchrony, time is the movement that consciousness can contain in representation.

But Levinas argues that this model of time and the kind of subject that it supports is not the only significance that time carries for us. If we begin with the lived experience of time, what stands out is its passing and how the self passively undergoes that lapse. Diachronous time resists representation, in a passing that cannot be reduced to insignificance: "the past bypasses the present.... It cannot be recuperated by reminiscence not because of its remoteness, but because of its incommensurability with the present. The present is essence that begins and ends, beginning and end assembled in a thematizable conjunction.... Diachrony is the refusal of conjunction, the non-totalizable" (OB 11). This is the movement of time in which the knower or the agent is immersed rather than being able to stand back from it, such that one might find oneself already entangled in a situation or already committed without having made a decision. Robert Gibbs describes this state as the interruption of representation: "My narration is broken into by something that I cannot make part of the story."[4] Diachrony is thus what unsettles the self in its incessant intentional activity, its comprehension of the world. Formal conceptions of time ignore diachrony in reducing time to what can be synchronized by consciousness. There are two different targets of Levinas's critique of formal time, which can be schematically identified with Aristotelian time and Kantian time.

The Aristotelian conception of time has dominated the history of Western philosophy and science (GDT 55). Aristotle describes time as an ordering of change, how we count or keep track of what is before and what is after.[5] Past and future are modifications of the present moment, the "now" that alone exists. Time as a whole is a "perpetual succession" of now-moments.[6] Aristotle thus describes a cosmological and public time, which can be spatially understood as the "number of change," or a series of present moments by which we measure change.[7] In this sense, the Aristotelian conception provides a foundation for modern scientific or objective time. Time becomes the linear order in which objects appear and events take place—a form (TaI 154–55).

Levinas's concern is that this account positions the subject as a self-possessed and observing knower, rather than as a subject that can find herself unexpectedly responsible for and to another person. In an early writing, Levinas associates the concept of a form with visibility and intelligibility: "The exteriority of things is tied up with the fact that we reach for them, that we have to come to them—that an object is given, but awaits us. That is the complete concept of *form*. A form is that by which a thing shows itself and is graspable, what is illuminated in it and apprehendable and what holds it together" (EE 39). Although he is not writing directly about time in this passage, there are strong connections between his project of deformalizing time and this description of a form. On Levinas's reading, Aristotle treats time as an organizing principle in physical reality, which can be studied apart from the subjectivity of lived experience.[8] Time becomes the structure populated by beings, which are fundamentally available to consciousness as objects of experience. Levinas contrasts "a time homogenous like space, made of invariable instants which repeat themselves, where all novelty would be reducible to these old elements, a spatialized time" with "duration which is pure change, without retrieving any identical substrate beneath this change" (ON 129–30). This is the distinction between Aristotle's account of time and Bergson's, where the latter emphasizes the irregular, meaning-laden movement of time. In defining the nature of time as the "number of movement," Aristotle inherits the Parmenidean idea that time structures a world of becoming, a falling away from or a degenerate form of what is. Levinas announces his "break with Parmenides," which is also a break with Aristotle, in contesting the idea that all future moments and all past moments could at least in principle be bound up into the unity of a changeless present (TO 42).

Levinas's Reading of Bergson, Husserl, and Heidegger on Time

Levinas is profoundly influenced by the critique that Bergson and Heidegger launch against this formal notion of public time, abstracted from lived experience and made present-to-hand—that is, time understood as a feature of the natural world and as a degraded copy of eternity.[9] Rather than attempt to give a compressed account of Bergson, Husserl, and Heidegger on time, this section will focus on what Levinas draws from each of them and his sometimes selective interpretations of those ideas. One of these key concepts is the Bergsonian rejection of a spatialized understanding of time, in which all moments can be made present. Behind or before this abstract, objective time is duration (*durée*): "a becoming in which each instant is heavy with all of the past and pregnant with the whole future. Duration is experienced by a descent into self" (GDT 55; see also ON 130–33 and GDT 7). Duration is the continuity between past, present, and future, such that the past and future animate and shape the present, which is lived out as an indistinct span of the self's particular, richly textured experience rather than a punctual, interchangeable moment.[10] Bergson emphasizes the experiential element of this layering of time: duration is "the continuous life of a memory which prolongs the past into the present, whether the present distinctly encloses the ever-growing image of the past, or whether, by its continual changing of quality, it attests rather the increasingly heavy burden dragged along behind one the older one grows."[11] What we might have understood as discrete moments are first experienced as a flux, as events in the process of becoming.[12] What it means to exist is to participate in this fluidity.

In the early essay "Hommage à Bergson," Levinas dramatically depicts Bergson's rejection of an Aristotelian-scientific conception of time as Zeus's attack on Cronos (HB 218).[13] The brute fact of time as part of the natural world, which annihilates all that it generates, is overcome by a temporality more intimately associated with human existence. Levinas reads this Bergsonian emphasis on becoming as a challenge to formal conceptions of time. Time is no longer the empty container for beings: duration is "not reducible to the substantiality of beings" or "the persistence of solids" (OUJ 223–24). Instead, the liquid movement of becoming is the primary quality of reality. This loosening of the traditional focus on beings in their persistence opens up the possibility of unseating the epistemic dominance of consciousness and questioning the normative dominance of the *conatus essendi*—my interest in preserving my own being, my quest for immortality (OUJ 228). If beings are not primary, consciousness may not always capture what is most significant, and my commitment to my own survival loses its normalized status. In Levinas's hands, then, Bergson's discussion of the *durée* at least gestures to the ethical significance of time, in destabilizing the self-possession of the subject.

By grounding time in duration, Bergson challenges the idea that time in its passing is a degenerate form of the timeless. Levinas credits him with this radical break from a tradition of privileging eternity: "for the first time in the history of ideas, [Bergson] tried to think time outside that failure of eternity" (FO 139; see also GDT 93 and PT 13).[14] This is a theme that Levinas positions at the center of his early essay "Time and the Other": "thinking time not as a degradation of eternity, but as the relationship to *that* which—of itself unassimilable, absolutely other—would not allow itself to be assimilated by experience; or to *that* which—of itself infinite—would not allow itself to be com-prehended" (TO 32). The hyphenation in the last word of this passage, as in Levinas's hyphenation of *maintenance*, emphasizes the metaphorical grasping at work in consciousness. Levinas argues that diachrony, time in its passing, exceeds the attempt to assimilate all that is present or could be represented. If time were merely a "degradation of eternity," its passing could be dismissed as insignificant, and we could conceptualize the present as a series of moments to be synchronized by consciousness. But its movement is the element of time that Levinas privileges. He therefore consistently criticizes the dominance of what he refers to as economic time, "where instants are equivalent and compensate for one another" (EE 8). A version of Aristotle's model, economic time allows for the public, linear measurement of time and what can be accomplished within it: "the time of clocks, made for the sun and for trains" (EE 101). Following Bergson, Levinas argues that one can retrospectively transform the passing of time into an abstract and measurable thing, but this is always derivative of the originary, subjective experience of time.[15]

In his own critique of Aristotelian time, Husserl engages in a deformalizing project in this sense of moving away from theoretical abstraction or objectification and toward a more originary internal experience of time.[16] The natural attitude and the scientific approaches that arise from it ignore the activity of consciousness in cognition, which leaves us with "empty logical-mathematical form[s]."[17] For Husserl, that originary experience of time involves the shading off of the present, or the now-point, both in the direction of what has just happened (retention) and in the direction of what is expected to happen next (protention). Rather than framing time with reference to a series of simple, well-defined points in a linear cosmological order, the internal constitution of time has depth and complexity that structures all of our experiences. Levinas praises Husserl for his attention to the experiential flux of time that is the ground for scientific or clock time, even if Husserl's concern is still with how intentionality makes sense of that movement and synchronizes it in representation (WH 76–77). Husserl's interest in what makes Aristotelian, formal time possible helps to open up the approach that treats time as a mode of human existence.[18]

In Heidegger's hands, that deformalization entails a consideration of how temporality should be understood in the light of the particular situation of human existence—not as an element of the natural world, but arising out of the finitude of our experience. Heidegger argues that temporality has the meaning of care (*Sorge*), in which past, present, and future are not points on a timeline, but how *Dasein* exists (or ek-sists, always standing outside of itself) in the world. The past has the character of thrownness, *Dasein*'s finding itself in a world that is already laden with meaning; the present consists of fallenness, a way of living in which

Dasein is surrounded by others, distracted from its most significant possibilities; and the future has the character of projection, in which *Dasein* is always incomplete and experiences the world as a domain of possibilities.[19] In other words, time is first and foremost understood in relation to *Dasein*'s existence, its way of being in the world, and only in a secondary way as an objective ordering of reality. Revealed in the affective moods of *Dasein*, such as anxiety or boredom, the significance of temporality is finitude, with which *Dasein* grapples with varying degrees of attunement and clarity. What Levinas takes from Heidegger almost entirely derives from his reading of this phenomenological analysis of time in *Being and Time*. Time neither provides the neutral framework in which beings are experienced, nor can it be treated as an object that could be present-to-hand. In Eric Severson's words, Levinas adopts and extends Heidegger's critique of the "subordination of time to the dominant logic of being."[20]

These major figures in Levinas's philosophical lineage—Bergson, Husserl, and Heidegger—contribute to the project of deformalizing time by focusing on how the human subject experiences time as itself meaningful rather than an empty structure within which events unfold or beings could be situated. The linear succession of moments that is variously called "clock time," "public time," "economic time," or "cosmological time" is derivative of this more subjective living out of time's passing. Despite these influences on Levinas's critique of Aristotelian time, he ultimately moves beyond them to argue for the close connection between diachrony and intersubjectivity—that when the ego confronts another person *as* other, as opposed to an abstraction or an alter ego, the other does not share our present moment. The other as other is not an intentional object, present before consciousness, but instead introduces a lapse of time. All of this means moving beyond the Husserlian account of time, which Levinas describes as containing "certain chiaroscuros," a dappling of what can be seen and what recedes from sight (DR 163). The present moment has intricate connections to the immediate past and the immediate future, and our reflections on that experience, or on the more distant past and future, require time, "a time that slips by like a flux. This metaphor of 'flux' lives off a temporality borrowed from the being [*étant*] that is a liquid whose particles are in movement, a movement already unfolding in time" (DR 163). That is, a Bergsonian becoming haunts the activity of consciousness, which can never entirely coincide with itself or take account of the time required for representation. But even that process of becoming can be made into an object of intentionality: "Time is the form of qualities that flow by as they are altered, a flux of quiddities identifiable through their order in time.... The instants go by as though they were things. They flow past, but they are retained or 'protained'" (GDT 108). Levinas notes that the Heraclitean image of a river or flux still frames time as a comprehensible entity, "a metaphor drawn from the world of objects" (GDT 108). Protention and retention, memory and anticipation, draw what is no longer and what is not yet back into the present as objects of cognition. In this sense, Husserl remains bound to the Aristotelian homology between knowledge and presence, the accessibility of objects in time to the synchronizing work of representation (FO 137).[21] There is no recognition that diachrony limits consciousness and initiates the ethical encounter with the other.

Levinas has a related challenge to Heidegger's understanding of time. Levinas's early critique is concerned with the abstraction introduced by temporal ecstasis, the way in which *Dasein* never quite lives simply in the present instant. But he increasingly focuses on how Heidegger's conception of time leaves no room for alterity, in which projection and thrownness are still focused on the individual ego in the present. The other appears primarily in the abstract form of "the they" (*das Man*), who threatens *Dasein* with a lived, habitual forgetting or concealing of the significance of temporality as care, and thus a forgetting of the significance of its own finitude. Intersubjectivity in *Being and Time* is most directly associated with the inauthentic privileging of clock time or everyday time, whereas *Dasein* as an individual, freeing itself from the influence of "the they," can disclose the primary significance of temporality. Tina Chanter discusses Levinas's evolving response to Heidegger as both an affirmation of Heidegger's critique of dominant philosophical understandings of time and an identification of how Heidegger's account remains beholden to those conceptions.[22] The crux of Levinas's rejection of Heidegger is the ethical significance of diachrony, in which the movement of time resists representation and thus unsettles the subject's epistemic dominance over his world: "As his reflections on time progress . . . Levinas will pay more attention to the past that was never present—an irrecusable past that signals a diachrony which is not captured by Heidegger's tendency to posit the ecstases as a unity capable of recuperating the alterity of time."[23] The significance of time for Heidegger remains a concern about how *Dasein* relates to itself, whether this self-relation is authentic or inauthentic, rather than opening up the relation to the other.

On Levinas's reading, this refusal of alterity culminates in Heidegger's focus on my own death, rather than the death of the other, a divergence that I discuss further in chapter 7.[24] Levinas reads this account of temporality as anchoring Husserl and Heidegger more closely to an Aristotelian view than it might first appear: the thinking, experiencing subject still has the capacity to contain past, present, and future in representation. As Yael Lin argues, that focus on the subject's capacities reinforces the assimilative dynamic of intentionality: "The inclination to gather the future and the past into the present (to re-present them) is only one aspect of the ego's tendency to assimilate the other into itself."[25] Without attending to diachrony, time still functions as the order within which the ego comes to know itself and its world. Even in Heidegger, then, Levinas finds a conception of time that supports the self-possession of the subject, whose relation to the world around it—and others in that world—is fundamentally a dynamic of assimilation.

Levinas's critique of Bergson is more muted. Where in his 1946 essay Levinas had positioned Bergson as a philosophical Zeus, engaged in patricidal battle against the Cronos of Aristotelian time, he also comes to associate Cronos with the synchronizing activity of narration, which greedily, incessantly devours everything exterior to it. Bergson's focus on free will and the spontaneity of subjectivity means that he participates in the tradition that subordinates time to the self-determining activity of the subject. For Bergson, the experience of duration opens up a sense of the progressive element of time, which is what allows for creative construction and transformation of the world: "the free act takes place in time which is flowing and not in time which has already flown. Freedom is therefore a fact, and among the facts which we observe there is none clearer. All the difficulties of the problem [of freedom and determinism], and the problem itself, arise from the desire to endow duration with the same attributes as extensivity, to interpret a succession by a simultaneity, and to express the idea of freedom in a language into which it is obviously untranslatable."[26] For Bergson, understanding time as duration opens up the possibility of freedom, which remains a paradoxical concept as long as time is reduced to the simultaneity of space—that is, drained of the transformative movement of duration. The immediate lived experience of freedom should lead us to understand becoming rather than static identity as the core of our lives. As Lin puts it, "It is not despite continuous change that our identity is *preserved*, but rather it is due to duration, the changes and evolvements that we undergo, that our identity is *formed*," and that identity continues to be transformed in an open-ended, indeterminate way.[27] But both identity-preservation and identity-formation are fundamentally self-regarding activities, so that time once again supports the I in her knowing and willing activity. For Levinas, time interrupts this complacency of the subject, who, preoccupied with her own existence and identity, has not yet confronted the question, "What right do I have to be?"

Thus Husserl, Heidegger, and Bergson each neglect how time opens up the encounter with alterity.[28] By contrast, Levinas emphasizes this ethical significance of time in various ways from his earliest to his last writings: from *Existence and Existents* (1947), "Is not sociality something more than the source of our representation of time: is it not time itself?" (EE 96); from *Time and the Other* (also 1947), "time is not the achievement of an isolated and lone subject, but that it is the very relationship of the subject with Other" (TO 39); from the lecture course "Death and Time" (1975–76), "Can one seek the meaning of death on the basis of time? Does this meaning not show itself in the diachrony of time, understood as a relationship to the other? Can one understand time as a relationship with the Other, rather than seeing in it the relationship with the end?" (GDT 106); and from his 1979 preface to *Time and the Other*, "Knowing conceals representation and reduces the *other* to presence and co-presence. Time, on the contrary, in its dia-chrony, would signify a relationship that does not compromise the other's alterity, while still assuring its non-indifference to 'thought'" (TO 31). Without this core significance of time as exposing the subject to alterity, our understanding of time remains beholden to the privileging of the present and the reduction of time's movement to a tool in the self-realization of the subject. Levinas's version of the deformalization of time reveals a lived experience that ultimately destabilizes these presumptions and so moves beyond the vestiges of Aristotelian time.

Kant: Time as a Pure Form of Experience

There is a second register of deformalization at work in Levinas's thought, which takes as its target a Kantian approach to time. As with Aristotle, Levinas criticizes the framing of time as contentless or insignificant for the subject. Whereas Aristotle gives us a metaphysical picture of time as a cosmic order, Kant understands time through the lens of transcendental idealism, in which time is not merely given to us by the external world but is one of the a priori conditions under which we can experience anything at all. Time is the not the content of any experience but the form that allows us to organize any possible experience, in both inner and outer sense. As a form of intuition, it functions as the condition under which sensations or thoughts emerge and can have meaning. Despite revising the kind of objectivity that time has, Kant shares with Aristotle a conception of time as a neutral order within which our experience of the world and of ourselves unfolds.

In the Transcendental Aesthetic of the *Critique of Pure Reason*, Kant argues that time is a pure form of sensible intuition. Time cannot, as Leibniz claims, be derived from our actual experience of sensations that we then relate to one another temporally, because for sensations to appear successively, they must already appear in time. Thus, according to Kant, time is merely the "empty" form within which the matter of experience appears to us; it is a condition for the possibility of experience.[29] In the Transcendental Deduction, Kant goes on to say that the perception of successive events also requires a persisting self-consciousness that can have and hold together successive experiences over time. Kant says that I must be able to relate the "I think" to all of my representations, or else no objective experience—of causally related objects in space and time—would be possible.[30] Apperceptive self-consciousness, which Kant distinguishes from the self that occurs (in time) in inner sense, is a formal condition for the possibility of experience. Such self-consciousness makes time consciousness possible, but it is not in time; it is distinct from the objects of both inner and outer sense. The apperceptive "I think" is the ground of synthesizing the diversity of events in time and is not itself affected by the movement of time.

Levinas's concern is that this abstract or formal understanding of time again neglects the originary dimension of lived time. The "I think" allows for "the gathering of the *sensed* into knowledge," according to the form of temporal order (PDIC 179). Despite the temporal diversity of what is sensed, it can be synthesized into intelligible representations (DR 161). Levinas emphasizes the Aristotelian roots of Kantian time, by drawing a connection between the power of apperception and the view of time as a degradation of eternity. In spite of the constant becoming of the world,

> the privilege of the present would still be maintained, whose sovereign expression is the Platonic theory of reminiscence, and thus a reference from thought to perception would be guaranteed; and thus, the privilege of eternity, as well as of a present-which-does-not-pass, would again be affirmed in the ideality of the idea; an eternity whose duration or diachrony of time would be only dissimulation or deformation or deprivation in the finite consciousness of man. A privilege also of the *I think*, "stronger" than time, which gathers the dispersal of temporal shades under the unity of transcendental apperception, the firmest and most formal of forms, stronger than all heterogeneity of contents—to identify the diversity of experience by embracing it and grasping it again identified in the knowing of the being into which it enters. (FO 149–50)

In synchronizing temporal difference, apperception is "stronger than time," and consciousness thus generates a kind of eternal present. But if the passing of time were *not only* a degenerate form of eternity, a falling away from the stability of the same, but instead imposed on the knowing subject some "concreteness 'older' than the pure form of time," the I's ability to synthesize his experience into a meaningful order would be disrupted (DR 176).

Diachronous time would then have a content that would overcome the presumed detachment of the knowing subject precisely because it does not smoothly deliver a perception or an idea that can be remembered or anticipated. For Levinas, this significance is specifically ethical:

> This meaning of a past that has not been my present and does not concern my reminiscence, and of a future that commands me in mortality or in the face of the other—beyond my powers, my finitude, and my being-doomed-to-death, no longer articulate the representable time of immanence and the historical present. Its dia-chrony, the "difference" of diachrony, does not signify pure rupture, but also non-in-difference and concordance that are no longer founded on the unity of transcendental apperception, the most formal of forms, which, through reminiscence and hope, joins time up again in re-presenting it, but betrays it. (DR 175–76)

Diachrony refuses to present an event that offers itself up as an object of the "I think" and instead raises the question of my right to persist in my being. Levinas claims that the history of Western thought, at least up to Bergson, represses or denies the impact that diachrony has on us, betraying that impact by reducing the passing of time to a formal structure. But diachrony opens up an encounter with alterity, a rupture of time that resists representation. By ignoring the significance of diachronous time, Western philosophy is then able to characterize the subject principally as an observer who makes sense of his experience and then attempts to impose his will on the world in the light of such knowledge.[31] For all its originality, Kant's critical philosophy does not revolt against that traditional set of assumptions, which allows time to function as the mere condition for knowledge.

Levinas's Reading of Rosenzweig on Time

Levinas takes up Rosenzweig's thought in idiosyncratic ways, but this section will focus on how he inherits Rosenzweig's claims to challenge Kant's view of time.[32] Levinas writes in the preface to *Totality and Infinity* that the *Star of Redemption* is "a work too often present in this book to be cited" (TI 28). The very title gestures to Rosenzweig's opposition between a Hegelian drive for comprehensive historical totality and the significance of the infinite, which lies outside of that history. This opposition is also expressed as the contrast between the time of paganism, in which human existence is governed by physical laws and an Aristotelian progression of present moments, and the notion of messianic time invoked in ritual and religious communities, in which past, present, and future are permeated by the relationship between human beings and the divine.[33] In Levinas's reading of Rosenzweig, time "receives its meaning from the horizon of religiosity" rather than providing the neutral form by which experience is assembled into a totality (PFR 137). Within a larger discussion of Rosenzweig's critique of Hegel, Levinas explicitly invokes the process of deformalizing the Kantian concept of time: "In Rosenzweig's work, the abstract aspects of time—past, present, future—are deformalized; it is no longer a question of time, an empty form in which there are three formal dimensions. It is as if Rosenzweig were saying: to think the past concretely, you have to think Creation. Or, the future is Redemption; the present is Revelation" (PJL 118). Levinas suggests here that Rosenzweig describes an originary temporality infused with significance, out of which emerges the conception of linear time as part of the observable world. The abstract idea of the past is derived from the idea of the world originating out of a divine power, the idea of the present is derived from the idea of the divine in the process of revealing itself in relation with the finite, and the idea of the future is derived from the idea of the fulfillment of a divine order. The chronology of public time is subordinate to this narrative of the relationship between human beings and God. This "philosophical audacity" challenges the idea that we experience cosmological, abstract time and then locate creation, revelation, and redemption—or any other narrative—within that structure (OUJ 233).

Having suggested the direction of Levinas's critique of Husserl, Heidegger, and Bergson in the previous section, I should mention briefly how he diverges from Rosenzweig, a critique that happens mostly implicitly in his writing. One aspect of this divergence is that Levinas very clearly prioritizes ethics above the relationship between the divine and the human. In discussing the relationship of finite beings to the infinite, Rosenzweig writes of the importance of human community, as in the redemptive character of communal prayer, in which the infinite breaks into the finite and the focus on individuals is superseded.[34] Levinas's focus is much more on the asymmetrical relationship with one other human being, where the moment of infinite demand does not form any part of a cosmological narrative of redemption.[35] This obdurate focus on responsibility as the one-for-the-other gives rise to Levinas's relative silence on the question of how the ethical moment should inform politics or religious faith. Nonetheless, Rosenzweig's deformalization of time—and particularly its derivation of finite or "pagan" time from the infinite or transcendent—undeniably influences Levinas's understanding of diachrony. Time has its own meaning and thus cannot function formally as a neutral framework within which the subject organizes her experience. More precisely, time cannot function *only* in this formal register, even if in our ordinary lives we mostly orient ourselves toward this derivative order of time.

The Significance of Diachrony

But what then is the content or significance of this deformalized time, for Levinas? It is at this point that the ambiguity in the genitive of that phrase "the deformalization of time" becomes important: time deforms the intentional activity of subject, such that the ego can no longer function purely as a synchronizing, apperceptive consciousness. In "Diachrony and Representation" Levinas links these two dimensions of deformalization:

> It was important to me above all to speak in this study of how, in the human intrigue, past, future, and present are tied together in time, without this being the result of a simple degradation that the unity of the One may somehow (I know not how) have undergone, dispersing itself in *movement*, which since (or according to) Aristotle supposedly lead us to time in its diachrony. On such a view, the unity of time would lose itself in the flow of instants, and find itself again—without truly finding itself—in re-presentation, where the past gathers together instants by way of the memory's images, and the future by way of installments and promises. But I have sought time as the deformalization of the most formal form there is—the unity of the *I think*. (DR 176)

He links in this passage Parmenides's privileging of being over becoming to Aristotle's cosmological conception of time, as a linear series of present moments, and then to the Kantian account by which the activity of consciousness binds this heterogeneity into a unity. Ultimately, a formal account of time presupposes a particular kind of subject—one capable of mastering becoming through representation. Levinas proposes as an alternative a deformalized time that undermines the self-possession of the subject: time is now the disturbance of how we typically order the world, not only in the sense that time loses its linear order but in the sense that the synchronizing activity of the detached observer cannot be sustained.

This idea of the contradiction between time in its passing and the organizing activity of consciousness appears as early as *Existence and Existents* (1947): "We must then try to grasp that event of birth in phenomena which are prior to reflection.... [I]t is reflection itself that thus characterizes all the events of our history in a purely formal way, laying them out as contents and covering over their dramatic nature as events" (EE 11). Challenging the synchronizing work of consciousness overturns the basic comportment of the subject, as a knowing, deliberating agent. Our originary relation to time is an undergoing, or, as Levinas puts it in *Otherwise than Being*, an "aging," in which we are utterly subjected to the passing of time (OB 52–53). It is only in a secondary sense that we come to master this passing through intentional activity. Originary or diachronic time is "patience itself," where patience has the connotation of passivity (GDT 7).[36]

Levinas insistently claims that the passivity of this "patience" is not the absence or the opposite of activity, an idea that sits easily within the domain of intentionality. Instead, this is a passivity that demands something of the subject. In the language that Levinas begins to use in his late work, the diachronic past is "immemorial" in its resistance to representation, but its inaccessibility does not negate its impact on consciousness. The immemorial past is not simply forgotten, a past that is so temporally distant that no one remembers it. It thus interrupts the familiar opposition between activity and passivity, which informs the basic dynamic of consciousness—the known object (*Gegenstand*) standing against the knowing subject—and of autonomy—the free subject imposing his will on a set of determined objects in the world. Time in its passing entangles the subject in a more complex kind of passivity, in which the subject "is unable to catch up with its origin and so is never fully present to itself," in Jeffrey Kosky's terms.[37] Diachrony puts us out of phase with ourselves, in a way that the powers of representation cannot recuperate. Levinas's argument for the possibility of this resistance to intentionality gestures to lived experiences of passivity. In "Useless Suffering," Levinas describes suffering as "not just a *datum*, refractory to the synthesis of the Kantian 'I think'—which is capable of reuniting and embracing the most heterogeneous and disparate data into order and meaning in its *a priori* forms—but the *way* in which the refusal, opposing the assemblage of data into a meaningful whole, rejects it; at once what disturbs order and this disturbance itself" (US 91). In the obscure last phrase of this passage, Levinas describes how suffering is both the sensation of disorder ("what disturbs order") and the disruption of any possible assimilation within consciousness. Suffering is certainly not equivalent to time, but with both concepts he emphasizes how intentionality gets destabilized, even if we retrospectively attempt to contain the impact of those experiences.

Levinas's understanding of diachronic time thus does not conform to the Aristotelian tradition of public or cosmological time, or the Kantian account of time as the formal condition of experience, which are committed to the centrality of the present and time's susceptibility to being synchronized in consciousness.[38] Although Bergson, Heidegger, and Rosenzweig are variously concerned with the significance of temporality in subjective experience, they do not emphasize the way in which diachrony opens up alterity, the specifically ethical significance of time. Michael Morgan describes Levinas's alternative as an original conception of temporality, beyond the objectivity of public-scientific time or the subjectivity of internally experienced temporality.[39] If time were only synchronic, every event could be reduced to a phenomenon, captured as an experience by consciousness. It would serve as a backdrop for beings, rather than challenging the power of representation. But diachrony introduces a kind of encounter that cannot be reduced to a representation: a responsibility to and for the other that cannot be charted on a linear timeline, initiated by any remembered act or promise. Time instead forces us to encounter what does not belong to the economy of presence and lack of presence. The other is not merely another intentional object present before me, and the other *qua* other does not share my present moment: "Time means that the other is forever beyond me, irreducible to the synchrony of the same. The temporality of the interhuman opens up the meaning of otherness and the otherness of meaning" (EoI 57). Diachronous time forbids the reduction of the other to an object of knowledge, or my responsibility to the other as a freely chosen commitment. In this sense it interrupts the complacency with which consciousness comprehends the world and itself.

The opposition between synchrony and diachrony thus maps onto the opposition between totality and infinity. The former aspect of time supports the activity of representation that binds events into a unity, whereas the latter opens up the possibility of a relation to that which resists representation or conceptual assimilation. The subject is exposed to the other in such a way that the other exceeds comprehension but is nonetheless in relation to the self. We encounter responsibility too late to be able to refuse it, to negotiate a different obligation, to make or retract a promise, or even to put limits on the scope of that responsibility: "Responsibility is anterior to all the logical deliberation summoned by reasoned decision. . . . In the ethical anteriority of responsibility, for-the-other, in its priority over deliberation, there is a past irreducible to a presence that it must have been" (DR 111). It is in this sense that the other addresses the self in the accusative—

and Levinas exploits the ambiguity of this term to refer both to the grammatical case (of being neutrally addressed) and to the more specific moral connotation of culpability. But diachrony is fundamentally an experience of a commitment that does not arise out of the subject's choices: "The responsibility for the other can not have begun in my commitment, in my decision. The unlimited responsibility in which I find myself comes from the hither side of my freedom, from a 'prior to every memory,' an 'ulterior to every accomplishment,' from the non-present par excellence, the non-original, the an-archical" (OB 10). For Levinas, the movement of time demonstrates the limits of our self-possession. The unlimited quality of responsibility lies in its an-archy, its lack of a determinate origin and governing structure. On Levinas's reading, responsibility thus cannot be defined by a series of obligations that can be ascertained by cataloging one's own actions, intentions, or particular relationship with the other. It precedes such questions, which Levinas consigns to the realm of justice—the domain in which we must treat the other as one person among others, whose interests must be weighed against other obligations. But the ethical itself does not allow this kind of calculation and limitation on my responsibility. Paradoxically, diachrony carries meaning precisely because its meaning cannot be thematized or made intelligible. Its significance burdens or imposes itself on the subject insofar as it escapes representation.

The deformalization of time leaves us with a signification that cannot be assimilated as just another intentional object, a neutral sensation, or experiential content that can be comprehended and integrated into an ongoing narrative of the knowing subject. In this way, diachronous time undermines the primary activity of intentionality, which Levinas associates with the autonomy of consciousness. Levinas describes Husserl's phenomenology as a "philosophy of freedom," where freedom is understood as the power of consciousness to constitute the world—to bestow meaning upon it (WH 84). But bestowing meaning entails the identification of objects by synthesizing them "across the multiplicity of mental life" (WH 59). That is, freedom is the activity of representation, itself made possible by the ability of consciousness to gather and reflect on its contents, "the secret of subjectivity itself, the condition for a free mind" (WH 77). Anything that could be significant to the subject would also then be intelligible:

> Signification, intelligibility and mind would reside in the manifestation and in contemporaneousness, in synopsis, presence, in essence which is a phenomenon, that is, a signification whose very movement involves thematization, visibility and the said. Any radical non-assemblable diachrony would be excluded from meaning. The psyche in the subject then consists in representation in its gift for synchronizing, commencing, that [is], its gift of freedom. . . . The psyche would be consciousness excluding any trauma, since being is in fact what shows itself before striking, what amortizes [*amortit*] its violence in knowledge. (OB 135, translation slightly modified)

In the last sentence of this passage, *amortir* refers to a softening or a cushioning of a blow, the buffer that allows the world to be represented as a set of phenomena. But diachrony breaks through the barrier between the subject and what it attempts to know and act on. It is in this specific sense that Levinas turns to the language of trauma, an encounter that cannot be represented and yet is significant for the subject.

This chapter began with Levinas's claim in 1988 that the "essential theme of my research is the deformalization of time" (OUJ 232). He continues that thought as follows: "Kant says that [time] is the form of all experience. All human experience does in fact take on a temporal form. The transcendental philosophy descended from Kant filled that form with a sensible content coming from experience or, since Hegel, that form has led dialectically toward a content. These philosophers never required, for the constitution of that form of temporality itself, a *condition* in a certain *conjuncture* of "matter" or events, in a meaningful content somehow prior to form" (OUJ 232). Formal conceptions of time characterize its movement as the frame or structure within which consciousness experiences beings or comes to know itself fully. In this sense, the future and the past can be integrated into the present. But time itself has no significance. In various ways, Levinas reads Bergson, Husserl, Heidegger, and Rosenzweig as offering alternatives to that notion of time, particularly by focusing on the subjective experience of the movement of time as the source of public or clock time.

For Levinas, however, these critiques do not escape the central assumptions of formal time, because they continue to privilege the subject's ability to synchronize the passage of time. It is only in attending to time in its diachrony that the philosophical tradition can radically undermine the sovereignty of the subject, and Levinas's positive claims about time begin from this idea: time has an ethical significance, one that dismantles the self-possession of consciousness. In breaking the dynamic of intentionality and opening up the encounter with alterity, then, deformalized time has the significance of trauma.

Notes

1. Chanter, *Time, Death, and the Feminine*, 195.
2. See, for instance, OB, 26–38, and DR, 159–72.
3. Augustine, *Confessions*, XI.20.
4. Gibbs, *Correlations in Rosenzweig and Levinas*, 30.
5. Aristotle, *Physics*, 220a.
6. Ibid., 219b.
7. Ibid.
8. Sugarman, "Emmanuel Levinas and the Deformalization of Time," 254.
9. See Severson, *Levinas's Philosophy of Time*, 13–18, and Lin, *Intersubjectivity of Time*, 33–41.

10. See also Cohen, *Levinasian Meditations*, 44–46.
11. Bergson, *Creative Mind*, 179.
12. As Nicholas de Warren argues, Bergson does not merely invert the privileging of being over becoming but argues that we should see being *as* becoming ("Miracles of Creation," 178).
13. See also Lin, *Intersubjectivity of Time*, 159–60.
14. See Bergson, *Introduction to Metaphysics*, 42–46.
15. See OUJ, 232.
16. See Hopkins, "Deformalization and Phenomenon in Husserl and Heidegger."
17. Husserl, *Ideas*, 26.
18. On the issue of how Levinas inherits the work of Husserl and Heidegger, see Drabinski, *Sensibility and Singularity*.
19. Heidegger, *Being and Time*, §65.
20. Severson, *Levinas's Philosophy of Time*, 98.
21. See also Durie, "Speaking of Time."
22. Chanter, *Time, Death, and the Feminine*, 143–55.
23. Ibid., 154.
24. Levinas has been accused of ungenerously reading Heidegger on this point and others, an accusation against which Chanter defends him in *Time, Death, and the Feminine*, 185–88.
25. Lin, *Intersubjectivity of Time*, 161.
26. Bergson, *Time and Free Will*, 221.
27. Lin, *Intersubjectivity of Time*, 22.
28. Ibid., 108–12.
29. Kant, *Critique of Pure Reason*, A51/B75.
30. Ibid., B131–32.
31. I use the masculine pronoun here deliberately—see Lloyd, *Man of Reason*.
32. For a more detailed discussion of Rosenzweig's influence on Levinas, see Gibbs, *Correlations in Rosenzweig and Levinas*; and Cohen, *Elevations*.
33. Rosenzweig, *Star of Redemption*, 345–46; see also Severson, *Levinas's Philosophy of Time*, 89–92.
34. Rosenzweig, *Star of Redemption*, 292–94.
35. See Lin, *Intersubjectivity of Time*, 144–57, and Gordon, *Rosenzweig and Heidegger*, 10–12. Gordon argues instead that Levinas radically reinterprets Rosenzweig's ideas on the significance of time.
36. Catherine Chalier echoes this idea: "time as vigilance and patience, time as awakening and disturbance" ("Levinas and the Talmud," 114).
37. Kosky, "After the Death of God," 240.
38. See Lin, *Intersubjectivity of Time*, 79.
39. Morgan, *Discovering Levinas*, 212–13.

2 The Traumatic Impact of Deformalized Time

ON LEVINAS'S READING, formal conceptions of time depict a neutral order within which we experience events and beings. These accounts correlatively naturalize a subject who comprehends and controls her surroundings. When Levinas identifies the deformalization of time as central to his philosophical work, he is thus engaged in the critique of the image of subjectivity presupposed by formal conceptions of time. Starting in the late 1960s, Levinas describes time's "meaningful content somehow prior to form" as traumatic: a responsibility for the other imposed on the subject, which consciousness is always too late to assimilate as a phenomenon (OUJ 232).

In *Otherwise than Being*, he describes diachronous time as a disruption of the activity of the knowing, willing subject. That notion of interruption or rupture is crucial to Levinas's use of the term "trauma" (*traumatisme*), which derives from the Greek word for a wound, particularly through piercing. To unpack the idea that time has an ethical significance, and why Levinas describes that significance as traumatic, in this chapter I draw on elements of the psychoanalytic discussion of trauma that illuminate Levinas's account of deformalized time. This is a connection that Levinas himself would avoid, given his wholesale rejection of psychoanalysis as a legitimate resource in understanding subjectivity. But Freud's work initiates a tradition of thinking about trauma that explores the undermining of the sovereign subject—specifically by destabilizing the subject's ability to represent traumatic events and thus create an orderly temporal narrative. In this way, psychoanalytic accounts of trauma enrich Levinas's use of the concept to describe the impact of deformalized time.

Time and Monsters

In the opening chapter of *Otherwise than Being*, Levinas refers to time as the "monstration of essence," in the context of discussing synchronous time as that which allows for the manifestation of all that is (OB 9). In this way of understanding time, the passing of time does not resist but instead supports this disclosure: "The getting out of phase [*déphasage*] of the instant, the 'all' pulling off from the 'all'—the temporality of time—makes possible . . . a recuperation in which nothing is lost" (OB 28). But diachrony introduces monstrosity or deformation into that synthesis, a significance that cannot be made present.[1] The strange intensity of Levinas's rhetoric moves from the everyday encounter—for instance, passing a stranger on the street—to its originary meaning of exposure to the other, an uncontracted responsibility to and for the other (OB 47). This vulnerability itself is a wounding, insofar as it overturns the basic dynamic of intentionality. Emphasizing the passivity of responsibility, Levinas calls it a "coring out" (*dénucléation*) of the subject (OB 64):

> in the saying this passivity signifies, becomes signifyingness, exposure in response to ..., being at the question before any interrogation, any problem, without clothing, without a shell to protect oneself, stripped to the core as in an inspiration of air.... It is a fission of the nucleus opening the bottom of its punctual nuclearity, like a lung at the core of oneself. The nucleus does not open this depth as long as it remains protected by its solid crust, by a form, not even when it is reduced to its punctuality, for it identifies itself in the temporality of its essence, and thus covers itself over again.... This being torn up from oneself in the core of one's unity, this absolute noncoinciding, this diachrony of the instant, signifies in the form of one-penetrated-by-the-other. (OB 49, translation slightly modified)

There are a couple of key dimensions to this description: first, the persistent use of embodied vulnerability as a way of thematizing denucleation, and second, the emphasis on diachrony within the encounter with the other. The language of fission, being torn up, and having a lung at one's core (entailing inspiration and expiration) gestures to the intensity of the encounter with the other, in which the I experiences otherness within himself, without being able to master what is foreign: "Time would ... be a disquieting [*inquietude*] of the Same by the Other, without the Same ever being able to comprehend or encompass the Other" (GDT 19). The for-the-other of responsibility breaks open the subject in his self-possession, and it is in this context that Levinas uses the term *traumatisme*.

Diachrony opens up the possibility of the self not coinciding with herself, and thus not being able to represent all that it encounters. John Llewelyn describes the *dia-* in diachrony as the cutting or interruption of my own linear narrative by the encounter with alterity *as* alterity.[2] Diachronic time introduces a discontinuity with formal time, a passing of time that cannot be recuperated back into the present: "this relation [diachrony] that is not knowledge, not something grasped, not intentionality" (IEL 296). But the *dia-* of diachrony also means the *dia-* of dialogue (PFR 144). We find ourselves responsible—answerable to and for the other—without having deliberated, decided, or acted in any particular way that would initiate that responsibility: "it is in the obligation for another which I never contracted—in which I have never signed any obligation, for never to man's knowledge have I struck a contract with another—that a writ was passed. Something *already concluded* appears in my relationship with another" (QA 96, emphasis added). In chapter 5, I will examine in more detail that peculiar claim that responsibility exceeds our conscious decision-making or voluntary action, having its origin in an immemorial past. For the present discussion of the traumatic significance of time, it is perhaps enough to say that the content of diachrony undermines the sovereignty of the subject, by impeding the reign of intentionality over everything exterior to the mind, and by introducing the uncanny passivity of an unchosen responsibility. Levinas refers to responsibility as an-archic to emphasize its distance even from a determinate moment of creation, a spatialized location along a linear chronology. Responsibility "is thus in a time without beginning. Its anarchy cannot be understood as a simple return from present to prior present, an extrapolation of presents according to a memorable time, that is, a time assemblable in a recollection of a representable representation. This anarchy, this refusal to be assembled into a representation, has its own way to concern me: the *lapse*" (OB 51). Bergson's emphasis on duration has become in Levinas's work the irreducibility of time's passing and how that lapse of time functions as the ethical limit of intentionality. I am concerned for the other without being able to comprehend or control the nature of that binding force. Levinas refers to this anarchic structure of responsibility as having the effect of a "traumatizing blow," which the synchronizing activity of consciousness cannot predict, amortize, or soften (OB 53).

Levinas's Aversion to Psychoanalysis

The terminology of trauma runs throughout *Otherwise than Being*, having first appeared in the 1968 essay "Substitution," a revised version of which forms the core of the book.[3] On my reading, trauma constitutes the substantive meaning of diachrony, in the wake of the deformalization of time. Somewhat heretically, I consider psychoanalytic discourse useful in interpreting the significance of trauma in Levinas's work—heretically, because Levinas categorically rejects psychoanalytic theory. His response to a question about Eros in a late interview is typical: "I am definitely not a Freudian.... I have never been a Freudian" (PJL 113). He characterizes psychoanalysis, in its focus on the opacity of the psyche, as a matter of "seeing or knowing," an attempt to bring what is unconscious to light (NM 167). That is, in spite of its recognition of the multiple ways in which the psyche is heteronomous and not even transparent to itself, psychoanalysis remains beholden to the idea that disclosing the truth of the subject's thought and behavior has therapeutic effects. Levinas reacts against the reduction of the other to a drama of transparency and obscurity, with much the same objection that he brings to dominant threads within modern Western thought: "The unconscious remains a play of consciousness, and psychoanalysis means to ensure its outcome, against the troubles that come to it from repressed desires, in the name of the very rules of the game. The play of consciousness does indeed involve rules, but irresponsibility in the game is declared to be a sickness" (OB 194n6). Resistance to intelligibility is still treated as a puzzle to be deciphered, although that goal remains only ever partially achieved by the analysand. Rationality and self-transparency remain the ideal, and even if irrationality, fantasy, and repression structure much of our psychic lives, they remain sources of pathology to be corrected or managed.

Levinas reportedly responded to a question about the significance of psychoanalysis for his work by asking "Is that not a form of pornography?"[4] Judith Butler remarks that this comment seems to imply that Levinas puritanically devalues psychoanalysis for its focus on sexuality, an interpretation that she ultimately refutes. His dismissal of psychoanalysis instead derives from a concern with voyeurism, in which scientific knowledge functions unreflectively as a form of objectification, and in which the main therapeutic task is the revealing of what is repressed.[5] One other element of his primarily gestural critique of psychoanalysis concerns its reduction of the psyche to embodied, involuntary impulses. Simon Critchley discusses a 1933 essay by Levinas called "The Understanding of Spirituality in French and German Culture," in which psychoanalysis is associated with a German tendency to privilege "embodiment, the body, the concrete I"—as opposed to the French focus on the rational mind. He reads psychoanalysis as identifying in our behavior determinate and perhaps even mechanistic motivations that can be systematically deciphered and redirected.[6] Tracing his own philosophical influences, Levinas mentions Charles Blondel, who "developed a specifically Bergsonian psychology quite hostile to Freud—a hostility which made a deep and lasting impression on me" (EoI 49). Richard Cohen notes that this hostility derives in part from the analyst's tendency to reduce the other person into a set of symptoms, thereby evading the ethical impact of proximity.[7] On Levinas's account, psychoanalysis remains committed to a tradition that positions the subject as either an ideal knower, capable of objective knowledge and autonomous action, or the object of knowledge. Neither pole of this dynamic allows for the disruptive impact of alterity.

Despite this strong disavowal of psychoanalysis, Levinas prominently uses language laden with psychological meaning—obsession, persecution, trauma, anxiety.[8] Although these concepts have been used in various contexts, psychoanalytic discourse has treated them as intelligible psychic experiences and thus carefully describes their characteristic structures and symptoms. In doing so, it has drawn out in more detail key elements of trauma to which Levinas only gestures in *Otherwise than Being* and other late writings. This is not to say that Levinas is implicitly relying on psychoanalytic accounts of trauma or that the two approaches are entirely congruent. There are, however, important resonances between Freudian accounts of trauma and Levinas's references to *traumatisme*.

Trauma: A Freudian Detour

Freud discusses trauma throughout his work, but he first uses the concept as a way of explaining the disorder of hysteria. In *Studies on Hysteria*, he and Josef Breuer famously claim that "hysterics suffer mainly from reminiscences," emphasizing the hold that past events have on the patient's present.[9] Those past events are not represented but acted out—or in Freud's later terminology, they are not remembered but repeated—precisely because they resist the cognitive processing required for representation.[10] Freud claims that it is somewhat misleading to refer to traumatic memories as memories at all, given the complex processes that create repetitive symptoms and prevent the person from incorporating the event into the ordinary stream of representations. Traumatic memories are not subject to the normal "wearing-away" process that allows one's perception of the event to take its place in a linear narrative. That cognitive incorporation involves being able to gain perspective on an experience, check the accuracy of a memory, and communicate its meaning to ourselves or others. Without such assimilation, traumatic memories retain their psychological intensity and are acted out compulsively and involuntarily.[11]

Levinas's references to trauma pick up elements of what has been called a prepsychoanalytic understanding of the disorder—an account that locates the origin of trauma in an external event, such as a battle or (to use Freud's favorite example) a train collision.[12] Originally psychological trauma was conceptualized through an analogy to physical trauma, where major injury is inflicted by an external force. Early psychologists speculated that psychological trauma was caused by concussion or physical wounds. In part because of concerns about malingering or fraudulent insurance claims, there were concerted efforts to locate in an observable event the etiology of what is now framed as post-traumatic stress disorder, and what has at various points in the last two hundred years been called hysteria, soldier's heart, shell shock, and traumatic neurosis. This prepsychoanalytic model of trauma struggled to resolve two primary questions: why psychological symptoms tend to have a latency period rather than manifesting themselves immediately, and why some people suffer from psychological trauma without ever experiencing a physical injury. Some soldiers in World War I, for instance, were diagnosed as suffering from shell shock after being in the midst of battle, but others displayed much the same symptoms without any direct experience of combat.[13]

Freud is able to address these two questions, but he confronts the additional question of how trauma fits into the basic picture of the psyche that he had developed. Until World War I, Freud conceives of dreams and pathological symptoms ultimately as expressions of the pleasure principle—as wishes, essentially—but he cannot explain how traumatic nightmares and other repetitions fulfill any wish or protect the psyche from pain. In the context of the treatment of soldiers, Freud returns to a consideration of how external events pierce and break open the psychical boundaries of the ego. For all the protective measures that the psyche employs—its "shield against stimuli from the external world" and coping mechanisms, such as projection, for internal stimuli—there are events that create stimuli too intense to be contained: "We describe as 'traumatic' any excitations from outside which are powerful enough to break through the protective shield. It seems to me that the concept of trauma necessarily implies a connection of this kind with a breach in an otherwise efficacious barrier against stimuli."[14] The apparently clear line between interiority and exteriority collapses, which undermines the psyche's normal methods of making sense of the world and of itself. In John Fletcher's words, traumatic experiences are "signifying traces" that "resist assimilation and binding into the ego's narcissistic structures and personal archives; they function as an internal foreign body and so give rise to deferred or belated aftereffects."[15] If someone had had time to be frightened, that would protect the ego against the violence of the event, but its very unexpectedness overwhelms the psyche. Fright appears only in a delayed form in traumatic symptoms, which arise as a reaction to the "internal foreign body" of the trauma.[16]

Here Freud distinguishes between anxiety (*Angst*), as the anticipation of some danger, and fright (*Schreck*), as the psychological response to unanticipated danger. Trauma results from a "lack of preparedness for anxiety," or more simply, a lack of anxiety in a situation that merits it.[17] The unexpectedness of the danger means that the protective mechanisms cannot "bind" or amortize the experience and thus protect the ego from its impact. Traumatic repetitions, such as flashbacks or nightmares, are attempts to "master the stimulus retrospectively, by developing the anxiety whose omission was the cause of the traumatic neurosis."[18] In other words, the psyche inflicts the reenactment of the traumatic event on itself, in an attempt to prepare and protect itself better against its shock this time around. But the traumatic event cannot be contained in the normal processes of dreaming, and the person merely re-experiences the fright without psychologically metabolizing it.[19] This breach of the ego's boundaries causes symptoms that cannot be explained by the pleasure principle alone. Freud is mystified by the fact that traumatic events are both driven from conscious memory and compulsively reenacted in dreams or flashbacks. This perplexity leads to his formulation of the death drive, a psychological force seeking the dissolution of the ego, as a way to explain the repetitive inflicting of painful (non)memories.

A disordering of time is intimately bound up with trauma. Repetitions of past events impose themselves involuntarily in the person's present experience, sometimes decades afterward. The threat of bodily harm or the witnessing of bodily harm to others, compounded with a sense of helplessness in these events, typically create a break in the person's basic perception of herself and the world. Although their approaches to trauma tend not to be Freudian, contemporary medical models affirm the central role that temporality plays in traumatic events and the symptoms that result. The National Center for Post-Traumatic Stress Disorder, part of the US Department of Veterans Affairs, has developed a questionnaire based on the *Diagnostic and Statistical Manual*'s current criteria to determine whether someone suffers from post-traumatic stress disorder. The relevant symptoms include what are collectively called intrusive recollections: "repeated, disturbing, and unwanted memories of the stressful experience; repeated, disturbing dreams of the stressful experience; suddenly feeling or acting as if the stressful experience were actually happening again."[20] The intrusion of the past in the present has broad repercussions for the person's life, including dissociative symptoms, avoiding situations that might remind the patient of the traumatic event, irritability, and hypervigilance.[21]

Unexpectedness is a crucial factor of what makes a traumatic event traumatic, and this suddenness disrupts the person's ordinary experience of the world and their place within it, which may provoke conscious or unconscious attempts to make sense of that event. But trauma also undermines the linear flow of time, the simple succession of past, present, and future—not only through flashbacks allowing the past to haunt the present, but by creating a sense of a foreshortened future, or disbelief that one's life could plausibly continue for very long. In his reading of Freud's evolving understanding of trauma, Fletcher emphasizes the passivity of the traumatized subject, specifically with regard to how memory is disordered: "Instead of a subject-centered process, 'I remember that event,' we need a formulation more like, 'This scene is remembered or remembers itself in me,' or even, 'This scene remembers me.'"[22] This repetitive displacement of the traumatized subject from the position of knower and agent remains true to Freud and Breuer's initial claim that "hysterics suffer mainly from reminiscences": "It is as though these patients had not finished with the traumatic situation, as though they were still faced by it as an immediate task which has not been dealt with."[23] The linearity of time is disrupted by a (non)experience that cannot be coherently integrated into the subject's memory. Such a disruption, carrying intense emotional investments, cannot remain isolated from the rest of one's psychological life. Instead, it causes an overwhelming disordering of the person's cognitive and affective integration. In this sense, trauma disrupts some of the basic ways in which we typically experience ourselves as agents in the world—as generally self-assured in our knowledge and memory, as emotionally self-possessed, as confident in our ability to make our way safely through the world and to act freely within it.

Post-Freudian Accounts of Trauma

Contemporary psychological accounts similarly describe the experience of trauma as a derangement of the person's basic sense of the structure of the world, both temporally and interpersonally.[24] When post-traumatic stress disorder was first defined in the third edition of the *Diagnostic and Statistical Manual* (1980), traumatic events were described as "outside the range of usual human experience."[25] Judith Herman notes that traumatic events are extraordinary not because of their rarity but because "they overwhelm the ordinary human adaptations to life."[26] Subsequent revisions have specified that such events are those that "involve actual or threatened death, serious injury, or sexual violence, or a threat to the physical integrity of self or others."[27] Traumatic events violate one's "inner schemata" of what reality is and should be, one's sense of a meaningful, basically secure world.[28] These experiences thus undermine familiar ways of navigating our lives. Cathy Caruth describes trauma as "a breach in the mind's experience of time, self, and the world."[29] This language serves as a reminder of trauma as a piercing wound, one with grave consequences for the rest of the subject's experience. Susan Brison describes the cumulative effect of those symptoms as an "undoing of the self"—a phrase that echoes Levinas's term *dénucléation*. One of the dimensions of that loss is the difficulty (but not impossibility) of constructing a coherent narrative about an event that is unspeakable.[30] She claims that in the wake of trauma, "one's basic cognitive and emotional capacities are gone, or radically altered. . . . This epistemological crisis leaves the survivor with virtually no bearings to navigate by."[31] As Brison writes, the traumatized person may experience herself as having died, because one's memory of one's past self is so discontinuous with one's present experience: "For months after my assault, I had to stop myself before saying (what seemed accurate at the time), 'I was murdered in France last summer.'"[32]

The loss of a familiar horizon has epistemic consequences, both for memory and in one's basic ability to make sense of the world. The unifying, meaning-bestowing activity of the psyche is disrupted: "trauma interferes with the synthetic function of the ego, with our very capacity to know."[33] In the therapeutic context, this factor contributes to the loss of a sense of agency on the part of the victim/survivor—including her ability to narrate her experience and trust that others will listen.[34] The feeling of disempowerment and profound disorientation is intensified by the intrusive re-experiencing of the traumatic event. The cognitive disruption caused by traumatic events generate experiences that impose themselves on the victim's life, and so create "a wide phenomenological spectrum" of at least partial knowledge of the traumatic event, including fugue states, repetitive enactments, and transference.[35] But this partial knowledge is something to be undergone rather than a form of mastery. At its most intense, trauma dis-integrates the ego's ability to organize its experience, but it remains a "demonic" presence in the lives of the traumatized.[36]

In sum, traumatic events resist metabolization by the psyche, to use Jean Laplanche's term.[37] Unlike events within the "range of usual human experience" or events that are unusual but predictable and/or harmless, trauma cannot be mastered cognitively and emotionally. Laplanche and Pontalis claim that in borrowing the term "trauma" from the medical discourse of bodily injury, psychoanalysis "carries three ideas implicit in it over to the psychical level: the idea of a violent shock, the idea of a wound and the idea of consequences affecting the whole organization."[38] This failure to "bind" the trauma, to integrate it into the rest of one's narrative, does not mean that the trauma cannot be remembered or represented at all, as some contemporary trauma theorists argue, but that traumatic events disturb the psyche's ability to remember such events normally.

One of the hallmarks of trauma, throughout the history of its diagnosis and treatment, is the damage it does to ordinary forms of representation and self-representation. These disruptions confirm the essential idea that traumatic events happen so suddenly and threaten the self's continued existence so intensely that consciousness is unprepared for them. They thus remain unmetabolized and not only resist being woven into the subject's autobiographical narrative but undermine the ability to tell such a coherent narrative at all. In other words, trauma collapses the "specular distance" associated with intentionality and thus breaches the boundaries of the conscious self (OB 99).[39]

Levinas's Use of the Concept of Trauma

These psychological descriptions of how traumatic events disrupt the ego elucidate how Levinas uses the concept, in three particular elements: the unexpectedness of the traumatic event, the "breach" in the boundary between the ego and the external world, and the resistance to narration that such an event poses for the subject. Those elements are intimately interconnected—not having time to prepare for an experience that the person perceives as life-threatening creates a psychological wound, a weight that imposes itself on the subject. This woundedness destabilizes the agency of the subject, in the sense of being powerless in that moment but also becoming more broadly hindered in their ability to make decisions, envision a plausible future, tell a coherent story of what has happened, experience themselves as a unified self across time, and generally feel at home in the world.[40]

Trauma thus dismantles the self-possession that Levinas associates with the *conatus*, the attitude of self-preservation whose animating impulse is to claim its own "place in the sun." Spinoza uses the phrase *conatus essendi* to refer to a natural self-love that motivates us to preserve our own being.[41] Levinas borrows this term to describe the narcissism and indifference to the other that generally characterizes human existence, until the encounter with the other interrupts the amoral complacency of that drive: the proximity of the other is "a putting into question within me of the natural position of the subject, of the perseverance of the *I*—of its morally serene perseverance—in its being" (DR 168). Levinas often illustrates this attitude by quoting the last two sentences of a fragment from Pascal, which in full reads: "Mine, yours.—'This is my dog,' said those poor children. 'That is my place in the sun.' Here is the origin and image of the usurpation of the whole earth."[42] But responsibility, in its denucleating impact, unsettles that ability to establish one's proper place. By unraveling the basic dynamic of intentionality, responsibility denaturalizes the natural standpoint of the *conatus*.

The term "trauma" enters into Levinas's discourse in the late 1960s and is particularly prevalent in *Otherwise than Being*. In the rest of this chapter, I give a close reading of passages principally drawn from that work, through the lens of trauma as it is psychoanalytically described, to draw out the ethical significance of diachrony.[43] Levinas's references to trauma overwhelmingly emphasize a form of passivity at the heart of responsibility—my inability to step away from, negotiate, or even comprehend my obligation to the other. That is, I find myself committed to the other without having agreed to that obligation. Diachrony and nonintentional exposure to the other are thus intertwined. In the highly condensed summary of the argument that opens *Otherwise than Being*, Levinas describes responsibility as "a response answering [*réponse répondant*] to a non-thematizable provocation [*provocation*] and thus a non-vocation [*non-vocation*], a trauma" (OB 12). Levinas juxtaposes two words that in both French and English derive from the Latin *vocare*, to call: to be provoked is to be called forth, as opposed to a responsibility that is deliberately taken up as a vocation. The nonvocation is not simply the refusal to take up a commitment but being seized by responsibility without having committed oneself. In this sense, responsibility is traumatic. Even the most automatic activity, the synthesizing activity of the apperceptive "I think," is suspended: "Ethics is the breakup of the originary unity of transcendental apperception, that is, it is the beyond of experience. Witnessed, and not thematized, in the sign given to the other, the Infinite signifies out of responsibility for the other, out of the-one-for-the-other, a subject supporting everything, . . . but charged with everything, *without having had to decide for this taking charge*" (OB 148, emphasis added). The other does not present itself as a phenomenon, but as a trace, a signifying lack or absence. And yet the other is not entirely absent, and we cannot be indifferent to the ethical demand made on us. Unlike a being that can be represented, responsibility "violently" assails us, without softening its impact by making itself known ahead of time (OB 135). Responsibility is not simply one possible experience among others, but instead it evades the processes by which I grasp intentional objects.

This is the interaction that Levinas describes as proximity—neither a neutral coexistence in which the other is present to ordinary experience nor an absence in which the other is insignificant to me, but an encroachment causing "incessant restlessness" (OB 81). This apparently spatial metaphor of proximity comes to have temporal significance: the neighbor does not share the "common time of clocks" with me, at least not *as an other*, but instead creates "a disturbance of the rememberable time" (OB 89). Proximity is an "arrhythmia in time, a diachrony" (OB 166). Lin comments: "in proximity the synchronic, tranquil, rememberable time of the subject is disturbed by the time of the other, and diachronic time is created."[44] Part of the trauma of diachrony is its interruptive force, the way in which it breaks in on an established order: in this case, the order of synchronic time and the subject presumed by that order. Rudolf Bernet discusses this as the transition from a self-possessed subject to one exposed to the other: "In substituting the time of hetero-affection for the time of auto-affection, and in substituting the time of passivity for the time of intentional representation, what Levinas is aiming for is a transformation of the egological transcendental subject into an ethical subject, one which is characterized not by her spontaneous, free power, but by a responsibility *for* the other which comes *from* the other."[45] Time in its passing opens up the experience of "hetero-affection," the encounter with the other in her proximity. As Levinas emphasizes, however, this passivity is "more passive still than any receptivity," so that responsibility involves the subject's being called out of himself without being able to locate the source of that obligation (OB 48).

It is in this sense that Levinas speaks of responsibility arising out of an "immemorial past," a past that has never been present—an unrepresentable source of obligation (OB 88).[46] The subject is bound by responsibility before being able to step away enough to treat that responsibility as one more experience to be observed, examined, and evaluated: "out of an unrepresentable past, the subject has been sensitive to the provocation that has never presented itself, but has struck traumatically" (OB 144). Responsibility exceeds the dynamic of intentionality in its temporal structure, by imposing itself before being made present to consciousness (OB 50–51). Levinas characterizes responsibility as "anarchic," because it lacks a determinable origin, but also because of its destabilizing effect on the subject (OB 123; see also FCW 31). It carries an obligation without being intelligible to the person who undergoes it. Responsibility based on moral principles or recognizing the other as an alter ego begins from self-knowledge and self-interest. The rhetoric of trauma instead indicates an encounter in which the self is radically exposed: "The 'me' does not begin in the self-affection of a sovereign I, susceptible in a second moment to feeling compassion for the other; instead, it begins through the trauma without beginning, prior to every self-affection, of the upsurge of another" (GDT 178). The priority of responsibility lies in the obscurity of its origin; we find ourselves responsible without having comprehended the justification for that commitment.

As in psychological accounts of trauma, this wound undermines the sovereignty of the subject by threatening the familiar barriers between self and other. Fabio Ciaramelli characterizes Levinasian trauma as the "deposing [of the subject] by the other, its exposure" (*dé-position par l'autre, son ex-position*).[47] The ego loses its position, its place in the sun, and is instead exposed in responsibility. Levinas uses the image of a Nessus tunic to describe this breach in the self's defenses. In Greek myth, the Nessus tunic was the instrument of Herakles's death, a poisoned tunic that, once put on, fused with one's skin and could not be removed (OB 109).[48] As Bettina Bergo comments, somewhat gruesomely if we have this reference in mind, "a traumatic event has the metaphoric effect of thrusting the outside inward, or peeling the inside back and folding it inside-out."[49] Trauma disrupts the supposedly impermeable boundary between what is internal to the self and what is external to it, and does so in such a way that the self cannot escape that exposure and the command contained within it.

Levinas anticipates the resistance of the ego to this inversion of sovereignty, which could only ever be a retrospective resistance. The traumatized ego attempts to comprehend its wound: "In consciousness equality and equilibrium between the trauma and the act is always reestablished. Or at least this equilibrium is sought in reflection and its *figures*" (OB 125). Responsibility is traumatic, however, precisely because it comes too late to capture the other in a representation. Levinas juxtaposes the force of the ethical demand with its fragility—the tendency to cover over or reduce that demand to a manageable phenomenon. The elusiveness of the trace raises the possibility that it may mean nothing to me, and Levinas intensifies this fragility by claiming that the extreme exposedness of the other's face simultaneously provokes both responsibility and violence, the refusal of responsibility. If the face could function as a cause, if it could be clearly identified as the origin and justification of a moral obligation, it would no longer be a trace. It would thus no longer have the binding power of responsibility, which preoccupies me because it cannot be reduced to an object of consciousness: "A trace lost in a trace, less than nothing in the trace of an excessive, but always ambiguously (trace of itself, possibly a mask . . .), the face of the neighbor obsesses me with this destitution. . . . Does this imperative force which is not a necessity come from this very enigma, this ambiguity of being a trace? In this enigma tends and distends the infinite, the nonoriginal and anarchic as well as infinite, which no present, no historiography, could assemble, and whose passing precedes every memorable past" (OB 93). In arising out of an immemorial past, it offers only a trace, rather than a form that could be present to intentionality. The demands for intelligibility may well follow the encounter with alterity, but at that point the breach has already happened: "In an approach [in proximity] I am first a servant of a neighbor, already late and guilty for being late. I am as it were ordered from the outside, traumatically commanded, without interiorizing by representation and concepts the authority that commands me. Without asking myself: What then is it to me? Where does he get the right to command? What have I done to be from the start in debt?" (OB 87). These questions attempt to establish a justification for responsibility, but Levinas's point is that if responsibility could be conceptualized in this way, it would have lost its binding power and become an idea to be grasped.

In this resistance to comprehension, responsibility has the force of a "surd," in Brison's terms,[50] an event that cannot be integrated into the world of established meanings: "Persecution is a trauma, violence par excellence without warning nor a priori, without possible apology [*apologie*], without logos" (OB 197n27). Persecution here is the unavoidable imposition of responsibility on the subject. The word "apology" is odd in this passage: whose apology for violence and persecution is Levinas denying? He seems to be using a transliteration of *apologia*, a defense or explanation, to mean that thought cannot position itself prior to this traumatic impact, to identify its source, make sense of the event of responsibility, and thus defend itself against the urgency of its demand.[51] There is a deliberate gesture to violence at the core of responsibility: "The ethical relationship is not a disclosure of something given but the exposure of the 'me' [*moi*] to another, prior to any decision.... Here, a sort of violence is undergone: a trauma at the heart of myself [*moi-même*], a claiming of this Same by the Other, backwards movement of intentionality" (GDT 187). Levinas uses the term "violence" in two different and opposing connotations. One is the violence of the *conatus essendi*, which is also implicated in the violence of intentionality—converting every other into an idea that can be comprehended, and in so doing reasserting the knowing subject's place in the sun. The second meaning is less typical, as in this passage: it describes the impact of responsibility on the self without ascribing that force to any identifiable source. The subject encounters responsibility as an intrusion in an existence otherwise governed by the epistemic complacency of intentionality and the moral complacency of the *conatus*.

As a for-the-other, responsibility is traumatic in the sense that something foreign—the demand that the other makes on me—has become an internal provocation to act: "There is a claim laid on the same by the other in the core of myself, the extreme tension of the command exercised by the other in me over me, a traumatic hold of the other on the same, which does not give the same [the self] time to await the other" (OB 141). Although Levinas tends to write about the traumatic *moment* of encountering alterity, in which I am struck by a responsibility that I cannot assume (in the connotation of converting into an idea or an object) and that I cannot *not* assume (in the connotation of taking up), this destabilizing of the self has broad implications for what subjectivity means: "This is a responsibility that does not leave me time: it leaves me without a present for recollection or a return into the self" (GP 71). In its "deafening trauma," diachrony unravels the constitutive role that synchronizable time plays in intentionality (OB 111). In these passages, Levinas links elements that are central to the psychoanalytic understanding of trauma: the unexpectedness of responsibility and its incursion on self-possession, which then profoundly problematizes the subject's ongoing sense of herself as an autonomous agent.

Divergences

However, there are two key elements of trauma as it is described within psychoanalytic discourse that do not arise directly in Levinas's references: repetition and "afterwardsness"(*Nachträglichkeit*). While Freud is struck by the repeated acting out of traumatic events, in Levinas's focus on the unexpectedness of each moment when the self is confronted by the other, there is no emphasis on how trauma causes symptoms over time and what those symptoms might be. Nonetheless, Levinasian trauma is an event that escapes representation and yet imposes meaning. It thus has the uncanny structure of the trace, as something neither present nor absent, as Chanter argues: "Trauma returns, but it is never fully present.... In a sense, it is *nothing but repetition*. Trauma is foreignness incarnate: absolute otherness, not being oneself, being outside oneself—and therefore no longer *being* in any of the recognizable meanings of the term. To undergo trauma is to fail to recognize oneself in the places one usually finds oneself."[52] The immemorial past is a past that cannot be located in a linear series of now-points, or synthesized through retention or memory into the lived experience of the present. As a trace, it offers no intentional object, but only imposes its force on the subject—that is, "nothing but repetition." This interruption happens repeatedly, given the insistent return of the *conatus* and the attempts of intentionality to make sense of trauma, as the following chapter will discuss in more detail. Nonetheless, Levinas's interest in trauma lies more in describing the quality of responsibility than in diagnosing or treating trauma as an ongoing psychological disorder.

A second element of the psychoanalytic discussion of trauma that is absent in Levinas's discourse concerns latency, or "afterwardsness." Freud contrasts the "old, naïve theory of shock" (in which trauma is literally a psychic wound caused by an unexpected force) with his mature psychoanalytic approach, which emphasizes the retrospective investment of meaning in an event. Traumatic events therefore only come to be traumatic through some level of interpretation on the part of the subject. Following the analogy with physical injury, prior to 1897 Freud attributes the symptoms of hysteria to traumatic sexual experiences in childhood, according to the profoundly misnamed seduction hypothesis. Freud's repudiation of the seduction hypothesis leads him away from the study of traumatic neurosis as the result of an external physical shock and toward the power of unconscious fantasy, governed by the pleasure principle. Although relationships with other people and real, shared events are still crucial to psychic life, those relationships and events are invested with meaning through the workings of the psyche, such that memories as well as present experiences and anticipations of the future are interpreted according to largely unconscious associations that have their origin in infancy or childhood. Psychoanalytic fantasies are "hybrid formations," consisting of mediated and unrecognized representations of a person's experience.[53]

Freud thus becomes increasingly interested in the peculiar temporal structure of trauma: while trauma can result from a train collision or experiences on the battlefield, it can also be triggered by events that appear to be quite ordinary but lead a person to experience an earlier event as psychologically overwhelming. Ruth Leys discusses this temporal complexity as "a dialectic between two events, neither of which was intrinsically traumatic, and a temporal delay or latency through which the past was available only by a deferred act of understanding and interpretation."[54] A paradigmatic case study is that of Emma in Freud's *Project for a Scientific Psychology* (1895). Emma suffers from hysterical symptoms at the age of twelve after hearing two shop-clerks laughing, and perceiving them to be laughing at her, or more specifically her clothing. Freud writes that "further investigation" reveals an earlier event, up to this point unconnected in her memory with the first one she discusses, that makes sense of her fear: that when she was eight, a shopkeeper "grabbed at her genitals through her clothes."[55] This initial event caused no trauma (in the form of overwhelming shame, fear, or guilt), according to Freud, because Emma did not invest any sexual significance into it. It is only when this incident is unconsciously associated with the shop-clerks laughing at her clothes, when she is four years older and more sensitive to sexualized behavior, that the earlier memory takes on traumatic power, which is then also attached to the trivial later event: "Here we have a case of a memory arousing an affect which it did not arouse as an experience, because in the meantime the change [brought about] in puberty had made possible a different understanding of what was remembered. . . . A memory is repressed which has only become a trauma by *deferred action* [*Nachträglichkeit*]."[56] Laplanche points out that a better English translation of *Nachträglichkeit* would be "afterwardsness," the sense in which an event is carried by the psyche long after it has happened, its significance is retrospectively invested into it, and its emotional charge is acted out in an unpredictable and indirect way.[57] That is, the afterwardsness of traumatic neurosis is not merely a matter of postponed action but an intricate temporal structure of later events influencing the meaning of earlier ones, as well as past events permeating the present.[58] That notion of a memory *becoming* traumatic through retrospective interpretation reveals the complexity of the psychological wound and the distortions of memory that result.

By contrast, in Levinas's work the force of responsibility does not gain its significance for the subject from either conscious or unconscious interpretation, because this is what separates a "non-thematizable provocation" from intentional objects (OB 12). However, implicit in Levinas's account is the idea that the encounter with alterity, and the diachronic responsibility that arises in that encounter, is particularly denucleating for a subject obsessed with her own nucleus, so to speak—a subject who understands herself as autonomous and self-possessed. He describes ethical trauma in the specific context of the transcendental subject who is wrenched out of that self-conception to become an ethical subject, in Bernet's terms. In this sense, proximity takes on the significance of trauma because it does not simply undermine the activity of consciousness but undermines it in the context of the assumption that consciousness cannot be resisted in this way.

Levinas is also intensely interested in the afterlife of the traumatic moment and how it comes to be understood—not in this case according to unconscious psychological structures, but through the various possibilities of responding to the imposition of responsibility: the moment of the ethical demand may be translated into justice, or it may be rationalized and dismissed. We can read Levinas's work as a whole as an analysis of these possibilities—particularly as they emerge in the Western philosophical tradition. His own philosophical reflection is an attempt to make sense of the incomprehensibility of the encounter with the other, which can only be thought retrospectively. He thus sets for himself the difficult project of thematizing trauma without draining it of its traumatic import.

Despite clear divergences in how trauma functions in the two discourses, various elements of psychoanalytic interpretations of trauma help to clarify some of the implications of Levinas's use of the concept. In the evolution of Freud's thought, he strives to capture both the immediate force of traumatic events and how the psyche responds to those experiences. Levinas's references to trauma emphasize the former aspect, what Freud calls the "naïve theory of shock," but the way that this shock destabilizes autonomous subjectivity resonates with the effects that psychoanalysis elaborates—the derangement of a linear temporal structure and the consequences for the ego's ability to know the world and act confidently within it.[59] It is certainly the case that Freud (and therapeutic work generally) is much more concerned with alleviating the suffering that the ego endures as a result of trauma, supporting the attempt to master the trauma retrospectively. But the careful description of that wound to the ego's boundaries amplifies the meaning of trauma in Levinas's discourse.

For Levinas, the significance of deformalized, diachronous time is the denucleating encounter with alterity, or the traumatic impact of responsibility, which breaks open the self-absorption of the subject, including his focus on his own freedom, intentional experience, and finite being. Interpreting what trauma means in Levinas's work raises the problem of his highly reflexive attempt to represent philosophically what resists representation and the impact that this resistance has on the subject. Particularly in his later writings, he criticizes the discourse of philosophy for turning every significant event into a set of themes that can be analyzed and evaluated. It thus frames those who engage in the work of philosophy as knowing subjects for whom all of reality at least potentially can be made intelligible. In this sense, Levinas's language has to work against itself, by finding terms that contort themselves to indicate their own limits and gesture to what cannot be captured. He attempts to make his language function as traces rather than signs, so that he can discuss the significance of responsibility as a trauma, while remaining attuned to the idea that trauma is precisely what eludes such representation (OB 189n25). The next chapter examines this immensely cautious and halting attempt to practice philosophy that does justice to the incomprehensibility of responsibility.

Notes

1. *Monstrare* is the Latin word at the root of both "demonstration" and "monster"; the link between them is the connotation of an omen, a warning, the sign of something foreign or uncanny.

2. Llewelyn, "Levinas and Language," 136.

3. Compare S, 90, where Levinas describes the suffering of substitution as "the original traumatism and return to self," with OB, 115–16; and S, 94, where the condition for the subject is "an anarchic traumatism this side of auto-affection and self-identification, a traumatism of responsibility and not causality," with OB, 123–27.

4. Quoted in Butler, *Precarious Life*, 140.

5. Ibid.

6. Critchley, *Problem with Levinas*, 45–46.

7. Cohen, *Ethics, Exegesis, and Philosophy*, 172.

8. See Critchley, *Ethics-Politics-Subjectivity*, 185–88, and Bergo, "Levinasian Responsibility and Freudian Analysis."

9. Freud and Breuer, *Studies on Hysteria*, 2:7.

10. Freud, "Remembering, Repeating, and Working-Through," 12:145–57.

11. Freud and Breuer, *Studies on Hysteria*, 2:10.

12. As Ruth Leys notes, modern European medical interest in trauma began with John Erichsen, a British doctor who treated survivors of train accidents and located the origin of trauma to a "shock or concussion of the spine" (*Trauma*, 3). Roger Luckhurst helpfully traces the intense legal, medical, and military debates that have shaped both early and contemporary definitions of trauma in *The Trauma Question*.

13. See Luckhurst, *Trauma Question*, 49–53. The concept of trauma remains unsettled, both within the microcosm of Freudian psychoanalysis and the larger frame of nineteenth-, twentieth-, and twenty-first century Western culture. There have been wide-ranging debates about whether trauma must be caused by firsthand physical injury, whether traumatic memory is more or less reliable than ordinary memory, whether trauma can be meaningfully understood as a collective or even cultural disorder as well as an individual affliction, and whether trauma is a culturally specific concept that is illegitimately deployed outside of those limits. The work of Leys, Fletcher, and Luckhurst all provide important genealogical analyses of these debates, by treating the idea of trauma as a historical formation whose significance is structured by a variety of cultural forces. See Leys, *Trauma*; Fletcher, *Freud and the Scene of Trauma*; and Luckhurst, *Trauma Question*.

14. Freud, *Beyond the Pleasure Principle*, 18:29. Leys notes that this metaphoric description of how trauma disrupts the line between the internal and the external is "quasi-military" in its emphasis on a protective shield around the psyche (*Trauma*, 23).
15. Fletcher, *Freud and the Scene of Trauma*, xiii.
16. Freud, *Beyond the Pleasure Principle*, 18:31.
17. Ibid.
18. Ibid., 32.
19. Lear, *Freud*, 154–62.
20. Weathers et al., "PTSD Checklist for DSM-5 (PCL-5)–Standard."
21. Ibid.
22. Fletcher, *Freud and the Scene of Trauma*, 53.
23. Freud, *Introductory Lectures on Psycho-Analysis*, 16:275.
24. There are significant tensions between psychoanalytic approaches to trauma and the contemporary framing of trauma as post-traumatic stress disorder, as more focus is put on the neurobiological responses underlying trauma, and which also defines the disorder primarily by its symptoms. See Luckhurst, *Trauma Question*, and Leys, *Trauma*.
25. American Psychiatric Association, *Diagnostic and Statistical Manual of Mental Disorders*, 3rd ed., 236.
26. Herman, *Trauma and Recovery*, 33.
27. American Psychiatric Association, *Diagnostic and Statistical Manual of Mental Disorders*, 5th ed., 272.
28. Horowitz, *Stress Response Syndrome*, quoted by Herman, *Trauma and Recovery*, 51.
29. Caruth, *Unclaimed Experience*, 4. She goes further to claim that as a result of its unexpectedness, the traumatic event is entirely *missing* from the person's experience—etched in the psyche in such a way that generates involuntary repetition without any cognitive access to that event. Leys takes Caruth to task for this interpretation of trauma, particularly in Caruth's attempt to support it by a reading of Freud's work. See Leys, *Trauma*, 229–97. I leave aside the issue of whether traumatic memories are unmediated, involuntary repetitions of past events or are mediated by other elements of the person's experience. These debates are tangential to Levinas's references to trauma.
30. Brison, *Aftermath*, 39.
31. Ibid., 50.
32. Ibid., xi.
33. Laub and Auerhahn, "Knowing and Not Knowing Massive Psychic Trauma," 288.
34. Brison, *Aftermath*, 49–54.
35. Laub and Auerhahn, "Knowing and Not Knowing Massive Psychic Trauma," 289.
36. Freud, *Beyond the Pleasure Principle*, 18:35.
37. Laplanche, "Time and the Other," 244.
38. Laplanche and Pontalis, *Language of Psychoanalysis*, 466.
39. Leys, *Trauma*, 9.
40. Herman, *Trauma and Recovery*, 35–37, 51.
41. Spinoza, *Ethics*, IVp7.
42. Pascal, *Pensées*, 21. For examples of Levinas's references to this phrase, see OB, vii; NC, 130; VF, 179; IFP, 53; DYF, 216; OUJ, 231; and PT, 23.
43. See also Bernet, "Traumatized Subject."
44. Lin, *Intersubjectivity of Time*, 123.
45. Bernet, "Levinas's Critique of Husserl," 90.

46. Maurice Merleau-Ponty also refers to the idea of an immemorial past, one that breaks open the smooth linearity of formal time (*Visible and the Invisible*, 244). See also Al-Saji, "The Temporality of Life," and Al-Saji, "'A Past Which Has Never Been Present.'"
47. Ciaramelli, *Transcendence et Éthique*, 185, my translation.
48. See Ovid, *Metamorphoses*, 9.188–97.
49. Bergo, "Levinasian Responsibility and Freudian Analysis," 263.
50. Brison, *Aftermath*, 103.
51. Robert Gibbs suggests that "for Levinas all discourse is an apology, an address to justify oneself to the other," but in this particular passage, Levinas seems to reject the possibility of justifying oneself in the immediacy of the encounter with the other (*Correlations in Rosenzweig and Levinas*, 164).
52. Chanter, *Time, Death, and the Feminine*, 221, emphasis added.
53. Fletcher, *Freud and the Scene of Trauma*, 91.
54. Leys, *Trauma*, 20.
55. Freud, *Project for a Scientific Psychology*, 1:354.
56. Freud and Breuer, *Studies on Hysteria*, 1:356.
57. Laplanche, "Notes on Afterwardsness," in *Essays on Otherness*, 260–65.
58. Fletcher, *Freud and the Scene of Trauma*, 71.
59. Freud, *Beyond the Pleasure Principle*, 18:31.

3   The Method of An-Archeology

LEVINAS'S PROMINENT USE of the concept of trauma provokes the question of how responsibility can be thematized at all, given its status as a trace rather than a phenomenon—an experience that can be unproblematically represented by consciousness. Through its rhetorical peculiarities, his philosophical style reflects his claims about the subject's encounter with what exceeds, frustrates, or otherwise interrupts conceptualization. This chapter will analyze Levinas's method of "saying and unsaying," with particular attention to his repudiation of narration in *Otherwise than Being*. Given that narration is one way to reduce the lapse of time to a unified representation, this methodological stance is intimately linked to Levinas's understanding of subjectivity. Emphasizing the impact that diachrony has on the subject requires him to examine how narratives—including philosophical narratives—fail, and thus what a more self-critical form of representation would be. Levinas's attempts to avoid positioning the subject as either the narrator or the object of narration result in his reticence on a number of questions that seem salient to his work. Various scholars have called Levinas to task for his refusal to speak more concretely on matters of justice, or to give a more robust argument about the source of moral authority. But his silence on these issues must be considered in the light of Levinas's methodological commitments to challenging the ideal of the sovereign subject and the understanding of time bound up with that ideal.

Saying and Unsaying

The first pages of *Otherwise than Being* introduce a distinction that is woven through the rest of the book: the event of saying and the "immobilized" content of what is said—the ideas, claims, or questions conveyed in language (OB 5). Although we tend to focus on the meaning of written or spoken words in order to comprehend them, Levinas characteristically insists on how language functions first as an address to the other. Anyone who greets another person, in even the most impersonal and superficial way, responds to an obligation to acknowledge the other (EN 88). Levinas argues that a greeting is an exposure of the self that responds to the vulnerability of the other, who faces the possibility of not being greeted—who may be treated as morally or socially insignificant. The other can be framed as an object to be studied or a rival for resources, neither of which challenge the basic logic of the *conatus*. Saying is the core of intersubjectivity, where addressing ourselves to the other is responding to other as other. Saying is thus "the proximity of the one to the other, the commitment of an approach, the one for the other, the very signifyingness of signification" (OB 5). Levinas's language of proximity and diachrony get at the peculiar tension of alterity—how the self is addressed by and provoked to respond to the other, precisely because the other is not merely present as an object of consciousness. The other as other is removed from that dynamic of intentionality but, as a trace, imposes an obligation on the self. Regardless of what is said, saying is a greeting and welcoming of the other in her proximity.

Levinas recognizes the ephemerality of the saying, from which the said arises, such that the force of the address inevitably congeals into the vehicle for that which can be conceptualized and represented. Saying becomes "the correlate" of the said, the instrument that facilitates the transmission of ideas (OB 6). Without this subordination nothing could be communicated. Levinas often uses the shorthand of "Greek" thought to refer to the "reduction of all experience, of all that is reasonable, to a totality wherein consciousness embraces the world, leaves nothing outside of itself" (EI 75). This is the paradigm of the detached knower who at least in principle can assimilate within consciousness all that exists. Such intelligibility depends on an idea or an event being made present to the knower, as Lin notes: "Only synchronic time is thinkable, since diachronic time is the realm of the immemorial, the irrecuperable, and the unrepresentable, which precedes history and meaning."[1] But this translation into intelligibility is also a "betrayal," by reducing alterity to an object of thought that is present before me (OB 6).[2] The said cannot on its own capture the ethical significance of saying, precisely because in language all signification "becomes a phenomenon, is fixed, assembled in a tale, synchronized, presented, lends itself to a noun, receives a title" (OB 42). In contrast, as responsiveness to alterity, saying is diachronous, occurring in the lapse of time between the self and the other.

Levinas's task is then to unravel this conceptual processing of Greek thought, such that the dynamic of responsibility can in some sense be represented philosophically without reducing it to the level of a phenomenon: "The *otherwise than being* is stated in a saying that must also be unsaid in order to thus extract the *otherwise than being* from the said in which it already comes to signify but a *being otherwise*" (OB 7). Having represented the trace in a philosophical claim, Levinas must double back and "unsay" that thematization to preserve it as a trace, rather than a being—even a "being otherwise"—that could be comprehended: "A face as a trace, trace of itself . . . an invitation to the fine risk of approach qua approach, to the exposure of the one to the other. . . . The thematization of a face undoes the face and undoes the approach" (OB 94). In such a thematization, the face is assimilated into a phenomenon and loses its ethical force. The immediate question that arises is how any discourse could possibly represent the saying without such a reduction. Especially in his late work, Levinas grapples with this question and experiments with what kind of philosophical method could capture diachrony in discourse, given the synchronizing work that would make diachrony intelligible as a concept. As Derrida asks about Levinas, "what does he do when he writes in the present, in the grammatical form of the present, to say what cannot be nor ever will have been present, the *present said* only presenting itself in the name of a Saying that overflows it infinitely within and without?"[3] In other words, how can the trauma of responsibility be represented without eliminating its traumatic impact?

This question echoes Derrida's influential analysis of *Totality and Infinity*, in the 1964 essay "Violence and Metaphysics," which contends that Levinas only seems to depart from the terrain of ontology, the philosophical discourse centered on being—or, even more broadly, writing in the tradition of the Greeks.[4] On Derrida's reading, Levinas attempts to situate his work unproblematically within the traditional opposition between Athens and Jerusalem—between a worldview that attempts to master the world epistemically and one that accepts the transcendence of the infinite.[5] Derrida acknowledges the challenge that Levinas poses to "Greek" philosophy: "In Greek, in our language, in a language rich with all the alluvia of its history—and our question takes shape already—in a language that admits to its powers of seduction while playing on them unceasingly, [Levinas's] thought summons us to a dislocation of the Greek logos."[6] Levinas uses the language and methods of philosophy, derived from Greek thought, to call into question the basic assumptions around subjectivity that he associates with the Greek intellectual tradition. Can "Greek" as a conceptual system, which contemporary Western philosophy has inherited, be used not only to critique itself but to unhinge its essential dynamic? In the 1964 essay, Derrida casts doubt on this possibility and calls into question the clarity of this binary opposition between Greek and Jewish thought, given that the distinction has its source within a Western intellectual tradition that identifies itself as Greek. In that discourse, Jerusalem functions as the constitutive "outside," and for that reason belongs to the "Greek" economy. The relation to the transcendent, which apparently exceeds reason, functions as an internal trigger within the system, a provocation to further investigation: "the philosophical pretention to nonphilosophy. . . . nothing can so profoundly *solicit* the Greek logos—philosophy—than this irruption of the totally-other; and nothing can to such an extent reawaken logos to its origin as its mortality, its other."[7] In that sense, nonphilosophy fits within the dynamic of philosophy reflecting on what seems to resist comprehension. Levinas's critique of the appropriative, assimilating violence within philosophical discourse would then participate in this violence. Gesturing to Levinas's references to eschatology in *Totality and Infinity*, Derrida argues that "escha*tology* is not possible, except *through violence*."[8] Levinas cannot use the tools of Greek philosophy, in their various Platonic or Hegelian or phenomenological iterations, without situating himself within that tradition, in which the critique of *logos* is already thematized and has its place.

Various scholars have argued that Levinas's rhetorical shifts from *Totality and Infinity* (1961) to *Otherwise than Being* (1974) in part respond to this careful deconstructive reading.[9] At the very beginning of the later text—but without referring explicitly to Derrida—Levinas explicitly addresses the issue of how a philosophical work can represent what interrupts the functioning of *logos*: "A methodological problem arises here, whether the pre-original element of saying (the anarchical, the non-original, as we designate it) can be led to betray itself by showing itself in a theme (if an an-archeology is possible), and whether this betrayal can be reduced; whether one can at the same time know and free the known of the marks which thematization leaves on this betrayal, even the unsayable. In this betrayal the indiscretion with regard to the unsayable, which is probably the very task of philosophy, becomes possible" (OB 7). The multiple hesitations here are significant. Levinas raises the methodological problem of whether discourse can capture multiple, countervailing movements: the transformation (betrayal) of the saying into the said, and then the examination and unsaying of that betrayal—"philosophy is called upon to reduce that betrayal," to attempt to return to the saying (OB 156).[10] He then only suggests that philosophy has this peculiar task of reflecting on the limits of representation, in its restless questioning of the status of its own discourse.

Philosophy is thus tentatively charged with both betraying the unspeakable status of responsibility—by treating the trace as a sign whose content can be articulated—and with betraying this betrayal, as Tina Chanter emphasizes in her reading of Levinas's method.[11] But that second betrayal, which calls attention to philosophy's reduction of the saying to the said and thus is a form of "unsaying" the said, can only ever be experimental and uncertain: "This reduction is then an incessant unsaying of the said, a reduction to the saying always betrayed by the said" (OB 181; see also OB 152). Levinas uses the metaphor of respiration to describe this process, in which saying is a "restless" opening (OB 180) to the other in which "the meaning shows itself, eclipses and shows itself" (OB 181). Saying and unsaying cannot be definitively accomplished within the said; instead, they function as an interruption disturbing the "sedimentation of the said."[12] This understanding of the goal of philosophical discourse entails that philosophy itself enacts a diachronic movement, in which not everything can be presented at once, rather than providing a synchronic, totalized account of reality: "The very discussion which we are at this moment elaborating about signification, diachrony and the transcendence of the approach beyond being, a discussion that means to be philosophy, is a thematizing, a synchronizing of terms, a recourse to systematic language, a constant use of the verb being, a bringing back into the bosom of being all signification allegedly conceived beyond being" (OB 155).[13] *Otherwise than Being* is then a demonstration of what this kind of convoluted, always incomplete philosophical reflection would look like. Describing this internal tension in Levinas's writing, Bettina Bergo argues that "the text *enacts* its own traumatization."[14] Levinas attempts to show in discourse the derangement of discourse effected by the diachronous encounter with alterity.

Despite this complexity of his later style, Levinas rarely makes explicit his methodological commitments. John Drabinski speculates that examining Levinas's methodology might be "the wrong question," because it asks about how a solitary thinker crafts the justification of a claim, rather than focusing on the passivity of the ego provoked to respond to the other.[15] Despite this risk, he claims that "Levinas ... continually returns to the question of method," one that is profoundly shaped by phenomenology—particularly Husserl's description of intentionality, in which the subject reaches out to the world.[16] Levinas intensifies this openness, in the ethical sense of proximity, to the point where the subject is characterized by "*intentionality disrupted by the reversal of intentionality*," which Drabinski names "the method of Levinasian thinking."[17] The tension between those two poles remains significant: philosophical discourse attempts to make sense of what resists thematization, and yet also to recognize its own limits in that endeavor.

Derrida's later reflections on Levinas's language emphasize the image of breaks in a thread that are retied in a series of knots. This image stems from the end of *Otherwise than Being*: "The interruptions of the discourse found again and recounted in the immanence of the said are conserved like knots in a thread tied again, the trace of a diachrony that does not enter into the present, that refuses simultaneity" (OB 170). The betrayal of alterity in philosophical discourse is interrupted by the reduction of that betrayal, but the reduction is itself reflected on and represented—in some sense the interruption is repaired. But its trace remains, in the form of a knot. Commenting on the preceding passage, Derrida emphasizes that "retying the thread" of representation calls attention to the break as well as to the repair that allows an idea to be intelligible: "Whether it severs or reties, the discourse of philosophy ... retains the trace of interruption despite itself. ... In order to re-mark the interruption, which is what E.L.'s writing does, one must *also* retie the thread, despite oneself, within the book not left intact by philosophy. ... Knotted threads are formed in it, recapturing the tears, but otherwise. They allow the discontinuous to appear in its trace."[18] This possibility of allowing the discontinuous to appear as a trace seems to be a revision of the argument in "Violence and Metaphysics," in which discontinuity served only as a provocation to the ongoing work of *logos*. But here the discourse of philosophy both records the breaks and restores unity.

The oscillation between the capturing of an idea in discourse and the rupture of discourse is not a Manichean battle between two fundamentally opposed forces. In its negative connotations, the term "betrayal" does not quite do justice to the complexity of this relationship between the saying and the said. Levinas argues in the last chapter of *Otherwise than Being* that the motivation for conceptualization and comparison arises out of the force of responsibility itself, with the recognition that the subject finds herself among multiple others with various needs. In relation to the saying, then, the said is not merely a degenerate, corrupted copy of living speech. Instead, that tension is closely connected to the interplay between the demands of justice and the infinite demand of the singular other. Proximity is the traumatic moment of infinite responsibility and *also* the "latent birth of knowing," with the entry of the third person (OB 157). The proximity of *the* other is complicated by the proximity of yet another, or seven billion others, which elicits a series of questions: "What then are the other and the third party for one another? What have they done to one another? Which passes before the other?" (OB 157). For Levinas, these questions belong to the domain of justice, in which "comparison, coexistence, contemporaneousness, assembling, order, thematization, the visibility of faces, and thus intentionality and the intellect" are necessary (OB 157; see also OB 160–61). In this way reason is not merely a betrayal in the sense of flattening the force of proximity, but also a betrayal in the sense of disclosing a meaning that stems from the initial impulse of responsibility itself. Thematization is a necessary response to trauma, but it can never completely recover from or eliminate that trauma.

This profusion of tears and knots between the said and the saying generates some of the opacity of Levinas's prose. As Critchley argues, "it is precisely in the play of binding and unbinding, the oscillation or ambiguity of the Saying and the Said, that the ethical Saying of Levinas's work is maintained."[19] Levinas's tortuous rhetoric in his later writings then carefully reflects the content of his account of normativity. Even by conceptualizing responsibility in terms of trauma, Levinas signals that the origin of responsibility and the specific demands that it places on the subject cannot be settled (EN 107, MoS 180). At particular moments in the text Levinas calls attention to this intense reflexivity in his writing: "Is it necessary and is it possible that the saying on the hither side be thematized, that is, manifest itself, that it enter into a proposition and a book? It is necessary.... But it is also necessary that the saying call for philosophy in order that the light that occurs not congeal into essence what is beyond essence" (OB 43–44). Levinas describes here the struggle to discuss the diachronous nature of the saying in philosophical discourse, which attempts to represent what is immemorial and thus resists representation. But in its self-critical stance, philosophy is positioned to also refuse the "congealing" of the infinite into the totality of the said. Philosophy can only perform this paradoxical project by "retaining an echo of the reduced said in the form of an ambiguity, of diachronic expression. For the saying is both an affirmation and a retraction of the said" (OB 44; see also OB 162). The activity of philosophical discourse is to represent the said *as a reduction* of the saying. This dual commitment generates "an endless critique, or skepticism, which in a spiralling movement makes possible the boldness of philosophy, destroying the conjunction into which its saying and its said continually enter" (OB 44). This critique insists upon the incompleteness of the reduction, and Levinas articulates this incompleteness in terms of time, as impermanence (OB 46–47). The saying does not coincide with the said and therefore cannot be represented entirely within it, which entails that philosophical reflection itself will be diachronous, moving between saying and unsaying: "Truth is in several times, here again like breathing, a diachrony without synthesis" (OB 183).

The tension between the need to disclose meaning and the excessiveness of the meaning that Levinas wants to convey generates this "spiralling" movement between saying and unsaying: "When stated in propositions, the unsayable (or the an-archical) espouses the forms of formal logic" (OB 7). Attached to the phrase "formal logic" is an endnote in which Levinas claims that "superlatives" are a way for meanings to show themselves in the lawfulness of logic but also interrupt that lawfulness (OB 187n5). This rhetorical structure deliberately invites the logical objection of self-contradiction, and in so doing attempts to call into question the proper domain of *logos*: responsibility "shows itself in the said, but does so only after the event, betrayed, foreign to the said of being; it shows itself in it as a contradiction" (OB 135). This peculiar instability of the saying is the movement of skepticism, which can be refuted by demonstrating its internal contradiction—it attempts to justify beliefs about our inability to justify beliefs. But logic deals only with propositions, as if meaning were contained entirely in the said. Levinas's claim is that skepticism arises repeatedly due to the diachrony of saying, which "puts an interval between the saying and the said" (OB 168). Skepticism can be refuted, but returns. He argues that it is "a refusal to synchronize the implicit affirmation contained in saying and the negation which this affirmation states in the said. The contradiction is visible to reflection, which refutes it, but skepticism is insensitive to the refutation, as though the affirmation and the negation did not resound in the same time" (OB 167–68). If saying could be reduced to a proposition, then the "implicit affirmation" of making a skeptical claim would be contradicted by the content of that claim. Reflection can make such a reduction, by translating the saying into a said. However, this reduction is incomplete, and further philosophical reflection, of the kind in which Levinas is engaged, marks that incompleteness. In this way, the significance of saying cannot be reduced to nonsense but also cannot be contained in a proposition. As a trauma or a trace, its impact lies in an unintelligibility that nonetheless intrudes on the subject.

Philosophy on Levinas's reading is a liminal enterprise, caught up in an endless series of self-reflections. Derrida famously describes the development of *Totality and Infinity* as "the infinite insistence of waves on a beach: return and repetition, always, of the same wave against the same shore, in which, however, as each return recapitulates itself, it also infinitely renews and enriches itself."[20] The repetition speaks to the difficulty of capturing responsibility, proximity, or substitution as concepts to be defined, analyzed, and put into circulation with other concepts. Reflecting on Hegel's suspicion about prefaces and Heidegger's caution about how to introduce ontological questions adequately, Levinas asks, "Should we not think with as much precaution of the possibility of a conclusion or a closure of the philosophical discourse? Is not its interruption its only possible end?" (OB 20). Levinas thus positions his text as part of an ongoing dialogue, demanding both exegesis and criticism.

Levinas's Rhetoric

Several recurring tropes in Levinas's writing reflect this understanding of the work of philosophy: his use of hyperbole or "exaltation," the reversal of dominant philosophical concepts, the provocation of the reader's response, and particularly the rejection of narration. These elements of his style speak to the difficulty of representing trauma *qua* trauma—or, more broadly, the difficulty that philosophy faces in thematizing the ethical.

Everywhere in his work, Levinas uses emotionally charged rhetoric to describe responsibility—including references to persecution, obsession, and denucleation. Paul Ricoeur refers to this tendency as a kind of "verbal terrorism."[21] But the intensity of Levinas's language attempts to push settled notions of subjectivity or responsibility past their familiar meanings. He contrasts a transcendental method, which tries to disclose an "immobile" foundation of an idea or experience, with his own, which "starts from the human, . . . which *ages* in the world, which withdraws from it in a way other than by opposition—which withdraws from it through the passivity of aging" (QA 88). Echoing Bergson, Levinas here rejects the possibility of distilling a foundation of being beneath becoming. Given this lack of foundation, Levinas claims that the process of justification depends on passing "from one idea to its superlative, to the point of emphasis. You see that a new idea—in no way implicated in the first—flows, or emanates, from the overbid. The new idea finds itself justified not on the *basis* of the first, but by its sublimation" (QA 88–89). Rather than exposing the conditions for the possibility of an idea or an event, the subject finds himself "aging," unable to represent all that it experiences due to the lapse of time. What Ricoeur calls "hyperbole" is what allows Levinas to challenge the dominant philosophical, political, and scientific assumptions that glorify the autonomous subject. Diane Perpich comments on the previous passage: "The older and more familiar notions of responsibility are not the *basis* on which a new account is built or justified; rather, hyperbole renders the older notions vulnerable or susceptible to showing responsibility differently and permitting a new sense (meaning and orientation) to emerge."²² The language of persecution and obsession emphasizes the passivity with which the subject undergoes responsibility, based on highly concrete experiences of encountering the other. Theodore De Boer refers to this rhetorical strategy as "exaltation"—a term that appears in the final pages of *Otherwise than Being*—that opens up a new meaning within a familiar concept (OB 181).²³ Exaltation within the said gestures to what disturbs the domesticating force of thematization, in which every possible event can be captured in a concept. Richard Cohen speaks of meaning being "exacerbated" in Levinas's work, to the point that the reader is "overloaded" by this meaning even as he comprehends it, in the diachrony of philosophical saying.²⁴ Levinas is thus playing off of a conceptual framework, a series of expectations about subjectivity, ethics, and relations to others, that he and his readers have inherited, and that he is attempting to destabilize.

Tracing his divergence from classical phenomenology, Levinas emphasizes the complex status of his own rhetoric: the for-the-other is not a "psychic content" neutrally accessible to consciousness (OB 183). Instead, "the human is brought out by transcendence, or the hyperbole . . . a hyperbole in which it breaks up and *falls upward*, into the human" (OB 184). The excessiveness of his language is here identified with the interruptive quality of responsibility, through which "the human" or a moral order breaks into the self-absorbed, amoral indifference of the *conatus*. The terms that he uses are charged with emotional resonances so that they cannot be merely treated as concepts to be comprehended. Their intensity gestures to the excessiveness of responsibility, its subversion of intentionality.²⁵

A second, related rhetorical trope that permeates Levinas's later writing is *renversement* or *retournement*; both terms tend to be translated as "reversal." Levinas describes the impact of responsibility as a "non-coinciding" that reverses the activity of consciousness: "There is the pain which confounds the ego or in vertigo draws it like the abyss, and prevents it from assuming the other that wounds it in an intentional movement when it posits itself in itself and for itself. Then there is produced in this vulnerability the reversal [*renversement*] whereby the other inspires the same, pain, an overflowing of meaning by nonsense. Then sense bypasses nonsense—that sense which is the-same-for-the-other" (OB 64). Throughout *Otherwise than Being*, the self-possession of the ego is invoked, only to be undermined. The preponderance of negative descriptions—what sensibility or time or the face is *not*—speaks to Levinas's attempt to unsettle our intellectual inheritance of these concepts, to call attention to and then turn against the presuppositions at work within them. *Renversement* means not only reversal but also has the connotation of inverting, overthrowing, or capsizing. Leonard Lawlor suggests that Levinas follows Husserl's "reversal of the natural attitude" in working backward from "common-sense" assumptions in everyday experience or philosophical discourse, for instance, to what lies behind those phenomena.[26] In doing so, Levinas challenges the legitimacy or the adequacy of those assumptions.

Reversal can thus be an inversion of some existing structure or belief, but also an overturning of the subject's power, in the sense of suffering a reversal. Levinas claims that the ethical "indicates a reversal [*retournement*] of the subjectivity which is *open upon* beings and always in some measure represents them to itself, positing them and taking them to be such and such (whatever be the quality, axiological, practical, or logical, of the thesis which posits them), into a subjectivity that enters *into contact* with a singularity, excluding identification in the ideal, excluding thematization and representation—an absolute singularity, as such unrepresentable" (LP 116). The directedness of intentionality, which treats anything that might be significant as an object of consciousness, is reversed in responsibility, where the other elides representation but still "enters into contact" with the self. Leslie MacAvoy comments that *retournement* connotes an "abrupt change in attitude or opinion, an about-face," in which the activity of intentionality is turned back from its intended object, which only ever appears as an immemorial trace.[27] That inversion of intentionality creates the sudden "bowling over" of *renversement*. These various meanings of "reversal" highlight the precise meaning of trauma in Levinas's thought: the dismantling of the power of intentionality.

The fact that Levinas emphatically positions himself against the philosophical lineage out of which he emerges generates an objection articulated by François Raffoul: "reversing a tradition is not necessarily the same thing as freeing oneself from it, and . . . Levinas's revolution owes perhaps more than it would like to admit to the egological tradition that it seeks to reverse, *precisely insofar as it determines itself as its reversal*."[28] The concern is that Levinas once again positions subjectivity as central, even if it is a subject in the accusative. According to Raffoul, replacing autonomy with heteronomy, or ontology with ethics, fails to call that traditional binary into question.[29] Levinas indeed sets up clear oppositions that structure his work: totality and infinity, being and otherwise than being, intentionality and responsibility. But Levinas also complicates these oppositions, by identifying cognition, for instance, as the outgrowth *and* reduction of responsibility (OB 157). In his account, autonomy points back, however obliquely, to the heteronomous moment in which I am commanded by the other, and that moment calls out for a subject capable of evaluating different forms of moral obligation. The significance of diachrony shifts us from a contradiction to an oscillation, in which the subject's ordinary self-possession is repeatedly interrupted by responsibility. The focus on the subject that Levinas maintains gives us a peculiar kind of response to the binary oppositions by which it has traditionally been defined. Often indirectly, his rhetoric reminds his readers of the continuing power of those assumptions, not only in philosophy but in the broader Western intellectual heritage. The strategy of reversal locates Levinas within a tradition, a language, and a conceptual structure that he tries to interrupt, but that is what philosophical work necessarily does, in Levinas's view.

At the level of rhetoric, Levinas refuses to provide a straightforward philosophical argument, much less one that leads to a set of ethical principles. Perpich notes the deliberate obscurity of Levinas's argumentative method in *Otherwise than Being*: "Nothing Levinas says about responsibility is empirically verifiable or justified in any of the usual ways relied on by philosophers, nor is it meant to be."[30] He describes what might in other contexts be called uncanny experiences: being held hostage by the other, being trapped within one's skin, and trauma. These dramatic descriptions call out for a response from the reader, to tease out what is recognizable in it in our particular interactions with the world. Levinas thus calls into question not only the foundational concepts of Greek philosophy but its traditional methods of representation, which presuppose a particular understanding of subjectivity, language, time, and embodiment.

In its unsettled quality, Levinas's discourse provokes the reader to engage with the text through her own ideas (including philosophical ideas) and subjective experiences. This may be part of why Levinas makes so few direct references to the history of philosophy in his mature writing. Particularly the phenomenological tradition and German idealism are everywhere assumed as the foundation challenged by Levinas's claims about responsibility, but in large part the reader is invited to reconstruct that buried but ongoing dialogue. The tone of the text calls out for a response on the part of the reader, and in so doing generates further interpretation, questions, and objections without any expectation of achieving a final conclusion: "books have their fate; they belong to a world they do not include, but recognize by being written and printed.... They are interrupted, and call for other books and in the end are interpreted in a saying distinct from the said" (OB 171). This claim affirms the idea that the text, as a thematization of proximity, is a betrayal but also a reflection on and resistance to that betrayal, which then invites the continuation of that work of thinking. Derrida emphasizes the fragility of this call to the reader: "The trace of this interruption within the knot is never simply visible, sensible, or assured.... You are never required to read or recognize the trace of interruption, it only comes about through you for whom it is freed, and yet he will have, wholly otherwise, obligated you to read what one is not obligated to read."[31] It is entirely possible to ignore the complexities of Levinas's writing and to demand that he articulate a set of clear positions and then justify them. But the density of his text reflects his understanding of the labor of philosophy, which resists being translated neatly into concepts. His writing thus reaches beyond itself, diachronically, and provokes its own interruption.

The Problem with Storytelling

This halting, restless style resists resolving itself into any clear narrative structure, even of the variety that philosophers tend to use. The "knotted thread" of Levinas's discourse reflects the diachronous movement of saying and unsaying without generating the kind of narrative that he refers to as an *épos*. Claiming disdain for stories is a highly traditional philosophical trope, even if such disdain is often accompanied by the selective deployment of stories, and the distinction between *mythos* and *logos* has been a constitutive boundary for the discipline of philosophy. The typical worry is that myth appeals to emotion or custom, without legitimating its representations or implied prescriptions through rational argument or empirical evidence. But this is not Levinas's worry about narrative. He focuses instead on how narration reduces diachrony to a series of representations, and in that sense the *logos* of philosophical arguments has much in common with the *mythos* of unphilosophical tales. In his later work, both storytelling and philosophical argumentation are associated with a synchronizing will to knowledge—to borrow a phrase from Nietzsche:[32] "the time that marks historiography, that is, the recuperable time, the recoverable time, the lost time that can be found again. As the time narrated becomes, in the narrative and in writing, a reversible time, every phenomenon is said, characterized by the simultaneity of the successive in a theme. In the remission or détente of time, the same modified retains itself on the verge of losing itself, is inscribed in memory and is identified, is said" (OB 36). Narration assumes an ego capable of synchronizing the events in its experience and discerning their significance. The totality becomes differentiated in time but is unified again in representation. In tracing the interweaving of narrative and knowledge, Michael J. MacDonald notes that the Latin root *narrare* derives from *gnarus* (knowing): "knowledge is formed by gathering the dispersed events of experience into the coherent order of a tale, story, or narrative."[33] This kind of knowing overcomes the lapse of time.

Levinas thus associates narratives with the synchronizing dynamic of intentionality. He adopts the term *épos* from the Greek, in which it refers to oral narratives and thus can mean a word, a story, or a song, but particularly the epic stories or songs that contribute to a cultural identity and tradition. He frequently associates the *épos* with the reduction of the saying to the said: "Essence fills the said, or the epos [*épos*], of the saying, but the saying, in its power of equivocation, that is, in the enigma whose secret it keeps, escapes the epos of essence that includes it and signifies beyond in the signification that hesitates between this beyond and the return to the epos" (OB 9–10).[34] Within the narrative, time functions as the supportive framework that makes the story possible, but it has no significance of its own. In other words, for Levinas the story is a form of comprehension, which once more positions both storyteller and listener as knowers rather than subjects who are ethically exposed in diachrony. Saying understood as an interruption of narration is in keeping with the characterization of responsibility as traumatic, resulting in the derangement of linear time.[35]

This suspicion about the presuppositions within narrative extends to philosophical discourse, so that in his late work, Levinas refuses to tell a developmental story by which the subject becomes ethical. From the 1930s until the 1960s, Levinas's writings typically employ a descriptive framework that begins with an isolated subject who then experiences the anonymous "rumbling" of the *il y a* (the "there is" in Levinas's early writings or the enjoyment of the world in *Totality and Infinity*—and only then comes to a more mature comportment and self-conception. Critchley goes so far as to discern a "divine comedy" in *Totality and Infinity*, "maybe even a theodicy" in which the birth of a child allows us to escape finitude.[36] This reading minimizes Levinas's argument that the future does not belong to the present, and that any resolution or reconciliation is undetermined. But it is entirely true that Levinas provides a relatively linear structure of ethical development in this text. Perpich argues that the narrative structure of *Totality and Infinity* is at odds with its conclusion: it is "an extended narrative that purported to show how a separated and atheist ego could nonetheless come to be commanded by and responsible for an other."[37] That responsibility does not come about as a result of the subject's choices, and the force of the other's command derives from its resistance to comprehension, "but the narrative form implies that one could in fact be *brought* to know, that a narrative could be produced that would show the ego to itself in the right light, despite [the text's] own attempt to position responsibility outside cognition and intentionality."[38] In contrast to *Totality and Infinity*, Levinas's rhetoric in *Otherwise than Being* rejects any clear narrative structure.[39] In the later book, narrative is insistently and negatively linked to history, as methods of representing past events and thus overcoming the diachronous lapse of time. Levinas also thwarts any expectation of the structure of a subject moving in any simple way from a childlike amoral solitude to the maturity of responsibility. The vestiges of a *Bildungsroman* of the ethical subject have been extirpated from Levinas's method by this point.

In its traumatic character, responsibility interrupts the mastery of consciousness over time and its correlative vision of subjectivity. This is the meaning of substitution, the condition of being for-the-other:

> Far from being recognized in the freedom of consciousness, which loses itself and finds itself again, which, as a freedom, relaxes the order of being so as to reintegrate it in a free responsibility, the responsibility for the other, the responsibility in obsession, suggests an absolute passivity of a self that has never been able to diverge from itself, to then enter into its limits, and identify itself by recognizing itself in its past.... These are not events that happen to an empirical ego, that is, to an ego already posited and fully identified, as a trial that

would lead it to being more conscious of itself, and make it more apt to put itself in the place of others. (OB 114–16)

Levinas here juxtaposes the idea of a self-conscious, autonomous subject capable of realizing his identity through telling his own narrative with the subject as subj*ected* in responsibility. If those experiences could be drawn into a narrative that constitutes the self-understanding of the subject, freedom would remain the essence of subjectivity, and that subject ultimately could not be denucleated by any trauma. At most this subject could recognize the other as an alter ego—another like myself—and thus deserving of respect or sympathy. This would be a subject incapable of ethics in Levinas's terms, because the challenge to one's right to be and to one's right to know would never arise. The ego's encounter with the other would be yet another experience to be assimilated into consciousness: "The unnarratable other loses his face as a neighbor in narration" (OB 166; see also IOF 9). But sympathy resulting from an analogical relation to the other has an intelligible foundation rather than an anarchic hold on the self.

Levinas's rejection of *épos* repeatedly associates it with the synchronizing activity of consciousness and the picture of autonomous subjectivity implied by that activity. The narrative becomes the source of illumination, or the structure that allows beings to be comprehended by a consciousness that remains unaffected by time: "It is only in the said, in the epos of saying, that the diachrony of time is synchronized into a time that is recallable, and becomes a theme. The *epos* is not added to the identical entities it exposes; it exposes them as identities illuminated by a memorable temporality" (OB 37). His language here, as elsewhere, calls attention to the ethical significance of subsuming other people as objects of knowledge, an activity mostly understood to be morally neutral in modern epistemology. For Levinas, the disclosure of the neighbor forecloses the possibility of being exposed in responsibility: "Proximity is no longer in knowing in which these relations with the neighbor show themselves, but do so already in narration, in the said, as an epos and a teleology" (OB 83). Proximity means being addressed by the neighbor, the stranger, the widow, or the orphan, rather than containing them within a concept—hence the contrast between responsibility and memory.

In this way, the traumatic quality of responsibility unsettles one of the central characteristics of autonomous subjectivity, as it has been dominantly defined in Western thought. The ability to represent the past accurately and to take those representations into account in decision-making has been held up as a marker of self-possession by figures as diverse as Nietzsche and Locke. In the context of a very different kind of project, Sue Campbell has examined how narrative memory has constituted this essential condition of personhood in modern Western culture, such that those whose memories are perceived as unreliable are excluded from the status of knowers, agents, and citizens: "Memory enters as a core cognitive ability, one of the abilities through which a human is configured as a person; and the kinds of activities that can be seen to be important to developing and maintaining this kind of core cognitive ability are activities involving self-narratives."[40] Having an untrustworthy memory—and trustworthiness here is socially conferred rather than simply discovered—consigns human persons to heteronomous status, and thus prevents them from taking up authoritative positions in the world. The political marginalization of women, children, the elderly, people of color, and people with disabilities (among others) has frequently been justified on the basis of such distrust. One does not fully take up the status of personhood without being able to remember reliably—and particularly to remember reliably events in one's direct experience. In discussing the contemporary politics of memory in the context of sexual violence, Campbell focuses on the entangling of power and epistemology, or what Levinas would call the sphere of justice. His concern is less with *which* subjects are seen as capable of telling reliable stories about themselves as he is with the general conception of the autonomous subject who is supposed to be capable of memory, storytelling, and legal responsibility. Levinas uses the connection between the ability to narrate one's experience faithfully and the status of autonomous personhood to gesture to the impact of traumatic responsibility. As Chanter claims, our understanding of time is closely connected to our understanding of the subject: "A concept of time informs the view that depends on maintaining the conscious, rational, dominating subject at the center of its account, and envisages the world as so many objects to be organized and orchestrated into a coherent plan."[41] By interrupting the subject's power to reduce the lapse of time to a synchronous narrative, responsibility undermines the self-possession and authority of the subject.

In addition to how narratives position subjects as narrators, Levinas argues that free activity and free subjects are all too easily assimilated as the objects of such narratives, along the lines of the Hegelian cunning of reason—in which the intentional actions of individuals fit within a larger, unintended unity. Even in its opposition to the determinism of mere things, the idea of free will still belongs to an order that treats all events as possible representations bound into a broader whole. For this reason, Levinas writes at the beginning of *Otherwise than Being*, the attempt to conceive what is otherwise than being "will look beyond freedom. Freedom, an interruption of the determinism of war and matter, does not escape the fate in essence and takes place in time and in the history which assembles events into an *epos* and synchronizes them, revealing their immanence and their order" (OB 8). In this sense the idea of the free subject does nothing to interrupt the totalizing power of narration, either in the position of narrator or as the object of narration.

Severson describes the dynamic of *Otherwise than Being* as a renarration of the ego, or a redescription of the subject as subjected, but it is more accurately depicted as a *denarration* of the ego—not a new story but a disordering of stories, the representation of the inability to represent responsibility.[42] As in the case of theodicy, which I discuss in the following chapter, Levinas acknowledges the force of the modern temptation toward a narrative structure (and our attachment to the assumptions that lie behind it) and argues for the importance of resisting this temptation. The rejection of stories happens repeatedly in *Otherwise than Being*, as in the characterization of the ethical demand as emerging out of an immemorial past: responsibility "appears as a plot without a beginning, anarchic" (OB 135). The wording here is precise: responsibility appears, to the extent that it can appear, as a plot that then undermines its own structure. Will Buckingham insightfully discusses the profusion of stories in Levinas's work, despite his frequently articulated suspicion about storytelling: in *Otherwise than Being*, he claims, "there is an unfolding, stuttering, always recommencing plot, a plot made up of breaks and fractures and disruptions."[43] This description of fragmentary stories harkens back to the image of the knotted thread, a discussion of the said and its interruption.

In keeping with the characterization of philosophy as a discourse that must turn back against its own representations, Levinas struggles to describe the relationship between responsibility and subjectivity without presuming an already-formed subject: "It is as though the first movement of responsibility could not consist in awaiting nor even in welcoming the order (which would still be a quasi-activity) but consists in obeying this order before it is formulated. Or as though it were formulated before every possible present, in a past that shows itself in the present of obedience without being recalled, without coming from memory, being formulated by him who obeys in his very obedience. But this is still perhaps a quite narrative, epic, way of speaking" (OB 13). Even in the articulation of responsibility as obedience, and thus a kind of receptivity and acceptance, a self-governed subject is presupposed at the center of the story. Levinas's concern is how to express intelligibly the impact of diachrony in the constitution of subjectivity, without depending upon the familiar set of assumptions at work in narration.

The account of trauma that Levinas gives in *Otherwise than Being* is itself fragmented and difficult to decipher. He writes of an originary trauma that inaugurates subjectivity—a for-the-other that is older than the activity of consciousness or the calculations of justice (OB 123). But there is also the trauma suffered by the sovereign subject, in which the *conatus* is interrupted and the ego is denucleated. Denucleation seems possible only for a subject with an already-formed sense of autonomy and self-possession, who has established her "place in the sun." On Joseph Rosen's reading, "the 'egological' self experiences alterity *as* traumatic ... alterity is only experienced as traumatic from within a logic of violence."[44] As in the narrative structure that governs *Totality and Infinity*, in this second chronology of trauma, the ego understands itself as self-possessed until the proximity of the neighbor or the stranger unravels that set of assumptions.

Levinas refers to both chronologies of responsibility, or explanations of how and when responsibility affects the subject, without rigorously distinguishing them. Elisabeth Weber argues that "the trauma which is repeated, or, more exactly, the trauma which in the encounter with the other recalls an earlier trauma, is trauma *because* it is reminiscent of an immemorial trauma."[45] This reconciliation of the two aspects of trauma would align Levinas's references to trauma with the psychoanalytic model of a traumatic event that recalls and gets its meaning from an earlier one. But Levinas himself does not describe this interplay between an initial and later trauma. Instead, he leaves open the question of where the trauma of responsibility is chronologically located. Its temporal priority lies in the texture of the subjective experience, in which the ego finds itself already obligated, without having made a commitment. In that sense responsibility is older than the ego: "The inscription of the order in the for-the-other of obedience is an anarchic being affected, which slips into me "like a thief" through the outstretched nets of consciousness. This trauma has surprised me completely; the order has never been represented, for it has never been presented, not even in the past coming in memory, to the point that it is I that only says, and after the event, this unheard-of obligation" (OB 148). I cannot step back from this authority, by which I find the obligation for the other already binding me, to identify the source of its hold on me. It cannot function as the *arkhe* or identifiable origin of subjectivity. Although Levinas offers an account of the trauma of responsibility, it is an account that calls attention to its own slippages and silences. In Weber's terms, Levinas's discourse "*opens up* the impossibility of remembering this speechlessness [the trauma of encountering the other]. *Otherwise than Being* 'stands' in this opening. In the trauma of this opening *there are words*.... This trauma is trauma because it opens anamnesis."[46] The anamnesis he offers, however, can only ever be partial and fragmentary—the anamnesis of trauma itself. Hence Levinas does not clearly separate a trauma that initiates subjectivity and a trauma that interrupts the logic of the *conatus*. This ambiguity reflects his broader refusal to provide a linear narrative of the subject's development.[47]

Nonetheless, his work *is* an anamnesis of a dimension of subjectivity that he takes to have been marginalized by and subordinated to the ideal of autonomy. Weber notes that in *Difficult Freedom* Levinas acknowledges the Nietzschean dictum that "forgetfulness is the law, happiness and condition of life" and then immediately rejects the finality of this dictum: "But here life is wrong" (SC 147). By calling attention to and reflecting on the trauma of responsibility, Levinas's philosophical project performs a response to that trauma—albeit a response that is not primarily oriented toward healing the wound of responsibility. One way to frame his fundamental criticism of Western philosophy is that it has been too anxious to recover from that rupture and in so doing has covered over its significance. His task is thus the undoing of that disavowal of trauma.

This leaves open the question of what it would mean to respond well in the wake of this denucleation. But if Levinas could provide any substantive account of that resolution, he would be fulfilling the desire for a narrative that would contain trauma rather than be interrupted by it. This complex, cautious thematization of traumatic responsibility is a form of working-through, in Freud's terms, in the sense that it interprets and reacts to a disruption of memory. Dominick LaCapra has argued that as a process working-through does not necessarily bring about "closure," by converting the traumatic event into one that can be accessed through the normal processes of memory: "Working through trauma involves the effort to articulate or rearticulate affect and representation in a manner that may never transcend, but may to some viable extent counteract, a reenactment, or acting out, of that disabling dissociation."[48] Working-through carries the enduring mark of the injury to which it responds.[49] Levinas's discourse attempts to make that trauma intelligible, to the extent that it can be made intelligible without entirely losing its status as a traumatic event (OB 156).

In this inversion of intentionality Levinas engages what is for him the core of the phenomenological tradition, the investigation of the meaning-making activity of consciousness. He comments in an interview on Husserl's identification of intentionality with meaning-bestowing: "The most fundamental contribution of Husserl's phenomenology is its methodical disclosure of how meaning comes to be, how it emerges in our consciousness of the world, or more precisely, in our becoming conscious of our intentional rapport with the world" (EoI 50). But he detaches signification (as he uses that term) from intentionality, such that the other is not merely an intentional object. Countering the idealist thread of phenomenology, Levinas claims that the ego does not bestow meaning on the other. De Boer describes Levinas's distance from transcendental and existential phenomenology in terms of how the other shows up to the ego: within traditional phenomenology, "exteriority can appear only within the circle of this meaning-giving center."[50] For Levinas exteriority unsettles the very capacity for meaning-*giving*. However, there is still meaning—a signification given by the other. Levinas is not rejecting Husserlian phenomenology here or adopting a prephenomenological account of experience so much as supplementing it, in the Derridean sense of that term: the picture of meaning within intentionality inadequately represents the kind of meaning that arises in the encounter with alterity. Whereas intentionality establishes the subject as a "meaning-giving center," alterity opens up the possibility of trauma, meaning imposed without warning or comprehension. Drabinski identifies Levinas's "most originary phenomenological question" as "What is the sense and origin of this traumatic awakening?"[51] The tension here is Levinas's insistence on responsibility breaking up the dynamic of intentionality, in which every event becomes a phenomenon. He attempts to depict what signification without comprehension would be, and to communicate this event in a way that is both intelligible and reflective of the necessary failure of intelligibility. Phenomenology is thus part of his method, but he is most interested in the point at which intentionality fails, or at which the ego encounters what cannot be integrated easily into a narrative.[52]

The Status of Metaphors

Thus far this chapter has focused on the general rhetorical and methodological characteristics of Levinas's later writing, but this section will examine Levinas's use of a particular cluster of images, which center on diachrony and trauma. It is important not only to unpack what Levinas means by these key images, but how he uses them, and what meaning they might have outside of his intent—how they put him into conversation with a longer philosophical tradition and a wider set of disciplinary lenses. When philosophy attempts to thematize what resists thematization, it must use the existing resources of language. To draw on a Gadamerian point, language necessarily employs a set of prejudices—a way of thinking and a way of life—to convey its meaning. Levinas tends not to make explicit an analysis of the tradition that shapes the grammar and vocabulary that is available to him and the conceptual structure that is implicitly expressed in them. For instance, his use of the idea of femininity notoriously suffers from this neglect, insofar as he deploys the trope without any sustained critical attention to how the gender binary has functioned and continues to function as an oppressive set of social norms (TI 154–56, 256–80). He claims that he uses the term "feminine" as a metaphor, without meaning to indicate by that term individual, living women. But those metaphors derive their significance from a larger philosophical and cultural narrative in which concepts of femininity *have* been used to define individual, living women—a tradition from which Levinas cannot entirely separate himself.[53] In this way as well, philosophical discourse must reflect on its own inherited conceptual systems and the limitations of those inheritances, and thus begin to unsay what it has said. At the same time, there is no way to communicate without employing those concepts.

Metaphors are transporters of meaning: an image carries an insight that perhaps can only be gestured at through such indirection. They may represent obliquely what resists representation, and in that sense fit a philosophical discussion of diachrony and alterity. Yet at several key points Levinas claims that his descriptions of substitution and vulnerability are "better than metaphors" (*mieux que des métaphores*) (TI 256; see also OB 110). He seems to be objecting to the way in which a metaphor appears to invite decoding, always remaining within the domain of intelligibility.[54] For example, Levinas rejects both a literal interpretation of the face (as a physical phenomenon) and a metaphorical one. Perpich suggests that both of these approaches carry the risk of treating the other as "a self-identical object, graspable by means of an image or concept."[55] His rhetoric struggles to find an alternative mode that breaks the epistemic assumption of an intentional subject, even on the part of the writer and the reader. Kathryn Bevis traces Levinas's use of the metaphors of dwelling and maternity and argues that "metaphor in Levinas is meant to *bear more than itself* in a relationship of infinite responsibility."[56] His metaphors would thus not point to a settled significance but, particularly in their hyperbole, unsettle the reader's assumptions about responsibility, sensibility, or subjectivity. Even in their intensity, Levinas's images of trauma and proximity are meant both as embodied experiences of exposure and as ethical concepts. In describing proximity, Levinas draws on the significance of maternity to characterize subjectivity more generally: "The one-for-the-other has the form of sensibility or vulnerability, pure passivity or susceptibility . . . psyche in the form of a hand that gives even the bread taken from its own mouth. Here the psyche is like the maternal body" (OB 67, translation amended). At some level the descriptions of the psyche in these claims must be read as metaphoric, but to read them *only* as metaphors would reduce away the immediacy of the claims.

Levinas does not trust traditional philosophical concepts and language to capture what lies beyond being, but he also does not entirely trust metaphors as literary devices, since images once again privilege the subject's power to comprehend the ideas sheltered within them, on his reading. There is no established rhetorical trope that allows Levinas to highlight the impact of diachrony, in which not everything significant can be represented to the knowing subject. These rhetorical convolutions reflect Levinas's philosophical struggle to represent how profoundly the trauma of responsibility interrupts the self-possession of the subject, even as a user of language.

The shifts in Levinas's discourse indicate the seriousness with which he approaches this rhetorical task. *Otherwise than Being* employs the language of temporality rather than spatiality, as a counter to phenomenological (and more broadly, modern philosophical) assumptions about the accessibility of beings to consciousness. *Totality and Infinity* (1961) relies heavily on the spatial opposition between interiority and exteriority, but as early as *Time and the Other* (1948), Levinas articulates a concern about how easily the spatially present is assimilated into the known: "The exteriority of the other is not simply due to the space that separates what remains identical through the concept, nor is it due to any difference the concept would manifest through spatial exteriority. The relationship with alterity is neither spatial nor conceptual" (TO 84). Despite this trepidation, Levinas continues to use spatial imagery, and particularly the language of height, to represent alterity up until the mid-1960s.[57] In "Transcendence and Height"

(1962), he claims that the other "challenges us from the greatest depth and the highest height—by opening the very dimension of elevation" (TH 17). The essay "Meaning and Sense" (1964) represents a transitional phase in his rhetoric, as he describes responsibility in temporal terms: the encounter with alterity means "literally, not to have time to turn around" (MS 55). But in the same text he uses the image of height to signify transcendence: "Height introduces a sense into being.... It is not because men, through their bodies, have an experience of the vertical that the human is placed under the sign of height; because being is ordained by height, the human body is placed in a space in which the high and the low are distinguished and the sky is discovered—that sky which for Tolstoy's Prince André, without any word of the text evoking colors, is all height" (MS 57). This passage is very much in line with the claims in *Totality and Infinity* about the face not being a phenomenon that can be captured in a list of characteristics (TI 187–94; see also EI 85). To explicate the way in which the face signifies without being a sign, however, Levinas draws in the central idea of the "trace" in the same essay and describes it as coming from an "utterly bygone, utterly past Absent" (MS 60). Even proximity should not be understood in spatial terms, but instead as the approach of the other that disrupts the linear ordering of present moments (GDT 138). From this point in his writing forward, he increasingly refers to diachrony to gesture to what exceeds representation.

This rhetorical wavering between spatial and temporal language concludes with the idea that space is the domain in which everything can be made present to consciousness, but the passing of time has at least the potential to destabilize this dynamic.[58] Although events in the past or future can be represented, the lapse of time itself resists the recuperating power of consciousness: "The trace qua trace does not simply lead to the past but is the very passing toward a past more remote than any past and any future which still are set in my time" (MS 63). This thought becomes in *Otherwise than Being* the immemorial past, "a failing of all presence, less than a phenomenon" (OB 90). Drabinski argues that in Levinas's later work, the trace does not so much *exceed* intentionality as call attention to the absence of an intentional object; it is "the impoverished and desolate presence of a radical absence."[59] That is, diachrony introduces the trace of something absent, rather than the overflowing presence of something higher than the ego. This description resonates strongly with the language of trauma, as a disturbance of memory that intrudes on the present. The significance of the ego's encounter with the other undermines the very activity of representation in memory, rather than being simply a particularly intense or surprising experience. As a trace, it can only be represented in convoluted, indirect ways. The shifts in Levinas's language indicate his awareness of how philosophical discourse negotiates the risk of reaffirming some element of autonomous subjectivity in the process of describing responsibility as the denucleation of the ego.

Given the prominence of his references to trauma in *Otherwise than Being* and other late writings, how the language of trauma functions must itself be examined. Levinas certainly draws on the emotional charge of the term but pays little explicit attention to the psychological context that lends the term its meaning. He is not interested in particular events (railway accidents, battles, sexual assaults) that generate psychological trauma, or how the symptoms that result from such experiences should be treated. Psychological descriptions of trauma are principally oriented toward determinate events within the lives of individuals or societies, and how people can meaningfully recover from those events so that their suffering is reduced.[60] These are concerns that from Levinas's perspective belong to the domain of politics and justice, arising only after the encounter with the other. In using the language of trauma, Levinas risks misappropriating the psychological specificity of this term: can the same word adequately describe both the generic ego's encounter with alterity and the forms of violence that individual human beings endure at particular moments and in particular places? LaCapra is wary of recent tendencies within philosophy and literary theory to blur the distinction between the particularity of loss and a structural situation in which all human beings experience absence or incompleteness. If the latter is called trauma, "mourning [the process of recovery] becomes impossible, endless, quasi-transcendental grieving, scarcely distinguishable (if at all) from interminable melancholy."[61] In this way, trauma becomes both glorified and trivialized, as an event that universally characterizes human existence (or perhaps only modern human existence), even in a repressed form. This abstract approach to trauma risks diluting the significance of psychological trauma and detracting from the need to both prevent and respond to concrete historical events.

On an initial reading, Levinas's references to trauma seem to position it as this kind of universal event that inaugurates subjectivity, regardless of historical context and individual experiences. Levinas uses the term to describe the impact of proximity on the self, but trauma is abstract in the sense that the self could be any self, the other could be any other, and the encounter between them has no determinate features. In his philosophical writing, his references to historically specific events tend to serve as examples of what goes wrong when we do not attend to the trauma of responsibility, not as psychological or cultural trauma itself. For instance, in "Useless Suffering," Levinas describes the events of the twentieth century—"two world wars, the totalitarianisms of right and left, Hitlerism and Stalinism, Hiroshima, the Gulag, and the genocides of Auschwitz and Cambodia"—as examples of suffering caused by the failure to respond adequately to the other *as other* (US 97). *Otherwise than Being* is dedicated to "the memory of those who were closest among the six million assassinated by the National Socialists," a specificity intensified by the Hebrew dedication that names "those who were closest." But that particularity spirals outward to include "the millions on millions of all confessions and all nations, victims of the same hatred of the other man, the same anti-semitism" (OB ii). The atrocities of the Shoah are thus linked to anti-Semitism as a whole, which in turn is identified with *any* hatred of the other. The hatred of difference and the violence caused by such hatred are described here as human phenomena, not the product of one culture or historical period. Although the rest of the text makes no reference to the genocides of the twentieth century, the dedications invite the reader to draw connections between "the hatred of the other man" and the otherwise ahistorical descriptions of saying, proximity, responsibility, and substitution.

In "Beyond Memory," a Talmudic writing from 1986, Levinas distinguishes between dangers that belong to the "domain of history"—the demands of tax collectors, censorship, legal limitations on one's profession—and dangers that arise, uncannily, within the sanctuary of one's home (BM 73). Levinas notes that the former category of threats particularly assails Jews in the Diaspora, always at the margins of political recognition, but he comments that in response "it is possible to walk, to wander, or to flee. Savagery and wasteland, the memory of which may yet fade" (BM 73). But the second category of violence is like being bitten by a snake, a threat that was unforeseen, which strikes without warning and where a person felt most at home: "the death of starving children thrusts us into the snake pit, into places that are no longer places, into places one cannot forget, but that do not succeed in placing themselves in memory, in organizing themselves in the form of memories. We have known such pits in this century!" (BM 73). In the context of particular historical events, Levinas precisely describes the traumatic disruption of memory that seems to take on an ahistorical, universal form in *Otherwise than Being*. But Levinas includes such events to highlight what happens when the other is reduced to an object; he is not primarily interested in the psychological effect that these determinate events have on their victims, witnesses, and perpetrators.

Without making a sustained argument in support of this conclusion, Levinas suggests that these collective traumas have resulted from the failure to respond to the other, or the suppression of the trauma of responsibility (PPH 63). In a discussion of German historians' attempts to come to terms with the Shoah, Eric Santner introduces the phrase "narrative fetishism" to describe "the construction and deployment of a narrative consciously or unconsciously designed to expunge the traces of the trauma or loss that called that narrative into being in the first place."[62] This kind of story- or history-telling denies the very need for working-through and in so doing forecloses critical reflection on the traumatic meaning of past events: "Far from providing a symbolic space for the recuperation of anxiety [working through trauma along a Freudian model], narrative fetishism directly or indirectly offers reassurances that there was no need for anxiety in the first place."[63] For instance, if the Final Solution can be framed as a response to the "Asiatic" savagery of Stalinism, the trauma that the Shoah presents for contemporary Germans can be contained by projecting its source elsewhere.[64] Levinas's work extends this idea to claim that particular, historical traumas themselves arise out of the deflection of trauma in its ethical significance—our tendency to protect ourselves from responding to the vulnerability and suffering of others. Levinas everywhere addresses the denial of responsibility in its diachronic, immemorial, traumatic nature in the history of Western philosophy, which has privileged the autonomy of the subject and deemed responsibility to be derived from that status. His project then reflects his attempt to respond to the trauma of responsibility more adequately, by naming and contesting the tendency to disavow it. But he draws no further connection between the contingent traumatic events that individuals undergo and the singular trauma of the subject encountering alterity.

Despite his tendency to use historical events merely as examples of how we can fail to live out the significance of responsibility, Levinas's thought is not ahistorical. His philosophical references to historical context are sparse, but he seems to assume that his readers will have the wars and genocides of the twentieth century in mind. Chanter considers the apparent ahistoricity of Levinas's discourse as a refusal to locate the interruption of the ethical in a particular event or set of cultural forces. To do so would be to reduce the ethical to something to be analyzed and comprehended by historians, anthropologists, sociologists, and psychologists: such representation

> would reduce it to an event—to an instant in the succession of instants, to the time of continuous history, where an instant is comparable to any other cross section of time. There is no need to refer to such an event, because there is another reference from which this saying acquires its energy—not only does it refer to an event, a discrete historical moment, an act, or a period of time that can be consigned to the past in the neat phrases of historians, but also, and more important, it refers to an interlocutor.[65]

In this way, Levinas's philosophical discourse appeals to and provokes our own experience of proximity in his sense of that term. It is not that we have to abandon the discourses of history or anthropology but that we should recognize that these disciplinary narratives cannot represent the singularity and urgency of the ego's exposure to the other. That moment becomes subsumed within concepts that are more easily articulated and examined by consciousness: "The caress of love, always the same, in the last accounting (for him that thinks in counting) is always different and overflows with exorbitance the songs, poems and admissions in which it is said in so many different ways and through so many themes, in which it apparently is forgotten" (OB 184). In the activity of *logos*, there is both a capturing of the ethical and a forgetting of it. This claim also contains a direct contradiction: is the "caress of love" always the same—universal and ahistorical—or always different?

On Levinas's reading, the peculiar power of philosophy is its ability to reflect on the status of the subject who analyzes, comprehends, and thematizes: "If philosophy has a tendency to fix the meaning of statements, to render accounts, its function is also not to allow its saying to rest in the said."[66] In this sense, Chanter argues, Levinas does not fall into an "unthinking universalism or ahistoricism."[67] Whatever the saying is or does, it does not originate from a historically determinate source, and it generates neither a description of a human ideal nor a universal set of ethical rules. It acts as an interruption of such discourses and an invitation to further critical reflection on their basic presuppositions: "by marking this turning of my response to the face of the other into a static principle that can take on the status of a universal, Levinas is by no means unequivocally endorsing universality. On the contrary, he is insisting on the need to bring it into question wherever and whenever there is a tendency for it to silence all other meanings."[68] Levinas thus engages in a complex negotiation with the particular and the historical—that which can be situated, thematized, and examined within a historical narrative. His references to trauma evoke the impact of being exposed to the other but resist reducing that moment of the ethical to an element of psychological pathology, or an event best analyzed by anthropologists or historians. His focus on the singular ego means that he tries to capture the texture of the lived experience of responsibility, and in that endeavor he employs psychological language without taking on the orientation of psychology or other empirical disciplines. Levinas's project is about the ethical, which is ahistorical in the sense of an anarchical disruption of what can be represented by memory or history. But the ethical moment is also highly particular, and historical events reflect the various ways we live out that moment.

Silence as a Rhetorical Trope

This oscillating movement generates some basic questions about where Levinas's thought leads. His emphasis on ethics as an unthematizable interruption of intentionality does not ground any determinate form of what he names justice. Although the trauma of responsibility opens out into the need to abstract away from the singularity of the other, to evaluate the different and sometimes competing vulnerabilities of multiple others, Levinas provides no algorithm for how responsibility might shape decisions that are made in the domain of justice. As Derrida notes, "Levinas does not want to propose laws or moral rules, does not seek to determine *a* morality, but rather the essence of the ethical relation in general. But as this determination does not offer itself as a *theory* of Ethics, in question then, is an Ethics of Ethics."⁶⁹ Moral principles would be ideas that reason could interpret, compare, and evaluate. There is nothing particularly traumatic about them, even if they may sensitize us to the moral significance of behaviors that we had previously considered utterly unquestionable, such as the justifiability of using fossil fuels or eating animals. Instead, Levinas focuses on what destabilizes our complacency as sovereign subjects by questioning not only the righteousness of our particular way of existing but our right to be at all. It is in this sense that we are addressed "in the accusative" by the other (OB 142). Perpich refers to this peculiar project as "normativity without norms," as Levinas examines the binding power of responsibility rather than constructing an ethical system based on foundational principles that would generate determinate normative rules.⁷⁰ The import of his thought is that any such set of norms will be provisional: "every particular norm is contestable, but the *moment* of normativity—*that the other makes a claim on me to which I cannot be entirely indifferent*—is incontestable."⁷¹ The process of figuring out what responsibility entails does not belong merely to the theorizing work of justice, but to justice informed or disturbed by a more indeterminate normativity.⁷²

Still, if we leave off the philosophical discussion with this vacillation between responsibility and justice, Asher Horowitz argues, we have only inadequately addressed the problem.⁷³ The paradox of unthematizable responsibility leading to decisions of justice is insufficient, on his reading: "Without the art of foreseeing peace, and foreseeing peace in the real society, the ethical relation that radically disturbs the state, but *only* disturbs it, continuously expanding rights in and against the eternal state, the eschatological vision necessarily implied by ethics, would be itself unethical."⁷⁴ Horowitz describes Levinas as subordinating the social situatedness of gender, race, religion, language, and culture (among others) to "radical situatedness"—our imbeddedness in intersubjective but asymmetrical relations with singular others.⁷⁵ In his emphasis on this radical situatedness, Levinas does not provide substantive resources for a justice that goes beyond the abstract universalism of interchangeable citizens-with-rights.

Levinas acknowledges the necessity of thematizing principles of justice, but cautions that these articulations and justifications should be ceaselessly challenged by the ethical. There are certainly forms of social organization and moral calculations that are incompatible with normativity as he describes it, but he avoids making claims about the domain that he calls the political. Justice is a kind of translation, not a degradation, of responsibility, but Levinas explicitly distances himself from the task of establishing the rules of ethics: "One can without doubt construct an ethics [a system of norms] in function of what I have just said, but this is not my own theme" (EI 90).⁷⁶ Any normative system will be complicated by his claims about the anarchic quality of responsibility. The ethical calls out for justice—the analysis of political interests, the adjudication of legal liability, and accurate historical narration, but it also destabilizes the assumption of the preexisting subject that grounds these various endeavors.

A second, related question is how the self becomes ethically significant, in addition to the other's infinite demand—so that we can begin to consider how the subject recovers from or responds to the encounter with alterity. Levinas's claim that responsibility is traumatic in character is an attempt to guard against the tendency to reduce others to morally domesticated objects or ideas. But in most psychological contexts, the discourse of trauma centers on what the traumatized psyche experiences and how it can heal from such a wound. No such discussion of recovery emerges in Levinas's work, even if his philosophical work can be read as a form of working through the event of responsibility. In the domain of justice, however, the needs of the self become morally significant, as I consider not only how to respond to *one* other's vulnerability, but also how to tend to the needs and interests of multiple others. To make these sorts of comparative decisions, assessing my own resources and how best to sustain myself in the face of those responsibilities becomes crucial. For example, the idea of respite from caregiving at some point becomes morally required. I may find myself responding to the other's need, but to take care of another person's specific needs in any long-term way, I must also consider how to take care of myself. In interacting with others, responsibility is translated into practical judgments. One can have duties to oneself that can be measured against one's duties to others.

It is at this point, when justice must translate the demand of responsibility, that we must consider how to transmute the trauma of ethical exposure into a process of decision- and policy-making. This is correlatively the point at which storytelling becomes legitimate, in the various ways it functions as a response to traumatic events: as historical representation, the preservation of the identity of a culture or a family, or therapeutic working-through. Psychological trauma is the interruption of the self's narrative and often the deauthorization of the self as a narrator, especially in the case of human-inflicted violence. For Levinas, although the suffering of others provokes our responsibility, it is as a matter of justice that our own suffering or particular experiences of trauma demand legal or psychological remedy. Judith Herman and Susan Brison have argued that such healing depends significantly on the opportunity to tell one's story to others and to have those stories heard sympathetically.[77] These retellings open up the possibility of the survivor reclaiming both a degree of agency, as the interpreter of her own experience, and the social affirmation of personhood that was threatened or destroyed by trauma. They typically begin to repair the perceived loss of autonomy that arises from the traumatic event itself, from psychological reactions to that event (including disruptions of memory), and from others' responses. But these considerations—precisely *how* to respond both to the suffering of others and to one's own—lie outside of Levinas's focus. He makes use of the medical or psychological description of trauma, but in a decontextualized way, by not considering trauma as a contingent experience that an individual happens to undergo. He does not repudiate the importance of the psychological, social, and political questions around recovery from trauma, but his project is concerned with calling attention to the urgency of responsibility that he sees as prior to those issues. Hence his references to trauma are highly circumscribed by his emphasis on the nonintentional quality of the encounter with the other.

A third worry that arises from Levinas's silence about the sources and content of norms is what Samuel Moyn describes as a "crypto-theology" at the core of his thought—an obscure gesture to a transcendent source of values, outside of all historicism, while simultaneously identifying the other as first and foremost a human other.[78] The ethical becomes privileged over and above the relationship with God, which Moyn argues is a direct inversion of the narrative that Rosenzweig tells of redemption and revelation, despite Levinas's claims about his close connections to Rosenzweig's approach to these issues.[79] Refusing to locate the source of moral authority in a religious or cultural context means that Levinas seems to be invoking one's infinite responsibility to the other as a universal, absolute value. If values are grounded outside of the contingency of history, culture, and human construction, there seems to be no way to interrogate the normative judgments or political decisions that apparently result from these values.

That concern about a crypto-theology that would uncritically legitimate politics is exacerbated by Levinas's tendency to draw a binary opposition between the dynamic of war, which dominates history, and the claim of responsibility, which breaks open that narrative. In various writings, he identifies Judaism as the "transfiguration of individual or national egocentrism or egoism into a vocation of moral conscience" (STI 117), and the State of Israel at least ideally embodies or holds out the possibility of such a transfiguration (SI 216–18). Suggesting that Israel occupies a position both in secular history and in an ethico-religious transformation of human existence clearly carries the risk of investing one political state with a divine purpose and thus justifying whatever means that state might employ to accomplish that end. Levinas's relative silence about the fate of Palestinians and other costs of the establishment of such a state intensifies those risks, even if he also articulates the dangers of Israel as an idea being co-opted and thus corrupted by being a state among other states.[80]

However, the gesture to what lies beyond history does not provide a substantive set of values that are ordained with absolute authority, which would then (if only we could know them fully) set history on a righteous path. Moyn's worry seems to be Nietzschean in origin: that Levinas constructs yet another shadow of God in referring to the infinite demand of responsibility. But this objection does not recognize the persistence and intensity of Levinas's refusal to establish a normative *arkhe*—in Derrida's terms, the source of "commencement and commandment."[81] The "vocation of moral conscience" is the experience of responsibility rather than the comprehension of the Good. Again, Levinas describes the opening of normativity rather than arguing in favor of a set of principles or values, and for that reason he is primarily engaged in examining dominant philosophical conceptions of subjectivity and the limits of those conceptions.

All three of these critical questions—whether Levinas's refusal to translate ethics into politics is ultimately irresponsible, whether he misappropriates the psychological trauma in ways that do not recognize the need for healing, and whether his ethics devolves into theology—arise from Levinas's obstinate silence about what comes after responsibility, in the historically specific domain of justice, where various kinds of narratives, rational argumentation, and empirical research can treat subjects as beings-with-attributes, can weigh responsibilities against one another, can make sense of concrete events, and can analyze political goals and priorities. As the previous sections have argued, this discursive commitment results from his refusal to treat subjects either as objects of narration or as narrators themselves. His emphasis on the an-archic moment of responsibility is in part a reaction against the "Greek" tendency toward totalization: treating all questions, including moral questions, as comprehensible. This conceptualization erases what is for Levinas the very core of the ethical, the exposure of the subject to the other. Without starting from this singular experience of the one facing the other, the subject becomes reduced to a series of categories subsumed within history—an object of empirical study. Levinas's silence is thus in keeping with his broader method and his understanding of the task of philosophy, even if (as he certainly recognizes) it calls out for supplementary responses, objections, and attempts to interpret and enact the work of justice.

The Pre-History of the Subject

Levinas's focus is on what exceeds and interrupts autonomous subjectivity as it has been articulated in modern Western philosophy, politics, and economics, among other discourses. Particularly in his later works, his rhetoric reflects and enacts the unraveling of autonomy to disclose the traumatic significance of responsibility, so far as this can be disclosed at all. The density of his prose speaks indirectly to the conceptual presuppositions that reach their limit at this point of describing how ethical subjectivity is constituted. Describing this encounter can only be represented through a failure—or at least a partial failure—of representation, in which the trauma is repeated rather than remembered. To do otherwise would be to elide the significance of what precedes the birth of the ego, a self-possessed subject capable of narrating any experience, as Drabinski claims:

"To write this pre-history is to write a history that cannot assume a narrative form. The very 'pre-ness' of a pre-history demands that such a writing break with reminiscence and memory."[82] The priority of exposure to the other by no means appears along a linear chronology in Levinas's analysis. His discourse is thus the fractured representation of what resists the representation of history.

It is perhaps too epic a way of speaking to refer to Levinas's focus as the "prehistory" of the subject. Its priority lies in its anarchy, its disturbance of narrative time, rather than a determinable chronological position. If the subject had no such pre-history, the ethical in Levinas's terms would be "incomprehensible" in the sense of "impossible": "Why does the other concern me? What is Hecuba to me? Am I my brother's keeper? These questions have meaning only if one has already supposed that the ego is concerned only with itself, is only a concern for itself. In this hypothesis it indeed remains incomprehensible that the absolute outside-of-me, the other, would concern me. But in the 'prehistory' of the ego posited for itself speaks a responsibility" (OB 117). The autonomous subject is not simply contrasted with the I subjected to responsibility, although Levinas sometimes seems to gesture to such an opposition. Instead, the subject defined by her intentionality arises out of the (non)experience of proximity, as the self of whom responsibility and then justice is demanded. However, proximity returns to unsettle the autonomous subject, to call into question her self-possession: "Signification as proximity is thus the latent birth of the subject. Latent birth, for prior to an origin, an initiative, a present designatable and assumable, even if by memory. It is an anachronous birth, prior to its own present, a non-beginning, an anarchy" (OB 139). This passage emphasizes the temporal disordering of subjectivity as Levinas conceives of it: a subject unable, even retrospectively, to give a coherent narrative account of her own identity. She thus cannot establish or know herself prior to her relationships to others, in contrast to various forms of social contract theory and epistemology—Hobbes and Locke among them—that have dominated modern Western thought. Derrida discusses this effect of the prehistory of the subject in specifically psychoanalytic terms: "Pre-originary hospitality, anarchic goodness, infinite fecundity, and paternity might still give way to allergy. This happens all the time and it entails forgetting, denying, or repressing what comes before the origin, according to the common practice of history. This negativity of repression would always remain, according to Levinas, secondary.... It would still attest, as if in spite of itself, to the very thing it forgets, denies, or represses."[83] As Levinas and Derrida use the term, allergy is the defensive reaction against the foreignness of the other, and that defensive reaction can take the form of denying or repressing the role that the other plays in subjectivity. But the ongoing activity of repression bears witness to this impact, and the significance of what is repressed returns to disrupt what is consciously avowed. As Derrida acknowledges, Levinas would reject the psychoanalytic vocabulary of repression, but both discourses focus on the limits of memory and the obscurity of the origins of subjectivity. For Levinas, the an-archic significance of responsibility generates the oscillation between ethics and justice, by which the pre-historical calls out for the historical, and the historical attests to what precedes it, even through repudiation.

These different conceptions of subjectivity privilege different relations to or experiences of time—as that which neutrally provides a form in which all events can be made intelligible, or that which disrupts all such narration. The dominant formal conceptions of time involve representing the past in such a way that individual subjects, or a collection of subjects, can understand what has happened, in order to articulate their present identities and deliberate about their future projects: "taking control of its past and future from the vantage point of the present."[84] But this account of subjectivity, in its narrative mastery over time, leaves out the register of responsibility. Levinas's method and language enact his alternative conception of the impact that diachrony has on the subject. The idiosyncrasies of his style—his emotionally charged language, his use of metaphor, the central image of trauma, and his refusal to delineate a vision of justice—all attest to the difficulty of philosophically representing what resists being reduced to a concept.

Notes

1. Lin, *Intersubjectivity of Time*, 111.
2. See also Perpich, "Figurative Language and the 'Face' in Levinas's Philosophy," 109–10.
3. Derrida, "At This Very Moment in this Work Here I Am," 16. See also Keenan, *Death and Responsibility*, 19–31.
4. Bernasconi and Critchley usefully remind readers that Derrida's approach is deconstructive rather than simply critical: editors' introduction, *Re-Reading Levinas*, xii–xiii.
5. Derrida, "Violence and Metaphysics," 79.
6. Ibid., 82.
7. Ibid., 152.
8. Ibid., 130.
9. Critchley, *Ethics of Deconstruction*, 12; Bernasconi, "Trace of Levinas in Derrida"; Bernasconi, "What Is the Question to Which 'Substitution' Is the Answer?," 249–50.
10. John Llewelyn remarks that "Levinas is, wittingly, hoist with his own petard as soon as he tries to explain to his readers what they are to understand" by responsibility (*Middle Voice of Ecological Conscience*, 29).
11. Chanter, *Time, Death, and the Feminine*, 227–29.
12. Ibid., 226.
13. See Derrida's discussion of the phrase "at this moment" in "At This Very Moment," 21–28.
14. Bergo, "Levinasian Responsibility and Freudian Analysis," 268.
15. Drabinski, *Levinas and the Postcolonial*, 20.

16. Ibid. Adriaan Peperzak refers to Levinas's method as a "transformed phenomenology" ("Levinas' Method," 111).
17. Drabinski, *Levinas and the Postcolonial*, 29.
18. Derrida, "At This Very Moment," 27.
19. Critchley, *Ethics of Deconstruction*, 129. See also Chanter, *Time, Death, and the Feminine*, 147.
20. Derrida, "Violence and Metaphysics," 312n7. Richard J. Bernstein extends this metaphor to describe "the movement of Levinas's thinking" in general ("Evil and the Temptation of Theodicy," 252).
21. Ricoeur, "Otherwise," 93.
22. Perpich, *Ethics of Emmanuel Levinas*, 119.
23. De Boer, *Rationality of Transcendence*, 66.
24. Cohen, *Ethics, Exegesis, and Philosophy*, 198.
25. In this sense Levinas's rhetoric overlaps with the psychoanalytic claim that ideas have affective charges as well as denotative or manifest contents.
26. Lawlor, "Intuition and Duration, 26–27.
27. MacAvoy, "Other Side of Intentionality," 112–13.
28. Raffoul, *Origins of Responsibility*, 165.
29. Ibid., 214–19.
30. Perpich, *Ethics of Emmanuel Levinas*, 121.
31. Derrida, "At This Very Moment," 28.
32. Nietzsche, *Beyond Good and Evil*, §24.
33. MacDonald, "Losing Spirit," 184.
34. Alphonso Lingis's translation of *Otherwise than Being* sometimes prints *épos* without an accent or in roman type, but in the original French, Levinas consistently italicizes and accents it.
35. Derrida uses this term *derangement* (derangement) in "At This Very Moment in the Work Here I Am." Although Derrida does not explicitly make this connection, it expresses two crucial features of trauma, its disordering or dis-arranging of "normal," representable events and the broader psychological impact of such disorder—the confusion and sense of helplessness in the face of a chaotic world ("At This Very Moment," 32).
36. Critchley, *Problem with Levinas*, 108–10.
37. Perpich, *Ethics of Emmanuel Levinas*, 117.
38. Ibid., 118. See TI 50–52.
39. See, for instance, Ciaramelli, *Transcendence et Éthique*, 86–129; Buckingham, *Levinas, Storytelling and Anti-Storytelling*, 109–12; Perpich, *Ethics of Emmanuel Levinas*, 117–18; and Ricoeur, "Otherwise," 83.
40. Campbell, *Relational Remembering*, 41. Thanks to Linda Martín Alcoff for bringing this work to my attention.
41. Chanter, *Time, Death, and the Feminine*, 162–63.
42. Severson, *Levinas's Philosophy of Time*, 241.
43. Buckingham, *Levinas, Storytelling and Anti-Storytelling*, 89.
44. Rosen, "From a Memory beyond Memory to a State beyond the State," 290.
45. Weber, "Persecution in Levinas's *Otherwise than Being*," 74.
46. Ibid.
47. See Bernet, "Traumatized Subject."
48. LaCapra, *Writing History, Writing Trauma*, 42.
49. Freud, "Remembering, Repeating, and Working-Through," 12:145–57.

50. De Boer, *Rationality of Transcendence*, 8.
51. Drabinski, *Sensibility and Singularity*, 8.
52. For a more detailed analysis of the relationship between Levinas's work and phenomenology, see Chanter, *Time, Death, and the Feminine*; Drabinski, *Sensibility and Singularity*; Cohen, *Ethics, Exegesis, and Philosophy*; and Bergo, "What Is Levinas Doing?"
53. Bevis, "'Better than Metaphors'"; Chanter, *Time, Death, and the Feminine*, 37–74, 241–60; Sikka, "Delightful Other"; Rosato, "Woman as Vulnerable Self"; Chalier, *Figures du feminine*; and Sandford, *Metaphysics of Love*, 47–49.
54. See Llewelyn, *Emmanuel Levinas*, 58, 178–98.
55. Perpich, "Figurative Language and the 'Face,'" 117.
56. Bevis, "'Better than Metaphors,'" 319.
57. For a close discussion of this evolution in Levinas's metaphors, see Severson, *Levinas's Philosophy of Time*, 108–227.
58. Despite this marked preference for the language of temporality in his later writings, Levinas still uses the language of height intermittently, as at the end of *Otherwise than Being*: "The emphasis of exteriority is excellency. Height is heaven. The kingdom of heaven is ethical" (OB 183).
59. Drabinski, *Sensibility and Singularity*, 216.
60. LaCapra, *Writing History, Writing Trauma*, 70.
61. Ibid., 69. See also Michael Lambek, who argues that the proliferation of discursive uses of the concept of trauma demands critical attention to the work that the concept is intended to do and which experiences are labeled traumatic ("Terror's Wake").
62. Santner, "History beyond the Pleasure Principle," 144.
63. Ibid., 147.
64. Santner is referring specifically to Eric Nolte's claims about the causes of the Shoah ("Vergangenheit die nicht vergehen will").
65. Chanter, *Time, Death, and the Feminine*, 232.
66. Ibid., 222.
67. Ibid., 239.
68. Ibid.
69. Derrida, "Violence and Metaphysics," 111.
70. Perpich, *Ethics of Emmanuel Levinas*, 124.
71. Ibid., 147–48; see also Perpich, "Don't Try This at Home."
72. For a discussion of the restlessness of Levinasian responsibility and Derrida's responses to that concept, see Michaelsen, "Tracing a Traumatic Temporality."
73. Horowitz, *Ethics at a Standstill*, 34.
74. Ibid., 35.
75. Ibid., 297.
76. Ibid., 10.
77. Herman, *Trauma and Recovery*, and Brison, *Aftermath*. See also Nelson, *Damaged Identities, Narrative Repair*.
78. Moyn, *Origins of the Other*, 230.
79. Ibid., 151.
80. Caygill, *Levinas and the Political*, 160–66.
81. Derrida, *Archive Fever*, 1.
82. Drabinski, *Sensibility and Singularity*, 188.
83. Derrida, *Adieu to Emmanuel Levinas*, 95.
84. Chanter, *Time, Death, and the Feminine*, 163.

4 Between Theodicy and Despair

LEVINAS'S CRITIQUE OF narrative and the conception of the narrating subject that underlies it leads him to the issue of how time is synchronized in the philosophy of history, where the process of abstraction from the singular other is most prominent. By interpreting the significance of disparate events and integrating them into a coherent account, the disciplinary approaches of history typically assume a formal conception of time, in which a linear chronology can be represented by consciousness. In other words, past events are treated as intentional objects. This synchronization of time entails generalizing from people's experiences, selectively emphasizing certain elements of what has happened, and drawing out themes from temporally or geographically remote events. From Levinas's perspective, the historian translates the immediacy of the face into an abstraction and so betrays it. The danger in this translation is the tendency to subordinate the singular to the totality and in so doing to neglect the suffering of the individual and the subject's implication in that suffering. Given this concern, Levinas predictably critiques Hegel's philosophy of history in the strongest possible terms.

The Hegel that Levinas most often addresses is the Hegel who posits a teleological unity to history, an account that dominates his *Lectures on the Philosophy of History*, a course that he taught five times between 1822 and 1831.[1] Hegel's understanding of time draws together ideas that characterize a Greek tradition of thought, as Levinas uses that term: the ability of consciousness to represent and understand all that is (or all that matters) and thus the identification of the self primarily with an observing, comprehending subject. Time then functions as the framework within which consciousness understands reality and itself, rather than posing a fundamental challenge to autonomy. For Hegel, the movement of time is subordinate—or becomes subordinated to—the drama of *Geist*, a drama that at least in principle culminates in moral, political, and epistemic fulfillment. Time itself is morally neutral, part of Nature and thus prior to moral concerns. But with this belief in perfectibility through history, the historian-philosopher generates a kind of theodicy that takes the form of an abiding belief in progressive history, in which conflict, suffering, loss, and death become necessary steps in the maturation of humanity. This presumption has remained influential far beyond the academic study of philosophy. Without such a belief in the underlying meaning of history, Hegel argues that we would be left in despair at the destruction wrought by moral and natural forms of evil. He thus establishes an opposition between the interpretive activity of history and the passivity of merely observing historical events without trying to make sense of them. This kind of exhausted resignation would be a repudiation of the essential capacity of *Geist*, to transform through reflection what is merely given. In this way cynicism about history—the denial of any overarching purpose—is a reversion to the determinism of matter, against the freedom of *Geist*.

But for Levinas neither theodicy nor despair is an appropriate response to suffering, and our humanity should not be measured by our ability to fit that suffering within a purposeful narrative. He sketches instead a third possibility, irreducible to autonomous activity or nihilistic despair, even as he acknowledges the gravitational pull of both of those possibilities. In this chapter I examine two related elements of Hegel's philosophy of history: the way in which history functions as a theodicy, and the capacity of *Geist* to transcend the destructive power of time. Levinas accepts the temptation of these ideas, but he contests their legitimacy in capturing the ethical significance of time. Levinas's references to the messianic responsibility of the subject challenge a moral order in which suffering signifies a sacrifice to a higher good and also offer an alternative to the denial of any moral order whatsoever, by emphasizing the obligation of each subject to work toward a fragile justice. Without reference to a historical totality, this privileging of responsibility in the encounter with a singular other in the present reinforces Levinas's privileging of diachrony. The subject is addressed by the other in the lapse of time, rather than being able to establish the reflective distance that would generate knowledge of a teleological history.

Hegelian History as Theodicy

Hegel's lectures on the philosophy of history begin with the claim that a philosophical approach to history consists of the "simple thought" that "Reason rules the world, and that world history has therefore been rational in its course."[2] Intimations of this idea arise in Anaxagoras's conception of the natural world as law-governed and in the Christian belief in Providence, and Hegel refers to these precursors to demonstrate the plausibility of his own view.[3] He acknowledges that the history of the world presents us with much that seems unreasonable and destructive, and that we can fall into moral nihilism in contemplating the ruin that results from human actions, even human actions carried out with the best of intentions: "when we see arising from [these actions] all the evil, the wickedness, the decline of the most flourishing nations mankind has produced, we can only be filled with grief for all that has come to nothing. And since this decline and fall is not merely the work of nature but of the will of men, we might well end with moral outrage over such a drama, and with a revolt of our good spirit (if there is a spirit of goodness in us)."[4] We can comfort ourselves more superficially by reminding ourselves that such suffering has been visited on others and that in any case there is no remedy for what is past. But a more substantive consolation can be achieved by converting our immediate horror at catastrophic events into an understanding of the broader purpose of those events. Hegel argues that we should confront the question that "necessarily comes to mind" as we "contemplate history as this slaughter-bench": "What was the ultimate goal for which these monstrous sacrifices [*ungeheuersten Opfer*] were made?"[5] *Ungeheuer* is a synonym for *unheimlich*—the uncanny—but with the connotations of something immense and unnatural. *Opfer* initially referred to an animal sacrificed within the context of a religious ritual, an obligation imposed on human beings by a divine order. By their nature, sacrifices must cause some degree of pain to demonstrate human faithfulness through their willingness to give up something of value in order to honor the gods. Sacrifices thus are deliberate acts by which an individual or a community chooses to undergo pain in order to worship the divine. But immense, monstrous suffering threatens the coherence of that theological structure: are these events best understood as sacrifices? Hegel's question is framed in a way that reaffirms the demand that reason makes of historical reality. He does not ask *whether* there is a goal behind this destruction or *whether* it should be understood in terms of sacrifice but *what* the goal was. However overwhelming and horrifying, losses have a purpose that explains and redeems them. Levinas characterizes Hegelian history as a narration in which "everything wicked forms a part of meaning" (IEO 146). Even the most destructive events fit into an intelligible order and lead to a higher good.

For this reason, Hegel describes philosophic history as "a theodicy, a justification of the ways of God," which allows for an "intellectual reconciliation" to a historical reality that often seems utterly irrational.[6] This kind of intellectual reconciliation honors the vocation of reason to understand the content of divine purposes, rather than superficially positing the existence of divine purposes without attempting to comprehend them—as in the belief in Providence. Whatever we undergo as existing material beings, as thinking beings we can stand back from those experiences and see them in the purposeful light of world history. Philosophic history thus addresses, somewhat unexpectedly, the problem of evil, the apparent disjunction between the experience of undeserved suffering and a belief in a moral order that would seem to disallow such injustice.

Of the various forms of theodicy that have arisen in Western theology, Hegel's philosophic history is most closely allied with one developed by Irenaeus, a second-century theologian who emphasized the pedagogical effect of suffering on the soul. Irenaeus argues that human beings were created in a morally immature state, but we have the capacity to develop virtue by living in an imperfectly just world: encountering moral challenges, making mistakes, and learning from them.[7] Any meaningful virtue requires this kind of hard-won wisdom. We reach spiritual maturity through what John Keats called "the vale of soul-making," rather than a mere "vale of tears."[8] We should not passively await salvation from the ordeals of human finitude, but instead we should see them as the "school" that transforms us morally and intellectually.[9] Irenaeus largely rejected the dominant tradition of Augustinian theodicy, which postulates as the root of evil a lapse from an initial state of moral purity and innocence. Instead, moral perfection results from a development that requires what Hegel calls the "magical power" of "tarrying with the negative."[10] In our immaturity, we may not see the purpose of suffering, but that suffering, if we respond to it properly, draws us out of immaturity. For Hegel, responding to it properly entails interpreting all of human history through the lens of the rational requirement that these evils are sacrifices within a larger order—putting to use the power of reason to transform reality into a just world.

The kind of evil that provokes Hegel to generate a theodicy is itself significant. It is not only the content of history but the condition of temporal existence itself that offends reason, in Hegel's terms. The passing of time is a destructive force, simply negating all that exists materially: "what was produced, the children of Time, were devoured by time."[11] In its obedience to natural laws, matter is fundamentally defined by its mortality, whereas *Geist* can transcend that vulnerability to make sense of its past experience and transform itself as a result of its past experience.[12] In this context, Hegel refers to the "devouring activity" of Cronos, limited by and ultimately overpowered by the law-giving force of Zeus. That capacity for self-reflection is concretely performed in the creation of historical narratives, which in their fully developed form interpret events rather than merely recording them. In this discussion, Hegel repeats a traditional conflation between two Greek gods: Chronos, the deity of time, and Cronos the Titan, father of Zeus, who ate his children to prevent them from usurping his power. In drawing together these two images, eating one's children (now not Zeus and his siblings, but all mortal beings) becomes characteristic of time itself. The myth underlines the unnatural brutality of Nature or the moral vacuum that precedes the institution of the law and then offends that law. As physical beings we are caught up in causal and temporal forces that open up the abysmal thought that we are no more than objects or the effects of some purposeless becoming. In miniature, the historical subsumption of natural time into a coherent narrative is a version of both Irenaean theodicy and the myth of Zeus and Chronos/Cronos, in which moral or spiritual development is imposed on barbarism only through a rejection of merely natural existence. Natural time is the negative force that we must overcome to avoid the despair that arises out of conceiving ourselves as merely material objects and to reach a more mature form of *Geist*—a free, thinking, self-determining being.

Such an account of time calls out for a theodicy that reaffirms a purposeful force more powerful than Nature. Levinas suggests that the myth of Cronos/Chronos expresses a paradigmatically Greek understanding of time, in depicting time as the destructive force that negates the present moment (HB 218).[13] This conception creates the idea of common, measurable time, or the series of punctual present moments described by Aristotle.[14] It becomes the way that the Western scientific worldview understands time, in which past and future are present moments that have gone by or are not yet, but are at least in principle accessible through representation. While this model of public time makes no overt reference to the psychological horror of Cronos eating his own children, the focus on the fleeting present carries along, as an undercurrent, anxiety about the mortality of those caught up in such a movement, an anxiety I will discuss in more detail in chapter 7. In this conception of the natural world, matter is governed by this destructive force and thus creates "nothing new under the sun."[15] Only *Geist*, as it realizes its historical, self-reflective capacity, can transform itself significantly and resist temporal annihilation.

But in searching for an overarching purpose for all that happens, *Geist* engaged in philosophic history must comprehend the "imponderable mass of wills, interests, and activities" as "the tools and means of the World Spirit for achieving its goal, to elevate it to consciousness and to actualize it."[16] Famously, Hegel refers to this synthesis as the "cunning of reason." It consists not only of a synchronous dimension, by weaving the private ends and actions of individuals into a coherent unity with a culturally determinate form of freedom, but also of the historical dimension of locating that culture within a teleological process. In this sense, the impact of time on individual human beings is overridden in the perfectibility of *Geist* as a self-reflective, maturing power.

According to Hegel, these capacities for synthesizing natural time reach their culmination in philosophic history, which actively interprets the events of history. No form of history can merely record facts, despite the popular image of the historian's task, because representing events at least begins to analyze what those events mean: "Even the ordinary, average historian, who believes and says that he is merely receptive to his data, is not passive in his thinking; he brings his categories along with him, and sees his data through them. In every treatise that is to be scientific, Reason must not slumber, and reflection must be actively applied."[17] The defining character of *Geist* comes into play in constructing a meaningful historical narrative—in selecting which events are significant and which are not, in interpreting what that significance is, and finding links between them. Part of what distinguishes philosophic history from other approaches is its capacity to reflect on its own interpretive assumptions. Through this reconstructive labor, rational reflection generates a recognizable structure of origin, development, and end. Historical narration provides an epistemic vantage point from which to ascertain a *telos*, which would then explain the suffering of individuals in relation to that purpose.

Freedom and Time

The rest of this chapter will trace both the lines of connection between Hegel's particular form of historical theodicy and Levinas's understanding of time, and the nuanced critique of Hegel that Levinas develops. But this critique begins with Levinas accepting the power of two key elements of this Hegelian picture of history: first, that freedom (as it has been dominantly understood in modern philosophy) requires overcoming the brute and brutal power of time; and second, that reason attempts to make sense of its experience, including historical experience, and that this effort requires treating suffering as an object to be understood in terms of a larger framework.[18]

In the early essay "Some Thoughts on the Philosophy of Hitlerism," Levinas discusses freedom and temporality in a way that resonates strongly with Hegel's opposition of *Geist* and matter. Just as Hegel identifies *Geist* by its ability to overcome the simple negation of time, Levinas describes freedom as spontaneity that is untrammeled by time. Our immediate experience of the past reveals the burdens that it places on us. Its very existence raises the possibility that even our deliberate actions are obscurely determined by forces that we do not recognize or control: "Time, the condition of human existence, is above all the condition of the irreparable. The fait accompli, carried off by a fleeting present, forever escapes man's grasp but weighs on his destiny. Behind the melancholy of the eternal flow of things—the illusory present of Heraclitus—stands the tragedy of an irremovable, ineffaceable past that condemns all initiative to be nothing more than continuation. True freedom, true beginning, would require a true present that is always at the apogee of a destiny, eternally resuming" (PH 14). Time puts past events out of our control. But if we are defined by events or forces that we cannot change, we may be merely the products of the past, rather than possessing any power to act spontaneously in the present. Catherine Chalier comments that time is a "figure of heteronomy more formidable" than the will of another individual: "How could one interrupt the infinite chain or series of events that connect one to the past? How could one really *begin* something and be free if the act one performs today is entirely determined by what was?"[19] It is only if we can overcome the passage of time that we might be entirely free. Levinas suggests that Christianity offers such a triumph over temporality, in the promise of redemption, or overturning the significance of one's own sinful past. Such spiritual purification is a "power given to the soul to liberate itself from *what it was*, from all that bound it, all that committed it, and recover its primary virginity" (PH 15). The "primary virginity" of freedom here lies in a complex relationship to

Geist in its historical dimension. This phrase imagines achieving a state of purity through the work of overcoming the destructive impact of time, through either spiritual redemption or intellectual reflection. As with Irenaeus, the moral ideal arises as the result of labor, not as an initial state of innocence.

The reflective distance of narrative representation would then reestablish the sovereignty of the ego. This same thought echoes in Levinas's later writings. In *Otherwise than Being*, consciousness is described as the activity of representation, which entails "rendering present anew and . . . collecting the dispersion into a presence, and in this sense being always at the beginning or free" (OB 165). That state of being at the beginning is accomplished through the work of consciousness, which represents all that surrounds it and therefore cannot be surprised or unknowingly affected by the past. This description again draws out Levinas's worries about the Greek ideal that positions the knowing subject as a narrator who can synthesize all that has happened and is in this way immune to the effects of diachrony. Levinas thus emphasizes the tension between the lapse of time and freedom in Western thought—a tension at the core of Hegel's teleogical history. The freedom of *Geist* rests on its ability to represent the chaotic plurality of historical events and reflect on their inner significance. Without this narration, *Geist* itself remains caught in the passage of natural time.

Despite his affirmation of Hegel's basic insight that diachrony threatens the achievement of autonomy, Levinas criticizes the synthesizing activity of history by claiming that the singularity of human experience is lost in historical narratives. To overcome despair, such narratives must be detached from the suffering of individuals and focus instead on the purpose within that destruction. In *Otherwise than Being*, Levinas emphasizes this abstraction in a description of Hegel's philosophy of history: "The multiplicity of unique subjects, entities immediately, empirically encountered, would proceed from this universal self-consciousness of the Mind: bits of dust collected by its movement or drops of sweat glistening on its forehead because of the labor of the negative it will have accomplished. They would be forgettable moments of which what counts is only their identities due to their positions in the system, which are reabsorbed into the whole of the system" (OB 103–4). Rosenzweig's critique of totality runs just below the surface of this passage, with an attention to the cost of such assimilation into the whole. Levinas is even more explicit as he discusses the activity of reason in comprehending reality: "The rational is syn-thesis, syn-chronization of the historical. . . . The thought of rational animality is accomplished in the *Idea* in which history presents itself. It is toward the idea that the dialectic tends, the dialectic in which diachronically traversed moments are recovered" (PA 79–80). Through this process, the identity of the subject is reaffirmed, as an observer to the radical changes within history, precisely "by making of disparate and diverse events a history—its history" (PII 48). In a sense, nothing prevents this synthesizing assimilation, and there is much in human cognition that seeks out such systematicity. Levinas's critique of Hegelian history then is along the lines of Heidegger's sardonic evaluation of a thought being "correct" (*richtig*) without getting to the originary and deepest significance of what it attempts to think. It may describe a powerful tendency of our thinking without capturing what resists such incorporation into an intelligible purpose. As Levinas asks in various ways in various writings: "The moment has come to ask whether this entry of each into the representation of the others, whether this agreement between thoughts in the synchrony of the given, is the unique, original, and ultimate rationality of thought and discourse. One must ask whether this gathering of time into presence by intentionality—and thus whether the reduction of time to the *essance* of being, its reducibility to presence and representation—is the primordial intrigue of time" (DR 164). This argumentative technique is phrased as a suggestion that appeals to a remainder that escapes the totalizing power of representation and suggests that time *also* subverts the synchronizing activity of consciousness rather than merely providing a structure for it. Levinas then typically offers a description of how time challenges the sovereignty of the intentional subject in a phenomenological analysis that evokes the subject's encounter with what exceeds comprehension.

In response to Hegel's view of history, Levinas accepts that time *can* be synchronized through representation, in history and memory, but he rejects the exhaustiveness of that reduction. Time can be domesticated to serve as the frame within which reality unfolds, shows itself, and is comprehended: "Truth is rediscovery, recall, reminiscence, reuniting under the unity of the recapture, relaxation and tension without a break, without a gap.... Time is reminiscence and reminiscence is time, the unity of consciousness and essence" (OB 29). In Hegel's terms, time can function as the negative element driving forward the fulfillment of *Geist* in its self-consciousness and freedom. Time in its very movement permits "a recuperation of all divergencies, through retention, memory and history" (OB 9).

But even as he affirms how time can be understood in this way, Levinas calls into question the neatness of this rational comprehension of history. Time is the "monstration of essence" but also shows its monstrosity, the diachronic lapse that makes us always too late to remain mere observers of the other's vulnerability (OB 9).[20] This alternative understanding of the subject's relation to time resists the pull of theodicy, by remaining attuned to the suffering of the other that provokes theodicy in the first place.

The Significance of Suffering

The language that opens Levinas's essay "Useless Suffering" resonates with the Hegelian attempt to evade despair in the face of suffering. He focuses on the helplessness inflicted by pain, which is both a perception and the "unassumable": suffering is a "backward consciousness, 'operating' not as 'grasp' but as revulsion....

The denial, the refusal of meaning, thrusting itself forward as a sensible quality: that is, in the guise of 'experienced' content, the *way* in which, within a consciousness, the unbearable is precisely not borne" (US 91). Intentionality is turned back against itself, its operations and its grasp thwarted by an experience that refuses to act as merely another experience—hence Levinas's suspension of these terms through the use of scare quotes. Its content is its resistance to being assimilated as an intentional object.

Pain can be represented in music and literature and stylized facial expressions on medical pain rating scales, but it also exceeds attempts to capture it as simply another sensation. It imposes on the person who experiences it a kind of passivity, beyond the "active reception" of perception (US 92). The pain of an injury or a migraine disrupts the voluntary activity of the self and reshapes the person as a patient. The sensation of pain is "a pure undergoing" that resists being gathered into any meaningful experience (US 92). For this reason, Levinas refers to pain as "absurdity," a moment of nonsense within sense or the "overflowing of sense by non-sense" (OB 74).[21] Elaine Scarry describes pain as having no object, of not being "*of* or *for* anything," and for this reason, it causes a "shattering of language," resisting representation.[22] Pain thus does not fit easily into the dynamic of intentionality, or the activity of reason as Hegel understands it. It offers no content to consciousness and overcomes (in its most intense forms) all other sensations. It is thus just an affliction.

Levinas accepts Hegel's claim that as we confront the helplessness of pain, we tend to look for "blessings in disguise," rationalizations that would convert this meaninglessness into meaning: "the pain of suffering can take on the meaning of pain that wins merit and hopes for a reward, and so lose, it would appear, its modality of uselessness" (US 95). Levinas's language here is extremely cautious: pain *can* take on this meaning and *apparently* lose its uselessness. Throughout this discussion, his claims remain at the level of describing—neither affirming nor rejecting—the various ways in which people try to establish a purpose in suffering:

> Is [pain] not meaningful as a means with an end in view, when it makes itself felt in the effort that goes into the preparation of a work, or in the fatigue resulting from it? One can see a biological finality in it: the role of an alarm signal manifesting itself for the preservation of life against the cunning dangers that threaten it in illness. "He that increaseth knowledge increaseth sorrow," says Ecclesiastes (1:18), where suffering appears at the very least as the price of reason and spiritual refinement. It is also thought to temper the individual's character. It is said to be necessary to the teleology of community life, when social discontent awakens a useful attention to the health of the collective body. Perhaps there is a social utility in the suffering necessary to the pedagogic function of Power in education, discipline and repression. Is not fear of punishment the beginning of wisdom? Do people not have the idea that suffering, undergone as punishment, regenerates the enemies of society and humankind? (US 95)

The term "regenerates" (*régénèrent*) in the last sentence has the connotation of rehabilitating criminals through the imposition of punishment. This example rounds out the catalog of apparently rhetorical questions and reports about what is commonly accepted about the purposes of pain—a catalog that attests to the strength and pervasiveness of our desire to find justifications for pain. These explanations attempt to register the tangible results that make pain worthwhile or justified. Immediately following this passage, Levinas gestures briefly to the limitations of these various attempts, with reference to the disproportionate, immoderate suffering produced by the judicial system itself, by war, by the oppression of the powerless by the powerful, and by natural disasters: "the bad and gratuitous meaninglessness of pain already shows beneath the reasonable forms espoused by the social 'uses' of suffering" (US 95). In other words, the desire for a purposeful order seems implausible in the face of our immediate experience of purposeless suffering.

In response to his own critique of such secular theodicies, he imagines a justification based less in mundane experience and more in theology, the idea of a cosmic order in which every evil is necessary to generate the highest good: "This is the kingdom of transcendent ends, willed by a benevolent wisdom, by the absolute goodness of a God who is in a sense defined by that super-natural goodness; or a goodness invisibly disseminated in Nature and History, whose paths, indeed painful but leading to the Good, benevolent wisdom should direct. This is pain henceforth meaningful, subordinated in one way or another to the metaphysical finality glimpsed by faith or belief in progress" (US 96). Behind the merely natural world and its brutal indifference to justice, a divine power provides reassurance of purposefulness even in the midst of destruction or moral chaos. The last sentence of this passage links this reassurance to the promise of historical completion, beyond the misery of temporal existence. The narrative structure requires some reason behind suffering, and this metaphysical form of theodicy gestures to a cosmic order that "would be destined to the atonement of a sin, or announce, to the ontologically limited consciousness, compensation or recompense at the end of time" (US 96). Our suffering would ultimately be useful, as part of a narrative that we cannot always glimpse. As Nietzsche claims in the *Genealogy of Morals*, we suffer not so much from suffering as from the meaninglessness of suffering.[23] The fact that this redemption comes at the "end of time," when finite beings will be united with the infinite, speaks again to the idea that the passing of time without such a *telos* threatens us with despair. Synchronizing historical events with reference to an intelligible purpose positions the subject as a participant and interpreter of a project, rather than being passively caught up in time.

Sounding quite a bit like Hegel, Levinas acknowledges the power of these attempts to subordinate suffering to a larger purpose that would make sense of it: "It is impossible ... to underestimate the temptation of theodicy, and to fail to recognize the profundity of the empire it exerts over humankind" (US 96). The essential work of reason, the finding of purpose within the given, has become a temptation and a governing element of our conceptual imaginary. The tendency to interpret suffering in terms of a teleological narrative survives even the death of God, in the "watered-down form at the core of atheist progressivism, which was confident of the efficacy of the Good that is immanent in being and destined to visible triumph" (US 96).

Identifying theodicy as a temptation calls into question the Hegelian claim that reason demands purpose-seeking and asks us instead to evaluate the desires and anxieties of reason itself. This approach means that Levinas does not directly launch arguments that address the traditional problem of evil, along Humean lines, as Paul Davies notes: Levinas "does not begin with, and never really sees the need for, an attack on the actual theoretical content of a theodicy. The description [of suffering] suffices, inviting us to infer the immorality of theodicy from its inability to address suffering as it is exposed in the description."[24] Arguing theoretically against a theodicy takes up the tools that Levinas wants to abjure, given his attention to the limits of reason in the realm of ethics. Conceptualizing suffering within a philosophical argument departs too quickly from the ways in which we are exposed traumatically to the suffering of others. If, as Davies claims, "theodicy will be the proper name of a philosophy that seeks to avoid *this* suffering," my suffering for the "unthinkable and unjustifiable" suffering that someone else undergoes, then there is a sense in which objections to theodicies participate in that same evasion.[25] Philosophical arguments deflect our exposure to the suffering of the other by translating the immediacy and urgency of that claim on us into an abstraction. Levinas's line of attack is therefore an attempt to disclose and reorient us toward the significance of suffering in its immediacy. Robert Bernasconi claims that Levinas's foremost philosophical concern is "the suffering human beings cause each other" and how philosophy has tended to contribute to that suffering—by glorifying the autonomy of the subject, through its forgetfulness of responsibility, and by rationalizing epistemic and political violence against the other.[26] In response, Levinas produces "an ongoing polemic against teleological philosophies of history" that justify the sacrifice of individuals for a greater good.[27] Levinas's response to Nietzsche calls attention to the suffering of others: we may suffer more from a lack of purpose for suffering than from our own pain, but in containing all suffering within a larger narrative, we deflect the ethical impact of the vulnerability and pain of others. In this sometimes subterranean argument, Levinas tries to evoke in his readers outrage at the attempt to convert others' suffering into sacrifices, by providing a careful phenomenological analysis of pain.

He recognizes that gesturing to the events of the twentieth century, to the immediate experience of suffering, or to the demand that another's suffering makes on us does not provide any guarantee against the desire to find a rational order within destruction and violence. In this vein, Oona Ajzenstat comments that the "critique of theodicy would harass theodicy continually; like skepticism harassing philosophy it would tear down any version of completeness or providence."[28] That interruption must happen repeatedly, given the tendencies of reason to try to repair those ruptures. From the perspective of philosophic history, to the person "who looks at the world rationally," there is no historical event or series of historical events that could destabilize the conclusion that "the world looks rational in return."[29] The critique of theodicy cannot directly undermine theodicy by producing even monstrous examples of moral evil. Hegel's philosophy of history is engineered to incorporate such examples within the thought of a purposive order. Levinas instead tries to unhinge the logic of theodicy, by appealing to that which provoked the need for theodicy to begin with: the brute experience of pain and specifically the pain of others. That pain *can* be integrated into a belief in teleological history, just as time can function as the monstration of essence, but such reductions leave a remainder. In this case, theodicy is a reaction to the demand made of us by the fact of suffering even as it attempts to reconcile us to such suffering.

Levinas tries to return his readers to that moment of provocation, the proximity of another singular being in distress, prior to any particular identification of that person as a fellow citizen, spiritual fellow-traveler, or family member, and prior to the narrative that finds an overarching purpose for that suffering. He recognizes that the temptation of theodicy will come into play but asserts the need to dismantle that same narrative. The uselessness and helplessness of pain calls out for a more immediate response, "a demand for analgesia [relief from pain], more pressing, more urgent, in the groan, than a demand for consolation or the postponement of death" (US 93). Pain itself remains useless, but the response of one subject to another is "the just suffering in me for the unjustifiable suffering of the other," a response that has ethical significance (US 94). This is not a translation of the absurd into something intelligible, but instead a dwelling with the exposure to the other. The other's cry for relief should not result in our own attempt to avoid the pain of being exposed to the other's pain, through the construction of a theodicy.

When Theodicy Abruptly Appeared Impossible

Despite the potential for a Hegelian philosophy of history to assimilate any example of catastrophe, Levinas argues that it is particularly in the historical context of the twentieth century that the ethical failure of theodicy should be obvious to us: "Perhaps the most revolutionary fact of our twentieth-century consciousness—but it is also an event in Sacred History—is that of the destruction of all balance between Western thought's explicit and implicit theodicy and the forms that suffering and its evil are taking on in the very unfolding of this century" (US 97). The attempt to reconcile historical events with the "simple thought" of a rational order within that history is interrupted, or should be interrupted, by the repeated, wide-scale, and deliberately inflicted suffering in genocide, war, and prison camps that are premised on a refusal of responsibility for the other (US 97). These instances of moral evil arose out of "exasperation of a reason become political and detached from all ethics" (US 97). Michael Smith and Barbara Harshav note that Levinas may be drawing on the Latin origins of the word "exasperation," which literally mean "to make rough or harsh." In the events of the twentieth century, reason becomes implicated in dehumanization and moral disaster, both in the form of technological or bureaucratic efficiency in support of violence and in the form of rationalizations of others' suffering.

But Levinas's larger claim concerns the contemporary cultural exasperation (as frustration and bewilderment) of thought in response to such rationalizations of evil (US 241n6). In another text, Levinas refers to 1941 as "a hole in history," a challenge to our ability to construct a coherent narrative of any kind, much less a progressive one (MS 93). He does not insist on the uniqueness of the Shoah and instead emphasizes the "universal meaning" that pervades the multiple moral catastrophes of the twentieth century, when "theodicy abruptly appeared impossible" (US 99). Theodicy here does not serve merely as a scholarly attempt to reconcile the experience of evil with the existence of an omnibenevolent divine power. Instead, its significance is its wider effect on how the subject responds to the other, and specifically how the subject allows herself to be addressed by the other's suffering. Levinas argues that these historical events should "reveal the unjustifiable character of suffering in the other, the outrage it would be for me to justify my neighbor's suffering" (US 98). Any such account subordinates the pain of others to a higher purpose, which then not only explains but frames that suffering as worthwhile. Carl Sachs comments that for Levinas the Shoah did not suddenly delegitimize theodicy as a theoretical position, but only revealed its impossibility: "the final solution did not actually render theodicy impossible. Rather, it is with Auschwitz that theodicy appears impossible. . . . Levinas' point is not that theodicy still remains possible but merely appears impossible, but rather that it was always impossible, and should have been seen as such."[30] Theodicy's particular kind of narrative about the other's suffering diminishes the urgency of the call that it makes on the subject, by conceptualizing that suffering as sacrifice. Hegel argues that philosophical history provides an antidote to despair in the form of a *telos*, by which destruction has a purpose, but this reassurance in Levinas's view generates a higher-order despair, that such a *telos* normalizes the suffering of others and thus anesthetizes us to the trauma of responsibility.

Framing suffering as a sacrifice, as a punishment brought about by individual actions or through original sin (as Augustinian theodicies do) or as a pedagogical activity (as Irenean theodicies do), is "the source of all immorality," the turning away from the suffering of the other (US 99). In Levinas's Talmudic writings, he claims that any such justification attempts to establish divine approval for those who directly perpetrate violence against others, and that such pardon would condone evil: "The world in which pardon is all-powerful becomes inhuman" (RA 20). Even God cannot intervene to pardon the evil that human beings do to each other.

There is a peculiar moment in an interview where Levinas reflects both the desire to find lessons in the past, to interpret and learn from ethical failures, and his more developed critique of that tendency. Asked about the significance of Judaism in his thought, he refers to grappling with the problem of evil in the wake of the Shoah:

> I myself was not at Auschwitz, but finally I lost my entire family there. Even now I ask myself if there is not a strange teaching—may God forgive me for saying this: a teaching of Auschwitz—strange teaching, according to which the beginning of faith is not at all the promise, and faith is not something one can preach, because it is difficult to preach—that is to say, to propose to the other—something without promise. . . . To tolerate Auschwitz without denying God, it is perhaps permissible to ask that of oneself. But perhaps also: there would even be an offense in contradicting the despair of those who went to their death. (IFP 77–78)

The passage begins with Levinas identifying himself as a survivor, in the moral uneasiness of having survived someone else's death. His hesitation in expressing a "teaching" from Auschwitz is intensified in the content of that teaching. The lesson, which might otherwise tempt us to see a pedagogical purpose in the suffering of others, is continuing religious faith in the face of such moral chaos, paired with the refusal of theodicy, a promise of a "happy end" that would make sense of that suffering (INO 197). The faith that Levinas references here is a stern kind of relationship with the ethical. He clearly refuses the idea of holding out a promise, or "preaching" to others the possibility of such a faith in this context, but worries also about the ethical implications of cultivating such a faith in oneself. The source of that concern is again the tendency of theodicy to generate indifference in the face of the other's suffering—"contradicting the despair" of those who were killed.

Levinas describes two ways of interpreting history: one recognizably Hegelian and one that counters the temptation to teleology and theodicy. The realization of *Geist* is both an epistemic achievement and a political one, and this mirrors the convergence between the good and the true that characterizes what Levinas calls Greek thought (MT 94). Levinas offers no direct argument against this picture of history. He only offers the suggestion that this totality does not exhaust what is significant in human existence, and that to ignore what resists this totality is to commit a certain kind of moral violence:

> Suppose for a moment that political life appears not as a dialectical adjustment which men make towards another, but as an infernal cycle of violence and derision; suppose for a moment that the moral ends which politics prides itself on achieving, but amends and limits by virtue of achieving them—that these ends appear steeped in the immorality that claims to sustain them; suppose, in other words, that you have lost the meaning of the political and the consciousness of its grandeur, that the non-sense or non-value of world politics is your first certainty. (MT 94)

If the *telos* of history requires and justifies such sacrifice, the teleological approach to history itself is contaminated—"steeped" in suffering and indifference to suffering—rather than having the moral force to redeem such sacrifices. Levinas explicitly links this perspective to the experience of Jews prior to their emancipation in eighteenth- and nineteenth-century western Europe, but the language that he uses—of losing the meaning of progress through politics—is very close to his description in "Useless Suffering" of the delegitimizing of theodicy in the twentieth century. There is no legitimate hope offered by a political or moral order that orients itself toward totality, in which justice is realized through the sacrifices rationalized by that vision.

On his own interpretation, Levinas writes at a historical moment at which traditional teleological narratives, at least those centered in Europe, have collapsed, and at which systems of moral rules have proven to be insufficient against moral catastrophe. As Hannah Arendt records with some distress, Adolf Eichmann defends his actions by referring, not entirely clumsily, to the categorical imperative.[31] The content of the hope that Levinas describes cannot be for the realization of a different normative code, one that would more perfectly reflect the demands of reason and thus create a just society (PO 109). Alasdair MacIntyre claims that Levinas's "normativity without norms" can only arise "as the end result of a history during which the relevant set of norms had lost whatever it had been that had once made those norms compelling. What remains is an awareness and a mode of response that can only be described through phenomenological techniques."[32] For Levinas, this description of subjective experience reaffirms that normativity remains—the sense of obligation to the other—without our being able to establish the source or parameters of responsibility. Indeed, normativity has its force precisely because it cannot be exhaustively reduced to a set of norms to be comprehended and evaluated. Levinas maintains, therefore, a restlessness at the heart of the ethical, as an alternative both to teleological history and nihilistic despair.

How then do we grapple with the "end of theodicy" (US 98)? If the root of immorality is justification of the other's suffering, our refusal to justify it by gesturing to a greater purpose is the opening of the ethical. Richard Bernstein argues that evil provokes our horror, but there are better and worse responses to that horror: "Everything depends on precisely how one interprets this horror of evil. If I interpret it as meaning that there is an economy here where evil *must* be counterbalanced by a good, then once again I am being seduced by the temptation of theodicy.... But there is another way (the Levinasian way) of interpreting how the horror of evil leads to the intimation of the good."[33] In contrast to Hegel's attempt to overcome horror by appealing a larger teleological narrative, Levinas proposes that horror at another's suffering is itself normatively significant. He recognizes the strength of the human impulse to resolve the purposelessness of suffering, but he suggests that maintaining horror in the face of suffering is the only justifiable response to it. This is another way of describing a moral order that breaks into the normalized amorality of the intentionality, in which holding oneself in the uneasy encounter with alterity requires refusing the tendency to transmute that exposure into a concept that might fit smoothly into a progressive narrative. This kind of unsettled response is a Levinasian version of working-through, in the wake of our exposure to *another's* suffering.

Levinas is careful, however, to avoid holding up the affective response of horror as a new moral ideal: "Is this horror of evil—in which, paradoxically, evil is given—the Good? Here it cannot be a question of a passage from Evil to the Good by an attraction of contraries. That would be an additional theodicy" (TE 183).[34] Our horror at another's suffering reflects our exposure to the other, which he identifies as the upsurge of holiness (EN xiii). But as soon as he indicates a possible conception of the good, he anticipates and undercuts the temptation to justify evil as what provokes the good of that response. Our finding the other's suffering unjustifiable or "unforgivable" is suffering that has ethical meaning (US 94). Levinas cautions that this useful suffering cannot be the purpose that redeems useless suffering: "It cannot give itself out as an example, or be narrated in an edifying discourse. It cannot, without becoming perverted, be made into a preachment" (US 99). Discussing Phillippe Nemo's work on Job, Levinas discusses evil as incomprehensible, in the sense of being "non-integratable..., a monstrosity, what is disturbing and foreign of itself" (TE 180). Hence it cannot be drawn smoothly into a narrative in which useful suffering overcomes evil.[35] Levinas here describes a much more complicated notion of hope than Hegel does; it is a hope that calls on each person as a singular being to respond to the vulnerability of the singular other. In this way, he evades the straightforward dichotomy between nihilism, in which we might well see ourselves as "duped by morality," and teleological history, in which meaning can be understood only by abstracting away from the suffering of individuals (TI 21).

Levinas's critique of theodicy stems from the intuition that the suffering of individuals is subordinated to the larger purposes of history, and that such a shift in attention ultimately rationalizes and normalizes further suffering. His worry, then, is that the ethical demand that one person makes on another gets entirely written out of the calculations of politics. Writing about the role of the state in "Peace and Proximity," he claims, "It is not without importance to know . . . if the egalitarian and just State . . . proceeds from a war of all against all—or from the irreducible responsibility of the one for the other, and if it can ignore the unicity of the face and love. It is not without importance to know this so that war does not become the institution of a war with a good conscience in the name of historical necessities" (PP 169). This passage articulates Levinas's broadest concern about Hegelian theodicy: although Hegel himself emphasizes that reason can only retrospectively form a meaningful narrative about the purpose of historical events, this activity lends itself to the justification of violence in the present and future, such that nations can engage in such violence in a state of moral complacency, "with a good conscience." Levinas's concern is about war and other political calculations undertaken without substantive and ongoing moral unsettlement about the justification for the political goal, its methods, and its consequences. Theodicy supports the insular dynamics of politics untroubled by the ethical demand to respond to the vulnerability of the other.

Historians as Survivors

Given his claim that Hegelian history should no longer be plausible to us, it is important to analyze what Levinas has to say about history more generally. His explicit references to history are often paired with references to memory, as tandem processes of representing the past. When Levinas uses the term "history," he most often emphasizes the interpretive, synthesizing activity that defines Hegelian philosophic history, the construction of a unified narrative to record disparate times and experiences in a way that makes them all simultaneously present before consciousness. The following passage from the lecture series "God and Onto-Theo-logy" is paradigmatic: "That which goes by, that which goes by temporally, or that which passes (i.e., the present, which is already past, which we must retain), is retained at first immediately; thereafter it is recalled thanks to memory; and finally it is rediscovered through history and reconstructed by history, or by prehistory. The rational work of consciousness is, from Plato to Husserl, *reminiscence*" (GDT 134). Like memory, history engages in a synchronizing project, so that a series of experiences can be made into an object comprehensible to consciousness. It thus directly negates the significance of diachrony.

Hegel treats the reflective distance that historians have from their material as supporting the work of rational interpretation. Levinas's version of this description is that history is "totalization itself," the movement of making sense of disparate events (TT 47). But over and above the epistemic labor of history,

Levinas emphasizes the personal position of historians with regard to the events and people about which they write, in describing them as "survivors" (TI 228). This term introduces a very different objection to empirical history than the one that Hegel raises. Hegel's point is that historians cannot be merely receptive, neutral observers of historical events, because knowledge is necessarily mediated by concepts. Levinas's point has a moral inflection to it. Historians are not merely receptive, neutral observers of historical events, because they are imbedded in a history of mortal human beings. Historians do not only survive an event (or live as the descendants of those who survived), but also survive those who have died. The deaths of those human beings are not episodes from which historians can stay entirely detached. Historians themselves are implicated as survivors, with all the ambiguous responsibility that this term carries: "My being affected by the death of the other is precisely that, my relation with his death. It is, in my relation, my deference to someone who no longer responds, already a culpability—the culpability of the survivor" (GDT 12). In chapter 7, I will discuss in more detail Levinas's claims about the significance of the other's death and the subject's position as a survivor, but in this context of identifying historians as survivors, he emphasizes their moral entanglement in the suffering and death recorded in historical narratives. Obviously, historians for the most part are not those who directly cause the deaths of others, and according to the standard legal concept of responsibility, they are entirely innocent. But as human beings representing the lives and deaths of human beings—even those far removed in time or place, they are called to bear witness by not allowing those deaths to be converted into abstractions.

On Levinas's reading, in producing a detached analysis of past events, historians negate the singularity of the dead (IT 29).[36] In *Totality and Infinity*, the identification between historians and survivors is extended to include "conquerors": "Fate is the history of the historiographers, accounts of the survivors, who interpret, that is, utilize the works of the dead. The historical distance which makes this historiography, this violence, this subjection possible is proportionate to the time necessary for the will to lose its work completely. Historiography recounts the way the survivors appropriate the works of dead wills to themselves; it rests on the usurpation carried out by the conquerors, that is, by the survivors" (TI 228). As with theodicies, here histories not only represent past events but also establish and normalize particular forms of subjectivity and intersubjectivity. And as with theodicies, the distance necessary to reflect on events requires assimilating the immediacy of the other into a concept. In the previous passage, Levinas's thought resonates closely with Walter Benjamin's warning that historical narratives reflect the interests of the powerful and thereby justify their past, present, and future actions: "The danger affects both the content of the tradition and its receivers. The same threat hangs over both: that of becoming a tool of the ruling classes. . . . *Even the dead* will not be safe from the enemy if he wins."[37] The wills of individuals are objectified as the raw materials for a narrative that reduces those lives and experiences to a comprehensible theme. Benjamin emphasizes the political exploitation of that theme, whereas Levinas's objection concerns the activity of totalizing comprehension itself. The violence arises even before the narrative is used in the service of any particular goal.

Teleological history in general participates in this broad form of ethical violence, by positioning the subject as a detached observer and narrator of others' suffering and by reducing the other to an abstraction.[38] History treats all that has happened as accessible to comprehension, with greater and lesser degrees of accuracy, and thus counteracts the passing of time (OB 36). It is organized into a set of ideas, linked by a plot or an explanation of causes and effects, in which the author or the reader functions as an observer, protected from any moral obligation. Historical events are "assembled in a tale," in which the temporal quality of the narrative only supports our ability to understand it, rather than diachronously resisting our knowledge (OB 42). But the ethical—"the invisible that is judgment"—unsettles the workings of politics that dominate history (TI 246).

Levinas's Version of Messianism

Despite this deeply critical attitude toward teleological history, Levinas occasionally refers in positive terms to eschatology and messianism. A great deal depends on what those terms mean in his discourse. Eschatology is literally the study of the *eschaton*, of last things or the end of the world, and Levinas uses this term mostly in writings from the 1960s. In the preface to *Totality and Infinity*, for instance, eschatology is positioned against the work of history, which serves the political purposes of creating a totalized image of human experience. In contrast, eschatology "does not introduce a teleological system into the totality; it does not consist in teaching the orientation of history. Eschatology institutes a relation with being *beyond the totality* or beyond history" (TI 22).[39] Eschatology resists the historical abstraction away from the lives of individuals and instead introduces the idea of moral judgment in the present. The relationship to the other happens outside of the realm of politics that makes up history and so reorients the ego to what does not fit within that totality: "Justice does not result from the normal play of injustice. It comes from outside, 'through the door,' above the fray; it appears as a principle exterior to history" (IT 30). It breaks open the logic of war that governs history, in which morality could only be a "dupe" (TI 23). Levinas writes in an essay from the same period as *Totality and Infinity* of work done for an unseen future, as "an eschatology without hope for the self or without liberation in my time" (TRO 349). In this way he attempts to contrast eschatology with how the totality of history sustains the *conatus*—by assuming a self-interested subject who relates to the world by attempting to comprehend and manipulate it.

However, in later writings Levinas rejects the language of eschatology in favor of messianism. In a 1981 interview, he distances himself from the teleological connotations of eschatology: "The term *eschaton* implies that there might exist a finality, an end (*fin*) to the historical relation of difference between man and the absolutely Other, a reduction of the gap which safeguards the alterity of the transcendent, to a totality of sameness" (EoI 66). Ajzenstat attributes this revision to Levinas's increasing commitment to undoing what she calls the dual "sacral systems" of spatialization and synchronization: "Both systems flatten out the gaps and diachronies of reality by seeing them under an all-encompassing rubric, a rubric under which reality can theoretically be seen 'in one place,' or 'all at once.'"[40] According to Levinas's later thought, the language of eschatology is too easily read as participating in the totalizing dynamic of history. It frames the *eschaton* as a *telos*, as a culmination that can be comprehended within the narrative of history, whether spiritual or secular. In *Otherwise than Being*, two brief references to eschatology identify it as part of the synchronization of time, by emphasizing the intelligible end of history over the significance of the lapse of time (OB 169, 171).

Levinas's later preference for the term "messianism" may seem equally vulnerable to this misinterpretation. The most common connotations refer to a messiah figure, who would liberate a people and thus bring about justice. In the 1981 interview in which Levinas affiliates himself with the language of messianism, he painstakingly criticizes that meaning. He accepts the term "only if one understands messianic here according to the Talmudic maxim that 'the doctors of the law will never have peace, neither in this world nor in the next; they go from meeting to meeting discussing always—for there is always more to be discussed.' I could not accept a form of messianism which would terminate the need for discussion, which would end our watchfulness" (EoI 66–67). Messianism cannot be reduced to a passive hope for finality, an end of history that would redeem all of its moments.[41] At the end of *Totality and Infinity*, he writes about a "messianic triumph" that certainly sounds like a resolution by which the temporal is united with the eternal. But in his later writings such finality is repudiated.[42] The thought of the messianic imposes more obligations—to respond to others, but also to think through what responsibility and justice mean—rather than establishing any form of complacency by providing a determinate goal or the means by which to reach that goal. In his difficult form of hope, Levinas dismisses "the popular concept of the Messiah," one that "represents him as a person who comes to put a miraculous end to the violence in the world, the injustice and contradictions which destroy humanity but have their source in the nature of humanity, and simply in Nature. However, popular opinion retains the emotional power of the messianic ideal, and we daily abuse this term and this emotional power" (MT 59). Popular or "apocalyptic" messianism seems to carry some of the same temptation that theodicy does, a hope for a morally ordered future that would bring an end to a history of suffering (MT 296n1).

The messianic shows up much more frequently in Levinas's Talmudic writings and lectures than in his philosophical work; it does not enter into his discussions of diachrony in *Otherwise than Being*. Nonetheless, various scholars have used the concept of "messianic time" to explicate the entangling between time and ethics in his later work.[43] Beyond the immediacy of the encounter with the other, and even beyond the mundane work of imperfect justice, the messianic is the open-ended, "unforeseen" hope for a future justice. In place of a longing for a past or future paradise (MT 67), Levinas develops an interpretation of messianism in which salvation, now barely recognizable in relation to the popular concept of it, is a permanent demand and an infinite responsibility on the part of each individual: "The fact of not evading the burden imposed by the suffering of others defines ipseity itself. All persons are the Messiah.... Messianism is therefore not the certainty of the coming of a man who stops History. It is my power to bear the suffering of all. It is the moment when I recognize this power and my universal responsibility" (MT 89–90).[44] Ipseity is subjectivity or selfhood, from the Latin root *ipse* (self), but as the core of Levinas's project argues, we should hear in this term the I in the accusative case—being addressed by the vulnerability of the other—rather than in the nominative, where the self is an observer, deliberator, and agent. To be accused is not only to be addressed neutrally, but to be held responsible. The diachrony of responsibility is significant here. We need not have done anything in particular to establish our responsibility for the other, and we do not stand accused of causing the other's suffering in any ordinary sense. But in being exposed to the other, we are nonetheless accountable to the other. That is essentially what Levinas means by the traumatic quality of responsibility, that in a primordial sense we cannot be indifferent to the vulnerability or suffering of the other. We come too late to "evade that burden." Levinas's version of the messianic thus emphasizes "acts of responsibility" in response to the suffering of others—a demand that involves neither waiting for a Messiah figure nor fulfilling the divine *telos* of human history through one's own actions.[45]

In this emphasis on each individual's responsibility in the present moment, Martin Kavka argues that Levinas inherits a tradition of messianism that runs through Maimonides, Hermann Cohen, and Rosenzweig. In Levinas's reading of this tradition, messianism entails the belief in "the real possibility for *any* person to attain [moral] perfection—if only for an ephemeral moment."⁴⁶ But moral perfection is not a determinate goal and cannot become a *telos*. Catherine Chalier adds that Levinas follows the Talmudic commentary of Rabbi Nahman, who identifies the Messiah as the person who suffers for the suffering of others, and in this sense can be anyone. As such this person is a "rupture" in the political logic of a world history that is defined by war and the temporary subsidence of war.⁴⁷

On the one hand, Levinas seems to say that this exposure to the other is constitutive of subjectivity, and so suffering for the suffering of others would be universal. But on the other hand he speaks of such responsiveness as "holiness" and "saintliness" and therefore as rare qualities that break through the ordinary complacency of the *conatus* (VF 171).⁴⁸ Again, the chronology of responsibility remains obscure. Levinas both describes our exposure to the other as primary and characterizes such exposure as traumatic. The messianic cuts through the tendency to cover over and diminish that exposure, and it does so in the present moment. In Chalier's words, the messianic is not principally oriented toward the remote future: "It lives in the here and now of the world despite and indeed because of its sound and fury."⁴⁹ By invoking *Macbeth* in this context, Chalier emphasizes Levinas's alternative to both a teleological history, leading to some ultimate redemption or perfection, and a despair in which the world is "a tale / Told by an idiot . . . signifying nothing."⁵⁰ Messianism is thus directly opposed to quietism motivated either by despair or by teleological optimism.

Above all, Levinas emphasizes the fragility of the messianic future. It is for this reason that he separates the often-theological vocabulary that he employs from the idea of reward or promise. Bettina Bergo argues that messianism as Levinas understands it contains a temporal duality, in which my responsibility in the present opens up a "groundless messianic hope" for justice in the future.⁵¹ This hope derives from my immediate responsibility to the other, rather than diminishing such responsibility by gesturing to a historical *telos*.⁵² Bergo notes Levinas's juxtaposition between the present obligation of individual human beings and the uncertainty of how such small acts will contribute to any cosmic fulfillment of justice: "The good will be realized in history, and we are necessary to its realization. We can not, however, explain how the good shall come to pass or why we are indeed a part of it. To believe this, for a Jew, is not so much to believe in the end of history. It is to believe in the contribution, and the necessity, of one's fellow humans toward this creation."⁵³ Each subject is singularly responsible for acting rightly, but without establishing the principles that would define that behavior or a vision of what such actions will ultimately accomplish. We will not arrive at a normative system of principles that could provide certainty about our own moral status and future.⁵⁴

The fragility of the messianic is intensified by the fact that responsibility can always be dismissed or subordinated to other motivations. Although Levinas argues that what it means to be a subject is to be responsible to the other, and that what it means to encounter the other is to be addressed by the authority of the face, he recognizes that this encounter does not determine how someone will act or think. The other is susceptible to being objectified and dehumanized; the exposure of the other's face both forbids and tempts the ego to violence (EI 86). Responsibility only ever interrupts our ordinary self-absorption, and we may cover over that interruption in order to seek refuge in the amoral complacency of the *conatus*. That choice to neglect the vulnerability of the other defines "evil" in Levinas's terms:

> It is evident that there is in man the possibility of not awakening to the other; there is the possibility of evil. Evil is the order of being pure and simple—and, on the contrary, to go toward the other is the penetration of the human into being, an "otherwise than being." I am not at all certain that the "otherwise than being" is guaranteed to triumph. There can be periods during which the human is completely extinguished, but the ideal of holiness [*sainteté*] is what humanity has introduced into being.... I have no optimistic philosophy for the end of history.... But the human consists of acting without letting yourself be guided by these menacing possibilities. That is what the awakening to the human is. And there have been just men and saints in history. (PJL 114)

Levinas draws out here only the possibility for the ethical (in his terms) to erupt within the ordinary moral complacency and egoism of our interactions with others, whether those actions are on the world stage or not. This unlikely, tenuous taking up of responsibility is "holiness," the exceptional that is possible at each moment for every subject.

Messianic responsibility aims toward a form of justice, even without knowing with any precision its content or how it might be accomplished. Once again privileging the ethical over the theological, Levinas describes "the state of mind that we normally call Jewish messianism" as a "subordination of every possible relationship between God and man—redemption, revelation, creation—to the instruction of a society in which justice, instead of remaining an aspiration of individual piety, is strong enough to extend to all and be realized" (RA 21). Our present responses to others in their vulnerability and suffering is the gravitational center of messianism, rather than beliefs about the nature of the divine, about the trajectory of history, about the perfectibility of humanity, or about the connection between the divine, the human, and the profane. Messianism orients us toward a justice animated by responsibility, not a vision of a future that would sacrifice attention to the singularity of the individual in the present.

Levinas explicitly contrasts messianic justice with the "universal order" that is the *telos* of philosophic history. While both refer to a universal justice, Hegelian history describes "conflicts between men, the opposition of some to others, the opposition of each one to himself" that lead to the triumph of Reason, or the fulfillment of *Geist* (MT 94). But for Levinas, justice is not an inherent purpose within human history.[55] The messianic form of justice perceives "the absurd element in history"—the irrationality of history, or the way in which political, religious, and ethical systems can produce and intensify suffering rather than transmuting it into a higher good (MT 96). For this reason, the universality of messianism "consists in serving the universe" or each subject confronting her infinite responsibility (MT 95). This form of messianism entails a restlessness shorn of metaphysical, eschatological reassurance—a moral demand without any promise of a happy end. Bernstein notes that there is no "adequate response" to suffering, nothing that would make suffering useful or worthwhile: "To think that there is, is to delude ourselves—to be seduced by the temptation of theodicy."[56] Yet the lack of an adequate response should, in Levinas's terms, impel us to respond to the other, however inadequately—to live out my excessive and inexhaustible responsibility in the suffering of the other (US 94). In this sense, messianism refuses both the despair that threatens human reason when it contemplates the slaughter-bench of history and the theodicy that Hegel proposes as a therapeutic response to that threat.

The "Madness" of Responsibility

In various writings Levinas refers to Vasily Grossman's historical novel *Life and Fate*, and one of the principal ideas that he cites from that book is the degradation of interactions between individuals in fascism and Stalinism. He characterizes the book as "a complete spectacle of desolation," giving no reason to hope for the secular redemption of universal justice (PO 107). Systemic political projects of both left and right that attempt to realize utopian ideals end in corruption, ideology, and oppression—"the impossibility of goodness as a government, as a social institution" (ibid.). This idea resonates with Levinas's claim in *Totality and Infinity* that eschatology does not enter into history, but instead interrupts it. Responsibility cannot be translated exhaustively into a moral and political order. If we ignore this idea and claim to comprehend the ideal toward which societies should move, the *telos* of history (however it gets defined) becomes the tool of violence against human beings. This is the link that Levinas repeatedly draws between totality and totalitarianism—to claim to comprehend what is good is to lose the traumatic force of responsibility and its unsettling effect on the subject as knower, agent, and citizen. In this way we ignore our exposure to alterity and are able to rationalize the suffering of the other, whether we inflict or merely observe such suffering. Grossman describes a dehumanizing world that could easily provoke the despair that theodicy tries to address, but is in fact the result of a certain kind of secular theodicy.

In spite of this bleakness, Grossman calls attention to the minute acts of generosity that happen in the midst of moral ruin—a woman giving water to an enemy soldier or the quiet camaraderie of those waiting to see political prisoners. Levinas comments on this juxtaposition between despair and hope: "[Goodness] is so fragile before the might of evil. Grossman writes that it is as if all the simple-minded tried to douse the worldwide conflagration with a syringe" (PO 108; see also BM 76–79).[57] Levinas calls this fragile kindness saintliness, a "mad" response that does not arise from political calculations or from rational deliberations about one's obligations to others (PO 109). Its source is unintelligible: there is no justification for the self's exposure to the other, and because we cannot identify the source of that obligation, responsibility arises diachronically. Even retrospectively, its hold on the ego does not fit into any linear moral narrative. For similar reasons, if messianic hope becomes established as a philosophical or political vision of the good, it loses its ethical force (BFO 120). In this way, diachrony produces in the subject a peculiar attention to the immemorial past and a peculiar hope for an unanticipated future.

Levinas's suspicion about narration and the kind of subject assumed by this activity animates his critique of Hegel's vision of rational history as a species of theodicy. Our exposure to the passing of time is our exposure to the other—a form of heteronomy, but one that refuses despair. The ethically significant past and the ethically significant future remain beyond representation, but this diachrony generates an infinite demand on the subject in the present, rather than paralysis or complacency.

Notes

1. A Hegel more attuned to endless self-difference and self-overcoming emerges, among other places, in the *Phenomenology of Spirit*. Thanks to Steven Taubeneck for a thoughtful commentary, centered on this point of how Hegel in other writings expresses ideas less at odds with Levinas's critique of theodicy, at the 2015 Pacific Division conference of the American Philosophical Association.
2. Hegel, *Philosophy of History*, 12.
3. Ibid., 14–18.
4. Ibid., 23–24.
5. Ibid.
6. Ibid., 18.
7. Ibid., 57.
8. John Keats to George and Georgiana Keats, 21 April 1819, 255.
9. John Hick revives a version of Irenean theodicy that combines a commitment to universal salvation with the idea that as a whole human suffering contributes to moral maturation (*Evil and the God of Love*).

10. Hegel, *Phenomenology of Spirit*, 19.
11. Hegel, *Philosophy of History*, 79.
12. Ibid., 20.
13. See also Lin, *Intersubjectivity of Time*, 159–60.
14. Aristotle, *Physics*, 220a5–26.
15. Hegel, *Philosophy of History*, 57.
16. Ibid., 28.
17. Ibid., 14.
18. Bernasconi, "Levinas and the Struggle for Existence," 176.
19. Chalier, *What Ought I to Do?*, 110.
20. It also makes us (as ethical subjects) too late to question the intensity or reality of someone else's pain, as Paul Davies discusses: "where must one start from in order to arrive at that question, in order to arrive at that as a philosophical problem (How do I know the other is in pain?)? . . . Levinas wants to describe the subject as a relation to the other in which this question *must not* arise!" ("Sincerity and the End of Theodicy," 171–72).
21. See also Brison, *Aftermath*, 103. In another text, Levinas refuses the language of irrationality or absurdity to describe what disturbs representation: "the irrational presents itself to consciousness and lights up only within an intelligibility in which it ends by being situated and defined" (EP 71). The concern here is that even the opposition of rationality/irrationality or sense/nonsense lies within the domain of intentionality, and Levinas's work consistently seeks language that is radical enough to break out of that economy.
22. Scarry, *Body in Pain*, 5.
23. Nietzsche, *Genealogy of Morals*, 3:§28.
24. Davies, "Sincerity and the End of Theodicy," 170.
25. Ibid., 171.
26. Bernasconi, "Levinas and the Struggle for Existence," 176.
27. Ibid.
28. Ajzenstat, *Driven Back to the Text*, 301.
29. Hegel, *Philosophy of History*, 14.
30. Sachs, "Acknowledgement of Transcendence," 280.
31. Arendt, *Eichmann in Jerusalem*, 136.
32. MacIntyre, "Danish Ethical Demands and French Common Goods," 14.
33. Bernstein, "Evil and the Temptation of Theodicy," 262.
34. Levinas's frequent rhetorical use of questions reflects the tensions in his philosophical method, in which the ethical resists representation; see Chanter, *Time, Death, and the Feminine*, 211.
35. Bernstein, "Evil and the Temptation of Theodicy," 260.
36. There are interesting parallels between the thematization necessary to history and the thematization necessary to philosophy, such that Levinas's descriptions of historians may well implicate his own project in significant respects.
37. Benjamin, "Theses on the Philosophy of History," 255.
38. See Critchley, *Ethics-Politics-Subjectivity*, 154–55.
39. See also Bernasconi, "Different Styles of Eschatology," 6–7.
40. Ajzenstat, *Driven Back to the Text*, 205.
41. Tina Chanter, among others, has raised questions about Levinas's use of the messianic in relation to politics, which "allows Levinas to affirm Zionism, without appearing to make a gesture that can be reduced to the merely political" (*Time, Death, and the Feminine*, 257–58). See also Bernasconi, "Different Styles of Eschatology," 13–14.

42. See Morgan, "Levinas and Messianism," 196.
43. Cohen, introduction to *Unforeseen History*, xxiii.
44. See also Bergo, *Between Ethics and Politics*, 170–71, and Ciaramelli, *Transcendence et Éthique*, 154–55.
45. Morgan, "Levinas and Messianism," 200. See also Kavka, "Reading Messianically with Gershom Scholem," 412–14.
46. Kavka, *Jewish Messianism and the History of Philosophy*, 7.
47. Chalier, "Messianic Utopia," 50.
48. For a discussion on Levinas's comments on saints and saintliness, see Guenther, *Gift of the Other*, 130–31.
49. Chalier, "Messianic Utopia," 50.
50. Shakespeare, *Macbeth*, 5.5.26–28.
51. Bergo, "Levinas's Weak Messianism in Time and Flesh," 227.
52. Although there are interesting lines of connection to Benjamin's "weak messianism," for Levinas the messianic does not arise as a result of deliberation or voluntary commitment, but as a demand that interrupts the self-absorbed flow of ordinary life. The messianic in Levinas's later work is not a matter of representing the past or the future in particular ways that would spur political action, but in being called to respond to others in the present.
53. Bergo, *Between Ethics and Politics*, 132.
54. See Perpich, *Ethics of Emmanuel Levinas*, 146–49, 196–98.
55. See Ward, "On Time and Salvation," 162.
56. Bernstein, "Evil and the Temptation of Theodicy," 266.
57. Levinas is paraphrasing Grossman here. The original reads: "The preacher declares that the heavens are empty.... He sees life as a war of everything against everything. And then at the end he starts tinkling the same old bells, praising the kindness of old women and hoping to extinguish a world-wide conflagration with an enema syringe" (*Life and Fate*, 410).

5   The Sobering Up of Oedipus

IN *ENEMIES OF the People*, a documentary film about the Cambodian genocide under the Khmer Rouge, the former leader known as Brother Number Two tells his subordinates, who tortured and executed political prisoners: "You did not have any intention, therefore you did not commit any sin."[1] Although we may well reject the claim that these agents of violence remained morally innocent, the idea that responsibility depends upon intentions dominates the moral and legal imaginary of modern Western thought. It is a claim that Levinas associates with the Greek tradition, and one that he insistently challenges. However, the undermining of this ingrained pairing of responsibility and decision also lies at the core of that most iconic of Greek tragedies, *Oedipus Tyrannos*. The shifting of Oedipus's self-conception within the play dramatizes Levinas's contestation of the voluntarist conception of responsibility, by making a claim of responsibility even in the absence of intention. Previous chapters have examined the significance of time in Levinas's account of subjectivity, and how the intricate temporal character of responsibility interrupts the subject's attempts to establish himself as an autonomous agent, knower, and narrator. As a way of examining the radicality of this conception of subjectivity, this chapter analyzes the "sobering up" that Oedipus undergoes through the course of the play in order to trace the contrast between responsibility in its dominant legal interpretation and responsibility in its Levinasian meaning (PA 89).

Oedipus lives out the unraveling of autonomous subjectivity that Levinas associates with responsibility in its traumatic force. At the climax of the play, Oedipus is confronted with the full significance of actions that had previously seemed morally permissible or even commendable, both in his own judgment and that of others: killing a stranger who had provoked him to violence, becoming the ruler of a city that he had liberated from its subjugation to the Sphinx, marrying its widowed queen, and having children with her.[2] He is specifically confronted with the fact that these actions, understood properly, did not carry the meaning that he had attributed to them, and that they therefore should be described as different actions altogether: patricide, accession to his father's throne, and incest. In this way he is forced to revise his basic understanding of who he is—not only his ancestry but his moral status and his very ability to control his own life. Despite his ignorance and lack of intent, Oedipus is held responsible by the gods, by the city, and by himself for these transgressions and the moral pollution that follows from them.

Sophocles portrays Oedipus not merely as an unfortunate character in the grip of fate, but as a figure who lives out the tensions between knowledge and ignorance, agency and vulnerability, and power and helplessness that characterize the human condition more generally. In the first half of the play, Oedipus is repeatedly praised as "the first of men."[3] After he learns the truth of his identity, the chorus uses the swift reversal of his fortunes as a warning for all human beings.[4] The universal vulnerability that Oedipus reveals is the condition of being responsible in the absence of intention and even counter to our intentions.[5] In this sense, *Oedipus* gives us a Greek variation on the idea at the core of Levinasian ethics. As one more symptom of human heteronomy, we come too late to comprehend and therefore control our responsibility. Although we may attempt to be self-contained agents responsible only for what we intend, our responsibility stretches beyond these limits. This Levinasian reading of *Oedipus* examines a point of convergence between the traumatic quality of the ethical and Greek tragedy, in their overlapping rejection of a modern legal understanding of responsibility. *Oedipus* thus challenges Levinas's identification of the Greeks with the glorification of sovereignty and demands that we examine the historical shifts within that tradition.

Levinas's Map of Athens

In an interview, Levinas describes Greek philosophy as fundamentally an epistemological project, one that generates a particular conception of the subject and his relationship to what surrounds him.[6] In the Greek account of knowledge, there is

> an equation of truth with an *intelligibility of presence*. By this I mean an intelligibility which considers truth to be that which is present or co-present, that which can be gathered or synchronized into a totality which we would call the world or *cosmos* . . . however different the two terms of a relation might appear (e.g. the Divine and the human) or however separated in time (e.g. into past and future), they can ultimately be rendered commensurate and simultaneous, the same, englobed in a history which totalizes time into a beginning or an end, or both, which is presence. (EoI 55)

As in the logic of intentionality, the methods of Greek philosophy frame the world as a series of objects that can be presented to consciousness, without any object or event significantly resisting or disrupting that intelligibility. Human thought has the task, therefore, of reducing away what interferes with the presence or presentation of what is—for instance, the passing of time. This model presupposes a sovereign individual who comprehends the world as so many objects of knowledge and is capable of manipulating them.[7] Knowledge functions as a kind of domination of what is known: "Cognition consists in grasping the individual, which alone exists, not in its singularity which does not count, but in its generality, of which alone there is science. And here every power begins. The surrender of exterior things to human freedom through their generality does not only mean, in all innocence, their comprehension, but also their being taken in hand, their domestication, their possession.... Reason, which reduces the other, is appropriation and power" (PII 50). The thing or the person is conceptualized and thus loses both singularity and alterity in being converted into an object of consciousness. The knowing subject is positioned as a detached observer whose right to know goes unquestioned, and that cognitive accessibility of the world is also a form of mastery.

Levinas's account of this Greek ideal of knowing, and how it influences dominant themes in modern Western thought, significantly agrees with feminist critiques of modern epistemology and moral theory. Seyla Benhabib famously describes the agent who functions as the foundation of liberal thought as "disembedded and disembodied," mirroring the idea of detached knower.[8] This subject is both generic, in the sense of being apparently interchangeable with any other subject, and gendered male, insofar as femininity has historically been framed as rendering people incapable of attaining the detachment and self-possession necessary for autonomy. In their exclusion from the role of moral and political agent, women are framed as supporting political life without substantively participating in it. As Benhabib notes, Hobbes's vision of individuals growing from the ground like mushrooms is emblematic, in the sense that mothers, or more generally the matrices out of which individuals emerge, disappear from view.[9] The autonomous subject is encouraged to forget his immersion in a history, culture, language, and network of intimate relationships. Benhabib argues that if we begin with this idea of a detached individual, moral and political theories inevitably structure relations with other individuals in terms of conflict: "The story of the autonomous male ego is the saga of this initial sense of *loss* in confrontation with the other, and the gradual recovery from this original narcissistic wound through the sobering experience of war, fear, domination, anxiety and death."[10] In these models, interactions with others tend to be framed as competitions with other adult male (fellow) individuals, including with metaphorical and literal fathers—as in Zeus's confrontation with Cronos or Oedipus's confrontation with Laius.

Cronos and Laius harbor murderous intentions toward their sons due to anxiety about future rivalry, and their sons (deliberately or accidentally) respond in kind. Like Laius, Oedipus is primed to perceive rivalries, particularly with other men: with Laius in a conflict about who will yield to the other at the crossroads, and with Creon and Teiresias over his authority to rule Thebes. He lives in a world dominated by individuals competing with each other for power. By contrast, images of fatherhood in Levinas's work have a quite different cast, as Lin argues.[11] For instance, Abraham profoundly loves Isaac, and his religious obedience, in his willingness to sacrifice him, is measured by the depth of this love. More generally, fathers try to protect their sons. In Levinas's account of fecundity in *Totality and Infinity*, the son both is and is not the father's future, an open-ended and indefinite promise (TI 267–69).

As a further contrast between Athens and Jerusalem, Levinas begins both of his major works with the claim that much of human experience is governed by the dynamic of war, and within that context, morality seems irrelevant and useless. The preface of *Totality and Infinity* starts with the sentence, "Everyone will readily agree that it is of the highest importance to know whether we are not duped by morality" (TI 21). On the second page of *Otherwise than Being*, Levinas discusses the *conatus* as "egoisms struggling with one another, each against all, in the multiplicity of allergic egoisms which are at war with one another and are thus together" (OB 4). From those skeptical starting points, both books attempt to find a register in which ethics interrupts the dynamic of narcissistic agonism, rather than merely suspending it and thus in some sense functioning symbiotically with it.[12] In this way, Levinas positions his work against the dominance of Athens, which provides the conceptual vocabulary and grammar from which modern Western thought begins and against which Levinas reacts.[13]

When Levinas speaks of Greek thought, he is typically referring to Plato and the intellectual orientation of Western philosophy, which privileges the autonomy of the knowing and acting subject. However, the primary conception of responsibility that emerges out of this discourse is precisely the one that is contested by the narrative trajectory of Sophocles's *Oedipus*. The play thus provides some justification for complicating the set of ideas represented by Athens.[14] If Oedipus as a character initially enacts a Greek mentality in Levinas's understanding of that term, *Oedipus* as a play depicts the collapse of that attitude.

Levinas tends to employ the figure of Odysseus to symbolize the Greek philosophical attitude that privileges knowledge as comprehension of what is (TI 27). Odysseus's adventure, through twenty years of war and wandering, leads ultimately to homecoming and the reappropriation of his role as husband, father, and ruler. Levinas describes the Greek conception of the subject in metaphoric terms—recognizable in Hegel's understanding of *Geist* and Husserl's idea of intentionality—that also apply to Odysseus: consciousness is an "adventure [that] is no adventure. It is never dangerous; it is self-possession, sovereignty, ἀρχή [arkhe]. Anything unknown that can occur to it is in advance disclosed, open, manifest, is cast in the mould of the known, and cannot be a complete surprise" (OB 99; see also NM 158). In *Totality and Infinity*, Levinas uses much the same language to describe the assimilative activity of comprehension: "Everything is here, everything belongs to me; everything is caught up in advance with the primordial occupying of a site, everything is comprehended. The possibility of possessing, that is, of suspending the very alterity of what is only at first other, and other relative to me, is the way of the same" (TI 37).[15] Levinas juxtaposes Odysseus's experience with the homelessness of Abraham (TRO 348). There is no binding command that exceeds human understanding, as in Abraham's case. This positions the knower as an active subject who imposes his will on the world but cannot be fundamentally destabilized by anything that might be encountered there: "Nothing can, or could smuggle itself into consciousness without being declared, without showing itself, and without letting itself be inspected as to its truth. Transcendental subjectivity is the figure of this presence: no signification precedes that which I give" (GP 60). Consciousness is directed out toward objects but ultimately confirms the dominance of the ego, a gravitational force that intellectually assimilates the world around it.

Oedipus as Tyrannos

Oedipus begins the play with this self-conception of the detached knower and its correlative picture of self-possessed agency, a subject who has through his own cleverness conquered various forms of passivity and vulnerability. He has renounced the entanglements of family by leaving home and establishing an adult identity. His bold actions—primarily outwitting and thus destroying the Sphinx, the monster outside the gates of Thebes—have earned him the position of the city's ruler. He is therefore a *tyrannos*, a term used in ancient Greece to describe a leader who has gained that status by any means other than direct inheritance, without any of the condemnatory connotations of the modern term "tyrant." Through most of the play, Oedipus takes himself to be capable of reaffirming his legitimacy as ruler by resolving this new blight that has befallen Thebes—widespread disease, famine, and stillborn children. But unlike Odysseus, Oedipus's homecoming has been unwilled and morally catastrophic, the consequences of which first emerge materially and are only later interpreted and understood—much too late for them to be avoided. After the collapse of this immense self-confidence, he comes to see himself as the monster within the gates of the city. In contrast to Odysseus's cunning, which leads to the triumphant reclaiming of his rightful place, *Oedipus* offers a more pessimistic view of what cleverness can achieve. Sophocles depicts the human condition as a state in which we understand ourselves and our moral state only retrospectively and can therefore never completely possess ourselves or control the consequences of our actions. The play thus offers a critique of the Greek ideal (as Levinas interprets it) that converges in significant ways with Levinas's own.

Sophocles's shaping of the myth intensifies the warning about human arrogance—specifically arrogance concerning the power of human knowledge to control reality—at the core of the Oedipus story. Oracles and seers play crucial roles in his version of the story, whereas in the brief summary of the myth that appears in Homer's *Odyssey*, they are entirely absent, and in Aeschylus's versions they play only a minor role.[16] Sophocles characterizes Oedipus as a determined investigator, surrounded by enigmatic messages that slowly unravel their meanings. As modern audiences do, ancient audiences approached the play already knowing its conclusion, and the action of the play is confined to Oedipus's gradual discovery of who he is and what he has done. Even at the beginning of the play, there is nothing that Oedipus can do to change the course of events. He is already caught up in the consequences of actions that he has voluntarily committed twenty years before but has not yet understood. Part of the nightmarish quality of the play—"that dreadful machine," as Bernard Williams calls it—is the implacable unfolding of Oedipus's fate, juxtaposed with his own mistaken sense of power.[17]

Through most of the play, Oedipus expresses no awareness of this helplessness, except perhaps indirectly in the intensity of his attempts to prove his authority as a leader. Jean-Pierre Vernant comments that Sophocles emphasizes this trait—the self-perception of Oedipus as the "one who knows"—by playing with the proximity of Oedipus's name to the Greek word *oida*, "I know."[18] Bernard Knox identifies Oedipus as the "*anthrôpos tyrannos*: self-taught, unaided, he seizes control of his environment."[19] Having heard the prophecy that he will kill his father, Oedipus assumes that this knowledge will allow him to avoid that fate. His ability to solve the Sphinx's riddle reinforces this fantasy that human cleverness leads to power of various kinds—political authority and divine approval among them. This reliance on his own quick-wittedness shapes his response to the present crisis facing Thebes. Even before his people appeal to him to save them from the plague, he has sent for guidance from the oracle: "You have not roused me like a man from sleep."[20] He demands quick and clear answers from Creon, Teiresias, and other interlocutors in the play, and the very pace of the dialogue accelerates as he gradually unearths the source of moral pollution in Thebes.

One element of this demand for knowledge is that after he hears that the city is being punished because it harbors Laius's murderer, Oedipus acts as if the past merely needed to be represented accurately in order to dissipate its impact on the present. He immediately demands information from the Thebans about the death of Laius and proclaims harsh punishment for any who withhold such knowledge:

> if you shall keep silence, if perhaps
> some one of you, to shield a guilty friend,
> or for his own sake shall reject my words—
> hear what I shall do then:
> I forbid that man, whoever he be, my land,
> my land where I hold sovereignty and throne;

and I forbid any to welcome him
or cry him greeting or make him a sharer
in sacrifice or offering to the Gods,
or give him water for his hands to wash.
I command all to drive him from their homes,
since he is our pollution, as the oracle
of Pytho's God proclaimed him now to me.[21]

In the language of command and authority, Oedipus unknowingly describes his own impending banishment. In microcosm, this passage represents the contrast between illusory power and real powerlessness that runs through the play. But at this point, Oedipus has no sense of this complexity. He takes up this task as a riddle to be solved, so that he will be able to fulfill the narrative of liberating Thebes from its suffering, in which he is the "champion" who "drive[s] pollution from the land."[22] The repeated phrase "my land" is emblematic of this tension: Oedipus thinks the city is under his control due to his accomplishments, but primarily and unknowingly he belongs to this land and to its history. His efforts in the action of the play are directed toward achieving an accurate representation of Laius's murder, but Sophocles's framing undermines the illusion of gaining even narrative control over events. In the play, time functions in a way that approaches diachrony in the Levinasian sense—a lapse of time that does not offer itself neutrally to the human powers of representation but instead interrupts the self-possession of the subject. Whatever Oedipus now wills, the repercussions of some events cannot be undone, even once those events are comprehended: "Time, the condition of human existence, is above all the condition of the irreparable" (PH 14). In this way Oedipus learns that he is not only a leader and problem-solver, but that he is bound by what has already happened. The significance of diachrony intrudes on his pretensions to autonomy.

The play is thus a narrative about the ways that not only Oedipus but all human beings "try, and fail, to write their own stories."[23] Teiresias warns of this failure when he claims, in response to Oedipus's exasperated insults, that Oedipus is the one who is blind: "Since you have taunted me with being blind, / here is my word for you. / You have your eyes but see not where you are / in sin, nor where you live, nor whom you live with. / Do you know who your parents are?"[24] Oedipus is unnerved by the question, given that he has fled from those he thinks are his parents to avoid the prophecy of patricide and incest. More generally Teiresias's question and the play as a whole challenge the belief that human beings are capable of defining themselves in the present and the future through their deliberate actions, rather than being determined by the past and the divine forces of fate, over which they have little control. Ancestry here stands for the power of the past as not only a limit to but a general undermining of the possibility of self-determination. Through his search for the murderer of Laius, Oedipus comes to understand the significance of his own name, which translates as "Swollen Foot"—a reference to the wounds caused by his parents' command to pierce his infant feet before abandoning him on the mountain to die. Jonathan Lear comments in relation to Oedipus's failure to question his own identity, "All Oedipus had to do was to think about the meaning of his name, wonder why anyone would have named him *that* and looked down at his feet."[25] But his curiosity does not extend to this question, and it is easy enough for spectators and readers of the play to imagine that they would have done better in his place—and thus to replicate Oedipus's overestimation of his own cleverness and control over his life story. Despite all his efforts to establish his own identity, Oedipus's name and his fate define him.

The play insistently calls attention to the problematic nature of time in the human attempt to understand and control reality. Even the predictable progression of time is distorted. Charles Segal emphasizes the collapse of linear, intelligible time in Oedipus's life: "For Oedipus, past and future are always getting entangled with each other. In the terrible circularity of his life pattern, he can never pull free of the maimed life in the past."[26] The critical role of oracles and Teiresias the seer in the play offer the possibility of synchronizing knowledge—aided by divine insight into the past and future—but instead, in their obscurity, reveal how past and future inhabit and preoccupy the present, in a way that subverts human control over events. Adding to the temporal confusion is the fallibility of memory. For instance, Oedipus's memory of what happened at "the place where three roads meet" is that he killed all of the travelers in the party, but the herdsman who had saved the infant Oedipus's life also happened to be attending Laius during that fight. He survived the attack and returned to Thebes to report Laius's death, and later to recite the story to Oedipus himself.[27] In that report he claims, perhaps exaggerating in order to explain his failure to protect Laius, that the party had been attacked by several robbers, while Oedipus was traveling alone and gave no reason to believe that he was a robber. Such uncertainties in the play are reminders of the limits of human knowledge, even concerning events in our own experience. Given Oedipus's trust in his own cleverness to establish the legitimacy of his rule, this finitude and fallibility threaten the basis of his power, and indeed his self-conception as a sovereign being who can outwit even the gods.

In his aptitude for solving riddles, Oedipus treats all that is unknown as a contingent and corrigible limit to comprehension, since all that is can be known. In other words, he embodies the Greek ideal of knowing as Levinas describes it. When he consults the oracle about the Theban plague and then Teiresias in order to illuminate the oracle's answer, he expects straightforward information in response. In this sense, Oedipus has little attunement to the significance of that which resists human understanding, as Lear notes: "oracles are vehicles of sacred meaning, which are necessarily opaque to human reason. For Oedipus, by contrast, the sacred is treated as a simple extension of the domain of practical reason. The oracle is treated like a hot tip from a very good source. Oedipus is living a life which denies the possibility of tragedy. He cannot recognize any dimension of meaning other than the one he already knows."[28] Oedipus lacks, in Levinas's terms, a sense of the *height* of oracles—how what they say exceeds the comprehension of human beings. Tragedy emerges from this disjunction between the limitations of human knowledge and the fact that we have to make choices under conditions of partial ignorance. Like the oracle, Teiresias frustrates this expectation of clearing up riddles, and in response Oedipus accuses him of conniving to usurp his throne and fleetingly suggests that Teiresias himself was responsible for Laius's death.[29] Oedipus attempts to frame this mystery, and those who refuse to help him solve it, in terms of identifiable political ambitions. He assumes his own actions are similarly governed by intention, and that he can best understand what has happened, and control what will happen, with reference to the domain of deliberate decisions. But in Oedipus's life, human intentions do not define the significance of the actions that proceed out of them. Even the best of human beings can only truly understand what he has done retrospectively, and we dwell in the terrible predicament of acting with only limited understanding and so being responsible for more than we intend.

In Sophocles's hands, the Apollonian injunction to "know thyself" requires confronting these limits experientially, through undergoing moral ruin. Oedipus is first assured of the power of human intellect and only retrospectively of its limits: "man's knowledge is not adequate to the field upon which he acts. That field is one constituted by the gods, and about this man can know nothing.... Reason marks the point of man's hubris: his belief that there is a symmetry between what he can know and what he can do. Man's reason, however, is nothing but cleverness, and cleverness runs out."[30] Paul Kahn's reading here emphasizes that the structure of the play reflects this subjective process of recognizing the essential finitude of human knowledge. Oedipus first attempts to solve the mystery of Laius's death, and only later does he become aware that he is implicated in that riddle. Adriana Cavarero comments that in answering the Sphinx's riddle about the nature of human beings, Oedipus recognizes *what* he is, utilizing abstract reasoning about universals, but he cannot accurately identify *who* he is, as a concrete being, born of a particular mother.[31] He has not yet recognized the ineradicable force of a particular, unwilled past in the willed present.

In contrast to Oedipus's shifting understanding of Apollo's command to know thyself, Jocasta consistently questions its legitimacy. In her attempt to defuse the conflict between Oedipus and Creon over the meaning of the pronouncements of Teiresias and the Delphic oracle, Jocasta casts doubt on the legitimacy of any prophecy. Rather than suspecting political machinations, as Oedipus does, she dismisses the very possibility of authoritative information about the future: "Why should man fear since chance is all in all / for him, and he can clearly foreknow nothing? / Best to live lightly, as one can, unthinkingly."[32] Once she knows who Oedipus is and what they have done, her recommendation of willful ignorance takes on more desperation: "I beg you—do not hunt this out—I beg you, / if you have any care for your own life. / What I am suffering is enough / . . . God keep you from the knowledge of who you are!"[33] At this point Oedipus, still attributing the actions of those around him to base motivations, suspects that she is ashamed of his lowly origins—an unwanted infant found on a mountain. Finally, rather than grapple with the consequences of human finitude, by which we have partial knowledge and partial ignorance, Jocasta kills herself. She thus represents an anti-Apollonian stance, disdainful and then fearful of knowing the truth.

Although earlier versions of the myth present Oedipus dying along with Jocasta once he knows who and what he is, in Sophocles's retelling there is a striking emphasis on Oedipus's reaction to what he has learned. A servant reports that as Oedipus blinds himself, he "shrieks out" that his eyes "will never see the crime I have committed or had done upon me."[34] His ambiguous language here invokes the central question of whether Oedipus is responsible for what he has done, but the play as a whole refuses any simple answer. Sophocles presents Oedipus neither as a pure victim of fate nor as a villain: he dwells in an intermediate space of responsibility, in which knowledge and self-determination are hemmed in and, even more strongly, subverted by what is outside our control. Vernant argues that Athenian tragedy needs to be understood in its historical context, as part of a cultural shift from "an ancient religious conception of the misdeed as a defilement attached to an entire race" to a more familiar legal concept of responsibility, in which the agency and intent of the individual is the primary focus.[35] Sophocles stages the central tension of the tragedy as the contradiction between Oedipus's intentions and the real significance of his actions. He is the author of his actions and yet "his actions elude him; they are beyond his understanding."[36] This uneasy interplay of sovereignty and determination permeates the action of the play, as the audience already knows but Oedipus does not. At the height of his power and his confidence, his helplessness is brought into relief, and it is only near the end of the play that Oedipus himself becomes aware of the limits of his self-possession.

For almost three hundred lines after the audience hears that Oedipus has blinded himself, we see him struggling with how to respond to his moral transgressions, which are both deeply sedimented in the past and fresh wounds to him. He still obeys Apollo's demand for self-knowledge, by giving voice to the "unspeakable" and "accursed."[37] It is in these lines that we see Oedipus accepting responsibility for his acts, even in his subjective innocence. Vernant reminds us that the messenger twice says to the chorus that Oedipus's self-blinding is his own, voluntary action, as opposed to the fate that he has undergone, but when Oedipus emerges from the palace, the dialogue complicates this distinction. The chorus asks him, "Doer of dreadful deeds, how did you dare / so far to do despite to your own eyes / what spirit [*daimon*] urged you to it?" Oedipus replies, "It was Apollo, friends, Apollo / that brought this bitter bitterness, my sorrows to completion. / But the hand that struck me / was none but my own."[38] His action is simultaneously destined and self-determined.[39] He has been polluted through his own unwitting error, and his punishment is both self- and divinely-inflicted. At the end of the play, Oedipus gropes toward an appropriate response to what he has done, which cannot be described neatly as either victimization by the gods or the result of sovereign intention.

Oedipus is finally displaced from his role as observer and judge by the chorus, by Creon, and by the gods, whom Creon consults through an oracle. But his narration of his moral crimes and his anticipation of the impact that they will have on his children display his capacity to mourn—that is, to begin to make sense of these events. This last scene of the play prefigures Oedipus's transformation from the agent of pollution to the agent of purification, capable of healing the city in a much more complicated way than he believed he would at the beginning of the play. Oedipus comes to function as a *pharmakos*, the sacrifice who expels pollution from the city, in his embodiment of both the toxin and the antidote to moral degradation.[40] He dramatizes the ambiguity of that role, which may be interpreted through a legal, individualistic lens as an innocent scapegoat or through an older, religious lens as the concentration of a community's moral impurity (its *miasma*).

Through his suffering within this moral framework, Oedipus gains the serene otherworldly wisdom displayed in *Oedipus at Colonus*. The last part of this narrative structure is deeply foreign to Levinas's account of the interruptive force of the ethical demand. But Oedipus does experience the inadequacy of understanding, that sense of coming too late to avoid responsibility, which for Levinas characterizes the response to the other, the beginning of ethics. The inability to tell our own story or to decide the meaning of our actions is a fundamental form of passivity, a nonvoluntarist responsibility. For Oedipus, knowledge shifts from an instrument of control to the demonstration of a profound moral vulnerability. He does not use his ignorance as an escape from responsibility, and at no time does he attempt to shift the blame to Laius and Jocasta, which (given their decision to commit infanticide) many modern audiences would find plausible. Instead, he holds himself objectively responsible and therefore morally polluting, even if his transgressions were entirely unintentional and thus subjectively innocent. In the shift from confident sovereignty to his status as the accused, Oedipus enacts the interruption of the ego by trauma.

It is in this inability to transcend his past that Oedipus raises the problem of moral luck, the paradox that we tend to hold people responsible for things that they cannot control, even though we simultaneously tend to believe that people can only be responsible for what they have freely chosen. Oedipus freely engages in actions that have meanings and consequences that are inaccessible to him. Thomas Nagel broadly formulates moral luck as operating "where a significant aspect of what someone does depends on factors beyond his control, yet we continue to treat him in that respect as an object of moral judgment."[41] More specifically, in the case of circumstantial moral luck, "a person can be morally responsible only for what he does; but what he does results from a great deal that he does not do; therefore he is not morally responsible for what he is and is not responsible for. (This is not a contradiction, but it is a paradox.)"[42] Famously, this problem seems to threaten the intuition that luck should be irrelevant to the moral status of one's actions. In the way that Sophocles has framed the plot, Oedipus has no way of avoiding his fate, despite his intent and best efforts, and yet he is held responsible for what he has done by those around him, and he holds himself responsible for it. One way to resolve the problem of moral luck is to refuse to blame Oedipus, but it then becomes difficult to establish the conditions under which anyone could be held responsible, given that we do not control the results of our actions, our circumstances, or the process by which we come to be the people that we are. The opposite resolution entails holding people responsible for what they have not chosen, which runs against dominant moral intuitions.

Sophocles does not so much resolve the paradox of moral luck as call our attention to it, by presenting Oedipus as a particularly extreme example of what Margaret Urban Walker describes as "impure agency": "agency situated within the causal order in such ways as to be variably conditioned by and conditioning parts of that order, without our being able to draw for all purposes a unitary boundary to its exercise at either end, nor always for particular purposes a sharp one."[43] Impure agents act voluntarily, and therefore should be held responsible at least partially for what they do, but they are also immersed in situations that they do not control, to the extent that the boundaries of responsibility remain unclear. Due to the blurriness of the distinction between what they control and what they do not control, such agents are permanently vulnerable to the experience of remorse, of revising their moral judgments about their obligations. In the character of Oedipus, Sophocles likewise challenges the assumption of human self-possession and describes a form of responsibility that outstrips intention. Early on in the play, Oedipus enacts our desire to tie praise or blame definitively to freely chosen actions or to deny free will through a deterministic vision of human action. But Sophocles then subverts that clarity by combining subjective innocence with objective guilt: Oedipus has committed these morally obscene acts in the process of trying to avoid committing them. His circumstances have conspired to undermine his intent, and voluntarist notions of responsibility do not adequately capture the complexity of his moral state.

This understanding of impure agency resonates with Levinas's critique of dominant notions of subjectivity, particularly in the sense that it is only retrospectively that agents may understand the significance and consequences of their actions. Levinas takes on the paradox of moral luck phenomenologically, by describing a subject who takes herself to be a pure agent in Walker's terms, concerned primarily with her own freedom, but whose self-conception is interrupted by an infinite ethical demand that introduces a fundamental, ineradicable vulnerability into our experience. Levinas is not primarily interested in establishing the parameters of agency—when someone can or cannot be held accountable for what she has done. However, he *is* interested in challenging the dominant conception of the subject as an autonomous agent. Impure agency under a Levinasian interpretation functions as a reminder of a responsibility that exceeds our freely chosen and willed actions.

Responsibility as Sobering Up

Whereas Sophocles challenges the voluntarist conception of responsibility in the period when it emerges in opposition to a religious conception of moral pollution, Levinas confronts this conception as a dominant cultural idea, in a historical period in which its legitimacy has gone largely unchallenged. But to the extent that Levinas associates this individualistic, sovereign form of subjectivity with Greek thought in general, he ignores internal tensions and historical shifts within ancient Greek culture. Levinas's critique of sovereignty certainly does not coincide with the ancient Greek religious idea of human lives being governed by fate, in which human beings should feel humility in the face of the gods' greater wisdom and power. But they both question the complacent self-possession of Oedipus as he first appears in the play—radiating confidence about his own cleverness and ability to control not only his own moral condition but that of his city. For Levinas, ethics is precisely the interruption of this narcissism: responsibility "steals into me like a thief, despite the taut weave of consciousness, a trauma that surprises me absolutely, always already *passed* in a past that was never present and remains ir-representable" (GP 75). To be responsible is to respond, and in that moment not to attend to who I am and what my obligations are, first and foremost, but instead to feel compelled by another's need.

Levinas struggles with the conceptual framework inherent in language to articulate this nonvoluntarist form of responsibility, and he does so by emphasizing how freedom is disrupted by temporality—or, more specifically, diachrony: "To say that the person begins in freedom . . . is to close one's eyes to that secret of the ego, to that relation with the past which amounts neither to placing oneself at the beginning to accept this past consciously nor to being merely the result of the past" (TOT 49). Levinas expresses two related concerns about defining the subject in terms of freedom: that either temporality will have no significance or that, if time does matter, the subject is stripped of both agency and responsibility, in his status as the product of forces that he does not control. Levinas refuses both poles of this binary opposition between freedom and determinism: "To be without a choice can seem to be violence only to an abusive or hasty and imprudent reflection, for [responsibility] precedes the freedom non-freedom couple" (OB 116). It is only from within the idealization of autonomy that any unchosen obligation appears to be enslavement. Responsibility does not fit in either of those two categories, but instead "sets up a vocation that goes beyond the limited and egoist fate of him who is only for-himself and washes his hands of the faults and misfortunes that do not begin in his freedom or in his present" (OB 116). We are provoked to respond to the other before all deliberation and choice, and in this sense are accountable beyond our intentional actions. In this sense, we do not write our own moral stories or establish the boundaries of our obligations.

The knowing subject is bound to the other—a bond that already obligates the self, rooted in a past that cannot be represented and thus even cognitively mastered:

> We have been accustomed to reason in the name of the freedom of the ego—as though I had witnessed the creation of the world, and as though I could only have been in charge of a world that would have issued out of my free will.... But the subjectivity of the subject [*un sujet*] come late into a world which has not issued from his projects [*ses projets*] does not consist in projecting [*projeter*], or in treating this world as one's project [*son projet*]. This "lateness" is not insignificant. (OB 122)

In juxtaposing the terms "project" and "subject" in this passage, Levinas plays with the ambiguity of passivity and activity within the self: are we the ones who throw, who create the world, or are we instead the ones who find ourselves thrown under an obligation to the other?[44] The very structure of temporality, in putting the past beyond our control, challenges our freedom as it has been understood within the liberal tradition (PH 14; see also OB 76). But the impact of diachrony intensifies this passivity, by making us latecomers who find ourselves exposed to the other prior to making any choice or commitment. Oedipus's descent through the action of the play is the disclosure of this dismantling of sovereignty under the force of a past that lies outside of his mastery.

Levinas occasionally uses the language of "creatureliness" to articulate this idea of emerging out of an (an-archic) origin that cannot be comprehended. Critchley interprets the creature as a "being who is always already in a relation of dependence to and distinction from the alterity of a creator ... [introducing] a passivity into the heart of subjectivity."⁴⁵ A creature is thus a subject bound by an immemorial past. Oedipus lives out at least a version of this passivity by only realizing the moral significance of his actions once it is too late to undo that significance. Responsibility is what has not been chosen but is still binding on us—a responsibility that does not depend upon one's intentions, or a "guilt without fault, as if I had to do with the other before knowing him, in a past that has never taken place" (IFP 52). Levinas does not deny free will in any of its philosophical variations as much as attempt to unseat it as the defining characteristic of the subject. Tracing the influence of diachrony, or the lapse of time that destabilizes autonomy, allows him to describe a different register of subjectivity, in which we are responsible beyond our deliberate actions.

In Levinas's terms, Oedipus's complex moral status is reflected in the natural attitude of the *conatus*: claiming "one's place in the sun" is a form of usurpation, or an attack on the other, outside of all intent. Our lateness as creatures is not only in being responsible, unable to avoid responding to the other, but in being addressed in the accusative. We realize after the fact that our very existence implicates us in the suffering of others. To describe this distinctly nonvoluntarist form of responsibility more concretely, in several late writings Levinas describes how the complacency of the *conatus*—our assumed right to be and to perpetuate that existence—comes to be challenged: "My place in being, the *Da-* of my *Dasein*—isn't it already usurpation, already violence with respect to the other? A preoccupation that has nothing ethereal, nothing abstract about it. The press speaks to us of the Third World, and we are quite comfortable here; we're sure of our daily meals. At whose cost, we may wonder" (VF 179). What had seemed a morally permissible or insignificant act suddenly has a past and a future that opens up the subject's culpability in the lives of other subjects who were previously distant or invisible.⁴⁶ A very similar passage draws out the contrast between legal responsibility and ethical responsibility:

> To have to answer for one's right to be, not in relation to the abstraction of some anonymous law, some legal entity, but in fear for the other. My being in the world or my place in the sun, my home—have they not been the usurpation of places belonging to others already oppressed by me or starved, expelled to a Third World: rejecting, excluding, exiling, despoiling, killing. Fear for all that my existence *despite its intentional and conscious innocence* can accomplish in the way of violence and murder. (PT 23, emphasis added)⁴⁷

As Oedipus does, one may enjoy the status of conscious or subjective innocence while being objectively responsible for the suffering of others, through actions whose moral significance has been obscured or ignored. Much in contemporary Western cultures trains us not to attend to the question "what right do I have to be?" and the emphatic grounding of responsibility in intent is part of that training—for instance, the belief that the world is fundamentally open to our comprehension, and that our position as consumers of the resources of that world is natural and self-evident.

Against this indifference to the other, Levinas claims that the *conatus essendi*, the activity of self-preservation, is itself a form of violence and in fact the "origin of all violence" (EN xii). Merely by living we engage in violence—intellectually by assimilating others around us into mere objects of thought and more tangibly by using resources that could be used to alleviate the suffering of others. Thus we are all, less dramatically and in much more normalized ways, in the position of Oedipus, realizing after the fact that we are responsible for consequences that we never intended. Levinas refers to this interruption of our moral complacency as a "sobering up" in which we are confronted by the thousand ordinary ways in which we cause others suffering and exploit their vulnerability (PA 89). Oedipus merely dramatizes the process by which the subject experiences himself as accused. It is only once he has taken his "place in the sun" that he perceives the traumatic meaning of what he has done. In calling the ethical an *interruption* of sovereignty, Levinas suggests that it is only retrospectively that we can ask about our own right to be. It is only retrospectively, in witnessing the vulnerability or the death of the other, that responsibility is "awakened . . . as if it was me who had killed" (HIB 78). Oedipus undergoes a transformation from self-assured sovereignty to the traumatized, persecuted, and denucleated subject, from the figure who can save Thebes by solving a puzzle to the one who is responsible not only for the catastrophe besetting his people but for two unspeakable moral crimes that inexorably define his own life and the lives of his family.

The audience's recoil against Oedipus's specific actions functions to cover over how the basic structure of his responsibility applies universally. The very triviality of our everyday actions helps to conceal their moral significance from us. The dominant account of responsibility generally limits praise and blame to actions we have voluntarily engaged in, but our actions—and, even more broadly, our ways of life—have meanings and consequences that are not intended and yet in which we are implicated.[48] A great many of us live on lands ceded or conquered from indigenous peoples, following mass death due to disease, war, and enslavement. A great many of us benefit from privileges accorded to us by our race, gender, class, nationality, religion, age, or sexual orientation. Much of this privilege is inherited privilege—our access to adequate health care, our reasonable hopes for our lives, and the opportunities open to us in education and occupation depend significantly upon the kinds of lives that our parents and grandparents led. We regularly consume products that were made in unsafe working conditions, by workers earning less than a fair wage. The processes of production and transportation of commodities entail the extraction of resources, the creation of by-products, or the risk of accidents that contribute to environmental degradation, the specific effects of which are much more likely to afflict those in poverty. When those products have been consumed, most of our waste is transported to sites (either within our own nation or outside of it) where the population is too politically and economically powerless to refuse it. But these actions—including buying food, driving, producing garbage, using electronic devices, and living in buildings powered by the burning of fossil fuels—are generally treated as morally neutral in developed societies. Levinas often emphasizes how existence in general usurps the resources that others need to live, but particular forms of existence intensify that usurpation, as he acknowledges in his references to how the lives of Europeans affect the lives of the global poor.

The subject's ignorance of being objectively implicated in the suffering of unseen others is a further mark of privilege. Peggy McIntosh and others have argued that one of the crucial elements of race- or gender-based privilege is its invisibility to those who enjoy that form of privilege, and an even broader invisibility of the influence of social forces in one's own life and behavior: "My schooling gave me no training in seeing myself as an oppressor, as an unfairly advantaged person, or as a participant in a damaged culture. I was taught to see myself as an individual whose moral state depended on her individual moral will."[49] We may recognize the brutality of racism, sexism, or heterosexism in past eras or on other continents, but the temporal or geographical distance can function as a protective mechanism against recognizing the continuing significance of these forces in our own lives. Like Oedipus, we tend to believe too eagerly that the past can be safely put behind us, and that individual actions thus gain their meaning from our deliberate intent in the present, rather than taking into account the historical context and consequences of those actions. Despite the fact that privilege is not chosen or even noticed, some of us are the beneficiaries of these inequities, and our everyday choices help to perpetuate them. We are thus implicated in them. Levinas uses Oedipus as an example of this inadequacy of the legal emphasis on intent:

> In doing what I willed to do, I did a thousand and one things I hadn't willed to do.... When ... the act is turned against the goal pursued, we are in the midst of tragedy. Laius, in attempting to thwart the fatal predictions, undertakes precisely what is necessary to fulfill them. Oedipus, in succeeding, works towards his own misfortune. It is like an animal fleeing in a straight line across the snow before the sound of the hunters, thus leaving the very traces that will lead to its death. Thus we are responsible beyond our intentions. (IOF 3)

The lack of intention does not function as a mitigation of responsibility, as it generally would in a legal judgment, but rather as the core experience of responsibility as Levinas understands it. We arrive at an understanding of our actions too late to control the consequences or meaning of them. It is indeed a matter of luck to be born into forms of privilege, but the "sobering up" of responsibility makes us aware of how we are accountable for what we have not deliberately chosen. Responsibility as exposure to the other signifies "my unintentional participation in the history of humanity, in the past of others which has something to do with me" (FO 150). The traumatic quality of responsibility means that we find ourselves accused by the other, complicit in a past that shapes the present, abruptly having to grapple with the question of our right to be. Levinas is most interested in that moment of normativity—that moment in which we are called out of ourselves, in which we are forced to ask, "What have I done?" or "How have I lived?" This is quite different from asking the present- or future-oriented question: "How should I act?" or "How should I live?"—which are the more typical philosophical questions.

Much discussion in moral philosophy focuses on individual agents confronting dilemmas about how to act in the abstract present or future—decisions about our obligations to hypothetical violinists with kidney problems or the potential victims of runaway trolleys. Such thought experiments provoke important reflections on our moral intuitions, and those reflections can certainly help to attune us to what is morally relevant in future actions.[50] But they predispose us to focus on well-contained, conceptually clear moral problems, and thus to neglect the moral significance of acts that we have already committed but not understood, and of our often unwitting or half-witting participation in larger, more complicated institutions and historical trajectories. Some of the impact we have on the world around us can be addressed by making different choices about the food we eat or the forms of transportation we use or the kinds of domestic and foreign policy we support, and these are questions about how to live more justly. But some of our impact on the world stems from factors over which we have no control, either because it has already happened (either through our own actions or those of others) or because we live within institutions that establish hierarchies of power regardless of any individual intent. Thomas Pogge, for instance, has argued that severe poverty constitutes a widespread violation of human rights, and that such impoverishment is the direct result of arrangements that advantage particular populations in wealthy nations. These arrangements are such that even assuming the best of intentions, the well-nourished, well-protected, and often absurdly comfortable lives of the wealthy contribute to the destitution of others: "In the present world it is completely beyond the capacity of affluent individuals to shape their economic conduct so as to avoid causing any poverty deaths in the poor countries."[51] Merely by living what are framed as morally ordinary lives, the privileged increase the suffering of the global poor and are in an objective sense responsible for that suffering. Such responsibility is not diminished by ignorance or the absence of malicious intent. Under those conditions, Levinas's question about what right we have to be at all becomes more intense.

But this vertiginous realization of the particular impact of one's own life on the lives of others is for Levinas ancillary to the larger issue of how *any* life—privileged or not—is disrupted by responsibility in his sense of that term. Becoming aware of how my daily activities impact strangers, widows, and orphans across the world exemplifies how the trauma of responsibility breaks open the *conatus*, but there is no form of existence that could be led in good conscience. Merely by being we are enmeshed in the "restlessness" of simultaneously being absorbed in our own needs and interests, which entails violence against others, and having that self-absorption interrupted by an exposure to the vulnerability of others (OB 82). In responding to the other, I find myself accused by and accountable to the other, regardless of my position in the world and any particular features of my existence.

This is a significant contrast with Oedipus's sobering up. He must reinterpret the significance of his actions, but for Levinas, responsibility extends not only to actions I have performed but not fully understood, but to what I have not done at all: "To be a self is to be responsible beyond what one has oneself done" (TOT 49). The past that is morally relevant to me is an "immemorial past," a "past that was never a present," not a past that I have up until now misunderstood (OB 88). The ethical demand does not gain its binding force from my recognition of how I have concretely contributed to the other's suffering. That thought remains beholden to the limiting of responsibility to actions that can be represented and claimed as one's own. For Levinas, it is valuable to attend to how habitual behaviors in our ordinary lives cause unintentional harm to others or participate in historical injustices, because it draws us into questioning our right to be in general. That latter question reflects the radicality of our exposure to the other, in which our responsibility arises from "nothingness" (TI 150). There is no narrative that explains or justifies my sense of obligation to the other. In contrast, Oedipus is capable, finally, of deciphering the source of his responsibility in his past actions and therefore of comprehending his fault. His responsibility derives not from the mere fact of being but from particular actions that were in some sense contingent. His question is not "What right do I have to be?" but "What have I done?" For Levinas, we may make our way toward the former question through the latter question—through a realization of how our ordinary existence is made possible by the toil and suffering of others or by depriving others of resources. But the calling into question of the *conatus* is of primary importance, and that traumatic moment is not tied to any determinate transgression.

Recovering from Trauma

If responsibility can be detached from its traditional anchor in intentions, the concept may seem to lose its meaning: how can we hold someone accountable for what she has not chosen and could not have foreseen or avoided? A Levinasian response entails separating legal responsibility, which is governed by established norms, from ethical responsibility, which speaks to the very possibility of normativity, the binding power that another being has over me regardless of my particular relationship to them or my past actions. This more radical approach to responsibility should not simply replace the legal conception. It is clearly important within the domain of justice to determine whether a law has been broken, who broke it, and whether that violation was committed intentionally or unintentionally in order to maintain stability in the larger society and to hold people accountable for their actions. There are good reasons why judicial systems should distinguish between murder and manslaughter—that is, killing with or without "malice aforethought," premeditation, or intent. There are also good reasons why judicial systems should distinguish first and second degrees of each of those crimes and establish penalties accordingly.[52] But Levinas's claim is that such judgments of guilt and impositions of punishments do not exhaust our responsibility. He is not pointing to the fact that we might have moral obligations that cannot be established as legal obligations. We have no legal obligation to yell "Fire!" in a crowded theater that is in fact on fire, although we may have a moral duty to alert others to immediate dangers. It may be morally incumbent on us to avoid causing others unnecessary emotional pain, but for the most part we cannot be held legally liable for such suffering. But the extension of moral responsibility in this sense beyond legal responsibility does not placate Levinas's concern.

If responsibility could be defined with reference to established judicial codes or moral principles, that would convert the ethical into one more idea to be comprehended, whereas for Levinas, responsibility exceeds any such epistemic mastery. Even moral commitments defined more broadly than our legal obligations are still modeled too closely, on Levinas's reading, on a set of doctrines that can be reduced to the said. He reacts against the narrowness of the legal understanding of responsibility by deliberately inverting its major elements.[53] Responsibility breaks up the economy of the sovereign, self-possessed self in the most extreme sense: divested of an originary and virile agency, the ego cannot even experience relief from the burden of responsibility by gesturing to determinism (DYF 207).

Levinas's account of responsibility means that the subject comes into being through responsibility, "a *sub-jectum*; it is under the weight of the universe, responsible for everything" and thus "a responsibility that rests on no free commitment" (OB 116). Again, we get an inversion of autonomy: "the condition for, or the unconditionality of, the self does not begin in the auto-affection of a sovereign ego that would be, after the event, 'compassionate' for another. Quite the contrary: the uniqueness of the responsible ego is possible only *in* being obsessed by another, in the trauma suffered prior to any auto-identification, in an unrepresentable *before*. The one affected by the other is an anarchic trauma, or an inspiration of the one by the other" (OB 123). In the ethical encounter, I experience responsibility prior to knowing what I might have done to incur such responsibility—that is the diachronic quality of responsibility. Richard Cohen argues that this is just what it means to be a subject: "selfhood emerges *as* the bearer of obligations and responsibilities for the other. The human self, in other words, is constituted by the inescapable exigencies of moral obligations and responsibilities."[54] Samuel Moyn points out that in this counterintuitive understanding of the self—that responsibility precedes autonomy—Levinas follows Descartes's distinction between "the order of the subject-matter" and "the order of the reasoning."[55] It is through experiencing ourselves as knowing, willing subjects that we come to be aware of what precedes knowing and willing: "The priority of the other in the order of the materials requires a discovery of this priority, which in turn mandates the priority of the ego in the order of discovery."[56] Like Oedipus, this understanding of responsibility can only be retrospective and in that sense traumatic, in its intrusion on the ego's sense of herself as a sovereign being and on the habitual attitude of the *conatus*.

Levinas's rhetoric emphasizes how the subject shifts between the excessive, incessant demands of the ethical and the calculations required within politics, in which my resources can be weighed and apportioned, and in which I can conceptualize interpersonal obligations abstractly, to the extent that the other is recognized as an alter ego. Neither pole of this oscillation can be reduced to or encompassed within the other. With the entrance of the third person, the political domain arises out of the ethical encounter, and ethics "cries out for justice," the political ordering and fulfilling of obligations (OB 158).[57] Speaking of the Greek theoretical tradition and the "ethical order" represented in biblical texts, Levinas claims that the two traditions "do better than converge. The relation with the other and the unique that is peace comes to demand a reason that thematizes, synchronizes and synthesizes, that thinks a world and reflects on being, concepts necessary for the peace of humanity" (PP 168). The trauma of responsibility calls out for a (Greek) subject who thinks and acts in response to this trauma. But Sophocles's text attests to the diverse understandings of responsibility *within* the Greek tradition, an internal contestation between a voluntarist conception of the individual, sovereign subject and an older, religiously oriented conception of the individual caught in the workings of fate. In challenging Oedipus's presumption of sovereignty, Sophocles gestures to a broader range of responsibility that overlaps with Levinas's critique of the ideal of autonomy.

Despite this convergence, there are clear and significant differences between Levinas's account of subjectivity and Sophocles's depiction of the human condition. That contrast opens up most obviously in the aftermath of Oedipus's realization of who he is and what he has done. His crimes have taken place in a spiritual and social context that allows him to make sense both of moral pollution and purification. He is accused and found guilty by his city, but he also begins to mourn his losses by speaking them aloud to the chorus and to wrestle with the question of how to expiate his crimes. This attention to the social aspect of justice, of the concrete calculation of moral consequences, separates *Oedipus* from Levinas. Two specific elements of this process of rectification or healing demonstrate the contrast with the Levinasian account of the ethical. First, in *Oedipus* there is little attention to the vulnerability of the other and the subject's responsibility to her. Our focus is instead on Oedipus, engaged in the process of figuring out what he has done and suffering for it. Although *Oedipus* represents the way in which responsibility exceeds intentions, and thus the "sobering up" of subjectivity, there is no real emphasis in the play on Oedipus's response to the specific needs and suffering of others. Oedipus attempts to respond to the tribulations of the Theban people, but he does so as a ruler. By the time he is implicated as the cause of their suffering, he is less focused on them than on what has unfolded in his own life. The play grapples with the question of whether human beings are in any simple sense the authors of their own actions, and whether we act wittingly or unwittingly. But for Levinas, the issue of moral agency is secondary to the experience of responsibility. Oedipus displays no such "obsession" with the vulnerability of the other (OB 55). His narcissism is interrupted, but it is not interrupted by the ethical, as Levinas understands it.

A second contrast with the Levinasian account of responsibility is the fact that Sophocles allows Oedipus a reflective process of mourning, one that culminates in his sanctification. The end of the play provides a measure of resolution, in which Oedipus begins to make amends for his moral transgressions and by going voluntarily into exile returns Thebes (at least temporarily) to political and social peace. The last scenes of the play show Oedipus working through despair to a kind of resigned acceptance of his own actions. In *Oedipus at Colonus*, written approximately twenty years later, Sophocles depicts Oedipus as almost a sacred figure for having endured so much. Even if others respond to him as an uncanny figure, he expresses certainty about divine protection: "O Holy Ones of awful aspect, / Whose throne, this seat, was my first resting place / In these lands; be gracious to me, be gracious to Apollo / Who, with the evil doom he cast upon me, / Promised me also this rest in the time to come / That I should find at last at the seat of the Holy Ones, / Sanctuary, and an end of my tormented days."[58] Oedipus's extraordinary suffering grants him an extraordinary status among human beings, an aura of being honored by the gods.

No such sense of resolution attends Levinas's understanding of responsibility. Sophocles thus presents us with the beginning of Levinas's analysis of the trauma of the ethical demand, but he does not locate that challenge to the ego's sovereignty within the anarchical realm of ethics. As he is told who he is, Oedipus begins to come to terms with the determinate actions that have caused the city and his family such harm. But Levinas describes a responsibility that does not depend on the particular identity of the subject, or the particular identity of the other, or the particular situation in which she finds herself. That indefinite and excessive quality of responsibility means that Levinas cannot provide even the minimal solace that Sophocles grants Oedipus. Oedipus, Creon, and the chorus are concerned with justice as reparation and purification, rather than the infinite, messianic vocation of "bear[ing] the suffering of all" (MT 90). The ethical remains traumatically interruptive of a teleological narrative structure, and there is nothing in Sophocles's vision that gestures toward the excessive responsibility represented in Levinas's work. It is for this reason that Critchley's characterization of Levinas's ethics as a "divine comedy" or "holy story" sits uneasily with the resistance to narrative in *Otherwise than Being*: the prospect of a resolution, whether happy or unhappy, collapses the anarchic quality of the ethical and reestablishes the subject as capable of standing outside of the movement of time to represent a purposeful, coherent series of events.[59]

For Levinas, the Greek worldview links knowledge to mastery over the world, "a matter of grasping in both senses of the term a being: to comprehend and to apprehend him, to unveil and dominate him" (BFO 117). Oedipus does indeed treat knowledge as a path to power—both his ascension to the throne of Thebes and his ability to govern well, particularly in this moment of crisis. Even the horrific truth about his life provides the bridge by which Thebes can overcome its pollution. I have argued in this chapter, however, that Levinas's understanding of the Greek worldview does not capture Sophocles's response to that emphasis on the knowing, observing subject. *Oedipus Tyrannos* serves as a warning of the limits of self-determination and a reminder of the power of fate, which overrides all human initiative and intent. In this way, Levinas and Sophocles are both questioning the sovereignty of the subject, but they do so from very different angles. Sophocles's understanding of fate has little resonance with the event of responsibility, in that fate anchors Oedipus in a determinate identity—he has to wake up to who he really is. The trauma of responsibility provides no such stability, even a tragic stability, of who the subject is and what she should do to live out that identity.[60]

To the extent that the play's conclusion brings about a sense of resolution for Oedipus and for Thebes, and catharsis for the audience, it runs against Levinas's description of the restless, inexhaustible nature of the ethical demand. That narrative completion belongs to the genre of tragedy rather than trauma, which exceeds all such conceptualization. Kathleen Sands claims that "tragedy is the beautiful representation of suffering that consigns trauma to a ritual space where, rather than being silently reenacted, it is solemnly voiced and lamented."[61] Tragedy attempts to make meaning out of what resists meaning. This containment of trauma within the framework of a tragic narrative mimics the betrayal of ethics in politics, a domain in which the ethical encounter is set within an intelligible, calculable context. Levinas's resistance to narration entails that he provides no definitive or permanent resolution to the rupture introduced by alterity. There is no "ritual space" that softens the blow of responsibility. Establishing such a structure would once again position the subject as the narrator, protagonist, or audience to a story that has a linear order of events and can be approached as an object of knowledge—that is, it would return us to the economy of Greek thought as Levinas interprets it.

Despite these significant divergences, however, at the core of the play the abysmal unraveling of Oedipus's sense of his own mastery enacts the trauma of the ethical response. *Oedipus* gives us a depiction of responsibility that undermines the fundamental conception given to us by modern ethical and political thought: that we are responsible for what we have freely chosen to do. The most striking form of this challenge arises in the case of actions in the past, over which we in the present have no control and even in that past present we did not intend.

The Incompleteness of Justice

How then do we respond to this dimension of responsibility, particularly in the concrete dimension of enacting violence against others merely by living one's life? The retrospective realization of responsibility introduces a need for mechanisms of restitution, a process that attracts little attention in Levinas's discourse. He instead focuses on the encounter between two individuals, before the excessive ethical demand is translated into questions of justice. In the dramatic collapse of his own sovereignty, however, Oedipus turns to his native/adoptive city. He narrates the moral trajectory that he has undergone, the shift in his understanding of who he is, and this narrative is importantly not a monologue but a conversation with the chorus. He begins to make sense of his trauma by representing it to others and by having others listen and respond to that narrative. *Oedipus* offers a way of situating the accused subject within a society, which has communal methods of apportioning responsibility and healing moral pollution. Oedipus's attempts to come to terms with his crimes place him back within an intelligible religious order, in which his monstrosity is understood as inherent to the human condition: "behold this Oedipus—, / him who knew the famous riddles and was a man most masterful; / . . . see him now and see the breakers of misfortune swallow him! / Look upon that last day always. Count no mortal happy till / he has passed the final limit of his life secure from pain."[62] As a community Thebes identifies Oedipus's unintentional responsibility as a general lesson about the need for humility before the gods. The trauma of responsibility provokes the need for social processes of healing.

But Levinas reminds us of the problematic tendencies of justice that remain isolated from the radical dimension of ethics. The search for justice by a community can bring about a sterile return of the moral order as the competitive interaction of sovereign individuals, or a privileging of a rigid narrative of that community's identity and goals. Levinas's work serves as a corrective to those temptations. On its own, however, his emphasis on the ethical does not provide an account of how we might adequately grapple with the abysmal responsibility that exceeds intention: how should that sense of responsibility be lived out? How should it influence our behavior toward others? our choices around consumption or occupation? our political commitments? It is precisely the unfathomability of our responsibility that distinguishes it from the economy of the *conatus*. Our ethical imperatives cannot be converted into an object of consciousness or imagined as leading us to a state of moral fulfillment. Levinas's distance from Sophocles's depiction of justice reflects his larger concerns about the temptation of theodicy or a resolution of suffering that would allow us to rest in moral complacency.

Without making the aftermath of trauma and the social restoration of justice the primary focus of his thought, Levinas's philosophical work enacts at least one form of that response to trauma. In his hands, this is a response deeply committed to maintaining the immediacy and urgency of responsibility, rather than domesticating it within a larger narrative that reinscribes the self-possession of the subject. His insistence on the radical quality of responsibility and his attempts to convey that radicality through philosophical (Greek) discourse are themselves social and cultural engagements, or invitations to dialogue, that aim toward justice, without offering an articulation of what that moral *telos* would be. Levinas's critique of the voluntarist account of responsibility and the kind of subject that underlies it is a rejection of this picture's completeness, not a rejection of its usefulness in the domain of justice. That critique stems from his refusal to treat responsibility as a determinate set of principles that could be known, examined, evaluated, and unambiguously followed or violated. In a sense, he radicalizes Oedipus's blindness, by not only placing the moral significance of our actions beyond human knowledge but also conceiving of responsibility as exceeding the self's past and present actions. We are left without even the framework of a divine order within which human folly unfolds—at least not a divine order that issues moral imperatives and is even marginally accessible to human knowledge. Even the idea of fate introduces a stability and divine order that allow Oedipus to know his identity and the obligations that stem from them. Responsibility as a form of trauma undermines such a moral order. Levinas rejects both modern assumptions about self-determination and the ancient Greek conception of fate: we neither choose our own identity (write our own stories) nor find ourselves determined by a fixed nature. Neither of those accounts of subjectivity allow for the traumatic character of the ethical. Levinas's focus, then, is not so much on the intersection between finite human knowledge and willful action as on a subject whose responsibility precedes and thus outstrips "the nets of consciousness," our attempts to establish ourselves as knowing, willing agents.

This understanding of subjectivity, in its diachronous exposure to the other, has far-reaching implications, given the foundational status of the modern identification of subjectivity with autonomy. The remaining chapters of this book examine the repercussions of Levinas's thought for how we understand embodiment, mortality, and our relation to nonhuman animals—for these are some of the principal ways in which the ideal of the autonomous subject is lived out more concretely. These discussions do not conclude with answers to the question about how to live out responsibility as Levinas conceives of it, but instead examine the breadth of the disruption that this thought introduces.

Notes

1. *Enemies of the People*, quoted in "Enemies of the People" (review), 31.
2. The people of Thebes are aware of the last three of these actions, and when Oedipus describes the incident at the crossroads, in which he kills Laius, there is no expression of moral outrage from either Jocasta or the chorus, until they know that this was an act of patricide.
3. Sophocles, *Oedipus the King*, 12.
4. Ibid., 64.
5. Vernant and Vidal-Naquet, *Myth and Tragedy in Ancient Greece*, 63.
6. Levinas typically contrasts Greek thought with Judaism, but sometimes separates Greek language from Greek wisdom. Robert Gibbs disentangles three different meanings of "Greek" as Levinas uses the term: (1) "Greek" as a political structure, the "rule of the universal" in which the individual is ignored and the other is conquered (political totalization); (2) "Greek" as an epistemic quest, in which all being can be known and represented (epistemic totalization or assimilation)—this is involves philosophical detachment, ignoring the trauma of responsibility; and (3) Greek rhetoric separated from the "clarity of reason" (*Correlations in Rosenzweig and Levinas*, 161–63). The first two meanings tend to receive more attention in Levinas's thought.
7. Levinas's description of the knower echoes in an epistemic key the isolation and complacency of the ego in the *conatus*. Both accounts draw on Rosenzweig's identification of the tragic hero as fundamentally alone, inwardly "buried in itself" rather than connected to others (*Star of Redemption*, 85–88). See also Oppenheim, *Speaking/Writing of God*, 13.
8. Benhabib, "Generalized Other and the Concrete Other," 157.
9. Ibid., referring to Hobbes, *On the Citizen*, 102.
10. Benhabib, "Generalized Other and the Concrete Other," 156.
11. Lin, *Intersubjectivity of Time*, 91, 161–66
12. Theodore de Boer articulates Levinas's project as starting from the question, "can the painful experience of freedom's failure convert the savage will to a rationality which is more than a ruse?" (*Rationality of Transcendence*, 22).
13. See Chanter, *Time, Death, and the Feminine*, 224–40.

14. This distinction has been challenged in other ways by, among others, Derrida, "Violence and Metaphysics"; Handelman, *Fragments of Redemption*; Gibbs, *Correlations in Rosenzweig and Levinas*; Chalier, "Levinas and the Talmud"; Ajzenstadt, "Levinas versus Levinas"; Bernasconi, "What Are Prophets For?"; and Meir, "Hellenic and Jewish in Levinas's Writings."
15. See also IOF, 9.
16. Cameron, *Identity of Oedipus the King*, 14.
17. Williams, *Shame and Necessity*, 69.
18. Vernant, *Myth and Tragedy in Ancient Greece*, 323.
19. Knox, *Oedipus at Thebes*, 110.
20. Sophocles, *Oedipus the King*, 13.
21. Ibid., 20.
22. Ibid., 16.
23. Bushnell, *Prophesying Tragedy*, 85.
24. Sophocles, *Oedipus the King*, 28.
25. Lear, "Knowingness and Abandonment," 49.
26. Segal, *Oedipus Tyrannus*, 86.
27. Sophocles, *Oedipus the King*, 41.
28. Lear, "Knowingness and Abandonment," 50.
29. Sophocles, *Oedipus the King*, 25–27.
30. Kahn, *Out of Eden*, 28.
31. Cavarero, *Relating Narratives*, 9.
32. Sophocles, *Oedipus the King*, 52.
33. Ibid., 57.
34. Ibid., 66.
35. Vernant, *Myth and Tragedy in Ancient Greece*, 81.
36. Ibid., 82.
37. Sophocles, *Oedipus the King*, 68–69.
38. Ibid., 69.
39. Vernant, *Myth and Tragedy in Ancient Greece*, 77.
40. Ibid., 128.
41. Nagel, "Moral Luck," 26.
42. Ibid., 34.
43. Walker, "Moral Luck and the Virtues of Impure Agency," 243.
44. See Davies, "Sincerity and the End of Theodicy," 173.
45. Critchley, *Ethics-Politics-Subjectivity*, 68.
46. This line of thinking is a point of convergence with Marx, as Levinas notes in various interviews, often immediately followed by a contrast between Marxism as an ideal and Stalinism as a reality. See, for instance, IFP, 81.
47. On this point, Jill Robbins describes the proximity of the other as a challenge to "my spontaneity and my—ultimately murderous—freedom" (introduction to *Is It Righteous to Be?*, 2).
48. There are limits to this rule: a person can be held morally and legally responsible for negligence or recklessness. But even this consideration concerns knowledge that *should* have been part of a person's decision-making.
49. McIntosh, "White Privilege," 10.
50. For a careful discussion of the uses of such case studies, see Davis, "Imaginary Cases in Ethics."
51. Pogge, "Severe Poverty as a Human Rights Violation," 17.

52. The United States Penal Code defines murder as "the unlawful killing of a human being *with malice aforethought*. Every murder perpetrated by poison, lying in wait, or any other kind of *willful, deliberate, malicious, and premeditated killing*" (US Penal Code, title 18, part 1, chapter 51, §1111, emphasis added). By contrast, manslaughter is "the unlawful killing of a human being *without malice*" (US Penal Code, title 18, part 1, chapter 51, §1112, emphasis added).

53. See Perpich, *Ethics of Emmanuel Levinas*, 119–20.

54. Cohen, *Ethics, Exegesis, and Philosophy*, 183.

55. René Descartes to Marin Mersenne, 24 December 1640, 3:163.

56. Moyn, *Origins of the Other*, 241.

57. See also Bernasconi, "Third Party."

58. Sophocles, *Oedipus the King*, 74.

59. Critchley, *Problem with Levinas*, 10.

60. Critchley discusses Levinas's rejection of fate or facticity as a central element of his response to Heidegger (*Problem with Levinas*, 30–67).

61. Sands, "Tragedy, Theology, and Feminism in the Time after Time," 83.

62. Sophocles, *Oedipus the King*, 76.

6 Anxieties of Incarnation

A YEAR AFTER Hitler came to power in Germany, Levinas published a short essay titled "Some Thoughts on the Philosophy of Hitlerism," which delineates the struggle between two movements within European thought: liberalism and Hitlerism. Somewhat surprisingly, Levinas treats Hitlerism as a philosophy, if a "simplistic" one. He interprets it as "the primary attitude of a soul faced with the whole of the real and its own destiny" (PH 13). Certainly Hitlerism was or is a form of ideology, but why should Levinas grace it with the name of what has systematically opposed dogmatism? Yet Levinas insists that the "awakening of elementary emotions" must be taken seriously as a worldview: the feelings that Hitlerism cultivates and expresses "predetermine or prefigure the sense of the soul's adventure in the world" (PH 13). This claim that Hitlerism should not be dismissed as a grotesque aberration from dominant European culture emerges even more sharply in Levinas's prefatory note to the 1990 English translation of the Hitlerism essay:

> the source of the bloody barbarism of National Socialism lies not in some contingent anomaly within human reasoning, nor in some accidental ideological misunderstanding. This article expresses the conviction that this source stems from the essential possibility of *elemental Evil* into which we can be led by logic and against which Western philosophy had not sufficiently insured itself. This possibility is inscribed within the ontology of a being concerned with being [*de l'être soucieux d'être*].... Such a possibility still threatens the subject correlative with being as gathering together and as dominating [*l'être-à-reassembler et à-dominer*], that famous subject of transcendental idealism that before all else wishes to be free and thinks itself free. We must ask ourselves if liberalism is all we need to achieve an authentic dignity for the human subject. (PPH 63)

Levinas's later critique of the modern understanding of the subject focuses on the characteristic that most clearly defines liberalism in the 1934 essay—the ideal of autonomy and its overcoming of time. In other words, he objects to how both liberalism and Hitlerism describe subjectivity, each privileging one element of mind-body dualism as the basis of identity. In their opposing concerns with autonomy and authenticity, or freedom and destiny, neither account leaves room for responsibility as exposure to the other. They instead remain beholden to the self-protective attitude of the *conatus*, and this thought lies behind Levinas's contentious claim that liberalism "has not sufficiently insured itself" against what he calls evil—a cultivated neglect of responsibility (PJL 114).

The contrast between Hitlerism and liberalism in the early essay is described in terms of the significance that the body carries in each one: as the inescapable determination of identity in the former, and as the mechanical-biological organism transcended by mind or spirit in the latter. Both conceptions of the body support related assumptions about the significance of time for the subject. A crucial aspect of autonomy is its capacity to overcome its immersion in the past and the influence of time as a force of nature. The Hitlerist identification of the individual with the body instead privileges the inescapability of an innate racial essence. The opposition between the two can be framed in terms of a subject who transcends the impact of time and a subject who is irrevocably tied to a particular origin. Both accounts affirm the assumption that materiality—in the form of the human body—undercuts the possibility of autonomy by chaining the subject to an unchosen past.

Levinas's later work attempts to undermine this traditional dichotomy between matter and spirit, even as he acknowledges its dominance, and opens up the possibility of understanding materiality as sensibility, the way in which we are exposed to the other. The idea of embodied humanity has seemed a contradiction in terms in modern philosophy: to the extent that we are only bodies, we are less than human. This issue of who counts as human and who is consigned to the status of subhuman or subperson has historically tended not to receive very much attention from philosophers. It instead plays itself out on battlefields, in detention camps, in courtrooms, in news reports, and on sidewalks, with racial identity functioning as one of the primary determining factors. Given the long history of racial prejudice, of attaching evaluative judgments to the raced body, the liberal denial of the significance of the body and particularly of biological race seems the most intuitive escape from racism.

But while Nazi Germany is a paradigm of the extremes of racist hatred, Levinas also argues that the dualistic picture of subjectivity that governs liberalism perpetuates hatred of the body and, by extension, those who are defined by their bodies. In his critique of the significance of the body in both Hitlerism and liberalism, Levinas avoids the characteristic anxieties around bodies (and particularly raced bodies) of modern European thought. His understanding of materiality reinforces a different way of thinking about the impact of time on the subject—in which diachrony refuses both the self-determination associated with liberalism and the biological determinism of Hitlerism.

The Glorification of Spirit: Liberalism

According to Levinas, modern liberal theory provides a vision of "man's absolute freedom with respect to the world and to the possibilities that invite his action" (PH 14). This freedom depends upon the primary identification of the self with the nonphysical mind or soul. The influence of external determinations—instincts, emotions, customs, others' opinions—can be regulated by reason. This idea of self-determination can be found in various forms in Kantian ethics, Cartesian epistemology, and Judaic and Christian theology: I am responsible for the person who I become, rather than merely a product of forces that I do not control. As I discussed in chapter 4, in the context of Hegel's account of *Geist*, Levinas claims that "infinite liberty" requires transcendence over temporality (PH 15). The passage of time limits freedom in this sense: events in the past are impervious to my will, however much I should wish them to be otherwise. In addition, temporality forcefully introduces the problem of determination, such that one's thoughts or actions might be the product of prior causes rather than the manifestation of a free will. The spontaneity of our decisions and the felt authenticity of our purposes may thus be illusory. A fully self-possessed mind would be able to represent all that it experiences, without being ruled by those forces or events. "True freedom" requires a present without a past, or without a significant past. In an essay from 1980, Levinas returns to this theme: "The modern is constituted by the consciousness of a certain definitively acquired freedom. Everything is possible and everything is permitted, for nothing, absolutely speaking, precedes this freedom. It is a freedom that does not bow before any factual state, thus negating the "already done" and living only from the new. But it is a freedom with which no memory interferes, a freedom upon which no past weighs" (ON 124). Freedom is defined by its spontaneity, in the sense of not being merely the result of the past. In that sense it is independent of "any factual state," continually creating itself in the present and projecting itself into the future.

The liberal identification of the human as an essentially intellectual or spiritual being rather than a merely material one allows for that detachment from the determinations of history. Time can be reversed and transcended, in the redemptive narratives of Judaism and Christianity, in the power to "repair the irreparable" through repentance and to "recover [the] primary virginity" of the soul (PH 14). In the secular discourses of the Enlightenment, autonomy based on rationality provides this kind of control over time. Reason privileges the spontaneity of the individual subject, insofar as it detaches authority from the dogmatic persistence of customary beliefs and values. The rational mind is able to question what has been held up as true or good, to evaluate justifications for alternative positions, and to generate its own commitments.

In its determination by natural laws and subjection to the passing of time, matter stands as the figure for all that opposes such transcendence. The fact that rational human beings are also corporeal becomes a serious source of anxiety in this tradition, not least as an epistemic problem of how to represent the self as both minded and embodied. Levinas describes the Cartesian position on the union of soul and body as "a miraculous intervention," an interaction that cannot be described coherently, much less verified (OB 142). He notes that Descartes conceives of the mind as a "thematizing thought" (OB 142), capable of "assembling into a system" its perceptions: "Here the subject is origin, initiative, freedom, present. To move oneself or have self-consciousness is in effect to refer oneself to oneself, to be an origin. Then a subject-origin which is also a subject of flesh and blood becomes problematic" (OB 78). Embodiment complicates self-determination, by introducing the passivity of a body that is a creature—that did not create itself, that is affected by forces that the will does not control, and that ages over time. Susan Bordo describes the characteristic anxieties of dualism by delineating four ways in which the body is framed in Western philosophy: "as *alien* . . . the brute material envelope for the inner and essential self"; "as *confinement* and *limitation* . . . exert[ing] a downward pull"; "as *the enemy* . . . the source of obscurity and confusion in our thinking"; and lastly "whether as an impediment to reason or as the home of the 'slimy desires of the flesh' (as Augustine calls them), the body is the locus of *all that threatens our attempts at control*."[1] Materiality takes on the character of something fundamentally alien to spirit, but we are intimately burdened with corporeality: "What does it mean, according to the traditional interpretation, to have a body? It means bearing the body like an object from the outside world. The body weighs on Socrates like the chains that bind him in the Athenian prison, confines him like the tomb that awaits him" (PH 17). The body is not just a physical object out there in the world, but closely attached to the self. Descartes notes in the *Meditations* that the self is not merely contained within the body as "a sailor is present in a ship," but struggles to define the "commingling" between the two different kinds of things more precisely.[2] Within this imaginary, the body jeopardizes the autonomy of the subject, and one dimension of that threat is how the body makes the subject vulnerable to the passage of time. The interest of Descartes and the Enlightenment generally in anatomy and medicine attests to the need to control this internal enemy, by understanding the body in mechanistic terms, "best known by being, after its death, dissected."[3]

The properly human is thus constituted by its separation from the merely natural or animal and particularly from what is animal within the human being. As Giorgio Agamben argues, this is historically how the human comes to be defined by modern European thought: "man is not a biologically defined species, nor is he a substance given once and for all. . . . He can be human only to the degree that he transcends and transforms the anthropophorous [human-bearing] animal which supports him, and only because, through the action of negation, he is capable of mastering and, eventually, destroying his own animality."[4] As the being rooted in nature rather than culture, as Hegel claims, animals are defined as that which needs to be surpassed, and the human is defined by this surpassing. The entangling of the human with the animal is erased—or, in Derrida's terms, "disavowed and foreclosed" through this process.[5] Neither the construction of the mind as transcending a merely mechanical or biological body, nor the construction of the animal *as* the animal can be recognized in its contingency. This means that those who are positioned as failing to achieve this transcendence over animality appear to be necessarily or naturally stuck in the status of subpersons. What it means to be fully human is to have overcome the merely given, but not every member of the human species is seen as capable of this transcendence. The devaluation of Nature and those beings defined by their association with Nature is a correlate of the idealization of the nonanimal.

Within this liberal imaginary, the rational mind retains the constant possibility of changing one's interpretation or reserving one's judgment. Its freedom is manifested in its skepticism, critical reflection, and reevaluation. No idea or value has so much authority that it cannot at some point be challenged and overturned. In this sense, every belief and judgment is provisional. Self-determination becomes the possibility of ceaseless self-creation or projection in new possibilities, untrammeled by anything that is merely given. According to Levinas's 1934 analysis, the seeds of Hitlerism lie in the reaction against this free-floating quality of the mind in liberalism. By positing an irrevocable commitment of the human being to the body—especially to the race of the body—Hitlerism puts an end to this intellectual wandering and demands "heroic" action in the world. That is, Hitlerism emerges in the tradition of Western thought as a revolt against its tendency to privilege the mind in its spontaneity and self-determination.

It is important to keep in mind that matter functions here as one element in the liberal fantasy, rather than as its outside. Modern Western culture is permeated by the Cartesian assumption that matter is merely inert stuff, impervious to interpretive manipulation and fundamentally outside the realm of discourse. But this too must be recognized as an intellectual inheritance, contingent on a certain understanding of matter and spirit. What is most interesting is the similarity of the body's framing in Hitlerism and liberalism, even if the body's significance is subject to opposing normative judgments, and the way that these complementary fantasies of the human generate parallel anxieties about purity and authenticity.

The Glorification of Matter: Hitlerism

In response to the possibility of permanent skepticism and rootlessness of liberalism, Hitlerism grounds identity in the imagined immanence of race, which appears to provide a fixed essence. By privileging the idea of an authentic, quasi-biological identity, Hitlerism refuses the genealogical question of how the idea of Aryanness or whiteness is constructed through historically specific processes. Levinas emphasizes how racism reacts against the perceived excesses of freedom in liberalism: "The essence of man lies no longer in his freedom but in a sort of enslavement. To be truly oneself is not to rise above contingencies, forever foreign to the Ego's freedom; on the contrary, it is to become aware of the ineluctable original enslavement unique to our bodies; it is, above all, to accept this enslavement" (PH 18–19). Race becomes the immutable, unchosen identity of the subject, and embracing that identity takes on normative force. To be Aryan means not only having a certain lineage but aligning one's behavior with the ideal of militant masculinity, for instance, that supposedly characterizes that lineage.

By analyzing the origins of Hitlerism, however, Levinas highlights the contingent quality of this "enslavement," the way in which this interpretation of identity emerges as a historically specific reaction against the ideals of the Enlightenment. In opposition to liberalism, Hitlerism retains a belief in the givenness of the body but denies human beings the ability to transcend this facticity: "The body is not simply a fortunate or unfortunate accident that puts us in relation with the relentless world of matter; *its adhesion to the Ego is valid in itself*. It is an *inescapable* adhesion that no metaphor could confuse with the presence of an external object, and nothing can alter the tragic taste of definitiveness of this union" (PH 18). The self is then identified with the body rather than the mind—the claims of blood could never be transcended by intellectual self-determination. The relentlessness of matter becomes the embodied racial identity of the ego. The normative judgment that arises from this worldview is to affirm this "fatality" and give up the illusion of liberation from matter (PH 18). The privileging of racial identity means that the human being is subjected to history in a way that the rational subject of the liberal tradition is not. The time privileged in Hitlerism is a fantasied time of the origin, or a time at which human beings expressed their racial essences purely, an ideal toward which the present and future should be directed. The contingencies of individual religious conversions, cultural assimilation, or contributions to society become irrelevant in this governing concern with racial origin. The biological *arkhe* of race carries irrecusable authority, an immanence to be embraced rather than overcome.

By inverting the normative hierarchy of mind and body, Hitlerism considers the transcendence of the body an illusion and a "betrayal" of identity. The freedom of the Enlightenment becomes associated with the danger of unending skepticism, as opposed to the nobility of "sincerity":

> Thought becomes a game. Man plays with his freedom and doesn't permanently commit himself to any truth. He transforms his capacity for doubt into a lack of conviction. Not being shackled to a truth turns into not wanting to engage oneself in the creation of spiritual values. Sincerity becomes impossible, bringing an end to heroism. . . . And in such a society that has lost its living contact with the true ideal of freedom, trading it for degenerate forms, delighting in the convenience this ideal offers and blind to the efforts it demands—in this kind of a society the Germanic ideal of man comes as a promise of sincerity and authenticity. (PH 19)[6]

The ideal human life, "the essence of the spirit," comes to be defined by the affirmation of an immutable identity—a determination by a bodily essence rather than the autonomy associated with the immaterial mind (PH 18). But this promise of authenticity assumes that the Cartesian dichotomy is itself natural and archic. The gravity and givenness of the body informs Hitlerism as much as it does liberalism, but with an inverted value.

The body glorified in Hitlerism is defined by its strength, rather than being the source of vulnerability emphasized in the liberal account. Here the givenness of corporeal identity is coupled with a fantasy of virility, including military and physical aggression, at least on the part of men. The self-critique and skepticism of the Enlightenment become framed as the corrupting influence of doubt. The embrace of militarism also casts moral questioning as a symptom of weakness— the suspicion that we may be "duped by morality" (TI 21). The project of racial purification requires not only the elimination of those framed as subhuman, but the elimination of moral compunction in the face of such violence—the vulnerability of responsibility. In this way embracing the "destiny" of racial embodiment entails a muscular rejection of other forms of passivity.

Hitlerism shares with liberalism an attempt to define what is truly or fully human in relation to what must be transcended or held at bay. The anxiety with purity now does not concern the mind's transcendence of embodiment but racial identity, expressed through bodily characteristics and behavior. A strange conceptual curvature allows Nazi fantasies of the intellectual and the animal to converge in a dystopian vision of degeneration. The racial stereotyping of Jews blends the anxiety about inauthenticity and intellectual rootlessness with fears of barbarism, so that images of capitalist corruption, communist activism, murder of Christian children, physical weakness, and sexual violence all somehow cohere into a single figure. In its utilization of ideologically driven anthropology and interpretations of evolution, Hitlerism generates its own version of the subhuman, which generates paranoia about the possibility of one who appears to be a human person but ultimately is not.[7] Agamben claims that nineteenth-century anthropology "functions by excluding as not (yet) human an already human being from itself, that is, by animalizing the human, by isolating the nonhuman within the human: *Homo alalus*, or the ape-man. And it is enough to move our field of research ahead a few decades, and instead of this innocuous paleontological find we will have the Jew, that is, the non-man produced within the man, or the *néomort* [literally, the "newly dead," or the person on the boundary between life and death]."[8] The devaluation here is not associated with matter as such or the givenness of the human body, but with the perceived content of that givenness—being Jewish or Roma or Slav, as opposed to of Aryan descent.

As it was lived out, Hitlerism sought to make real this imagined hierarchy, to separate clearly the human from the subhuman by creating the *Muselmann*, the prisoner who can scarcely be recognized as human, whom Emil Fackenheim describes as a product of Auschwitz: "that skin-and-bones person who can no longer feel or think but still, if barely, stands or walks until he drops to the ground."[9] In the charged context of writing as a survivor, Primo Levi famously comments: "Their life is short, but their number is endless; they, the *Muselmänner*, the drowned, form the backbone of the camp, an anonymous mass, continually renewed and always identical, of non-men who march and labour in silence, the divine spark dead within them, already too empty to really suffer. One hesitates to call them living; one hesitates to call their death death, in the face of which they have no fear, as they are too tired to understand."[10] The fantasy of revealing the subhumanity of those deemed to be racially inferior creates the reality of the camps, in which the *Muselmann* represents not merely the generic state of being defined by one's body, but a status that no longer counts as fully human. They are "non-men" whose lives are so stripped of the normal indicators of humanity that their deaths are not quite deaths. The creation of the *Muselmann* then fulfills the narrative of racial struggle in which one's racial origins define one's essential identity and in which the healthy are protected from the degenerate.

In the early essay, Levinas describes Hitlerism as the culmination of the initially inchoate identification of the raced body as the essence of the self and of the suspicion that the intellectual freedom of liberalism leads to moral corruption. However, the question that Levinas later confronts is whether liberalism is also implicated in the violent constitution of the human through a series of projective fantasies and correlative anxieties—even if now what is essentially human is defined in relation to the transcendence of the mind rather than the immanence of the body. Levinas's attempt to reconceive the meaning of embodiment, to provide (in Critchley's words) "another thinking through of facticity," challenges the logic of dualism underlying both liberalism and Nazi anti-Semitism, in which the polarity of transcendence and immanence gives rise to anxieties about maintaining the purity of the human essence.[11] Those anxieties then express themselves in the various discourses and practices of racism within liberal societies.

Overturning the Dichotomy

In his later work, Levinas's critique of the concepts central to the Western philosophical tradition takes up the elements of liberalism described in the Hitlerism essay: the "infinite liberty" of the subject, made possible by the isolation of the mind or spirit from materiality and by the transcendence of temporality (PH 15). Critchley notes that the same paradigm of subjectivity operates in philosophical idealism and liberalism—"the subject as self-constituting, self-positing, self-legislating, and constituted by reflection," and this is the conception of subjectivity that Levinas continually challenges.[12] That critique calls our attention to some of the same ideas that Levinas had used to express the Hitlerist reaction against liberalism—sincerity, pain, being bound to the body. This section is a reading of how Levinas appropriates these terms, which seem to operate unproblematically within the debate structured by the poles of liberalism and Hitlerism. But he transforms their meaning to show the inadequacy and ethical violence of both positions and to provide an alternative outside of this economy.

The term *sincérité* in Levinas's description of Hitlerism signifies the commitment to an essential identity and the actions determined by that identity. Levinas refers to the example of "the deadlock of physical pain" as undermining a liberal identification of the self with the mind alone: "doesn't the sick person feel the indivisible simplicity of his being as he tosses and turns on his bed of suffering?" (PH 17–18). In the undergoing of pain, the "spiritual" subject may try to transcend the body, but the effort required to "revolt" against the body indicates the ineradicability of embodiment. "Sincerity" recurs in *Otherwise than Being*, where it again refers to an "irreversable given" in the experience of the human subject (PH 20): "Responsibility for the other, in its antecedence to my freedom, its antecedence to the present and to representation, is a passivity more passive than all passivity, an exposure to the other without this exposure being assumed, an exposure without holding back, exposure of exposedness, expression, saying. This exposure is the frankness, sincerity, veracity of saying" (OB 15). Sincerity here signifies the passivity of the embodied subject, exposed to the other and unable to avoid the force of responsibility. Sincerity retains the connotation of gravity, an immutable force binding me to myself.

In "Useless Suffering" pain is similarly described as "a submission" that does not allow consciousness to take up an intentional object (US 92). It simply imposes itself as pain (OB 55). In this sense, the body does not allow for self-determination. There is a contorted passivity in Hitlerism—the need to affirm the enslavement of embodied racial identity and on that basis to engage in virile, heroic action. The perceived justification for the aggressive defense of purity, in the form of military conquest and genocide, is the embracing of an identity that is given rather than chosen. Given these resonances, a worrying implication is that Levinas's later work, like Hitlerism, may be romanticizing an enslaving corporeal *arkhe*, against which all the ideals of the Enlightenment are betrayals.

On a superficial reading, Levinas merely repeats the traditional association of the body with passivity and determination, particularly in the series of associations that he draws between embodiment and exposure. Sensibility is repeatedly contrasted with the grasping, intentional activity of knowing. Sensation is "vulnerability, enjoyment and suffering, whose status is not reducible to the fact of being put before a spectator subject" (OB 63). Alphonso Lingis comments that "our sensibility is . . . a sensitivity to being wounded and outraged" (OB xxxiii). In these descriptions, Levinas intensifies the traditional connection between passivity and embodiment, and in so doing reconceives its significance. The nature of the body's vulnerability is not fundamentally to disease, injury, or aging in the most literal sense (much less racial degeneration), but instead the exposure of responsibility: "An animate body or an incarnate identity is the signifyingness of this non-indifference [to the other]. Animation is not better expressed by the metaphor of inhabitation, the presence of a pilot in the helm of his boat, a vital principle immediately assimilated with a directive principle, or the virility of a logos and a command. Animation can be understood as an exposure to the other, the passivity of the for-the-other in vulnerability" (OB 71). In this passage Levinas repeats Descartes's rejection of the simile that likens the mind in the body to a pilot in a ship, but not for the Cartesian reason that this model overlooks how the mind and body are "commingled."[13] Levinas rejects the idea of consciousness directing mere flesh, which once again characterizes the subject as autonomous in his conquest over elements of Nature, including his own body. The Lockean idea that the body is a form of property, and indeed the model for all other forms of property, reinforces this conception of subjectivity that inhabits a body without being incarnate in any significant sense.[14] Subjectivity is precisely what is distinguishable from flesh. But for Levinas, the vulnerability of the body is the opening of responsibility within the otherwise amoral dynamic of intentionality. The body is not a thing to be possessed and controlled or the mark of one's authentic identity, but our relation to alterity.

The passivity of corporeal subjectivity has ethical significance, and thus introduces instability into the identity of the subject rather than grounding any determinate essence. His treatment of the body in *Otherwise than Being* exemplifies this intricate reweaving of the tradition that ultimately undermines the dualism of mind and body: "The concept of the incarnate subject is not a biological concept. The schema that corporeality outlines submits the biological itself to a higher structure; it is dispossession, but not nothingness" (OB 109). Whereas Hitlerism treats a supposedly biological identity as primary and immutable, Levinas describes incarnation as an exposure to the other that unsettles any fixed identity for the subject. The body's status as a biological specimen, an object of knowledge or ground of identity, is derivative of this anarchic quality, in which embodiment is "not nothingness" in the sense that it breaks open the complacency of the *conatus* without destroying or enslaving the subject. In Levinasian responsibility, there is still an emphasis on passivity, but this is not a natural essence that demands affirmation. The passivity of the body is its sensitivity to the proximity of the other. As Levinas emphasizes, this vulnerability is not even merely receptive, which would reestablish the binary opposition between agency and objecthood: it is the passivity of finding oneself responsible, or having to respond, without having chosen or willed anything that might warrant that obligation. Thus Levinasian sincerity refers to a self stuck inside of its skin in a way radically different from a racial essence. It is as a singular being whose identity and place in the world has been called into question that I respond to the other, not as a particular being whose identity can be willfully embraced as a vocation. Sincerity is now "the breakup of essence," not an affirmation of a fixed essence (OB 14).

For this reason, pain has a different meaning for Levinas than it does in Hitlerism: it is not an experience that belies the disembodied ideals of liberalism in favor of the givenness of the body. In *Otherwise than Being*, pain takes on ethical significance, as a sign of our exposure to the other: "Pain penetrates into the very heart of the for-oneself that beats in enjoyment, in the life that is complacent in itself, that lives of its life. To give, to-be-for-another, despite oneself, but in interrupting the for-oneself, is to take the bread out of one's own mouth to nourish the hunger of another with one's own fasting" (OB 56). The exposure of responsibility is the experience of pain in the sense that my enjoyment and my complacency are disrupted by the need of the other. Levinas's reading of pain locates it squarely in an intersubjective context: my own hunger is bound up with the hunger of another, and the aging of the body functions as a reminder of diachrony in its ethical significance.

But Levinas intensifies the peculiarity of incarnation further: the body carries the ambiguity of self-centered enjoyment and ethical exposure to the other. Embodiment itself has no fixed meaning, but oscillates between the standpoint of the *conatus* and the standpoint of responsibility: "The subjectivity of sensibility, taken as incarnation, is an abandon without return, maternity, a body suffering for another, the body as passivity and renouncement, a pure undergoing. There is indeed an insurmountable ambiguity there: the incarnate ego, the ego of flesh and blood, can lose its signification, be affirmed as an animal in its *conatus* and its joy.... But this ambiguity is the condition of vulnerability itself, that is, of sensibility as signification" (OB 79–80, translation amended). Incarnation is the coring out of the subject in responding to the need of the other, without being able to pause to weigh the context of that need or my obligation to fulfill it. But at the same time incarnation is being a body with my own needs and desires (see TI 147–51). In John Drabinski's words, the body becomes "the ambivalent site of obligation."[15] Even more radically, as embodied beings we live in ways that visit violence on others, often beyond the horizons of our awareness. In the last sentence of the preceding passage, Levinas claims that this dual nature of incarnation is indissoluble. Embodiment provides no stable essence that might identify me either as a self-concerned being-with-desires or as a being attuned to proximity.

Levinas's mature claim is that neither the sovereignty of the mind nor the givenness of the body is privileged as an archic identity for the human subject. The obligation to which the body binds us is instead a denucleation or a "dispossession": finding ourselves responding to the needs of another before we have decided that we have a duty to respond.[16] There is no determinate essence that would define who we are or how we should act, in contrast to liberalism and Hitlerism. We should understand the body "neither as an obstacle opposed to the soul, nor a tomb that imprisons it," but instead as "the bearer of the world . . . blocking rest and lacking a fatherland" (OB 195n12). Levinas rejects the dualistic presupposition that the body either determines our existence or we manage to transcend that determination. Both worldviews generate an account of the origin and ideal of subjectivity that function as a "fatherland"—an identity constituted through the exclusion of others who are framed as incapable of fulfilling this ideal. Levinas's description of the body clearly references the conception of materiality dominant in the Western tradition, but also takes its leave from it.

For Levinas, the body still functions as a source of heteronomy and thwarts the attempts of consciousness to achieve self-possession. Sensibility is the subject's inability to represent herself and the other within synchronous time and comprehend all of her experiences. Insofar as the pathologies of persecution, obsession, and trauma represent the encounter with alterity, their value is ultimately positive. But this is no mere inversion of values in the mind-body dichotomy, as Hitlerism is. Although the body is still understood in terms of passivity, in opposition to consciousness, it is "a passivity more passive than all passivity" (OB 15). Given the dominance of the dualist model, Levinas's conception of the ethical significance of embodiment may sound unintelligible. What would it mean for a body to be more passive than all passivity? Addressed by the other, the self is called on to respond and cannot avoid that demand. In that sense, the subject is neither an object controlled by external forces nor a source of spontaneous action. We find ourselves always already responding to the other, obeying a command that cannot be represented in memory. Being a passive object in the traditional sense locates that being in a continuum of causes and effects in a linear time frame, and being a subject invokes the freedom of existing in the present and projecting oneself toward the future. But exposure to the other introduces the complication of diachrony, the lapse of time that resists representation and so resists the logic of objectivity and subjectivity assumed in representation.

Skin, Breathing, Aging

To clarify how the body takes on ethical significance, I will focus on three elements of embodiment that Levinas discusses in some detail in *Otherwise than Being*: being in one's skin, breathing, and aging. These are ways that we interact with the external world and experience various forms of vulnerability. These biological processes can be made into the objects of consciousness, as in the case of the medical disciplines of dermatology, pulmonology, or geriatrics, but they are also experiences outside of the control of the ego, thus opening up the "hither side" of consciousness. In each case, Levinas emphasizes the passivity involved, which is never merely receptive but responsive. Responsibility is "beyond the normal play of action and passion in which the identity of a being is maintained" (OB 114). The self experiences himself as accused in his responsibility, without having acted in any way to justify that responsibility and without having time to evaluate his level of obligation.

The extended discussion of responsibility that forms the core of *Otherwise than Being* repeatedly uses the image of being too tight in one's skin. Levinas frequently refers to skin as inherently vulnerable, in its permeability and exposure to the world, but in this description one's skin also functions as a constraining force, holding the self in the uncomfortable position of proximity: "In its own skin. Not at rest under a form, but tight in its skin, encumbered and as it were stuffed with itself" (OB 110). Skin provides no ground for identity or a sense of belonging, but instead generates restlessness. In this way the two experiences of being in one's skin—being vulnerable to the other and being stuck within one's skin—impose a passivity that does not protect the self from accusation.

These images describe the embodied correlate of the psychological states of persecution, obsession, and denucleation—what it means to be a subject is to be unable to be at home with oneself. That restlessness results from the condition of proximity, in which I am always too late to avoid my responsibility to the other. As Jacob Meskin puts it, "the individual body already testifies to an other 'within' itself ... *without* the dialectical overcoming of such otherness."[17] This is not the one dedicating itself to the other, or recognizing in the other some shared human nature. As an incarnate being, the self is exposed from the start to the other, within itself. Having a body or being a body—language conspires to constrain the possibilities of understanding the body outside of dualism—means being vulnerable to the other: "It is the living human corporeality, as a possibility of pain, a sensibility which of itself is the susceptibility to being hurt, a self uncovered, exposed and suffering in its skin. In its skin it is stuck to its skin, not having its skin to itself" (OB 51). The condition of embodiment is the condition of self-dispossession, or the blurring of the self's boundaries. In the typical ambiguity that Levinas uses to remind readers of the fragility of responsibility, the skin is also what protects the rest of the body from threats—infection, heat, dehydration, and so on. But in its simultaneous vulnerability to the outside world, its permeability is ethically significant.

Levinas frequently uses the image of breathing to represent this permeable boundary of the self, in which the other is in me, or I am for-the-other (OB 68–69). Breathing is not merely the mechanical bodily process that makes possible the functioning of organs and ultimately conscious experience. He emphasizes that this state is inherently unsettling: "a peculiar dephasing, a loosening up or unclamping of identity: the same prevented from coinciding with itself, at odds, torn up from its rest, between sleep and insomnia, panting, shivering" (OB 68). The images here mix the spatial and the temporal. The proximity of the other introduces the lapse of diachrony, the inability of the ego to be present to itself in its inability to represent the other. Like eating, breathing seems to be a claiming of external resources in the service of self-preservation, but in that process the *conatus* is interrupted (OB 181). Breathing means taking into the self what is exterior to it and thus opening up an exposure to the world within the very core of the self.

We are not obligated to interpret respiration, or embodiment more generally, in these ethical terms, as Levinas acknowledges:

> To be sure, breathing is said more simply in terms of biology: answering a fundamental need for energy, it brings to the tissues the oxygen necessary for the functioning of the organism, and eliminates the waste. Air and the oxygen it contains are then treated like wood and iron; air can be healthy or unhealthy, conditioned air or liquid air; oxygen is carried in the baggage of astronauts like fresh water on ships. But the relationship to air by which the experiences expressed in these truths are formed and stated is not in its turn an experience, despite the status of objectivity it acquires even in the philosophical language that describes the signification of these experiences—by going behind these experiences, or reducing them to the horizon of their thematization. (OB 181)

The process of respiration *can* be understood merely as a mechanical or biochemical operation governed by natural laws. But Levinas's claim is that this conception of respiration, and the ability to articulate this conception, depends on a prior relationship to air (or to the outside of the subject) that cannot be thematized and therefore is not a phenomenon. Inspiration and expiration in this sense are the openness to what lies outside the self, with all the vulnerability that this exposure entails. Lisa Guenther notes Levinas's invocation of the Greek word *psyche* to describe the subject: "The word 'psychism' is rooted in the Greek *psuchein*, to breathe; it is also related to the word *psyche*, or soul. The diachrony or delay between self and Other is . . . the opening of the self to inspiration by an Other who is already gone by the time I have opened."[18] What it means to be a self is to be exposed to the other, and the incarnation of the psyche demonstrates that exposure.

The third element of embodiment to which Levinas regularly refers in *Otherwise than Being* is aging, which constitutes a particular kind of vulnerability to diachronous time. Matter records a different kind of temporality than that of consciousness. Paraphrasing Augustine, Levinas writes: "To speak of consciousness is to speak of time. It is in any case to speak of a time that can be recuperated" (OB 32). But the effects of time on matter cannot be recuperated: bodies are inscribed by diachrony as they age. The passivity of the process of aging "is the contrary of intentionality" or of the self-determination of consciousness (OB 52). Aging is the most literal way in which the subject is subjected to the lapse of time—as embodied beings we undergo the passing of time despite the powers of memory and history. For Levinas, this impact of time on the embodied subject carries ethical meaning insofar as it points to the limitations of self-determination. The thriving antiaging industry serves to indicate the intensity of the desire to control the effects of time on the body, and the contemporary cultural anxiety about aging may well be strengthened by the association between autonomy and personhood. Aging tends to increase our dependence on others, but in addition to these tangible consequences, the aging body symbolizes the vulnerability of the self to natural forces. In the weakening of heart muscles, shrinking of brain matter, cellular damage or mutation, and loss of bone density, we undergo the lapse of time rather than being able to master it. In aging, our bodies are determined by causal processes that we can analyze and attempt to counter, but Levinas argues that this form of passivity at least gestures toward the ethical passivity by which we respond to the other, outside of all commitment.

Levinas's discussions of being in one's skin, respiration, and aging all point to the complexity of his treatment of the body, in which the body is not "mere matter" along dualist lines but has ethical meaning. In various ways, embodiment disrupts the self-possession of the ego and opens it to the demands of the other: "Subjectivity is here all the gravity of the body extirpated from its own *conatus*" (GDT 188). Once more, he exploits the traditional associations between the body and heaviness, but the weight here is ethical rather than material.

Even as Levinas challenges dualism as a way of understanding the subject, he transforms it into a metaphor of *inter*subjectivity. As Descartes conceives of it, the distance between consciousness and flesh is insurmountable. In essence, they are entirely distinct kinds of things—hence, all of the objections to interactionism. Levinas uses this tension to describe the restlessness of the for-the-other: "What seems incomprehensible in a humanity of flesh and blood to the Cartesian conception—the animation of a body by thought, which is nonsense according to the intelligibility of a system, in which animation is understood only in terms of union and dovetailing and requires a *deus ex machina*—outlines signification itself: the-one-for-the-other. In the subject it is precisely not an assembling [of mind and body], but an incessant alienation of the ego" (OB 79). The ego is unsettled by what it cannot comprehend as another phenomenon. In proximity, the one and the other "mark two Cartesian orders, the body and the soul, which have no common space where they can touch, and no logical *topos* where they can form a whole" (OB 70). In this passage, Levinas once again denies the possibility of "common space," of synchronizing the other, to emphasize the ethical significance of diachrony. The other is neither temporally nor spatially present to consciousness. The problem with

Cartesian interactionism becomes the diachronous proximity that maintains the other *as* other.

Freedom and the "Rehabilitation of Heteronomy"

Part of Levinas's reconception of the body requires critical reflection on what autonomy has come to mean in the liberal tradition. In the Hitlerism essay Levinas's references to freedom follow a fundamentally modern understanding of the concept—"the power given to the soul to liberate itself from *what it was*, from all that bound it, all that committed it" (PH 15). This is the ability to define oneself apart from heteronomous influences, including historical and social ones. Epistemically this self-determination means that skepticism is the dominant attitude, such that any belief is subject to questioning and revision. As he shifts into expressing (without yet explicitly criticizing) the anxiety about inauthenticity from the perspective of Hitlerism, Levinas distinguishes between "the true ideal of freedom" and "degenerate forms," in which transcendence becomes a refusal of all stable identity, belief, and commitment (PH 19). His genealogical analysis of Hitlerism culminates with the idea that its ideal "contests the very humanity of man" (PH 21). This language seems to indicate that Levinas endorses the "Christian liberal" identification of freedom with the untrammeled liberty to choose one's own identity.

However, in *Otherwise than Being* and in the prefatory note to the Hitlerism essay (written in 1990), he sketches out a more complicated relationship to the liberal understanding of freedom. The familiar opposition between freedom and enslavement that dominates the Hitlerism essay is called into question as he sets responsibility for the other apart from "strict book-keeping of the free and non-free" (OB 124). Responsibility is not a limitation on my freedom but arises prior to it, and thus challenges the foundation of the liberal subject as it has been imagined by modern Western thought.[19] Responsibility is neither chosen nor imposed on us through some natural determination (OB 124). The subject's freedom arises out of and is tempered by responsibility, and Levinas sometimes translates the language of freedom into that of election, the singularity by which I am infinitely responsible (INO 193; see also GDT 181). In speaking of responsibility as a "passivity more passive still than the passivity conjoined with [or opposed to] action," Levinas wonders if this election into responsibility can coherently be called freedom, without invoking the connotations of autonomy and sovereignty, and he is careful to distinguish responsibility from voluntary commitments (OB 115–17).

In a late interview, he describes his work as "a rehabilitation of heteronomy, insofar as it is conceived only in terms of slavery" (DFT 273). Within the modern philosophical tradition, the alternative to freedom is slavery, or being tyrannized by another. Levinas notes that racial identity under National Socialism is an embrace of "fatality," a "shackling to the body," and a refusal of liberation as liberalism understands it (PH 18). It thus inverts the value judgments of liberalism without challenging the traditional conception of heteronomy as enslavement. Levinas's rehabilitation of that term involves recasting our understanding, such that heteronomy can be distinguished from "servitude or bondage" (PJL 172).[20] It is instead responsibility to the other, or the very birth of the subject, prior to her self-possession: "To say that the person begins in freedom, that freedom is the first causality and that the first cause is nobody, is to close one's eyes to that secret of the ego, to that relation with the past [an immemorial past] which amounts neither to placing oneself at the beginning to accept this past consciously nor to being merely the result of the past" (TOT 49). This passage from Levinas's Talmudic readings echoes the claims that he makes in *Otherwise than Being*. This kind of embodied heteronomy cannot be reduced to the passivity of affirming a given identity or embracing enslavement to the biological. The liberal story of self-determination—in the sense of consciousness fashioning its own identity through its deliberate commitments—and the Hitlerist story of determination—in which my identity is forged independent of all choices—are complementary fantasies, and neither of them can make sense of a responsibility that precedes autonomy, an embodied vulnerability that provokes me to respond to the other.

Implications for Race

Levinas's antidualist understanding of the embodied self demonstrates how both liberal and Hitlerist views of the body contribute to modern racism. It is admittedly strange to use Levinasian resources to critique how racism results from the parallel anxieties concerning the body that arise out of liberalism and Hitlerism. For all the attention that Levinas pays to violence against the other, he has little to say about historical forms of oppression. He refers to anti-Semitism and racism more generally as manifestations of the "hatred for the other man," but he tends to focus on how this more general hatred arises out of the *conatus* and is interrupted by responsibility (OB v). The other that he has in mind is a singular other, unmarked by categories of race, ethnicity, gender, disability, age, or immigration status. To locate the other in those categories of identity, which would begin to tell a narrative about who that person is, would be essentially to highlight the phenomenal characteristics of the face rather than allowing oneself to be addressed by the authority that is the face. Hence Levinas rarely discusses particular histories of oppression and how they influence the present. However, the modern European concept of race intersects with a series of associations between the human ideal, dualism, and personhood, and Levinas offers important resources in analyzing and criticizing those ideas. Reading Levinas's discussion of embodiment as an alternative to dualism provides a diagnosis of how the raced body functions in both liberalism's denial of how the body shapes identity and Hitlerism's affirmation of that bodily identity.

In the early essay Levinas sketches out an explanation for the popular appeal of Hitlerism in Germany and in so doing offers his own idiosyncratic genealogical critique of race as a cultural idea. In the concept of race as it specifically functions in anti-Semitism, the workings of fantasy must be recognized behind the facade of an identity that purports to be beyond such contingency. The history of the concept of race has been well-documented in contemporary critical race theory, with an emphasis on the fact that the concept *has* a history and is neither natural nor necessary. First used widely in the eighteenth century, the term takes on scientific significance in the late eighteenth and nineteenth centuries, in a development contemporaneous with and inextricably linked to European conquest, colonialism, and the institution of slavery in the Western hemisphere. Central to the idea of distinguishable races is an essentialist assumption that one's racial identity is founded on "something fixed, concrete, and objective."[21] Given dominant cultural assumptions that framed difference as a form of degeneration from an ideal, scientific racism produces a hierarchical ranking of human populations and the normative demand for the preservation of the so-called higher races in their purity.[22]

The attempt to establish clear boundaries between groups of people is particularly complicated in the case of European Jews. Anti-Semitism might be understood first and foremost as the hatred of the other, but a crucial component of this hatred is an anxiety regarding ambiguous identity—a fear about the permeability of the barrier between neighbor and foreigner. As Vincent Pecora argues, Jews were framed as internal foreigners, an identity that raises questions about the authenticity and purity of everyone else's identity:

> [The Shoah] represents an uncanny episode in the enlightened West's need to define itself against its others. It is precisely because the Jews, perhaps more than any other people defined a priori as alien to the West and its traditions, are understood to have infiltrated the culture of reference at its core, that they represent the most destabilizing threat to their host culture. The image of the Jew as a "parasite," which runs throughout National Socialist dogma, would be impossible without the Jews' characterization as internalized aliens, as the enemy within. Their eradication must be seen, then, as a project spawned . . . by their embodiment of the non-West within the West, the internal difference that the West simultaneously most wishes to disavow and can never manage to disavow fully.[23]

The idea that Europe has a determinate identity, understood either in terms of biology or intellectual progress, requires the creation of the foreigner or the barbarian. The virulence of anti-Semitism derives at least partially from the fact Jews might easily be seen as part of European society. A foreigner unmistakably identifiable as a foreigner poses different problems. It is precisely at this point of the blurring of racial identity that the eradication of ambiguity, which in Hitlerism takes the form of the eradication of the ambiguously foreign, appeals to anxieties about protecting the purity of the human ideal, in the form of a master race.

One obvious alternative to the reification of race is the liberal claim that racial distinctions are ultimately insignificant, given the historical construction of this concept and given the ability of the mind to transcend both the constraints of the body and an irrational set of customs or superstitions. Levinas characterizes the entire "liberalist world" as one in which a person "does not choose his destiny under the weight of history. He does not know his possibilities as troubled forces churning within, that already orient him on a determined track" (PH 16). The very idea of destiny now becomes the result of individual choice, not—as for Oedipus—because fate works through the choices of individuals, but because autonomous subjects determine their own futures. In Naomi Scheman's words, the subject is "unfettered by history."[24] At least in principle, such subjects can treat as irrelevant the particular characteristics of the body, inherited from one's ancestors and interpreted through the lens of cultural prejudices.

But race does not become insignificant merely through establishing its contingent and epistemically unjustified status. Its contingency does not detract from its power or a society's attachment to it, although the recognition of the genealogy of a concept might facilitate critical reflection about its use.[25] The association of historical contingency with insignificance, or a lack of authority, repeats the Enlightenment conceit that the mind can be liberated from "external" influences, including the influences of time and embodiment, to follow the authority of reason alone. But a concept might retain authority, in the sense of power over our understanding and behavior, without possessing scientific or moral legitimacy. In denying the significance of race and thus abandoning the attempt to understand its continuing power, liberalism remains vulnerable to unacknowledged prejudices, and in this way does "not sufficiently [insure] itself" against Hitlerism (PPH 63). That is, individuals may be constrained by a racist history precisely because they believe that they have transcended its significance in the present.

The projects of modern colonialism and slavery display this uneasy coexistence between the ideal of individual self-determination and the perpetuation of racial hierarchies, which structure who counts as a person capable of self-determination. Various scholars have criticized Levinas's own brand of Eurocentrism, in which he depicts Europe as a culture dominated by the interplay of Athens and Jerusalem.[26] Cultures outside of Europe receive almost no attention in his work, a narrowed focus captured by his comment that "humanity consists of the Bible and the Greeks. All the rest can be translated: all the rest—all the exotic—is dance" (IRM 18). The claim that everything outside of the Bible and Greek philosophy can be translated, apparently without remainder, into those discourses seems to justify an assimilation of the foreign that would be an extension of the assimilation of the other. His emphasis on the decontextualized singularity of the other costs him the opportunity to reflect critically on how alterity is lived out politically, and how it arises in his own discourse. Levinas dogmatically inherits here the charged distinction between civilization and barbarism, between mature and immature cultures.

Despite this stance, he repeatedly criticizes the ongoing effects of European imperialism. This includes the violence inflicted by and justified with reference to spreading the ideals of the Enlightenment: "liberating truth of its cultural presuppositions . . . can be a pretext for exploitation and violence" (MS 58). As he argues in "Peace and Proximity," a just state based on intellectual "lucidity"—the solidarity of common beliefs and a shared identity—has failed to prevent the horrors of the twentieth century. This is a liberal vision of peace premised on a contract that dissipates the conflicts that arise among essentially self-interested individuals. But Levinas links this Hobbesian picture to a Socratic one, in which individuals can only unite through acknowledging what is true. Society is built not through conquest but through persuasion, an echo of the propagation of ideas that Levinas associates with liberalism in the Hitlerism essay (PH 20): "Peace on the basis of the Truth—on the basis of the truth of a knowledge where, instead of opposing itself, the diverse agrees with itself and unites; where the stranger is assimilated; where the other is reconciled with the identity of the identical in everyone. Peace on the basis of the truth, which—marvel of marvels—commands humans without forcing them or combating them, which governs them or gathers them together without enslaving them, which, through discourse, can convince rather than vanquish" (PP 162). This version of peace, in which individuals are not enslaved but instead are "masters" of ideas, leaves no room for the force of proximity (PH 20). Subjects and citizens form an "organism—or a concept—whose unity is the coherence of its members, or a comprehensive structure" (PP 165). But within this totality, others are alter egos, conceptually interchangeable with the self, rather than being singular others, for whom I am responsible regardless of their citizenship or other categories of identification. In its emphasis on assimilation through shared belief or a shared human nature, liberalism does not remove itself far enough from the logic of war, in its neglect of the ethical as Levinas understands that term.

These internal tensions manifest themselves in the continuing racism that pervades liberal societies. In conjunction with the spread of liberal epistemological and political ideas, colonial discourses limited the universal application of these ideas.[27] Every rational being is seen as capable of self-determination, but not every human being is seen as fully rational or capable of transcending his body. Within modern liberalism, subpersons identified primarily as raced bodies are framed as heteronomous, as opposed to the autonomy of apparently raceless people—this is the first privilege of whites. To be defined by one's body is to belong to nature or animality, whereas mindedness offers the possibility of self-determination. But self-determination requires a foil. Race is the remainder of a theoretical approach that denies the authority of the body over the mind and yet requires an other against which to measure its freedom. In more practical terms, as Charles Mills describes, the status of persons in a racialized society requires the existence of subpersons: "white Lockean, Kantian, Millian persons who own themselves and their efficient nature-appropriating labor, who are rational noumenal duty-respecting beings, whose individuality must be respected by the modernist liberal state, emerge not merely in contrast to but to a certain extent on the backs of nonwhite subpersons thousands of miles away, whose self-ownership is qualified and whose labor is inefficient, whose phenomenal traits limit their rationality and consequent moral autonomy, and for whom, accordingly, slavery and despotic colonial rule are appropriate."[28] Whites are generally defined as self-possessing and rights-bearing persons, but this philosophical, political, and economic designation is defined through its contrast with various forms of heteronomy. This conceptual opposition then works to justify a racialized political, economic, and educational hierarchy by which subpersons are exploited for the benefit of those who are considered persons. Mills distinguishes the status of the subperson from that of mere objects or nonhuman animals: "it is an entity which, because of phenotype, seems (from, of course, the perspective of the categorizer) human in some respects but not in others. It is a human (or, if this words already seems normatively loaded, a humanoid) who, though adult, is not fully a person."[29] The construction of the Orient is one such mechanism for establishing and sustaining a racial hierarchy, in which human beings are divided into persons and subpersons, as are the discourses surrounding slavery and white supremacy in the Western hemisphere. More mundanely, such exclusivist strains are manifested and perpetuated by the construction of white Americans or Europeans as self-determining individuals and of people of color as immigrant hordes, a criminal class, or uncritical fanatics led astray by barbaric theology.[30] The designation "person" then functions not merely as a descriptive but also as a normative concept, with one racial group perceived as actualizing an ideal that others are perceived as failing to achieve.[31] This imagined failure then serves as the justification for paternalism, discrimination, exploitation, and oppression.

The anxiety that characterizes liberalism is the need to transcend what is merely animal within human beings, and this anxiety is most easily allayed by the separation of humans over and against those who are labeled subpersons. But the idea of distinguishing persons from subpersons parallels the Hitlerist anxiety about maintaining pure, unambiguous racial identities. In both cases, there is a need to set against the truly human what does not belong in that category—the animal, the Jew, the foreigner. Racism is at least partially an artifact of the attempt to define the human, whether the ideal and essence of humanity is located in a biological identity or an intellectual one. In the liberal tradition, it produces a characterization of the subperson on the basis of what the ideal of rational autonomy cannot tolerate: a being subject to its own history and materiality. But these are vulnerabilities, Levinas reminds us, that belong to human beings in general. In the glorification of different kinds of invulnerability—autonomy or authenticity—the exposure to the other is devalued, and the hatred for the other persists, in the form of racism and other prejudices that project weakness or dependence onto marginalized, dehumanized groups.

Thus the reification of biological race and the denial of the significance of race must both be contested, and the anxious logic of dualism subverted. Levinas develops this overturning of traditional dualism in *Otherwise than Being* by investing the biological with ethical significance—not as Hitlerism does, by claiming that we must affirm a fixed biological identity, but by drawing out the manner in which the body refuses to serve as the ground of identity. In this way, the body reflects the denucleation of the subject by the ethical demand of the other. As Levinas describes it in the Hitlerism essay, the passivity of racial identity—the need to embrace a biological destiny to which one is enslaved—sets up a desire to maintain the purity of that identity, expressed also in the desire to defend one's fatherland. The virtues that emerge out of this anxiety are virility and invulnerability. It establishes a certain kind of place in the sun, an identity and an origin worth defending. In this particular sense, liberalism does not provide a radical alternative to Hitlerism. In the European philosophical tradition, one's place in the sun is defined primarily in epistemic and moral terms rather than biological ones. The subject is identified as a conscious mind and autonomous agent whose bodily particularity is irrelevant. Yet the identification of subjectivity with consciousness creates a structurally similar anxiety with maintaining purity in order to protect that identity, here expressed as an anxiety about how embodiment or other forms of heteronomy, including intersubjective influences, might contaminate consciousness. But if subjectivity *is* embodied subjectivity, the impact of responsibility challenges both the liberal goal of autonomy and the Hitlerist goal of racial authenticity.

The History of Creatures

Levinas's rejection of the idea that the body can serve as the ground of identity means that he refuses to grant ethical significance to the other's particular historical situation—how her race, gender, sexual orientation, age, religion, language, immigration status, or ability intensifies or protects against vulnerability of various kinds. These factors are relevant in political deliberations, but the other *as* other has no determinate identity or history. Levinas thus avoids engaging in what Drabinski calls "incarnate historiography," attention to how history constitutes the significance of bodies, or that bodies bear a history: "Perhaps the color of the Other and the color of the vulnerable body signify the specificity—and thus not singularity—of obligation, designating terms of responsibility that bear historical violence, memory, and pain into the upsurging moment of encounter."[32] In Levinas's insistence that the face is not a phenomenon, that I do not perceive it as a set of physical characteristics, he also denudes the face of the historically particular aspects of the other's vulnerability (IOF 9). He therefore excludes from the ethical encounter the historically particular aspects of how the subject may be implicated in that vulnerability. Both the self and the other are typically unmarked and uncategorized for Levinas. In proximity, consciousness recedes to the point that the facts of my identity and the facts of the other's identity are insignificant. But this means that he consigns the critique of social and political oppressions to irrelevance in the ethical encounter itself, although they may come into play within the calculations of justice.

He rejects the idea that the singular other could be reduced to a representative of an identity category. This would again convert the other into a phenomenon to be comprehended: "To catch sight, in meaning, of a situation that precedes culture, to envision language out of the revelation of the Other (which is at the same time the birth of morality) in the gaze of a human being looking at another human precisely as abstract human disengaged from all culture, in the nakedness of his face" (MS 59). He argues that "the birth of morality" in the encounter with the other lies outside of history, stripped of the categorizations that would locate the other in a specific context and in a specific relation to the self. Adriaan Peperzak identifies this "un-worldly" aspect of alterity as Levinas's central claim: "the other does not fit into any horizon. The other disrupts all contexts, worlds, totalities, and encompassing horizons. . . . The other makes a hole in the world."[33] This is another form of the claim that the other does not share a present with me and instead imposes a diachronic limit to representation, in its very alterity. I do not approach the other as another manifestation of universal human nature, interchangeable with the self. The other does not form part of any totality that could be comprehended. But Drabinski objects to the consequent narrowness of Levinas's conception of alterity: "the Other comes to me, not just as a singular face who signifies without context, but as an embodied being whose appearance to me is irreducibly saturated with historical meaning. . . . When we *notice* the color of the Other, so to speak, our responsibility takes on particular, specific characteristics that, without that worldliness, might have remained simply empty—even if profound—senses of ethical obligation."[34] The other comes to be singular *and* particular, her embodiment signifying both as a universal form of vulnerability but also in the sense of occupying a highly specific location in contingent hierarchies and relations of power.[35]

Levinas's neglect of the particularity of the body thus repeats some elements of the assumption that he attributes to Hitlerism: that the body has no significant history apart from its origin, that its identity remains unaffected by social, economic, or religious forces. These considerations would add another dimension of heteronomy of the kind that Levinas describes—the historically incarnate body is neither entirely self-determined nor the pure result of external forces. These historically specific influences form part of Simone de Beauvoir's description of embodiment as an open-ended situation, "our grasp on the world," within which what is materially and culturally given interact, and which the self interprets in his relations with the world.[36] From Levinas's perspective, however, if the other could be described exhaustively within a historical context, and if my own characteristics and forms of privilege could also be described, we would inhabit a synchronous space, in which our burdens and possibilities could be compared. He does not deny that the individual *can* be described in these terms, but his project reacts against the completeness of this account of the other, which he takes to have dominated modern Western culture. His work is intended as a corrective to the one-sidedness of identifying the other only as a phenomenon to be recognized and studied, as Chanter notes: "Levinas acknowledges that bodies are inscribed by meaning and history, that they signify at the level of representation, that they are encoded by society, but refuses the idea that such signification completely circumscribes them or exhausts their effects."[37] The issue is how Levinas's attempt to correct a deficiency in dominant ways of understanding the other can help attune us to both historically specific and universal forms of vulnerability.

At stake in the other's singularity is her diachrony, that as other she cannot be incorporated into a narrative that would locate her within a particular historical trajectory. He contrasts embodiment as he interprets it with Merleau-Ponty's notion of the "fundamental historicity" of the body, by which the body and its movements are invested with meaning in its intersubjective context: this "assembling into a world of the subject and of its world . . . is enacted in the said" (OB 70). For Levinas, this kind of analysis reestablishes the dynamic in which the other is synchronized as an intentional object for a knowing subject. But incarnation is an exposure, "not a transcendental operation of a subject that is situated in the midst of the world it represents to itself" (OB 76). In this embodied relation of proximity, the other *as other* is unmediated by conceptualization.

Drabinski argues for a closer integration between the singularity of the ethical demand and the "worldly memory of race and nation."[38] Levinas makes some room for this possibility at certain moments when he describes responsibility as extending beyond the scope of my chosen and willed actions: "In my responsibility for the other, the past of the other, which has never been my present, 'concerns me': it is not a re-presentation for me. The past of the other and, somehow, the history of humanity in which I have never participated, in which I have never been present, are my past" (PJL 176). I am implicated in what happens to the other and what has happened to the other. In this sense, I am a survivor of others' deaths. The events of human history are not merely episodes to be neutrally represented but address me in my singularity. Similarly, in his references to how ordinary life in developed societies establishes itself only through usurpation, at the cost of intensifying the vulnerability of and causing suffering for the global poor, he opens up a connection between empirical vulnerability of the specific other and the decontextualized vulnerability of the singular other. But these glimpses of how one could take account of the historicity of the body are never developed substantively in Levinas's work. He more often consigns these questions to the realm of the political, of which he says relatively little. The call to respond to the other as an embodied being whose vulnerability is historically encoded belongs, in his account, to the work of justice informed by proximity. The issue is whether the other can approach me in "the context-neutral life of the face-to-face," or whether this imagined encounter, in its treatment of individuals as generic in their singularity, is not itself saturated with a historically European understanding of ahistorical, abstract relations between individuals.[39]

Against parallel charges from feminist scholars, Perpich defends Levinas's adherence to the other as singular, rather than considering alterity in the form of racial, ethnic, or gender difference. The recognition of the importance of identity—contesting the interchangeable ideal subject who functionally has turned out to be male, European, heterosexual, of an elite social class, and so on—has the clear political purpose of authorizing various sorts of voices and historical experiences, and thus denaturalizing sedimented political hierarchies. But Perpich notes that "even as such a politics seeks recognition for a given group in virtue of the oppression and marginalization experienced by its members, it re-marks those same subjects precisely in terms of the categories through which social and economic subordination operates."[40] The individual becomes the bearer of a fixed identity, which has probably derived much of its content from a history of oppressive identifications. Levinas is deeply attuned to how such categories may not be used in liberatory ways—not only in the usual connotation of political oppression but in his ethical sense of reducing the other to an object of knowledge. Perpich argues that the other is not merely a stranger, but someone who does "not share even the *lack* of a common community that makes two people strangers to each other."[41] The other does not share the present moment with me and hence cannot be captured as a phenomenon.

This does not mean that the other's identity is entirely irrelevant to ethics as Levinas conceives of it. As he emphasizes toward the end of *Otherwise than Being*, responsibility demands the processes—legal, political, economic, and social—that recognize the other as an individual, whose needs and interests can be weighed against those of others: the immediacy of proximity "calls for control, a search for justice, society and the State, comparison and possession, thought and science, commerce and philosophy, and outside of anarchy, the search for a principle" (OB 161). But that search for a principle must be informed and complicated by the anarchic force of responsibility that responds to the other in his singularity.

In place of a historical consideration of my own embodied existence or the other's embodied existence within the ethical encounter, Levinas focuses on the idea of creatureliness. He borrows the theological notion for ethical purposes, without appealing to a narrative that would once again identify a fatherland, a Creator to worship, or a *telos* for human existence.[42] To be a creature means to find oneself responding to a demand without being able to represent its own origin or the origins of that demand: "in creation, what is called to being answers to a call that could not have reached it since, brought out of nothingness, it obeyed before hearing the order. Thus in the concept of creation *ex nihilo*, if it is not a pure nonsense, there is the concept of passivity that does not revert into an assumption.... The oneself has to be conceived outside of all substantial coinciding with oneself" (OB 113–14). Creation introduces the lapse of diachrony that does not allow everything to be represented to consciousness and that opens the subject's vulnerability to the other. Creatureliness is thus about an irreversible *lateness*, being embedded in a history that one does not control. Michael Fagenblat reads creatureliness in explicitly ethical terms: "To become an ethical creature is to dispel oneself of the fantasy of being a moral creator responsible for one's free acts."[43] The fantasy is that we create our own moral identity, rather than being responsible for and to the other in ways that we come too late to control. As with Oedipus, creatureliness is the interruption of autonomy.

Thus far the passivity of creatureliness overlaps significantly with how various forms of identity function, as historically invested markers of meaning that individuals do not choose and over which they have minimal control. But Levinas is interested in an immemorial history rather than an empirical one that could be analyzed by the methods of the social sciences. We cannot represent the origins of our own subjectivity, but always come too late to comprehend and thus control our exposure to the other: "a responsibility not resting on any free commitment, that is, a responsibility without freedom, a responsibility of the creature; a responsibility of one who comes too late into being to avoid supporting it in its entirety" (S 91). For Levinas, it is *my* creatureliness that is my concern, my being imbedded in a longer history—but that longer history is an immemorial one that sets up an infinite, undetermined responsibility, rather than obligations incurred by a particular history. Describing the passivity of the subject, he speaks of "an attachment that has already been made, as something irreversibly past, prior to all memory and all recall. It was made in an irrecuperable time which the present, represented in recall, does not equal, in a time of birth or creation, of which nature or creation retains a trace, unconvertible into a memory. . . . The oneself is a creature, but an orphan by birth or an atheist no doubt ignorant of its Creator, for if it knew it it would again be taking up its commencement" (OB 104–5). We experience our creatureliness without being able to represent it. In the language of trauma, Levinas gestures at how responsibility intrudes on our experience without our being able to comprehend it. Guenther claims that in this state of ignorance we are capable of betraying our creatureliness and claiming our "own originality, autonomy, and mastery."[44] The disavowal of our origins may be more motivated than accidental, however, in the context of modern ideals of subjectivity that glorify the autonomy of a subject who is not beholden to his past.

Just before the preceding passage from *Otherwise than Being*, Levinas gestures to maternity as the condition of creation, reminding the subject of the inability to "posit itself" (OB 104). As I will discuss in more detail in chapter 7, in his later work maternity more typically stands for the exposure of the one-for-the-other, giving up one's own resources to meet the needs of others. But for Levinas the maternal also occasionally represents the immemorial past of creation, out of which subjectivity emerges. Guenther describes this experience of creatureliness in terms of this passivity of finding oneself "of woman born": "As one who is born to a mother, I am unable to form myself or posit my own existence; already in the womb, I am exposed to an Other who bears me. . . . As one who is gestated in the body of a woman, I am passive, sensible, and exposed to the Other before I have a chance to find (or lose) myself."[45] What it means to be a creature is to stand in this kind of relation to an unrepresentable, anarchic past, to be passive and beholden in ways from which I cannot detach myself, not even to evaluate that obligation.[46] In this sense, the general character of human embodiment carries ethical meaning, in a way that helps to dismantle the meanings that raced bodies have historically borne. Levinas's suspicion about how particular identities have been assimilated into the logic of intentionality stands behind his stubborn focus on the singularity of self and other.

Beyond Dualism

Both liberalism and Hitlerism seek an archic identity in one or the other of the poles of Cartesian dualism. Both worldviews also set up a fantasy of invulnerability, in which the autonomy of the mind or the purity and strength of the raced body must be maintained. But these opposing ideals generate accompanying anxieties about what might threaten autonomy or authenticity, or symbolize instead heteronomy and inauthenticity. The figure of the subperson—the being onto whom defining traits of heteronomy or inauthenticity are projected—grounds modern racism, whether that being is understood in terms of her immersion in nature and irrationality, or in terms of her status as an internal foreigner who might cause the degeneration of the master race.

Levinas's critique of the dualistic understanding of the self in *Otherwise than Being* is an extension of the critique that he sketches in the 1934 essay: we must resist the search for an *arkhe* either in materiality or in mind. We are indeed incarnate beings, but we should understand this condition in ethical terms, as the disruption of identity rather than the foundation for it. Subjectivity is rather a "knot," first and foremost a responsiveness to the other rather than a being striving for autonomy or authenticity (OB 77). In contrast to the ideal of mastery, he offers an understanding of ourselves that is fundamentally heteronomous: vulnerable to physical forces, time, and above all to the ethical demand of the other. But given his conception of the incarnate subject, however, his account shares with those liberalism and Hitlerism an inattention to the historical context of embodied identity. None of these approaches can substantially examine the way in which subjects emerge out of a particular history. Levinas leaves this kind of analysis for the work of justice, in which responding to the vulnerability of the singular other entails understanding the ways in which that other is vulnerable in historically specific ways, and thus how I as an individual or my society as a collective agency must react to those needs. But this oscillating relationship between responsibility and justice remains unstable and unpredictable, bereft of governing principles that might specify *how* our creatureliness should be translated into practical, political action.

This chapter has raised the issue of how embodiment functions as a source of anxiety as long as the ideal of personhood is autonomous subjectivity and how the concept of race and the practices of racism in modern societies reflect this cluster of ideas. Levinas's discussion of an ethically significant embodiment interrupts that narrative and its repercussions. Sensibility as the opening of responsibility profoundly destabilizes both the liberal ideal of self-determination and the Hitlerist ideal of authenticity; as embodied creatures (in Levinas's sense of that term), we do not inhabit a fatherland of any kind, whether grounded in a nonphysical mind that establishes self-determination or in a racialized body that establishes a destiny. As a way of dismantling the racism generated by the anxieties that attend both ideals, Levinas's alternative conception of the body emphasizes our constitutive, unavoidable exposure to the other, which calls into question every attempt to claim one's place in the sun.

Notes

1. Bordo, *Unbearable Weight*, 144–45.
2. Descartes, *Discourse on Method and Meditations on First Philosophy*, 99.
3. Scheman, "'Though This Be Method, Yet There Is Madness in It,'" 95.
4. Agamben, *Open*, 12.
5. Derrida, *Animal That Therefore I Am*, 113. As I discuss more carefully in chapter 7, Derrida implicates Levinas in these anthropocentric processes of disavowal and foreclosure.
6. This debate on the durability or flexibility of identity is also at work in the complementary critiques of postmodernism and various forms of fundamentalism in recent decades.
7. The terms "subhuman" and "subperson" designate overlapping but not interchangeable concepts: in general, I use the term "subhuman" in contexts where biological hierarchies are invoked, and "subperson" where the subject's status as a knower, agent, and citizen is more germane.
8. Agamben, *Open*, 37.
9. Fackenheim, *To Mend the World*, xxxviii; see also 25, 215.
10. Levi, *Survival in Auschwitz*, 90. The American edition has a more triumphal title than the original Italian *Se questo è un uomo* [If this is a man].
11. Critchley, *Problem with Levinas*, 34.
12. Ibid., 30–31.
13. Descartes, *Discourse on Method and Meditations on First Philosophy*, 98.
14. Locke, *Second Treatise of Government*, 5:§27.
15. Drabinski, *Levinas and the Postcolonial*, 31. See also Guenther, "Flair Animal," 222.
16. See Ziarek, "Rethinking Dispossession."
17. Meskin, "In the Flesh," 174–75.
18. Guenther, *Gift of the Other*, 105.
19. See also TOT, 46.
20. On the distinction between enslavement and Levinasian election, see Chalier, *What Ought I to Do?*, 73–84.
21. Omi and Winant, "Racial Formation in the United States," 183.
22. See West, "Genealogy of Modern Racism," and McWhorter, "Sex, Race, and Biopower."
23. Pecora, "Habermas, Enlightenment, and Antisemitism," 167.
24. Scheman, "'Though This Be Method, Yet There Is Madness in It,'" 87.
25. On the vigorous debate in critical race theory about the status of race as a concept, see Zack, *Race and Mixed Race*; Appiah, "Race, Culture, Identity: Misunderstood Connections," 30–105; Outlaw, *Race and Philosophy*; and Mills, *Blackness Visible*.
26. See, for instance, Drabinski, *Levinas and the Postcolonial*, 1–10.
27. Mills, *Blackness Visible*, 2–4.
28. Ibid., 128.
29. Ibid., 6.
30. Judith Butler notes the contrast between the American soldiers who receive obituaries in American newspapers and those whose deaths in the wars of Afghanistan and Iraq (among others) not only go ungrieved but are positioned as "ungrievable," because their lives are not deemed worthy of this kind of attention (*Precarious Life*, 35).
31. The very need to assert that "Black Lives Matter" speaks to the continuing power of the racial hierarchy that divides persons from subpersons.
32. Drabinski, *Levinas and the Postcolonial*, 41.
33. Peperzak, "Levinas' Method," 123.

34. Drabinski, *Levinas and the Postcolonial*, 42.

35. A great deal of scholarly work discusses Levinas's neglect of the ethical significance of the sexed body. See, for instance, Perpich, "Sensible Subjects"; Chanter, *Time, Death, and the Feminine*; Sandford, *Metaphysics of Love*; and Ziarek, *Ethics of Dissensus*, 47–62.

36. Beauvoir, *Second Sex*, 29.

37. Chanter, *Time, Death, and the Feminine*, 92.

38. Drabinski, *Levinas and the Postcolonial*, 127.

39. Ibid., 44.

40. Perpich, *Ethics of Emmanuel Levinas*, 183.

41. Ibid., 187.

42. See Gibbs, *Correlations in Rosenzweig and Levinas*, 210–11.

43. Fagenblat, *Covenant of Creatures*, 103.

44. Guenther, *Gift of the Other*, 127.

45. Ibid., 125.

46. In *Totality and Infinity*, creation functions as an interruption of totality: "the idea of creation *ex nihilo* expresses a multiplicity not united into a totality; the creature is an existence which indeed does depend on an other, but not as a part that is separated from it" (TI 104). That is, an an-archic creation cannot be captured by a causal narrative, in which the creature is merely a product of its creator. The apparent nonsense of the subject arising out of nothing foils the attempt to construct a coherent representation of one's origin, and thus a ground of some determinate essence that would define a human ideal, whether that ideal is understood as biological terms or as the transcendence of the biological.

7 Rethinking Death on the Basis of Time

IN THIS CHAPTER, I draw out the implications of Levinas's argument that the body is ethically significant and the relationship between his understanding of the body and his emphasis on diachrony. In its very susceptibility to illness, injury, and aging, the body reveals our radical exposure to others. His refusal to consider the particularity of the body—its race or gender, for instance—as part of this ethical significance certainly limits the usefulness of his understanding of embodiment to political questions, as he employs that term. In addition, feminist philosophers have been wary of the implications of Levinas's direct references to femininity in his discussion of responsibility. But given the strong cultural associations around embodiment, physical reproduction, and mortality as markers of heteronomy, his work challenges some of the dominant framings of maternity and femininity more generally. Maternity has tended to be identified in the Western cultures either as a degenerate copy of some more perfect form of creation or as a symbol of angelic self-sacrifice. I argue that both conceptions are grounded in the logic of the *conatus essendi*, in its preoccupation with the ego's mortality, the most obvious reminder of the human immersion within the passing of time. Levinas's dismantling of a subject governed by the *conatus* and his refiguring of embodiment thus provide at least indirect resources in rethinking the meaning of maternity.

In ancient philosophical and theological sources in the West, physical reproduction is the defining activity of femininity, positioned as the natural center of women's lives. Women who are not engaged in childbirth and childrearing are still measured by their past or future maternity or their refusal to become mothers. There is thus a history of mutually supporting interpretations of what reproduction and femininity signify. Two elements of that entanglement may appear to be in tension with each other, given that one devalues the role of women and the other glorifies it. But both are rooted in an anxiety about who we are as embodied and temporal subjects. First, physical reproduction is insistently and negatively compared with other forms of creation that are gendered in masculine ways. Maternity becomes understood as the process of giving birth to merely mortal beings, provoking anxiety about the persistence of one's being. Symbiotically, maternity has also functioned as the sentimentalized space in which the brutal competition for survival within the public sphere is suspended. Both conceptions of maternity hinder women's ability to claim the status of rights-bearers, moral agents, religious leaders, and authoritative knowers. But if embodiment and temporality have ethical significance, as our vulnerability to the other, we can reconceive of maternity outside of the logic of the *conatus* and its enabling exception of feminine self-sacrifice.

The Logic of the Conatus in the Human Animal

Levinas frequently articulates the activity governed by the *conatus* in specifically Darwinian[1] terms: "To be: already an insistence on being as if a 'survival instinct' that coincided with its development, preserving it, and maintaining it in its adventure of being, were its meaning.... The life of the living in the struggle for life; the natural history of human beings in the blood and tears of wars between individuals, nations, and classes" (EN xii).[2] In this Darwinian-Hobbesian account, human beings share with other animals an instinct for self-preservation, which entails not only defending oneself against attacks from others but aggressively securing resources for oneself at the expense of others. The perpetuation of one organism requires the suffering and death of others, and the self-absorbed concern of the *conatus* rationalizes this violence. Levinas seems to embrace in this description the understanding of the natural world that has prevailed since the middle of the nineteenth century, in which nature is "red in tooth and claw."[3] As in the Tennyson poem from which this phrase is drawn, this ubiquitous and ultimately meaningless violence sharply diverges from the Western theological picture of nature as an orderly and purposeful creation of an intelligent and loving God. Levinas depicts an organism that treats its own preservation as its overriding goal, which entails its indifference to the welfare of others. This "instinct" then motivates pervasive "savagery," not only among individuals but among wider groups (EN xii). If the struggle for survival is indeed instinctual, a Hobbesian state of nature would undergird all human interactions. The only form of sociality or peace would be one that presupposed war as a default condition, and morality would indeed be only a distracting illusion from that struggle (TI 21).

But Levinas complicates this now-familiar conception of nature. He does not directly challenge the Darwinian claim about the instinctual basis of animal behavior (including human behavior), and he does not take up a Nietzschean skepticism about contingent interpretations of nature masquerading as objective descriptions of nature. However, he does argue that this instinct for self-preservation does not exhaustively explain human experience.[4] Into this anxious narcissism and indifference to the other there arises, as an interruption, "a vocation of an existing-for-the-other stronger than the threat of death" (EN xii), or "the proposition of a human more human than the *conatus*" (GDT 22; see also GDT 169). Humanity here is the suspension of the *conatus*, so that concern for others becomes possible. The trauma of responsibility destabilizes the power of the motivation to preserve ourselves, but this disruption is neither a replacement for nor a kind of maturation beyond a primitive instinct. Our self-centeredness and our concern for others exist in an uneasy tension—hence the fragility of responsibility and the repeated nature of its trauma.

There is an interesting parallel between this description of the human breaking into the animalistic dynamic of the *conatus* and the creation narrative in Genesis, as it is generally interpreted in Jewish theology. In that reading, creation is not the formation of the universe from nothing, but instead the imposition of a moral order on a chaotic, unformed void. Creation is the beginning of a moral structure, in which the concepts of law, obedience, and responsibility have meaning. Michael Fagenblat describes this moral (rather than cosmological) interpretation of Genesis as the process by which "a moral point of view is engendered amid the chaos of mere existence."[5] Correlatively, the human emerges in the midst of animality. But such an order is always vulnerable to being overwhelmed by the possibility of moral disorder: "The world is therefore always at risk of degenerating into elemental indifference. The created world, unlike elemental existence, must accordingly be actively sustained and regenerated."[6] That moral disorder is the logic of the *conatus*, which governs the inhuman but instinctual behavior of human beings, and which leaves no space for the questions of how I should treat the other and whether my own existence and the use of resources that sustains that existence are justifiable. The subject's confrontation with those questions is the opening of the fragile moral order, within each individual. That moral attention always risks devolving back into the indifference of the *conatus*, in which concern for the vulnerability of the other is occluded by a concern for my own existence.

The *conatus* can be characterized as both complacent and anxious in its narcissism: complacent insofar as it never questions its right to preserve its own existence, to secure for itself "its place in the sun," but anxious insofar as it perceives this continued existence as threatened by rivalry with others and by natural forces. These anxieties are thus framed by the dyad of life and death, in which both terms refer narrowly to one's own life and death—one's own being or nothingness. In contrast, Levinas describes responsibility as an *ethical* anxiety, by which that complacency is interrupted, at two related levels: my concern is for the mortality of the other, and I am implicated in that mortality. I become attuned to how establishing my place in the sun is a *usurpation* of the other's place, and I become attuned to how *having established* my place in the sun *has already usurped* the other's place. What had been the unquestionable, amoral drive behind my actions becomes morally problematic. But Levinas acknowledges that this reorientation of attention appears only fleetingly in the history of Western thought.

The dominant motivation of the *conatus* involves securing the boundaries of the self against external threats to the ego's sovereignty, and mortality represents the most catastrophic form of the collapse of that sovereignty.

Following Rosenzweig and others, Levinas suggests that the history of Western philosophy provides a set of responses to this anxiety, but that those responses are generally deflections of the reality of death.[7] These deflections include reducing death to the death of the physical body—thus treating the true self as immortal—and by conceiving of an individual's death as a necessary part of an intelligible totality.[8] In these conceptions of death, the history of Western philosophy tends to reflect a kind of sublimation of the *conatus*. If knowledge can reflect what is rather than what becomes, then the things that come into being and pass out of being, and the processes of birth and death, have no ultimate meaning. If ideas or an immaterial part of the self belong to what is, then mortality has been overcome. If individual efforts contribute to broader projects that are carried forward by others, they have in some sense transcended death. The life of the mind is preserved, in spite of all appearances. But that reassurance still responds to and therefore attests to the anxiety of the *conatus*—that death is the annihilation of the self, in the face of which any talent or strength or wit or luck is powerless.

The *Phaedo* is emblematic of some of these deflections. Socrates's last philosophical dialogue concerns the immortality of the soul (*psyche*). Having argued emphatically in the *Apology* that we can know nothing of death—a claim that Levinas affirms—he concludes here that the rational soul animates the body but is separable from it: "when death comes to a man, the mortal part of him dies, but the immortal part retires at the approach of death and escapes unharmed and indestructible."[9] Famously, Socrates's final words imply that in dying he is cured of the disease of material existence: "Crito, we ought to offer a cock to Asclepius. See to it, and don't forget," Asclepius being the divinity to whom people appealed for healing from illness.[10] The content of Socrates's argument reflects his indifference to his own death, including his flippant response to Crito's inquiry about how he should be buried: "Any way you like, replied Socrates, that is, if you can catch me and I don't slip through your fingers. He laughed gently as he spoke, and turning to us went on, I can't persuade Crito that I am this Socrates here who is talking to you now and marshaling all the arguments. He thinks that I am the one whom he will see presently lying dead, and he asks how he is to bury me!"[11] Earlier in the dialogue Socrates claims that philosophy is the process of learning how to attend solely to the world of ideas and to purify oneself of the distractions of the body and the material sphere it inhabits.[12] In reference to this attempt to transcend the natural, Jacques Rolland claims that "death must be understood as the very fulfillment of the philosophical exercise, as the very fulfillment of the theoretical."[13] Death becomes a release from the burdens of physical existence, but this is a death that is a purification and a transformation, rather than an annihilation.

Maternity, Life, and Death

Socrates's light-heartedness about his own death arises from the conclusion that death is only the death of the physical body, rather than the death of the true self. Plato's representation of Socrates functions as the perpetuation of his ideas among those who survive him, which Diotima holds up as true immortality in the *Symposium*. Plato puts into Socrates's voice Diotima's claim that the reproduction of ideas, which happens to occur almost entirely between male philosophers, outstrips the limitations of the degenerate form of immortality offered in physical reproduction, which involves women: "those whose procreancy is of the body turn to woman as the object of their love, and raise a family, in the blessed hope that by doing so they will keep their memory green, 'through time and through eternity.' But those whose procreancy is of the spirit rather than of the flesh—and they are not unknown, Socrates—conceive and bear the things of the spirit."[14] Diotima speaks as a priestess imparting her wisdom to Socrates, but she does not fit within this taxonomy, in its distinction between men drawn to sexual reproduction and men drawn to intellectual reproduction. The latter relationships between beautiful souls produce "something lovelier and less mortal than human seed."[15] She asks, rhetorically, about poets and the creators of laws: "who would not prefer such fatherhood to merely human propagation.... Who would not envy them their immortal progeny, their claim upon the admiration of posterity?"[16] There is a complex rejection of physical reproduction at work here.[17] The imagery of childbirth has been detached from its material, mortal domain to represent what happens in intellectual creation, but the imagined immortality resulting from intellectual creation is then deployed as the standard against which physical procreation seems to be only a degenerate copy.

The *Symposium* thus simultaneously appropriates and devalues the power of reproduction, by exalting intellectual creation and claiming it for men, while women are capable of giving birth only to beings caught in the flow of time, in the fleetingness of becoming. As Adriana Cavarero argues, Diotima herself is an example of women engaging in intellectual reproduction, but she, like the flute girls, is absent from the scene, her ideas reproduced through and displaced by Socrates.[18] The authority of her claims derives in part from the fact that she is a priestess (and Socrates has vouched for her wisdom), but the content of her claims excludes women from participating in the highest forms of reproduction. Diotima uses the imagery of maternity, the "theme and metaphor of pregnancy, parturition, parenting."[19] But ultimately it is Socrates who is the midwife of ideas, who adopts that imagery to show how mortals can attain real immortality, rather than the mere appearance of it. (Male) philosophers give birth to the children who matter most, whereas maternity in its embodied form—and by extension femininity as a whole—remains implicated in death. Cavarero characterizes this philosophical appropriation as a "symbolic matricide" that claims the traditional power of women for men: "In Diotima's speech maternal power is annihilated by offering its language and vocabulary to the power that will triumph over it, and will build its foundations on annihilation itself."[20] Insofar as women are identified by their connection to the material world and its becoming, they are incapable of supporting any legitimate form of immortality. Luce Irigaray traces a tension within Diotima's speech between a divinity associated with becoming itself, in the creative, "demonic" fecundity of love, and the value attached to immortality, as a teleological product of that love.[21] In the latter account, women can function only as a tool in the service of reproduction and only toward a degenerate form of immortality.[22]

The temporal character of human existence animates this concern with immortality—how to attune human beings to what is rather than what merely becomes, and through such attunement to allow them to be defined essentially by that transcendence, to the point where the physical death of the body is a cure and a release. Immersed as it is in the passing of time, the mortal body is framed as a source of evil or weakness in comparison to what is presumed to be eternal.[23] The role of women in this production of the mortal child then forecloses the possibility of participating in this kind of transcendence, with the ambiguous exceptions of Diotima and the hypothetical philosopher-queens of the *Republic*. Furthermore, the association between maternity and mortality comes to characterize femininity in general.

A similar theme sounds in the shared creation narrative of Western monotheisms, where Eve is a primary symbol of femininity, the mother of all humanity, and the figure responsible for bringing death into the world. Her disobedience results in the conjoined punishment of desiring her husband and experiencing pain in childbirth—the term "pain," in the historical context in which these texts were written, encompassing not only the pain of labor but high rates of maternal and infant mortality in childbirth. Eve's maternal role is dangerous both to herself and to her children, which metaphorically includes all human beings.[24] Her flawed, painful reproduction is a corrupted imitation of the creative power of a divine father. That entwining of birth and death comes to define the degeneracy of earthly, embodied life.[25]

To the extent that women have been culturally defined by their reproductive role, they also represent the repetitive cycles of nature and the private sphere, sequestered from the more permanent accomplishments recorded in human history. In this sense, femininity is defined by its association with many of the animal functions within human life—most directly, menstruation, pregnancy, lactation, and childrearing. But this association tends to be extended to any experience that we must passively undergo, as embodied beings: infancy, weakness, and aging, in which lack of independence can be read as being "unmanned." The autonomous subject is defined by his self-possession, independence, and individuality, his ability to establish and maintain his separation from others. The subject's interactions with others are first and foremost rivalries rather than relations of dependence. The idealized (masculine) subject results from the disavowal and projection of various forms of vulnerability and heteronomy. Self-determination requires the overcoming of an existence governed by time and natural forces, an existence primarily associated with women.

Within this broad conception, women live only at the margins of public life in order to sustain its activities, by producing and caring for heirs, workers, and citizens. As feminist scholars have long noted, however, cultural norms of femininity in the West have also contained the element of glorified sentimentality, spirituality, and morality: women as "angels of the hearth"—an idealization that has carried and continues to carry limitations based on race, class, immigration status, gender expression, and sexual orientation. Out of this lineage, we get a complex set of characteristics associated with femininity. On the one hand, female bodies are framed as belonging to the natural world in all of its presumed heteronomy, and on the other, women (at least those recognized to be embodying femininity) are framed as hypercivilized, the caretakers of moral virtue and religious faith, and thus they are supposed to act as noncombatants in the competition of industry, politics, or war.

In describing the struggle for existence, Darwin emphasizes the importance of individuals not only surviving but reproducing successfully, which (by his account) involves males competing for sexual access to females. He ascribes to human females an entirely different instinctive comportment toward others: "Woman seems to differ from man in mental disposition, chiefly in her greater tenderness and less selfishness. . . . Man is the rival of other men; he delights in competition, and this leads to ambition which passes too quickly into selfishness. These latter qualities seem to be his natural and unfortunate birthright."[26] As presumably the natural and more fortunate birthright of women, tenderness and selflessness provide solace from the various fields of battle. But this anomalous behavior does not so much interrupt as support the larger competition between men.

In a prescient critique of the Cult of True Womanhood, Mary Wollstonecraft argued that the sentimentalized celebration of "the eternal feminine" is intimately connected to the degradation of women: "my own sex, I hope, will excuse me, if I treat them like rational creatures, instead of flattering their *fascinating* graces, and viewing them as if they were in a state of perpetual childhood, unable to stand alone . . . the soft phrases, susceptibility of heart, delicacy of sentiment, and refinement of taste, are almost synonymous with epithets of weakness."[27] The virtues of femininity come to be centered around sacrifice for others, particularly children and husbands, to the extent that good mothers abandon their own goals, desires, and interests to support the projects of those around them.[28] Above all, these virtues have been dominantly imagined to come naturally to women but simultaneously used to exclude women who cannot or choose not to conform to the cultural ideals of femininity from the protections that accompany presumptions of feminine fragility and dependence. Contemporary Western visions of maternity, reflected in Mother's Day cards, marketing for cleaning products, and handbooks on pregnancy and parenting, still tend to reinforce these ideals and their supposed ground in a feminine nature. The glorification of the self-sacrifice of mothers elevates women above the narcissism of the *conatus* but traps them within its economy as the constitutive exception to that brutality.

Much of what Levinas has to say directly about femininity notoriously repeats this conservative logic that glorifies the gentle, supportive, and secondary role of women in men's lives. In *Totality and Infinity*, the idea of the feminine arises in the discussions of *eros* and fecundity, where mothers are the means that bring about the filial relationship "with the absolute future, or infinite time" (TI 268). As keeper of the home, the woman is described as establishing a domain of intimacy, in which she is an "other whose presence is discreetly an absence, with which is accomplished the primary hospitable welcome" (TI 155). A woman is not a peer or a rival in the public sphere but instead provides comfort in the private space of the home. Her very elusiveness is part of her softness and allure (TI 257). The erotic relationship with the feminine is not itself ethical, but it makes possible the father's ethical relationship with the son, who is both "my own and not-mine" (TI 267), who belongs to an unpredictable future which is "yet . . . my adventure still" (TI 268). This ethical relationship to the future through the figure of the son is a "triumph of the time of fecundity over the becoming of the mortal and aging being" (TI 282). Levinas's claim here is not that the father is made immortal through the son, but that the meaning of time is no longer confined to the inexorable passing away of individuals. It instead can have the ethical significance of "pardon," the messianic possibility of bringing about a moral ideal in the future.[29] But mothers and daughters have no substantive part to play in this moral drama.

Beauvoir was one of the first philosophers to criticize Levinas's account of the feminine as perpetuating a dominant Western interpretation of the function of women—agents solely in the domain of reproduction and otherwise elusive and irrelevant.[30] In identifying women as the necessary backdrop to the narrative centered on fathers and sons, Levinas reinforces the idea that the heterosexual dyad naturally forms the basis for the family, that families perpetuate themselves in patrilinear structures. Irigaray comments that for all of Levinas's concern with alterity, he replicates the traditional marginalization of female otherness: "Although he takes pleasure in caressing, he abandons the feminine other, leaves her to sink, in particular into the darkness of a pseudoanimality, in order to return to his responsibilities in the world of men-amongst-themselves."[31] Women do not enter the scene of fecundity as ethical subjects. In Irigaray's critique, Levinas's pervasive anthropocentrism and androcentrism mark the limits of his radical rethinking of the ethical. Women make possible but do not participate in ethical interactions between (male) subjects. While reading Levinas's references to the feminine more generously than Beauvoir and Irigaray do, Chanter argues that by positioning the feminine outside of ontology, he privileges the disruptive potential of femininity without critiquing the political effects of this designation: "to leave the feminine forever unthought, to condemn it to the impossibility of ever being thematized, is to allow it to do its work in the absence of recognition. Levinas's use of the feminine . . . risks maintaining it as a safe haven for the masculine thought which would arise up out of it."[32] This role of "a delightful lapse in being" consigns women to the perpetuation of life and angelic selflessness and excludes them from fully ethical relationships with others.[33]

Levinas's patriarchal framing of the "eternal feminine" in *Totality and Infinity* thus repeats a traditional sentimentalization and naturalization of motherhood (TI 258). They support the interruption of the self-absorbed world of brutal competition by the human, or the moral concern for the other. But women themselves do not centrally represent the human—hence Irigaray's reference to a "pseudoanimality" that characterizes femininity. In Levinas's account, women oppose the brutality of the *conatus* through their nurturing presence, which Guenther calls "a tired myth of women's suffering."[34] Nothing about the feminine in these earlier writings fundamentally departs from the sentimentalized role that women are assigned under the Darwinian assumption that men are governed by the basic anxiety of self-preservation. It is elsewhere—not in Levinas's direct references to femininity but instead in his treatment of how diachrony and embodiment have ethical significance—that we can read in his work the possibility of overturning the demand for maternal selflessness in the face of the struggle for survival, and the anxiety about mortality at the root of such demands. In other words, in challenging the supremacy of the *conatus*, Levinas revises how we should understand time and death, and this rethinking disrupts problematic associations between maternity and mortality.

Whose Mortality?

Rolland characterizes the issue of death in Levinas's work as "a side concern perhaps but a recurrent one."[35] Levinas's concern emerges out of his dissatisfaction with how traditional philosophical accounts of death support the conception of the autonomous subject, as knower and agent. Throughout his writings, Levinas consistently maintains that death is the "utterly unknown," an idea that he inherits most directly from Rosenzweig (PD 121). Death is not only something contingently unknown but fundamentally unknowable. As conscious beings, we are entirely passive in relation to death, in its defiance of representation. In this sense death presents a limit to the knowing subject in the same way that alterity does—by functioning as a trace rather than a phenomenon to be represented. It is something to be undergone, rather than narrated. Against Heidegger, Levinas argues that mortality does not have significance only as the annihilation of my existence or the end of my possibilities: "In an existence determined by death, in this epic of being, there are things that do not enter into the epic, significations that cannot be reduced to being" (GDT 61). Levinas explicitly positions Heideggerian ontology against Kant's antimetaphysical ground for ethics, in order to draw out the possibility of significance irreducible to phenomena or that which appears to consciousness. For Kant, we cannot know whether freedom, God, or immortality exist, but we nonetheless are practically justified in the belief that they are real. We can only know the world subject to our conditions of knowing it (space, time, and the categories), and because those are only applicable to phenomena, the truths of metaphysics exceed our knowledge. However, our beliefs in God, freedom, and immortality are validated practically through our immediate sense of moral constraint (the fact of reason). In Levinas's hands, Kant thus offers a divergence from the "comprehension of being" that governs philosophy. Along parallel lines, Levinas suggests that death has a meaning that does not fit into *Dasein*'s confrontation with being and nothingness, and this is a meaning that cannot be reduced to an intentional object.

In Heidegger's account of death, *Dasein* is always out ahead of itself, projecting itself forward into the future, and death thus means "the possibility of absolute impossibility."[36] Confronting that annihilation of *my* possibilities, which no one else can experience, allows me to encounter myself authentically, in awareness of *Dasein*'s essential relation to nothingness. I must come to terms with death as "always essentially my own."[37] Ordinary social rituals around death obscure its significance: "The They is characterized by the fact that it *chats*, and its idle talk (*Gerede*) is an interpretation of this being-toward-death that is a fleeing-death, a distraction.... One dies, but no one in particular dies.... One dies, but not I, not just now.... We console ourselves as if we could escape death. Public life does not want to let itself be troubled by death, which it considers a lack of tact" (GDT 48). In the neutrality and generalization of claiming that "one dies," I am distracted and "tranquillized" from thinking through the individuality of my own death and the impact that this future event casts over my life.[38] Death is treated as one far-off possibility among others, rather than the possibility that structures my whole existence, including the temporality of existence. Throwing off "the illusions of the 'they'" allows *Dasein* to live out "the possibility of being itself . . . in an impassioned freedom towards death."[39] The deaths of others cannot have this kind of meaning for me.[40] An authentic relation to death would then grasp it as "an ever open possibility" that essentially characterizes *Dasein*, and this requires turning away from the intersubjective dimension of death (GDT 47).

Levinas objects to two related ideas in this Heideggerian account of being-toward-death: first, that death should be read as "the most proper, or ownmost possibility" of *Dasein*; and secondly, that the death that concerns me is ultimately my own death (GDT 51). Both of these claims adhere to the concerns of the *conatus*, in which the primary significance of mortality is *my* annihilation. To speak of the "possibility of impossibility" is still to define death in terms of the possibilities and projects of *Dasein*. But for Levinas, death is a matter of passivity, and he therefore inverts Heidegger's phrase to say that death is the "impossibility of possibility" (PD 122).[41] It unravels any possible project that *Dasein* might have. For Heidegger, authentic being-toward-death allows *Dasein* to see its existence for what it is, an event of being held out over nothingness, and to take up possibilities in the light of that awareness. For Levinas, my own death imposes a passivity that can only be undergone.

Levinas frames the divergence between his own view and Heidegger's as the opposition between "the identical in its authenticity, in its own *right* or its unalterable *mine* of the human, in its *Eigentlichkeit* [authenticity], independence and freedom, and on the other hand being as human devotion to the other, in a responsibility which is also an election" (DYF 211). While he acknowledges the power of Heidegger's challenge to dominant concepts of death and time, by not treating death as one event that might be catalogued among others, Levinas claims that Heidegger continues to understand death in terms of the meaning that *my* death has for me, the end of *my* possibilities. Being-toward-death is still a form of "virility" or mastery: "death announces an event over which the subject is not master, an event in relation to which the subject is no longer a subject. . . . Death in Heidegger is an event of freedom, whereas for me the subject seems to reach the limit of the possible in suffering. It finds itself enchained, overwhelmed, and in some way passive" (TO 70–71). The bodily passivity that Levinas invokes here is linked to the way in which we are (traumatically) impacted by the death of others. Whereas for Heidegger death is "an isolating possibility, since it is a possibility that, as my ownmost, cuts all my ties with other men," for Levinas it is instead precisely the event that opens up my relation to the other (GDT 51).

Even though others' deaths can be depicted straightforwardly as events in my experience, these representations do not exhaust their significance. Clearly, observing someone else's death *can* produce a description of how death transforms the living face into a mask, the living body into an unresponsive corpse: "Death is the *no-response* [*sans-réponse*]. Those movements [of the living] both hide and inform the vegetative movements. Death strips that which is thus covered over and offers it up to medical examination" (GDT 9). So we observe, as Socrates's friends observe, the death of someone else as the draining away of life. However, Levinas's claim is that this identification of death with the annihilation of an organism is too narrow. Death opens up a meaning that is not simply a phenomenon to be observed: "The experience of death that is not mine is an 'experience' of the death of *someone*, someone who from the outset is beyond biological processes, who is associated with me as someone.... The death of someone is not—despite everything that seemed so at first glance—an empirical facticity... it is not exhausted in this appearing" (GDT 12). The quotes in the first sentence of the passage introduce a paradox: whatever experience we have of someone's death exceeds a phenomenon that can be represented synchronically, as just another event passing indifferently before the gaze of consciousness. Instead, the self is affected by this event in such a way that the other's death becomes my concern, and I become implicated by it, with the "culpability of the survivor" (GDT 12). The Darwinian echoes of the *conatus*, in which everyone is most concerned with their own survival, is inverted, such that surviving is not a mark of success. It instead calls my right to be, or the justification for my survival, into question (DR 169).

Levinas argues that the reaction of Socrates's friends to his death, despite his rational derivation of the immortality of the soul, attests to this excessive significance: "they weep without measure: as if humanity were not consumed or exhausted by measurement, as if there were an excess in death" (GDT 9).[42] In response, Socrates likens them to the women he has sent away so that he could die in "good-omened silence."[43] Levinas refers to Alexander Kojéve's remark that Plato is noticeably absent at this death scene, and thus his account leaves open the question of whether he would have wept—"whether he was convinced about immortality by the proofs of the *Phaedo*" or whether such proofs adequately address the meaning of death (PD 124). The careful description of Socrates's dying moments seems to run against the argument that little attention should be paid to the body in its mortality. His death is not simply a transition from a bodily state to a disembodied afterlife, it is "a source of emotion contrary to every effort at consolation" (GDT 9). Levinas's reading here is idiosyncratic, in the sense that he puts no emphasis on the fact that it is Socrates's friends, who have a particular history with him and strong emotional bonds to him, who react in this way. Instead, it is *any* other—"the first one to come along" (PD 129)—who compels us to responsibility and to respond to her death as an outrage and a murder. In this simultaneous resistance to representation and imposition of meaning, death functions as a limit to philosophy rather than its fulfillment, and above all as the limit to what philosophy can comprehend.

We encounter death and are called to think through its meaning by others' deaths, first and foremost (GDT 8). This is part of what Levinas means by referring to the observer of a death as a survivor. We are survivors in the uninteresting sense that someone has outlived another person, but there is also a moral resonance of this term, that in witnessing a death—or anticipating it, in responding to the mortality of the other—the self is implicated in it: "In the guiltiness of the survivor, the death of the other [*l'autre*] is my affair. . . . The death of the other is not only a moment of the mineness of my ontological function" (GDT 39). The death of others should not be understood—or understood exhaustively—in terms of how I relate to my own mortality. In a sense, where Heidegger objects to the tranquillizing effect that "the They" has in relation to the significance of my death for me, Levinas protests against the tranquillizing effect that the philosophical glorification of the sovereign subject has had on the significance of the death of others.

He does not deny that one's own death is of concern, and in *Totality and Infinity* describes death as simultaneously "absurd" and "malevolent," an event that makes no sense and yet seems always to have a destructive intent behind it, even if my death is due to accident, illness, or age (TI 234). In these passages, Levinas emphasizes the subject's passivity in relation to her own death, in the sense that she can neither intellectually master death nor avoid it (TI 234–35). Death resists the intentional activity of consciousness and puts an end to enjoyment and freedom: "In its deep-seated fear life attests [to] this ever possible inversion of the body-master into body-slave, of health into sickness. *To be a body* is on the one hand *to stand* [*se tenir*], to be master of oneself, and, on the other hand, to stand on the earth, to be in the *other*, and thus to be encumbered by one's body" (TI 164). Here aging is not yet the reminder of the ethical impact of diachrony but the transition from self-determination to objecthood.

But my concern with my own aging and death forms part of the logic of the *conatus*. Even if I find myself unable to perpetuate my own being, it does not shift my attention away from that fundamental concern: "My death, always premature, places in check the being that, *qua* being, perseveres in being, but this scandal does not shake the good conscience of being, nor the morality founded upon the inalienable right of the *conatus*" (BC 175; see also PD 128–29). My own death functions as a limit on my action, but without forcing me to confront the trauma of responsibility, which challenges my right to be. Levinas argues that the meaning of death arises fundamentally in the death of the other, in the bad conscience even of the ego who may be legally innocent in that death: "does the relationship to the death of the other not deliver its meaning, does it not articulate it by the depth of the affection [*la profondeur de l'affection*], from the dread that is felt before the death of the other? Is it correct to measure this dreaded thing by the *conatus*, that is, by the persevering-in-my-being, by comparing it with the threat that weighs upon my being—that threat having been posited as the sole source of affectivity?" (GDT 13) Being-toward-death treats the "dreaded thing" as my own death, from which secondary emotions like anxiety arise, but this conception is still preoccupied with the end of my existence.⁴⁴ In this sense, Heidegger does not break radically enough from the tradition of Western philosophy that conceives of death as either annihilation or a transition to some immaterial form of existence.⁴⁵

If death is to be understood outside of this binary, Levinas claims, we must shift philosophical attention from the scandal of my death to the death of the other, which I cannot neutrally witness: "every death is a murder, is premature, and there is the responsibility of the survivor" (GDT 72). This does not mean that I have caused or that I can prevent that death, but instead that I am commanded "not to remain indifferent to that death, not to let the other die alone; that is to say, to be answerable for the life of the other, or else risk becoming the accomplice of that death" (FO 148). Levinas draws a moral equivalence here between being concerned for the death of the other and not allowing him to die alone. Inversely, my indifference morally implicates me in that death. That death cannot be merely another phenomenon, from which I stand back as an observer; the "nets of consciousness" are infiltrated by this vulnerability. In this sense, the other's mortality disrupts the narcissism of the *conatus*. It questions my right to pursue my own preservation and approach the world as a series of beings to be comprehended: "The death of the other man puts me in question, as if in that death that is invisible to the other who exposes himself to it, *I*, through my eventual indifference, became the accomplice; and as if, even before being doomed to it myself, *I* had to answer for this death of the other, and not leave the other alone in his death-bound solitude" (FO 145–46). The mortality of the other addresses me in the accusative. The possibility of indifference to the other—ranging from overt violence against the other to the objectification of the other as a phenomenon—would be a willingness to let the other die, and to let the other die alone. The other addresses me, then, with an imperative of "responding through one's presence to the mortality of the living" (PD 127–28). I am called out as singularly responsible for the other, and in this sense death, now in the form of the vulnerability of the other, individualizes me (GDT 12, 43). But it is not living authentically in the light of my own death, away from the chattering of "the They," that brings about this individualization. The self who stands accused is not at that moment a being with possibilities but finds herself responding to the other's need.

Levinas's claims about death form a complex knot of ideas. Descriptively, he argues that I find myself implicated in the other's witnessed or potential death even as I am concerned about my own continued existence. Intensifying this ambivalence is the idea that the other's vulnerability "tempts" me in two contradictory directions:

> the relation to the Face is both the relation to the absolutely weak—to what is absolutely exposed, what is bare and destitute, the relation with bareness and consequently with what is alone and can undergo the supreme isolation we call death—and there is, consequently, in the Face of the Other always the death of

> the Other and thus, in some way, an incitement to murder, the temptation to go to the extreme, to completely neglect the other—and at the same time (and this is the paradoxical thing) the Face is also the "Thou Shalt not Kill." A Thou-Shalt-not-Kill that can also be explicated much further: it is the fact that I cannot let the other die alone, it is like a calling out to me. (PJL 104)

The face is vulnerable, exposed to the possibility of being abandoned to die unnoticed and unmourned. This exposure "thus" provokes a violent reaction from me, where violence may well be simply my indifference. This inference goes unexplained, but surely the attitude of the *conatus* lies in the background. If I must compete with others in order to survive, the weakness of the other is the weakness of a rival and can only invite aggression. However, "at the same time" the very exposure of the face demands my nonindifference and impresses on me the command not to kill. The suspension of the *conatus*, like the creation of a moral order out of chaos, can only ever be the fragile interruption of that state.

Within this suspension, my own death is of concern only in a secondary sense. Levinas draws a contrast between Heidegger's understanding of death and the Marxist humanism of Ernst Bloch, who discusses our orientation to the future in terms of justice, the hope and labor that transform "the misery and frustration of the neighbor" (DB 35). The work of the individual in bringing about justice can only ever be partial, given the finitude of any given individual. This work is therefore permeated by "melancholia," an awareness of this lack of fulfillment, or the gap between what is and what should be. On Levinas's reading, this means that our anxiety about our own death emerges out of our obligations to others, a "fear of leaving a work undone" (DB 39–40). My own death at least partially derives its significance from the fact that I am accountable for responding to others, and my concern for myself arises as a question of justice. Levinas's emphasis on the interruption of the *conatus* means that anxiety about one's own death is not eradicated, but this interruption opens up the question of what is to be dreaded most (GDT 10). If the significance of mortality is no longer an exclusive attention to my own anticipated death, then the subject who can die is already a quite different kind of subject, for whom time is not merely a threat to my capacity for self-preservation but opens up ethical anxiety.

Thinking Death on the Basis of Time

In his late work, Levinas articulates his challenge to traditional philosophical understandings of time and death as the attempt "to think death on the basis of time rather than time on the basis of death" (GDT 106). Our understanding of death should be shaped by the ethical significance of diachrony, rather than considering time primarily as the force that imposes mortality upon human beings. This shift in orientation means that we focus on the death of the other, rather than our own. This is most clearly a rejection of Heidegger's analysis of being-toward-death. But Levinas is also rejecting the older tradition of seeing time as a "degradation of eternity," or becoming as a degenerate copy of being (TO 32). In this approach, time belongs to a world marked by finitude: beings fleetingly come into and pass out of existence. Levinas suggests that this interpretation of time reinforces the dynamic of the *conatus*, which positions the preservation of my own life and thus the anticipation of my death as fundamental and organizing ideas. These are the claims that Levinas challenges, in refusing to "think time on the basis of death."

But it is less clear what it would mean, alternatively, to "think death on the basis of time." All of Levinas's discussions of diachrony lie behind this idea, in which time is not a linear series of present moments or the neutral condition for the possibility of experience. Time disrupts the power of consciousness to represent intentional objects and arrange them into a narrative, and exposes the subject to "the hither side of being," what cannot be reduced to a being present to consciousness—alterity (OB 43). Time is thus "nonrest," "disquietude" and "disturbance," not as a threat to my continued existence but as a threat to the complacency with which I exist, my presumed right to exist (GDT 109–10). Diachrony opens up the possibility of the one-for-the-other, where the other concerns me but is not assimilated into consciousness: "Time, rather than the current of contents of consciousness, is the turning of the Same toward the Other" (GDT 111). Diachrony is precisely the resistance to synchronization that would once again position the knowing subject as sovereign amid a world of objects to be studied and used. Levinas's paradoxical task is to try to describe the significance of diachrony without reducing it to an idea, shorn of this traumatic force: "How to lend a meaning to time, when for philosophy identity is the identity of the Same, when intelligibility thrives in the Same, when it thrives on being in its stability as the Same, when it thrives on assimilating the Other into the Same—when every alteration is senseless, when understanding assimilates the Other into the Same?" (GDT 107). In the context of inheriting a tradition that treats temporal difference as a lapse away from being, Levinas attempts to disrupt the tendency to reduce diachrony either to nothingness or to a being that can be comprehended.[46] Death in the light of *that* understanding of time is first and foremost the mortality of the other: "Death, in the face of the other man, is the mode according to which the alterity that affects the Same causes its identity as the Same to burst open in the form of a question that arises to it. This question—the question of death—is unto itself its own response: it is my responsibility for the death of the other" (GDT 117). Here the *conatus* in its self-containment is not merely thwarted but destabilized, as the significance of death cannot be reduced to either the promise of continued life or the negation of that hope. The fundamental question is no longer how to preserve my own being, either physically or through some intellectual or material legacy, but how I am implicated in the vulnerability of the other (PD 125).

In elaborating how to think death on the basis of (diachronous) time, Levinas makes use of highly traditional ideas about how the significance of death illuminates the distinction between human and nonhuman animals. Returning to the claim that the *conatus* governs a Darwinian competition for resources,[47] Levinas argues that the human is this ethical interruption of the animal concern for itself: "Is there no thinking that goes beyond my own death, toward the death of the other man, and does the human not consist precisely in thinking beyond its own death?" (PD 126). He reinforces the separation between the human and the animal in terms of their relationships to death, but here the contrast is not that one possesses an immortal soul, while the other belongs entirely to the natural world. It is instead that the human being is capable of suspending his obsession with his own existence and his own death, in his concern for others. In "Dying for . . . ," Levinas contrasts the Heideggerian discussion of death, as dissolving all relations to others, with an interpretation of a biblical verse, "the funeral chant of the prophet [Samuel] weeping for the death of King Saul and his son Jonathan in combat: 'Saul and Jonathan were lovely and pleasant in their lives, and in their death they were not divided; they were swifter than eagles, they were stronger than lions'" (DYF 215). Levinas's reading of this passage puts no particular emphasis on the fact that Saul and Jonathan are father and son. He instead draws out of this metaphor the specific way in which the human interrupts the *conatus*, by being (unlike animals) concerned for each other even in death: in this way they were "swifter than eagles" and "stronger than lions." In relation to one another, the human is a "surpassing . . . of the animal effort of life, purely life" (DYF 215). The key term in this passage is "effort," the striving for one's own survival, and how responsibility unsettles this striving. This is not the promise of an afterlife, as a transcendence of the merely natural world. Having reinterpreted what death means, he refuses to provide an alternative fantasy of mastering death.

In the history of philosophy, animality tends to be identified with the physical condition of mortality, in opposition to the (possible) immortality of the human psyche, but Levinas here associates animals with a certain kind of existence, wholly governed by the *conatus*—and thus anxiety about their own deaths and indifference to the deaths of others. Although the boundary gets drawn in various ways, the boundary between the human and the animal does not coincide with the delineation of species but is internal to human beings themselves. A typical account might claim that our instinctual behavior, emotions, and bodies may belong to nature, but something in us transcends those constraints. Similarly, Levinas discusses the human as an eruptive force within the default animality of existence. Responsibility strikes us in the midst of our ordinary self-absorption and indifference to others. Despite the internal character of this divide, Levinas avoids the dualism of associating embodiment with the *conatus*. It is in our very passivity and vulnerability as embodied creatures that we are exposed to the other. Although Levinas is inheriting elements of a traditional separation between the human and the animal, or the spiritual and the natural, he deploys these elements in ways that at least partially challenge that tradition.

A second revision of dominant ideas about death arises in Levinas's discussion of *Antigone*. Levinas generally has little praise for Hegel, but he reads Hegel's analysis of burial obligations in *Antigone* as a reflection of the need to not allow the other to die alone, or to be abandoned in death. Hegel reads Antigone's insistence on burying her brother as devotion to the divine law that demands that relatives act to supplement "the abstract natural process by adding to it the movement of consciousness, interrupting the work of Nature and rescuing the blood-relation from destruction."[48] Rather than allowing scavengers and other natural processes of decay to return the corpse of Polyneices to the earth, Antigone takes on the obligation of burial as a ritual that "makes him a member of a community which prevails over and holds under control the forces of particular material elements and the lower forms of life."[49] Burial allows Polyneices to be recognized as part of the divine moral order, rather than merely as an organism within the physical world. The burial need only be symbolic, rather than actually protecting the corpse from decay. The sentry guarding Polyneices's body reports that "Someone just now / buried the corpse and vanished. He scattered on the skin / some thirsty dust; he did the ritual, / duly, to purge the body of desecration."[50] On Levinas's reading, it is the fact that any ritual at all is performed that allows the individual's existence to be affirmed and fulfilled as part of the human community: "The family cannot acknowledge that, with death, he who had been a consciousness is now submitted to matter, that matter has become the master of a being that was formed, that was a self-consciousness. One does not want this conscious being to be given over to matter, for the ultimate being of a man, the ultimate fact of man, does not belong to nature" (GDT 85). Levinas refers to the earth in this ritual as a "maternal element" that once more embraces the corpse (GDT 86). This return to the earth is quite different than the material decomposition of the body. It instead marks the separation between the natural and spiritual worlds: "the blood relatives effect a destruction of death and bring about a sort of return, as though there were a fulfillment, as though beneath terrestrial being there were a subsoil to which one returned and from which one came" (GDT 86). The dead person thus avoids "the dishonor of anonymous decomposition"—in other words, being treated as if he were only an animal (GDT 86).

Levinas's reading of Hegel on this point emphasizes how the funeral rites reflect the obligations of the survivors of the dead. Antigone refuses to allow Polyneices to be dead alone, in stubbornly demonstrating her nonindifference to his death, in contrast with Ismene's more practical obedience to Creon's order, even as she privately mourns. As with Socrates's friends, Levinas assigns no significance to the particularity of the relationship between Antigone and Polyneices (although Antigone herself insists on this point), but instead focuses on the interpersonal effect that death has on those who witness it.[51] He also resists the idea that burial returns the dead person to a divine community, insofar as this narrative makes death "intelligible," part of a coherent account that survivors can tell about a kind of life persisting beyond the event of death (GDT 89). In Chanter's words, this makes death "an intraworldly event" rather than the limit of knowledge.[52] But within this critique, Levinas approvingly cites the idea that survivors are caught by an obligation to respond to the other, even in death, which forbids indifference to the other's death and so becoming complicit in it. In his account, this response to death is emblematic of the emergence of the human within animality.

If death is understood in terms of the ethical significance of diachrony, the lapse of time that unhinges the activity of consciousness, it no longer can be reduced to the annihilation of a being. Death does not function as a symptom of the subject's immersion in becoming. This would once again position time as a "degradation of eternity" and the subject as ideally capable of representing and thus intellectually overcoming the lapse of time. But if the lapse of time cannot be collapsed in this way, and instead carries its own significance, diachrony introduces a resistance to what can be comprehended and a challenge to the status of the observing, self-contained subject: "It is impossible to *receive* time's blow; it is more like receiving the blow, or force, of time and waiting still; it is to receive without receiving, without taking upon oneself, to endure that which still remains outside in its transcendence and yet to be affected by it" (GDT 115). This is another description of trauma, as an event that imposes meaning on the subject without being available for representation. Rolland comments that death undermines the autonomy of the subject: "In time thus thought, death comes to be twice inscribed. First, as the mortality of the another person . . . which would be the concrete modality by which, within the subject, the same does not rejoin the same but offers itself passively and gratuitously to the service of another. It is next inscribed with my own death, the nonsense of which "would guarantee" in some fashion that this passivity will not be inverted into activity, or that this disquiet will not finish by finding rest."[53] The subject's own death challenges the possibility of sovereignty, whether that is understood as the ability to enact one's will in the world or as the power of comprehending the world. But the death of the other overturns the complacency of the *conatus* that accompanies even the ideal of such mastery. Given Levinas's attempt to radically alter our understanding of time and death, in order to call attention to where and how the *conatus* is suspended in ordinary human existence, dominant cultural conceptions of reproduction and maternity also shift in ways that Levinas himself did not examine closely.

Rethinking Maternity

As long as the *conatus* remains the primary motivating force in human thought and behavior, anxiety about one's own death positions maternity as either a degenerate form of reproduction or merely instrumental in supporting one's interests. In the latter case, the self-sacrifice required of the good mother is glorified as an exception to the greedy self-centeredness of competitive survival, but this angelic attitude does nothing to interrupt the basic economy of the *conatus*. Levinas admittedly uses the language of sacrifice to describe responsibility as the advent of the human within the animal, an "excessiveness of sacrifice" that prioritizes the other over the ego (DYF 217). The sacrifice of oneself for another seems to have no place in a world governed by individuals concerned only for their own needs, unless ultimately sacrifice comes back to some form of egoism. Claire Katz attributes Levinas's interest in sacrifice to his attempts "to provide the argument for understanding the possibility of the ethical in the shadow of a world that seems to make ethics impossible. Thus, sacrifice in the form of nurturing and feeding the other becomes a substantial part of his ethics. The possibility of sacrifice demonstrates that the *conatus essendi* can be interrupted."[54] Sacrifice is the "madness" of responsibility, in which the other takes priority over the ego. The risk in using this kind of terminology to describe the human, over and above the animal, is romanticizing sacrifice particularly by women, who have been historically coerced into subordinating their projects and desires to those of others.

This risk is intensified by the fact that Levinas consistently uses maternity as an image for exposure to the other in his late writings. The contrast with the significance of the feminine in *Totality and Infinity* is stark: maternity is the very situation of responsibility rather than the preparatory condition for that relation.[55] In *Otherwise than Being*, maternity signifies the one-for-the-other, the "psyche in the form of a hand that gives even the bread taken from its own mouth" (OB 67). The psyche is like a "maternal body," a body that shelters and nourishes another within itself during pregnancy or in less direct ways afterward.[56] There is nothing voluntary about this prioritization of the fetus/child's needs over the woman's. Under the right circumstances, women can choose whether to become pregnant, but within pregnancy itself, responding to the needs of the fetus happens without deliberation or choice. Levinas repeatedly uses "maternity" and "vulnerability" as equivalent terms, with the qualification that vulnerability here is understood as the vulnerability of responsibility, being bound to the other's need (OB 108).[57] The psyche is a hand that gives the bread *taken* from its own mouth, in the sense that the self clearly has needs and interests of her own, but attention to those needs and interests is suspended.

A "natural" feminine selflessness or devotion to the needs of the child has been glorified in various ways in the history of European cultures, but for Levinas, maternity is not an emotional attachment to the child. He describes it more as bodily pain or restlessness caused by the fact that another is carried within the self: maternity is "the groaning of the wounded entrails by those it will bear or has borne" (OB 75). Perpich remarks that this is "a passage whose imagery is as unsentimental as any ever written about pregnancy."[58] Subjectivity as the feeling of being too tight in one's skin is another way of expressing the claim that we are exposed to others in a way that has not been chosen, as if the other were inside the subject already, making a claim that is unavoidable. Despite these images of maternal suffering in the midst of sustaining and nurturing others' lives, the Levinasian image of maternity cannot be identified simply with the virtue of self-sacrifice. The feminine is no longer associated with "welcoming" the other as if she were a gracious host; the psyche is now a hostage to the other.[59] The violence of this language emphasizes that this is not even an instinctive generosity, much less the result of moral deliberation and free commitment.

Levinas takes this exposure one step further to make the radical, counterintuitive claim that we are not only responsible *to* the other person but answerable for their actions. Again, Levinas separates how legal notions of responsibility operate in the domain of justice from the responsibility that Levinas describes as substitution (OB 111–18). The latter is a responsibility that does not emerge from any intention or voluntary act, but is instead the trauma of finding oneself responsible beyond one's choices: "a responsibility for others, to the point of substitution for others and suffering both from the effect of persecution and from the persecuting itself in which the persecutor sinks. Maternity, which is bearing par excellence, bears even responsibility for the persecuting by the persecutor" (OB 75). The woman bears the other, who burdens her with sleeplessness, unpredictable internal punches and kicks, and in general a sense of not being at home in her own body. The boundaries of responsibility similarly remain obscure. Guenther notes the problematic proximity between the exalted figure of the Madonna in Western cultures and this description of vulnerability: "there is more than an echo here of the patriarchal image of the Good Mother: a quiet and patient martyr who bears my suffering and even my sins without protest."[60] "Good mothers" take responsibility for and bear even what they have not done. But she reminds us that Levinas refuses this interpretation by separating what he means by maternity from "a guilt complex (which presupposes an *initial* freedom)," from "a natural benevolence or divine 'instinct,'" and from "some tendency to sacrifice" (OB 124). None of these causal explanations do justice to the trauma of responsibility, in which we find ourselves always already exposed to the other, regardless of our emotional attachments, natural instincts, or personality traits.

At its most extreme, Levinas describes maternity not only in terms of vulnerability but as a concrete physical danger:

> The feminine in its feminine phase, in its feminine form certainly may die bringing life in the world ... the "dying" of a woman is certainly unacceptable. I am speaking about the possibility of conceiving that there is meaning without me.... It is that human possibility which consists in saying that the life of another human being is more important than my own, that the death of the other is more important to me than my own death, that the Other comes before me, that the Other counts before I do. (QDE 27)

Levinas clearly borrows the content of the image of maternity from the Western patriarchal tradition, which has simultaneously exalted and degraded women, as both transcending the brutality of the public sphere and being immersed in the natural world. Katz notes that in this passage Levinas quickly conflates the feminine with the maternal, and his "references to maternity and his description of the feminine reinforce historical, cultural, and philosophical views of women that have shaped their lives and often confined them to oppressive and abusive situations."[61] Levinas affirms and employs those associations uncritically.

However, Levinas uses these images in ways that resist traditional constructions of femininity. Katz argues that he does not offer this description of maternal sacrifice as a feminine ideal: "Rather than advocating death in childbirth, it seems Levinas has instead identified the very real risk in childbirth."[62] What it means to be "like a maternal body" (*comme un corps maternal*) is to find oneself in a situation where one's own life, health, and comfort are risked in supporting the needs of another (OB 67).[63] The subject finds herself responsible for the other, being for-the-other. Both Katz and Guenther emphasize that this reading of the ethical significance of the maternal body is not a normative stance on empirical women's choices about whether to become mothers or whether to continue their pregnancies: questions in the abortion debate about the legal rights of pregnant women and the potential legal rights of fetuses belong to the domain of justice.[64] Levinas's late claims about maternity also do not prescribe any particular style of parenting or family structure, but they do describe a dimension of subjectivity that has been marginalized in Western thought. The normative content of Levinas's association between maternity and the interruption of the *conatus* is that we should attend to responsibility, understood in this way, and allow it to complicate ethical and political systems that frame human beings purely as individual, sovereign, self-created subjects.

In this sense, Levinas is not appropriating the image of maternity in the same way that Plato does in the *Symposium* or the *Phaedo*—claiming the power of reproduction for the (masculine) pursuit of philosophical knowledge, and in so doing degrading the merely physical form of reproduction that has been culturally associated with women's bodies. Instead, Levinas describes the most human part of the psyche as being like the incarnate vulnerability of maternity. Since the body in its very susceptibility is ethically significant, the maternal body's intensification of that susceptibility—the ways in which maternity is the condition of the one-for-the-other, where the other is not external to the self but also not assimilated into the self—functions as a metaphor for responsibility.[65]

In other words, the language of maternity supports Levinas's broader challenge to the ideal of the sovereign subject, with its accompanying assumptions about embodiment, vulnerability, and death. The body as sensibility is not a specimen for dissection or a heteronomous object that stands in the way of the autonomous will. These various ways of interpreting the body lie easily within the discourse of intentionality, which leaves the agency of consciousness intact. The sensible body is instead sensitive and attuned to the needs of others, without having chosen those commitments. In this way, understanding embodiment as an ethical vulnerability inverts the subject's self-absorbed concern for his own being (OB 75). Given how dominant conceptions of maternity support and reinforce anxieties about mortality, Levinas's rejection of those assumptions of what time and embodiment mean allow us to also reconceive maternity and femininity more generally.

The Responsibility of One Mortal for Another

Despite Levinas's traditional identification of maternity with bodily vulnerability and the activity of nurturing, his peculiar use of these ideas challenges the ideal of the (masculine or masculinized) autonomous subject. This is particularly true when we consider the metaphor of maternity in conjunction with his claims about the ethical significance of death and time. The vulnerability of feminine bodies has been normalized and sentimentalized within social and political systems that assume the priority of the *conatus*. In disqualifying women from the competitive brutality of industry, war, and politics, such virtues have been traditionally and dominantly deployed to disempower those defined by their position outside of the public sphere, whether that position has been one of degradation toward animality or glorification toward divinity. When he writes directly about femininity in his early work, Levinas participates in this instrumental positioning, but by providing an alternative notion of the embodied self and the ethical significance of mortality in *Otherwise than Being* and other late writings, he helps to undermine it.

First, by emphasizing the vulnerability of every body, Levinas's conception of the ethical does not consign women alone to the role of a constitutive exception to greed and narcissism.[66] Even though he describes the incarnate experience of the maternal body, there is no restriction of this kind of ethical experience to female bodies. *Every* psyche is like a maternal body, bearing the other within itself. Moreover, subjectivity itself is founded on this vulnerability, rather than being positioned in fundamental opposition to it. In its ambiguous connections to moral decision-making and the practical work of justice, responsibility arises out of the experience of temporal, embodied beings, concerned for the welfare of others. Maternity then is no longer singled out as the foil to self-centeredness and ruthlessness. Instead, human beings in general are called to respond to the needs of others and called to respond even as they also manage the demands of justice.

Levinas also at least gestures to an interesting ambivalence in the experience of subjectivity: we are metaphorically both children and parents, and both images draw out forms of vulnerability. We are creatures in the sense of finding ourselves as part of a larger history—in Levinas's terms, addressed by an immemorial past—and unable to represent our own origins. This diachrony sets up the "lateness" of responsibility that unsettles the autonomy of the knowing subject. Levinas invites us to understand ourselves as children, marked by what Guenther refers to as the "anarchy of birth," in which we are in relation prior to being conscious of that relation, much less choosing it.[67] But children are not simply products of their parents or a broader history, and part of the anarchical character of birth is that it opens up an unpredictable future: "The future of the child to whom the pregnant woman will someday give birth does not quite belong to her, even if it does implicate her in a future of responsibility. As in Levinas's account of paternity, the future of the child is the future of a stranger; it exceeds the parent's own powers of representation and expectation."[68] Within this anarchic temporality, we find ourselves addressed by the other and so implicated in the other's vulnerability. In that sense, the subject undergoes a quasi-maternal experience of bearing the other within herself. In shifting between those positions of child and parent as he describes subjectivity in its ethical exposure to the other, Levinas refuses to privilege either one as primary. Instead, every subject experiences both the passivity of creatureliness and something like the restless responsibility of maternity.

By framing bodily experience not only as the precursor to the ethical but as itself ethically significant, Levinas offers a new way of conceptualizing maternity, in which reproduction neither raises nor alleviates anxiety about one's own death. Reading Levinas's work on embodiment in this way by no means erases the problematic use that he makes of the concept of femininity. However, it opens up the possibility of undoing the subordination of maternity to paternal creation, according to the order that remains obsessed with eternal being and its pale imitation, the perpetuation of our being. If death is not primarily understood in terms of the ego's annihilation, maternity need not be understood in the interdependent terms of animality and angelhood. As temporal, material beings, we are exposed to the other and not in possession of ourselves. In this sense, embodied existence in general carries ethical weight, and there is no need to project onto women an exceptional, marginalized, and ultimately subordinate status. Instead, human subjectivity becomes "the responsibility of one mortal for another" (GDT 117). This is Levinas's attempt to think death on the basis of diachronous time. The reinterpretation of embodiment in all its vulnerability—now ethical rather than purely physical vulnerability—allows us to break open the logic of the *conatus*, and to challenge the ideal of the masculine subject and the disavowals of heteronomy that such an ideal generates.

Notes

1. Matthew Calarco notes that Darwin himself is more nuanced in his description of animal behavior—that the "struggle for existence" was not always and everywhere a Hobbesian war of each individual organism against every other, but rather includes cooperation and altruism within social groups ("Faced by Animals," 117–18).
2. Darwin discusses the "struggle for existence" in natural selection in *The Origin of Species*. Herbert Spencer first referred to this process as producing the "survival of the fittest," a phrase that Darwin incorporated into the fifth edition.
3. Tennyson, "In Memoriam A. H. H.," 135.
4. Bernasconi notes that in arguing for the incompleteness of Darwinism and its necessary interruption by responsibility, Levinas "opposes one of the most dominant tendencies of modern political thought," a tendency that predates Darwin ("Levinas and the Struggle for Existence," 171).
5. Fagenblat, *Covenant of Creatures*, 38.
6. Ibid., 39.
7. Rosenzweig, *Star of Redemption*, 9; see also Gibbs, *Correlations in Rosenzweig and Levinas*, 36–37.
8. Gibbs, *Correlations in Rosenzweig and Levinas*, 36.
9. Plato, *Phaedo*, 106e.
10. Ibid., 118a.
11. Ibid., 115c–d. The contrast between Socrates and Antigone on the question of burial is revealing, although neither is concerned with the literal welfare of the body. Antigone argues that we have obligations to those who have died—that our relation to them does not end at their deaths, that these obligations are established by divine law, and that they are lived out through social custom. We can read Plato as tacitly supporting the first part of this stance, despite Socrates's nonchalance about what happens after his death, in writing the dialogues at all and in the attentive representation of Socrates's death.
12. Ibid., 64a, 67d–68b.
13. Rolland, "Death in Its Negativity," 464.
14. Plato, *Symposium*, 208e–209a.
15. Ibid., 209c.
16. Ibid., 209c–e.
17. See Irigaray, "Plato's *Hystera*," 243–364.
18. Cavarero, *In Spite of Plato*, 92.
19. Ibid.
20. Ibid., 94. See also DuBois, *Sowing the Body*.
21. Irigaray, "Sorcerer Love," 37–38.
22. Ibid., 40.
23. See Cohen, *Levinasian Meditations*, 41–43.

24. *New Oxford Annotated Bible*, Gen. 3:16.

25. I am all too briefly summarizing here a dominant interpretation of the Genesis narrative, but there has been lively and rich scholarly debate about how to read this text. See, for instance, Brenner (ed.), *Genesis*; Trible, *God and the Rhetoric of Sexuality*; and Meyers, *Discovering Eve*.

26. Darwin, *Descent of Man*, 326. See also Grosz, *Nick of Time*, 73.

27. Wollstonecraft, *Vindication of the Rights of Woman*, 76.

28. Rich, *Of Woman Born*.

29. See Gibbs, *Correlations in Rosenzweig and Levinas*, 237–38; and Fagenblat, *Covenant of Creatures*, 92–94.

30. Beauvoir, *Second Sex*, xxii.

31. Irigaray, "Questions to Emmanuel Levinas," 113.

32. Chanter, *Time, Death, and the Feminine*, 255.

33. Ibid.

34. Guenther, *Gift of the Other*, 112.

35. Rolland, "Death in Its Negativity," 462.

36. Heidegger, *Being and Time*, 232.

37. Ibid., 223.

38. Ibid., 234.

39. Ibid., 311.

40. See Chanter, *Time, Death, and the Feminine*, 202.

41. See also Cohen, *Levinasian Meditations*, 67–68; Derrida, *Aporias*; and Keenan, *Death and Responsibility*.

42. See also Rolland, "Death in Its Negativity," 465.

43. Plato, *Phaedo*, 117e.

44. Levinas frequently links Heidegger to the attitude of the *conatus*, in a series of readings that Heidegger scholars have challenged. For instance, Levinas typically reads *Sorge* (care) in terms of preserving my own existence: "The possibility for man to get his identity from somewhere other than the perseverance in his being, to which Heidegger accustomed us; that is, from elsewhere than this *conatus* where death strikes its blow to the highest of all attachments, the attachment to being" (GDT 103). Even in Levinas's most sympathetic readings of Heidegger—in "Dying for . . . ," where he traces the link between *Jemeinigkeit* (mineness) and concern for others—he still draws the contrast between the profoundly antisocial nature of authentic being-toward-death in Heidegger and his own emphasis on mortality as opening an ethical relation to the other: "In 1927 it appears to us [Heidegger's students] as if he were beginning with a kind of Darwinian struggle for existence. *Dasein* is a being for whom this, his being, is an issue. Later he changed this a little: *Dasein* is a being for whom the meaning of being is a concern" (BTD 136). Chanter argues that Levinas's criticisms are "based on a sustained critique of Heidegger," in which he both applauds Heidegger's attempt to overturn dominant ideas in the history of Western philosophy and recognizes the limits of that attempt (Chanter, *Time, Death, and the Feminine*, 185–86).

45. Chanter, *Time, Death, and the Feminine*, 216–17.

46. See also DR 173: "Responsibility for the other man, being answerable for the death of the other, devotes itself to an alterity that is no longer within the province of re-presentation. This way of being devoted—or this devotion—is time."

47. And perhaps also reproduction, in a genetic form of immortality. See Dawkins, *Selfish Gene*.

48. Hegel, *Phenomenology of Spirit*, 271.

49. Ibid.

50. Sophocles, *Antigone*, 170.
51. Ibid., 196.
52. Chanter, *Time, Death, and the Feminine*, 219.
53. Rolland, "Postscript," 236.
54. Katz, *Levinas, Judaism, and the Feminine*, 143.
55. For closer analysis of Levinas's references to maternity, see Chanter, *Time, Death, and the Feminine*; Chanter (ed.), *Feminist Interpretations of Emmanuel Levinas*; Katz, *Levinas, Judaism, and the Feminine*; Rosato, "Woman as Vulnerable Self"; and Guenther, *Gift of the Other*.
56. One empirical resonance of the image of the bread taken from the mother's own mouth is the fact that during pregnancy and lactation, more calcium is transferred to the fetus/child than women can absorb through their diets, thus depleting their own reserves of calcium and resulting in significant bone loss (Kovacs, "Calcium and Bone Metabolism in Pregnancy and Lactation").
57. In a footnote, Levinas draws an etymological connection between the Hebrew word *Rakhamin*, mercy, and *Rekhem*, uterus: responsibility is "a mercy that is like an emotion of maternal entrails" (NI 147). Once again, Levinas does not directly associate maternity with mercy, but instead claims that responsibility is *like* a maternal emotion. Katz comments on this passage and a related one from *Nine Talmudic Readings* that Levinas once again privileges the maternal body as an image of responsibility (and particularly the moral emotion of mercy) without pathologizing maternity or emotion more generally—as in the diagnosis of hysteria (*Levinas, Judaism, and the Feminine*, 131–32).
58. Perpich, *Ethics of Emmanuel Levinas*, 129.
59. See Fagenblat, *Covenant of Creatures*, 122.
60. Guenther, *Gift of the Other*, 111.
61. Katz, *Levinas, Judaism, and the Feminine*, 143.
62. Ibid., 164n43.
63. Guenther discusses this phrase carefully and notes that Alphonso Lingis's English translation of *Autrement qu'être* omits the word "like" to render the phrase as "Psyche is the maternal body." Guenther argues that the simile works "to destabilize any strict correlation between women and mothers, or between motherhood and responsibility" (*Gift of the Other*, 7). See also Katz, *Levinas, Judaism, and the Feminine*, 142.
64. Katz, *Levinas, Judaism, and the Feminine*, 142; see also Guenther, *Gift of the Other*, 141–63. Levinas's reading of maternity interestingly complicates a tendency within moral debates around abortion to treat the woman and fetus as two competing rights-bearers. Given his focus on the experience of the mother, it also opposes the problematic tendency among abortion opponents to identify with the fetus: see Frye, "Some Reflections on Separatism and Power." One of the rhetorically powerful elements of Judith Jarvis Thomson's argument is its resistance to this tendency; she guides the reader's moral imagination to identify with the person who unwittingly and unwillingly becomes the life-support system for another person ("Defense of Abortion").
65. In this way, Guenther argues, Levinas retains an emphasis on the embodied significance of maternity without thereby participating in its sentimentalization as a "fixed biological or even social identity" (*Gift of the Other*, 139).
66. See Katz, *Levinas, Judaism, and the Feminine*, 143–44; and Guenther, *Gift of the Other*, 139.
67. Guenther, *Gift of the Other*, 99.
68. Ibid., 100.

8   Animals and Creatures

THE PREVIOUS TWO chapters have raised a cluster of issues about the implications of Levinas's understanding of embodiment for the relationship between human and nonhuman animals, particularly given his emphasis on the subject's status as a creature. Levinas defends a very traditional form of anthropocentrism, which leads him to the conclusion that animals fall outside of the ethical encounter between the self and the other. He thus has very little to say about animals. But in the wake of his radical reconception of subjectivity—as heteronomous, embodied, and ineradicably affected by time—the question of how human creatures relate to nonhuman ones demands more attention than he is willing to give it.

In *Beyond Good and Evil*, Nietzsche criticizes the Stoics for interpreting the natural world according to their own needs and desires but mistaking this interpretation for objective observation of an independent reality: "while you pretend rapturously to read the canon of your law in nature, you want something opposite, you strange actors and self-deceivers! Your pride wants to impose your morality, your ideal, on nature—even on nature—and incorporate them in her; you demand that she should be nature 'according to the Stoa,' and you would like all existence to exist only after your own image."[1] Nietzsche has in mind here the claim that the goal of human life can be attained by adapting oneself to the rational laws governing the cosmos, expressed in Cleanthes's proposition that human flourishing is "living in agreement with nature."[2] As with many idols, Nietzsche's mockery calls into question the authority of nature, by refusing to accept it as something that we simply discover. Instead, he argues that nature is a construction, shaped by what various systems of thought have wanted it to be. But the authority borne by the term "natural" depends on the covering over of this interpretive process. In other words, nature needs to be perceived as unmediated by human conceptualizations of it in order to be invested with normative power. Premised on the forgetting of how we shape what is taken to be true or good, this kind of reverence provokes Nietzsche's genealogical objection.

Unlike the Stoics, Levinas does not attribute any normative authority to the natural world. As he writes in various places, the human is what interrupts the dynamic that governs all things in nature, in its Hobbesian-Darwinian struggle of all against all. Responsibility is the "shattering of indifference—even if indifference is statistically dominant" in a world defined by "violence in the guise of beings who affirm themselves 'without regard' for one another in their concern to be"

(EN xii). In Levinas's work, the concept of animality, which is primarily used to refer to the animality within human beings, is defined by a compulsive focus on one's own needs and a deafness to the needs of others. In contrast to the Stoics, acting ethically—to the extent that Levinas defines what this would be—requires resisting the internal momentum of the *conatus* and its rationalizations, and attending to the disruptive force of responsibility, "a preoccupation [*préoccupation*] with the other" (EN xii). That term "preoccupation" succinctly expresses two key dimensions of Levinasian responsibility: that subjectivity begins in the one-for-the-other, so that by the time that I attempt to make sense of my obligations to the other, I have already responded to the demand of the other; and that I am concerned for the other, unable to maintain the indifference of the *conatus*. But such preoccupation as the beginning of normativity is the suspension of the natural rather than the realization of a moral ideal in nature.

Despite the evaluative distance between the Stoics' conception of nature and Levinas's description of animality, Nietzsche's suspicion applies equally to both, and leads to the question of what function animals play in Levinas's larger account of subjectivity, and what makes that function seem so natural. What gives anthropocentrism its purchase in Western philosophy and Western culture more generally? Why should that commitment maintain this privileged place in Levinas's discourse, when in so many other ways he attempts to unseat the dominant ideal of the self-possessed subject, whose status is bound up with a disavowal of animality? This chapter is a reading of Levinas's anthropocentrism, for which he has been thoroughly criticized, and the tensions within that position. Given the anarchical status of responsibility in his account, his refusal to treat nonhuman animals as morally considerable seems arbitrary and inconsistent with the rest of his project. Part of the trauma of responsibility is that we find ourselves to have committed violence against others, simply through living our ordinary lives, and thus find ourselves accused when we had thought ourselves morally innocent. Levinas's unapologetic anthropocentrism sits uneasily with this anarchic quality of responsibility, in which I cannot predict who or what will accuse me in this way. More concretely, I draw on the work of Cora Diamond and Jacques Derrida to call attention to the ambiguities that operate in dominant attitudes toward animals, including in Levinas's account. These lines of fissure emphasize the various forms of projection used to establish a supposedly clear distinction between human and nonhuman animals. I read Diamond and Derrida as providing a genealogical analysis of animality, with the same intent that Nietzsche had, of making "fixed ideas" questionable.

Nonetheless, Levinas's description of responsibility in its relation to diachronic time opens up possibilities that go unheeded in many contemporary discussions of animal rights and animal welfare. His critique of the ideal of autonomy has implications not only for how we understand subjectivity, but for our attention to the conditions that make existence possible, and for how we think about responsibility. His approach to responsibility reveals some of the limitations of contemporary debates in animal ethics, which tend to invoke the characteristics that human and nonhuman animals share, including the capacity to suffer. For Levinas, such observable characteristics do not answer the issue of how we find ourselves obligated in the first place. His reflections on the limits of philosophical discourse suggest that determinate traits will not decide our exposure to the other: the face is not a phenomenon. For Levinas, what it means to be a creature is to find oneself addressed by the other, but without having time to identify the source of that address or evaluate its legitimacy. How we conceptualize moral obligation cannot ignore that disruption of the conceptualizing, thematizing work of consciousness. In this sense, Levinas's approach to responsibility offers a new way of understanding our relation to nonhuman animals and the limits of philosophical arguments around this issue.

Framing Animality

Levinas's anthropocentrism has been well-documented and discussed extensively in secondary scholarship.[3] His references to the other, however marginalized (the widow, the orphan, the stranger), consistently signify a human other. His challenges to the metaphysical humanism of the Western philosophical tradition lead him to an alternative humanism defined by our responsiveness to the other human being.[4] In this sense, Levinas resists what Freud calls the second great cultural trauma of modern thought—the Darwinian claim that the human being as one species among others, continuous with other living things.[5] Levinas is most interested in precipitating a cultural shift in our self-understanding that is anti-Darwinian, to the extent that he associates the animalistic struggle for survival with the *conatus*. He repeatedly discusses the ethical as the interruption of self-absorption, or the upsurge of the human within animality: "the human breaks with pure being, which is always a persistence in being. This is my principal thesis. A being is something that is attached to being, to its own being. That is Darwin's idea. The being of animals is a struggle for life. A struggle for life without ethics" (PM 172). But this struggle for life is also a dominating motivation in human life, so that the drama of the *conatus* and its interruption takes place within human beings, rather than between human and nonhuman animals. Levinas's claim here is not quite that human beings are radically separate from animals, but that within the human animal ("human" here understood as a biological concept) arises the possibility of humanity (where "humanity" is now an ethical concept). Levinas focuses so intently on human intersubjectivity that John Llewelyn notes that "almost always when he touches upon the subject of animality he is thinking of the animality of man."[6] But even this dimension of his anthropocentrism is highly traditional—the recognition of some trait or behavior in human beings that is attributed to a thread of animality within the human psyche, as in Freud's reference to the German proverb, "Man is a wolf to man."[7] There is a complex dynamic of projection at work in the use of an animal metaphor to describe the violence of human interactions, somehow without calling into question either the presumed nature of animals (specifically, wolves) as violent or the boundary between humans and animals. Levinas consistently describes animality through references to violence, aggression, and amorality, even as he locates these tendencies within human beings.

As its base, hunger is the driving force of the *conatus*, associated with "covetousness," the gaze of "reasonable or wily animals," and "an incessant chasing after things" (SH 4). Levinas moves from literal hunger to its epistemic analogy, the drive to represent what is external to consciousness and thus assimilate it. As knowers, we do not so much leave behind our cunning as hunters as sublimate it. Levinas argues that practical and even philosophical knowledge stems from the motivation to satisfy more immediate hungers in order to control the resources that satisfy such needs: "There is an affinity between . . . ontology and the good practical sense of men troubled by hunger, seizing upon things, perceiving; men called to take before consuming and thus to acquire and to store, to keep themselves in their houses, at home and to build and assure themselves of the presence of things and to represent these, and gradually to touch the very sources of the celestial light which one day shall be reduced to their physico-chemical essence" (SH 8). The assumption that what *is* can be made accessible to human consciousness leads to the practical mastery of objects in the world. Through this process, what seems to be transcendent—the stars in their grandeur—becomes intelligible under the "industrious gaze" of human beings (SH 7). This destruction of the "visible gods," the disenchantment of Nature through the work of reason, appears to be "the end of animality and stupidity [*bêtise*]" (SH 8). But for Levinas, this epistemic and technological mastery over the natural world is instead an extension of the prevailing attitude of animality, the *conatus*, which he associates with the figure of Messer Gaster, Rabelais's caricature of the desiring ego—"without ears, like a hungry stomach" (TI 134).[8] The *conatus* is specifically deaf to its exposure to others. But Levinas's intent in all of these references to animals is to describe human tendencies, or the inhuman tendencies endemic to the human.

Levinas's scattered remarks about nonhuman animals themselves uncritically replicate the assumptions that a clear distinction can be drawn between human and nonhuman animals and that this boundary designates the proper realm of moral considerability.[9] Among other recent scholars, Derrida argues that this boundary is anything but epistemically self-evident or morally innocuous. Anthropocentrism instead has a determinate history that normalizes violence against nonhuman animals: Levinas's subjects "are 'men' in a world where sacrifice is possible and where it is not forbidden to make an attempt on life in general, but only on human life, on the neighbor's life."[10] The suffering of animals becomes habitually seen as morally justified and practically necessitated by human interests, and in this sense, such suffering becomes (almost) morally invisible. Hence Derrida's claim that Levinas, like the most dominant strains of Western thought, does not "sacrifice sacrifice."[11] Ultimately, he is unwilling to give up the instrumentalization of animals for human ends.[12] In this way, Levinas participates in a general negation of the moral considerability of animals. Both the deaths and the highly managed lives of animals (particularly those in factory farms)—"an artificial, infernal, virtually interminable survival"—apparently should not, on his account, invoke an immemorial obligation that is at the center of Levinas's thought.[13]

For Derrida, the Darwinian trauma that claims that human beings belong to one species among others has not fundamentally disrupted a "denial or disavowal" of animality, which has become only more powerful in the structures of human existence in the last century and a half.[14] In the denial of any proximity to nonhuman animals, violence against them is normalized and made invisible in various ways. The killing of animals happens under government regulation in "meat-processing" facilities that employ low-income and especially immigrant workers and that are isolated from the bloodless spaces in which we buy and consume food. The contradictions involved in these processes indicate the cultural tensions that run through the attempt to establish nonhuman animals as morally inconsiderable: "No one can deny seriously any more, or for very long, that men do all they can in order to dissimulate this cruelty or to hide it from themselves; in order to organize on a global scale the forgetting and misunderstanding of this violence"—a violence that is both the destruction and manipulation of populations.[15] Levinas almost entirely ignores such violence and so implicitly treats such practices of production and consumption as morally permissible.

When Levinas is pressed to respond to the issue of the suffering of animals in an interview, he quickly prioritizes the suffering of human beings by claiming that our compassion for animals arises out of a "transference to animals of the idea of suffering" in humans (PM 172). This stance echoes Kant's claim that we should not harm animals unnecessarily because it will desensitize us to the moral implications of harming human beings.[16] We have no "immediate duties"—either direct or indirect—to animals, but our obligations to other human beings generate norms of behavior toward animals: "our duties towards them [animals] are indirect duties to humanity."[17] Inflicting suffering on animals does not amount to any direct wrongdoing, except insofar as that act makes such violence habitual and easier to inflict on human beings: "a person who displays such cruelty to animals is also no less hardened towards men."[18] Like Kant, Levinas attempts to establish an impermeable moral boundary between human and nonhuman animals, but this boundary runs counter to the psychological tendency that they both acknowledge: our behavior toward nonhuman animals shapes our behavior toward human animals.

Derrida puts pressure on this tension by rejecting the attempt to draw a clear distinction between human and nonhuman animals, on the basis of language or nonmechanical responsiveness (for instance). He revives Bentham's claim that the right question about animals is not "Can they think?" or "Can they talk?" but "Can they suffer?"[19] For Derrida, in this respect Levinas does not radically challenge the prejudices of the Western philosophical tradition: "Would it suffice for an ethics to remind the subject (as Levinas will have attempted) of its being-subject, its being-host or hostage, and thus its being-subject to the other, the Wholly Other or to any other [*au Tout-Autre ou à tout autre*]? I do not believe so. This does not suffice to break the Cartesian tradition of the animal-machine with neither language nor response."[20] Levinas participates in this Cartesian tradition to the extent that he refuses animals the possibility of response and of responsibility—they are capable only of instinctual behavior, motivated entirely by the "law of being" (PM 175). In place of a decisive separation between humanity and animality, Derrida proposes thinking of the boundary as "more than one internally divided line; ... as a result, it can no longer be traced, objectified, or counted as single or indivisible."[21] He is at pains to distance himself from the position that there is no significant difference between human and nonhuman animals. The claim that the line cannot be drawn in any simple way does not amount to the claim that it cannot be drawn at all. But the characteristics of that line are immersed in a contingent history, which need to be submitted to a kind of genealogical analysis.[22] Levinas's exclusion of animals from the ethical sphere belongs to that contingent history, for all his resistance to the ideal of the sovereign subject, an ideal that in its projection of embodiment, temporality, and determinism onto animals is profoundly entangled with anthropocentrism.

Despite this near-exclusive focus on human experience, Levinas's approach to ethics also opens up a more complicated account of the relationship between human and nonhuman animals. His "rehabilitation" of heteronomy, his emphasis on the ethical significance of embodiment, and his claim that the perpetuation of the I's existence involves violence toward others all raise profound challenges to anthropocentrism, particularly in its connections to the ideal of sovereignty. Levinas's claims about alterity cannot be simply extended to animals, living things, or all things in general.[23] However, given the anarchic quality of responsibility, it is unclear how he can draw well-defined boundaries around who counts as my neighbor.[24] Such uncertainty is itself ethically significant.

Consumption as Usurpation

In the project of unsettling anthropocentrism, one resource offered by Levinas's thought begins from an idea discussed in chapter 5: that my very existence functions as a form of usurpation, in the sense that in living my ordinary life—eating, driving, heating my house, using devices powered by electricity or batteries, buying clothes—I am consuming resources that others lack and thus contributing to the degradation of others' lives. These actions may also contribute to institutions and practices specifically founded on the exploitation of others.[25] The others whom Levinas has in mind are always human others, but the concern about usurpation leads to a larger set of questions about the resources that I consume. By eating I am not only taking the food from the mouth of another, and enjoying the fruits of another's alienated labor, but more or less directly deriving nutrients from other living things.[26] This Levinasian interpretation of eating overlaps significantly with Marx's analysis of commodity fetishism, in the sense that the history by which commodity is produced—principally, the labor power of human beings—is obscured. In resisting this erasure and the accompanying feeling that consumption is morally neutral, we become aware of an ethically complicated history behind the products that we consume, where the processes of consumption had appeared to be ethically neutral. And we are "sobered up" to this significance only retrospectively. As Derrida emphasizes, one must eat in order to live, and therefore "the moral question is thus not, nor has it ever been: should one eat or not eat, eat this and not that, the living or the nonliving, man or animal, but since *one must* eat in any case and since it is and tastes good to eat, and since there's no other definition of the good [*du bien*], *how* for goodness' sake should one eat well [*bien manger*]?"[27] To the extent that responsibility always *interrupts* the *conatus*, its force is traumatic both in being unexpected and in sobering up the ego to what it has already done, the accusation that has been launched against it. The challenge to the ego's right to be, and to do what is necessary to survive or merely to fulfill its desires, comes after its complacent pursuit of those ends. But even after this sobering up, there is no set of choices that would guarantee one's moral innocence.

Contemporary discussions concerning the ethics of eating reflect both the desire for moral purification and its impossibility. Simply choosing not to eat animals, or animal products more broadly, or plants produced without the use of pesticides or genetic modification, does not disrupt one's entanglement in how consumption depends upon forms of injustice, as Lisa Heldke argues: "I cannot even choose a diet in which I am not complicit in the oppression of others. I can, however, choose to withdraw support from systems that oppress and exploit workers, animals, and the soil."[28] There is no question of *whether* I am complicit in the exploitation of others (both human and nonhuman), but only of *how* I am complicit and which choices within that framework could diminish that exploitation. That critical reflection can only happen retrospectively, and with the ongoing awareness of how my existence depends upon structural inequalities, systematized violence (particularly toward animals), and ecological devastation. For Heldke, this complicity highlights the relational nature of the self, and how eating, among other activities, impacts those around us, even if those relationships happen to be invisible to us: "It is not a matter of *deciding* to become involved with others' lives [including those of nonhuman others], but of recognizing the ways in which I am inevitably a part of them.... I must recognize that I cannot choose to become involved or not, but can only choose (to some extent) the nature of my involvement."[29] This relational structure means that I can never eat with an entirely good conscience, in Levinas's terms. In his comments about the usurpation of resources from the Third World, he emphasizes how our complacency about not only getting enough to eat but satisfying quite ordinary desires comes at a cost to others: "In the Old Testament there is the sixth commandment, 'Thou shalt not kill.' This does not mean simply that you are not to go around firing a gun all the time. It refers, rather, to the fact that, in the course of your life, in different ways, you kill someone. For example, when we sit down at the table in the morning and drink coffee, we kill an Ethiopian who doesn't have any coffee" (PM 173).[30] Consumption is thus a usurpation, and an unavoidable usurpation undergirding the continuation of our lives, and of the lives of our children and parents and friends. The kind of usurpation in question widens (in a way that Levinas would reject) when we consider not only the lives of human beings but the lives of animals and plants. In that case, we stand accused not only of the taking of food from others, but the eating of animals or food produced through farming and distribution practices that destroy habitats or introduce toxic chemicals into the soil, water, and air.

Levinas seems to acknowledge at least some of this moral uneasiness around eating animals at the beginning of the short, strange essay "The Name of a Dog, or Natural Rights." This is almost the only text in which he focuses explicitly on nonhuman animals, as opposed to the animality of human beings (although that theme is also at work in this essay, which concludes with a recollection of his time as a prisoner of war in Germany). He begins with a quote from Exodus: "'You shall be men consecrated to me; therefore you shall not eat any flesh that is torn by beasts in the field; you shall cast it to the dogs' (Exodus 22:31)" (ND 151). There is a trifold distinction in this passage, among the "beasts in the field [or the heath]," the dogs, and "consecrated" human beings. Levinas wonders whether the verse refers to the domesticated dog, who has lost "the last noble vestiges of its wild nature, the crouching, servile, contemptible dog," or the dog whose domestication may be deceptive: "in the twilight [*entre chien et loup*] (and what light in the world is not already this dusk?), does it concern [refer to] the one who is a wolf under his dogged faithfulness, and thirsts after blood, be it coagulated or fresh?" (ND 151–52). The colloquial phrase for twilight—literally, "between dog and wolf"—evokes the uncertainty of the boundary between day and night or the familiar and the threatening. There is an uncanny ambiguity about whether dogs are fully domesticated, trustworthy members of the household or whether they might unpredictably revert to savagery. Levinas says of dogs in a separate interview: "A dog is like a wolf that doesn't bite. There is a trace of the wolf in the dog" (PM 172). But he makes clear in both the interview and "The Name of a Dog" that he is not referring only or even primarily to dogs. In the light of the fact that this discussion of Exodus leads into his memories of a Nazi prison camp, in which a dog named Bobby is only one who treats the prisoners as human, this uncertainty about dogs and wolves is the fragility with which responsibility, or the good, interrupts the "law of being" in human beings. The suspension of the *conatus* is never definitive or absolute, but it always bears the risk of falling back into the war of all against all and moral complacency in the midst of that violence.

Levinas invites this connection between the uncertainty of canine behavior and the uncertainty of human behavior, but his discussion slides over the difference between domestication, through which dogs are trained to no longer behave like wolves, and the possibility of the ethical eruption of the human within the animal. However, this is supposed to be the clear boundary between human and nonhuman animals—that humans are capable of responding ethically to the other, whereas dogs only follow their manipulated instincts. The shadowy quality of this distinction continues in Levinas's discussion of eating. The idea that human beings are consecrated, designated as sacred beings, or belonging to a moral order, is juxtaposed with an anxiety about the proximity between human carnivory and "butchery": "the sight of flesh torn by beasts in the field" may be "meat too strong for the digestion of the honest man who, even if he is carnivore, still feels he is watched over by God" (ND 151). The "bloody struggles" of wolves or other beasts are repeated in hunting games and war. Even the act of eating meat in the ritualized, mediated setting of the "family table"—"as you plunge your fork into your roast"—may call to mind that violence between or within species (ND 151). Levinas emphasizes here the uncomfortable moral status of eating meat, which can only through various religious limitations be distinguished from the violence of a dog-eat-dog world.[31] Despite his prevailing anthropocentrism, in this essay he opens the question of whether those distinctions between animal and human violence in the act of eating hold up under scrutiny.

Still, Levinas concludes that dogs are only tamed wild animals, who receive the flesh "torn by beasts in the field" from human hands, so that those human hands may remain morally pure. This also entails that the dog remains unconsecrated and experiences no guilt as it eats: "by virtue of its happy nature and direct thoughts, the dog transforms all this flesh cast to it in the field into good flesh" (ND 152). On Levinas's reading, dogs cannot suffer from a bad conscience, because they do not seem to be addressed by the other. Training that builds on instinct drives them to act as predators or pets. As Derrida notes, dogs in this essay come to stand for all nonhuman animals, regardless of the wide variations between animals, in terms of cognitive functioning, communication, and social behavior.[32] Levinas therefore seems to assert that "the animal" is incapable of responsibility. By invoking this distinction, he withdraws from the thought that our existence is premised not only on violence toward other human beings, but toward living things in general. For Levinas, those particular kinds of usurpations seem to be justified, even if they generate fleeting moral qualms, because only human animals can respond rather than merely react.[33]

The Problem of the Face

But the question of whether animals are capable of responding is not the right question for Levinas, just as the specific characteristics of the other do not determine my obligations to her. The issue is whether human beings might have responsibility *to* or *for* nonhuman animals, not whether nonhuman animals in general or which kinds of nonhuman animals are capable of responsibility. Responsibility does not depend on reciprocity, in the asymmetrical encounter with the other. When Levinas is asked about this in an interview, the question takes the form of whether animals have faces. He responds by affirming the "priority of the human face" over nonhuman animals, in whom "the face is not in its purest form" (PM 169). But Levinas does not typically use the language of "purity" to describe the face or suggest that there might be relative levels of "facedness." David Clark notes the strangeness of talking about "an absolute demand and responsibility—which is what the face usually connotes in Levinas's work—that is also partial."[34] Strangely, then, animals may have faces, but a comparatively weak form of that authority. This claim resonates oddly with Levinas's claim that the face is not a phenomenon that could be conceptualized and then compared to other phenomena.

Unlike the response to the other, whose command is binding *not* because I recognize a shared characteristic, Levinas asserts that the obligation that I may feel toward the animal rests on the "transfer" of the experience of suffering from human to nonhuman animals (PM 172). Perpich argues that Levinas generally refuses a utilitarian focus on suffering as the ground of responsibility, because in his account no "quality or capacity, no matter how important or distinctive, is that in virtue of which I am responsible to or for an other."[35] This is clearly true in the case of human others, but when Levinas speaks of the choice not to eat meat or the desire to spare animals unnecessary suffering, it is precisely their shared capacity for suffering that he cites. Our obligations to animals, such as they are, arise through an analogy to our own experience: "It is because we, as human, know what suffering is that we can have this obligation" (PM 172). The moral feeling that we have toward animals is grounded in the self-regarding focus of the *conatus*, simply extended to others, rather than its interruption. This analogical transfer produces "pity" without raising the fundamental question of my right to exist (PM 172). No traumatic obligation arises from the encounter with the nonhuman animal.

There are anomalous passages, specifically about the suffering of hunger, in which Levinas appeals to a similar analogy as the basis for responsibility between human beings.[36] Once again, he characterizes the concern with another's hunger as the "bursting" of the human into the animal concern with one's own hunger (SH 10). The animating force of this sense of obligation is a "transference which goes from the memory of my own hunger to the suffering and the responsibility for the hunger of the neighbor" (SH 11). Although hunger is perhaps the most primitive expression of the self-interestedness of the *conatus*, we may also recognize hunger in another person and by analogy feel bound by that need that mirrors our own. Levinas claims that although we are anesthetized to many things in modern life, we remain "strangely sensitive in our secularized and technological world to the hunger of the other man . . . [which] awakens men from their sated drowsing and sobers them up from their self-sufficiency" (SH 11). The sobering up depends here upon an identification between my past experience of hunger and the other's present suffering. This derivation of responsibility drains it of traumatic force and frames the other as an alter ego.

More typically, Levinas avoids drawing such analogies between the self and the other, so that the other does not devolve into a being-with-attributes: "All the others that obsess me in the other do not affect me as examples of the same genus united with my neighbor by resemblance or common nature, individuations of the human race . . . fraternity precedes the commonness of a genus" (OB 159). Appealing to commonality would again premise one's sense of obligation upon a recognition that is present to consciousness or a contract to which the autonomous subject has committed himself, even implicitly. That is, the diachronic, traumatic significance of responsibility would be muted if we comprehended the other as the possessor of certain morally significant traits. Unlike human others, however, nonhuman animals *can* be understood as beings-with-attributes, including sharing the capacity to suffer. But Levinas's account simultaneously suggests that their suffering has little moral standing in comparison with human suffering—even more specifically, in the face of human hunger, which can be justifiably sated by the eating of animals.

In this sense, nonhuman animals are phenomena in a way that the human face is not, with attributes and capacities that can be recognized. Perpich notes that Levinas could acknowledge the possibility of an "animal politics," in which certain actions or practices are justified with regard to animals.[37] But in his conceptual framework there is no such thing as animal *ethics*. Levinas's refusal to grant animals faces (at least in their purest form) seems to replicate the structure of the very problem of the *conatus* to which his project responds, which Levinas refers to as evil: the failure to see the other as a source of ethical authority, in the specific sense of diminishing the other to a phenomenon to be comprehended or manipulated.

However, in Levinas's account, the question of what makes a being morally considerable is unanswerable. There is no definitive attribute that causes or justifies the I's response to the other. Levinas gestures in this direction under sustained questioning about whether animals have faces: "I cannot say at what moment you have the right to be called 'face.' The human face is completely different and only afterwards do we discover the face of an animal. I don't know if a snake has a face. I can't answer that question. A more specific analysis is needed" (PM 171). For all his avowed confusion, Levinas's language here is careful. A right is a possession proper to a particular kind of being—by virtue of being a citizen or a certain kind of organism, we have rights. But a face does not belong to this order of political recognition, in which our mutual obligations, freedoms, and protections can be constitutionally articulated. Nonetheless, Levinas clearly distinguishes the authority of a human face from the ambiguity or impurity of an animal face (in this case, a snake). He is certain that humans have faces but uncertain about whether snakes do. Bob Plant comments sardonically on Levinas's claim that he cannot yet answer this question, "Precisely what sort of 'analysis' Levinas has in mind remains unclear."[38] What sort of study would establish whether snakes have faces, if the face is not a phenomenon?

As the autobiographical reflections of "The Name of a Dog" essay indicate, part of Levinas's ambivalence stems from the historical context of twentieth-century genocides, violence frequently normalized through a dehumanization that was explicitly also a bestialization. Clark suggests that Levinas refuses to grant moral considerability to dogs—even to the singular dog named Bobby, who earned the title of the "last Kantian in Nazi Germany" (ND 153)—because "the sentimental humanization of animals and the brutal animalization of humans are two sides of the same assimilating gesture."[39] Given the history of racist identifications between those designated as subhuman and nonhuman animals, allowing any permeability in the boundary between human and nonhuman animals seems to court the possibility of degrading politically or socially marginalized human beings—even if belonging to a species is not the ground of the other's transcendence or diachrony, on Levinas's account. He recalls that his fellow prisoners, separated from other French prisoners of war because they were Jews, were "stripped . . . of their human skin": "We were subhuman, a gang of apes . . . despite all their vocabulary, beings without language. . . . How can we deliver a message about our humanity which, from behind the bars of quotation marks, will come across as anything other than monkey talk?" (ND 153). The prisoners were excluded from being able to *address* anyone; being able to produce words does not guarantee the traumatic authority of saying.[40] Words can be treated as only mechanical repetitions or degenerate imitations of speech in all of its sociality. In his language of "monkey talk," Levinas reinforces the anthropocentric assumption that only human beings legitimately use language and can speak, but his claim is also that the address of even the human other is ignored or foreclosed in the midst of interhuman violence.

Given this historical context, Levinas resists any fluidity between the categories of the human and nonhuman. However, the tensions that run through "The Name of a Dog" link what Clark calls the "animalization of humans," the dehumanization of the prisoners by German soldiers and bystanders, with the "animalization of animals," the degradation and violence visited on nonhuman animals. This normalized exclusion from moral considerability also underlies Derrida's neologism *animot*: "The animal is a word, it is an appellation that men have instituted, a name they have given themselves the right and the authority to give to the living other."[41] Naming becomes a form of domination. Animals are subject to conceptual assimilation in order to become "a variably meaningful figure in service of configuring and consolidating the exemplarity of the human."[42] This is the kind of assimilation that Levinas refers to as the totalizing activity of consciousness, in which the other functions as a way of reflecting the self. Levinas's own ambivalence about the animalization of animals arises in his characterization of Bobby as bearing witness to the humanity of the prisoners, even nonlinguistically, through the embodied joy of his greetings: "jumping up and down and barking in delight" (ND 153). Bobby's witness prefigures Levinas's own witness, even if the latter "has always already usurped Bobby's place in our reading of it."[43] Bobby has a name and is thus recognized at some level as an individual, but this recognition does not extend to seeing him as an other. In the internal tensions in his writings about animality, Levinas enacts his own claim that "one cannot entirely refuse the face of an animal"—but one can mostly refuse it (PM 169).

Both Llewelyn and Derrida claim that Levinas's perplexity about whether the snake has a face raises serious issues for Levinas's larger work, in the sense that perhaps a tradition of religious anthropocentrism structures and lends its authority to what seems to be the anarchical moment of responsibility. In Levinas's inability to articulate definitively who or what has a face, Derrida sees the collapse of Levinas's ethical project:

> declaring that he doesn't know where the right to be called "face" begins means confessing that one doesn't know at bottom what a face is, what the word means, what governs its usage, and that means confessing that one didn't say what responding means. Doesn't that amount, as a result, to calling into

question the whole legitimacy of the discourse and ethics of the "face" of the other, the legitimacy and even the sense of every proposition concerning the alterity of the other, the other as my neighbor or my brother, etc.?[44]

In other words, how can we make justifiable claims about responsibility, and who addresses me in such a way as to provoke that responsibility, if we cannot define who has a face?

Agnosticism

In Levinas's defense, his uncertainty is significant, in the sense his response is consistent with his claim that the face is not a series of attributes that could guarantee the I's response to the other. Perpich argues that Levinas's refusal to draw a conceptual line between a face and a nonface reminds us that the significance of a face "is not reducible to its visual or perceptible form. It is a liminal figure, a structure that 'undoes' its own form."[45] The face has no place in a causal order, as one phenomenon among others. Levinas claims that "the face is not a force. It is an authority" (PM 169). The face is not an object that *possesses* either force or authority that could be examined and verified. It *is* an authority—it *is* the demand or the accusation, by which we are obligated and bound to the other. The question of the source of this authority is the wrong question: if we could explain what allows the other to speak to us in this accusatory way, responsibility could be reduced to an identifiable cause (such as the other's vulnerability, mortality, or suffering). Then Levinas would be giving us a version of utilitarianism. What makes the face an authority is that it eludes the activity of consciousness, as Perpich argues: "while it is a mistake to think that [Levinas's] view is that the face of the other is entirely unknowable in the usual sense, as if we simply had no access to the other at all, it is equally problematic, however, to assimilate the exceptional presentation of the self in a face and the ethical commandment that translates this expression to something that we then *know* or that is incumbent on us or claims us in the same way that a belief or a knowledge claim."[46] The face is not intelligible but it also imposes its significance: this is the structure of trauma. It is entirely in keeping with Levinas's claims about the face that he cannot articulate who has one, even if this renders his philosophical account of responsibility incomplete.

But this lacuna leads to the issue of why a nonhuman animal would be categorically barred from commanding us in this way—why the animal has only an "impure" face. This question is only intensified by remembering that Levinas uses the language of the face only to gesture to the ethical significance of the other, how I am addressed by the "extreme precariousness" of the other (PP 167). I need not be able to see the face of the other in order to encounter this address, but instead might only have to stand behind someone in line to see "their raised shoulders with shoulder blades tense like springs, which seemed to cry, sob, and scream."[47] If the face is not a set of determinate characteristics, or even necessarily a face, we cannot say in advance what or who will address us in an ethical sense. Barbara Jane Davy notes that Levinas's claims about the face or the eyes speaking are metaphorical and "should not be forced back into literality.... If an eye can speak why not a leaf?"[48] The non-literal status of an eye or the naked skin of the face speaking allows Levinas to preserve its status as a trace, that which arises out of the immemorial past, binding the self absolutely and eluding the synthesizing, representing "nets of consciousness."[49]

Levinas wants to draw a clear line between the anarchical moral command of the other (human) person, and the kinds of obligations that are compatible with the *conatus*—such as compassion for animals through an analogy with our own experiences. But if responsibility is anarchical, this line cannot hold. Derrida reads Levinas as excluding animals from moral considerability on the basis of their inability to use language,[50] but Peter Atterton objects that "this wrongly conflates what Levinas calls 'expression' with some form of linguistic behavior.... The face does not require language."[51] The saying is how the other *addresses* me, with or without words. So this boundary turns out to hinge on the question of whether I am addressed by the nonhuman animal, rather than objectively identifiable characteristics that it may or may not possess, or experiences that I may or may not share with it. In his commitment to anarchic responsibility—the utterly unpredictable way in which the other makes a claim on me—Levinas's anthropocentrism seems like an arbitrary limitation on who or what can address me. Matthew Calarco argues that Levinas should be "committed to a notion of *universal ethical consideration*, that is, an agnostic form of ethical consideration that has no a priori constraints or boundaries."[52] No being can be excluded in advance from at least the possibility of being morally considerable, particularly because moral considerability does not rest on the characteristics of that organism but on whether the I is addressed by that being. It is there that the diachronic quality of responsibility becomes significant—the origin of my responsibility is immemorial, and that responsibility breaks in on me in such a way that I cannot step back to analyze its legitimacy and then either affirm or reject its binding power. The traits of the other do not serve as the ground of justification for that experience of exposure. For this reason, the kind of being who could make that claim on me remains undetermined.

One reason to remain agnostic about what or who can address us is Levinas's association between the physical vulnerability of embodiment and the moral vulnerability of exposure to the other. Levinas's description of the subject as embodied and vulnerable has some affinity with the Darwinian trauma that unsettles humans' belief in their superiority over other animals. Both accounts challenge the power of consciousness to distance human beings from a merely natural existence and thus also challenge the ideal of self-possession. For Levinas that claim to self-possession belongs on a continuum with the struggle for survival that characterizes the natural world, and so he looks for a more radical kind of break from the *conatus*. If animality is understood not simply in terms of self-interested aggression, but *also* as the sensibility of embodiment, then it is as animals that we are exposed to the other. Guenther argues that Levinas's emphasis on the body as the "site of enjoyment and suffering, of sensibility and nonsense" runs counter to the idealization of the sovereign subject in modern Western thought, an idealization maintained through the projection of heteronomy on nonhuman animals: "the most relevant distinction for an ethics of exposure would not be between human and animal, but rather between the sensible animal (human or otherwise) and a certain (characteristically human) denial of sensible animality. The ethical challenge would not be to rise above one's animal self-interest, but rather to resist closing off one's animal-human exposure for the sake of a safer, more protected and self-possessed model of consciousness."[53] Levinas's principal concern is the disavowal of responsibility, and thus the disavowal of exposure, that allows the subject to conceive of itself as sovereign. Guenther here contrasts the need to "rise above one's animal self-interest" and the need "to resist closing off one's animal-human exposure." But Levinas is clearly interested in both, although he would only recognize the use of the term "animal" in the first instance. If we reject his identification of animality with the *conatus* (recognizing it as a historically contingent, highly questionable interpretation of the natural world), and adhere to his connection between vulnerability and sensibility, the ethical interruption of self-interest *is* one's "animal-human exposure." To the extent that the body in its vulnerability has ethical significance, it is as animals that we are capable of or open to responsibility. This line of argument approaches the claim that we share something morally significant with animals—a life of sensible vulnerability. But the crucial idea is that disavowing the animal supports the ideal of self-possessed sovereignty, in which our exposure or liability is clearly defined, and we can comprehend our moral obligations. The core of Levinas's project runs counter to that deflection of responsibility, the conception of subjectivity that it protects, and the moral complacency it produces.

Establishing who or what is morally considerable amounts to a form of conceptual mastery over responsibility (a negation of its diachronic and traumatic quality), and I have argued in this section that this standard cannot be clearly drawn in Levinas's account. But the permeability of this boundary, or the existence of multiple lines of convergence and divergence between human and nonhuman animals, does not negate the legitimacy of his project, as Derrida suggests. This uncertainty about who counts as the other reflects the larger fragility of responsibility in Levinas's thought, in which the vulnerability of the other may provoke either violence or the interruption of violence, and in any case is not a matter of establishing the truth about any being. Discussing philosophical disagreements about the range of morally considerable organisms, Calarco comments that "these efforts ... are useful for highlighting how particular entities (individualistic criteria) or networks of interaction (holistic criteria) might have an ethical claim on us," but that this debate also misses something crucial: "*it proceeds as if the question of moral consideration is one that permits of a final answer. If ethics arises from an encounter with an Other who is fundamentally irreducible to and unanticipatable by my egoistic and cognitive machinations, then how could this question ever be answered fully?*"[54] This reading of Levinas emphasizes the need for repeated interruptions of political calculations by the unsettled ethical question of whether I have a right to be. On the one hand, societies must establish laws and individuals will act according to determinate judgments about who is morally considerable, but on the other, these judgments remain open to the traumatic authority of a form of responsibility that precedes the interpretation of constitutions, debates about the rights of citizens, and other forms of moral reasoning. Levinas's project centers on that ethical rupture of political calculations.

For Levinas, one of the most pernicious side effects of reducing ethics to a normative system, or a set of principles that can be rationally examined, is the tendency toward moral complacency, in which the subject is always already protected against the trauma of responsibility. One might perceive obligations but encounter them as deriving from one's actions or commitments, not as diachronous, immemorial claims that arise from no action or intent of my own. For this reason, Levinas emphasizes that any existence, no matter how carefully it is morally navigated, is implicated in the usurping violence of the *conatus*. There is no way to avoid this moral complicity, even if choices around consumption can minimize one's carbon footprint, one's participation in factory farming, or one's investment in environmentally unfriendly corporations. Vegetarianism or veganism as practical responses to this concern carry the risk of a good conscience, ignoring the broader issue of the symbolic sacrifice of animality in preserving anthropocentrism.[55] There is no unassailable answer, however ascetic, to the question of how to "eat well." This uncertainty should not lead to paralysis or resignation, but instead to a restless questioning of the adequacy of our moral calculations. The uncertainty of responding well to others (which others?) also means that there is no method by which we can reliably cultivate attunement to others, human or nonhuman. As Levinas's discourse suggests, however, philosophical discussion of these issues has some role to play in inviting us to challenge our right to be and to consume and then *how* we consume.

The Limits of Moral Arguments about Animals

This question of whether I am addressed in this moral sense by "the animal" in general, by any species or genera of animals, or by any singular animal (as in the case of Bobby or Derrida's cat in *The Animal That Therefore I Am*) has prompted discussion in far-flung pockets of contemporary philosophy—obviously in debates around animal ethics, but also increasingly in philosophy of mind and in political philosophy.[56] Despite his anthropocentrism, what Levinas can contribute to these debates is a reminder about the limits of philosophical discourse in capturing the dynamic of being morally compelled by another. What does the activity of theoretical representation, analysis, and evaluation, which has been taken to be essentially and definitively human, distort or neglect when applied to the subject of nonhuman animals and their relation to human beings?

More specifically, the tendency to draw boundaries around morally considerable organisms on the basis of particular characteristics ignores the set of questions that Levinas raises around authority—the source of normativity. Once again, the issue of methodology engages what sort of subject is presupposed by certain kinds of argumentation. If arguments around animal ethics reaffirm the ideal of the sovereign subject, capable of comparing and contrasting the traits of human and nonhuman animals, they miss the emergence of responsibility as Levinas describes it and therefore fail to address the dominant refusal to consider nonhuman animals as morally considerable. In this way, Levinas's project converges with some of the work that Cora Diamond has done to evaluate the approaches of animal rights and animal welfare advocates. In her early paper, "Eating Meat and Eating People," and again in her more recent "The Difficulty of Reality and the Difficulty of Philosophy," Diamond argues that utilitarian attempts to advocate for animal welfare fail to take animal suffering into account in important respects. Without disagreeing with their conclusions, she claims that the procedure of such arguments deflect the moral significance of animals by reducing them to a set of abstract characteristics. Even the capacity to suffer can be domesticated in a concept—we call it sentience. With this term "deflection," Diamond suggests that mainstream philosophical arguments engage in a kind of motivated distraction from the core of the issue around animals. She accuses philosophers of sheltering us (and themselves) from the vulnerability bound up with sentience:

> The awareness we each have of being a living body, being "alive to the world," carries with it exposure to the bodily sense of vulnerability to death, sheer animal vulnerability, the vulnerability we share with them. . . . Is there any difficulty in seeing why we should not prefer to return to moral debate, in which the livingness and death of animals enter as facts that we treat as relevant in this or that way, not as presences that may unseat our reason?[57]

This passage is part of Diamond's reading of J. M. Coetzee's novel *The Lives of Animals*, in which she is interested in illuminating how the central character, Elizabeth Costello, is wounded, rather than being merely philosophically troubled, by the reduction of animals to morally inconsiderable beings. The "vulnerability we share with them" can be read literally as the shared characteristic of mortality, but Diamond describes vulnerability in terms that bring her very close to what Levinas means by ethical exposure—the unseating of reason. John McDowell comments on her argument that our inability to capture this exposure to the significance of animals "dislodges us from comfortably inhabiting our nature as speaking animals, animals who can make sense of things in the way the capacity to speak enables us. The special kind of animal life we lead comes into question."[58] The fact that the lives and deaths of animals may dislodge us from our status as knowing, speaking beings seems significantly aligned with Levinas's challenge to sovereign subjectivity and the sorts of moral reasoning proper to that subject.

In the face of such wounding, Peter Singer's utilitarian argument against eating animals, in extending moral considerability to nonhuman animals on the basis of their ability to feel pain, does not capture our "fundamental moral relation" to animals.[59] The recognition of a being as sentient is not the source of our obligation, as Levinas's experience in a prisoner of war camp (among many other examples) attests, and so the argument that animals are sentient beings or have interests of their own is "in the wrong dimension."[60] For Diamond, these arguments tend to be ineffectual in part because our conception of personhood is bound up with a whole host of social conventions about moral considerability: "We learn what a human being is in—among other ways—sitting at a table where WE eat THEM. We are around the table and they are on it."[61] We do not discover the difference between human and nonhuman animals so much as inherit it and perpetuate it in our way of life. The problem with utilitarian arguments is that they ignore that it is not the capacity to suffer itself that creates moral obligation, and thus what is likely to shift how most people think about animals is not a philosophical argument that points out such a capacity. What matters is instead the significance that the suffering being holds for us, what it is to us. The conclusions of utilitarian arguments may be correct without being able to gain traction with the dominant moral intuitions of contemporary culture and without questioning the ideal of the sovereign subject that is entangled with anthropocentrism, because they neglect the anarchic source of normativity as Levinas describes it. Our complacency about our right to be, and to eat or otherwise sacrifice animals in perpetuating that existence, shapes whether we will perceive the suffering of animals as morally problematic.

To draw out the complexity of the significance attributed to animals, Diamond discusses, again using literary examples, evocations of the "extraordinarily confused and conflicting ways"[62] that animals show up in human life: as pets, as food, as predators, as vermin, as experimental subjects, as service animals, as entertainment, as "fellow creatures."[63] This last kind of comportment, treating animals as fellow creatures, does not rest on the recognition of biological similarity or any other characteristic about the animals in question: "It does not mean, biologically an animal, something with *biological life*—it means being in a certain boat, as it were, of whom it makes sense to say, among other things, that it goes off into Time's enormous Nought, and which may be sought as *company*."[64] It is instead a matter of the much less philosophically crisp notion of what those lives mean for us—whether there is any possibility of taking their suffering or their well-being seriously. How we respond to suffering depends on how that suffering is heard and received, and Diamond acknowledges that our cultural training and perhaps individual sensitivities shape our moral attunements.

In her critique of animal welfare arguments, Diamond echoes a constant theme in Levinas's work: that moral obligation is not created through the intellectual recognition of moral considerability or any of the traits that might qualify an organism for moral considerability. If we could establish sentience as a standard of moral considerability, we could more or less clearly delineate our moral obligations, without attending to how our reasoning powers are put out of play by the address of the other. That is, such abstract arguments once more position the moral reasoner as a knower and judge. The face of the other demands our response, but not as a physical set of features, or a presence that could be empirically verified. A face reduced to its features would no longer make a moral demand. Instead, as Levinas says, "the face is a trace of itself, given over to my responsibility" (OB 91). As a trace, the face cannot be the conceptual foundation for a moral judgment. It operates in a different register than deontological or utilitarian arguments about our abstract, universal duties to others or to ourselves. As a singular subject, I am addressed by or exposed to the singular other. Although that exposure may have to be transformed into the calculation of my relative obligations, the exposure itself is not reducible to a set of characteristics, which can be neutrally examined and weighed by the knowing subject: "this is not about receiving an order by perceiving it first and obeying it subsequently in a decision, an act of will. In this proximity of the face, the subservience of obedience precedes the hearing of the order" (FO 151). Proximity generates the lateness of comprehension and moral deliberation, in the sense that we respond *before* consciously understanding the demand of the other.

Surrounding this shared rejection of objective characteristics as a basis for moral considerability, there are significant divergences in Levinas's and Diamond's accounts, specifically with regard to the role of cultural training in our moral attunement. In her Wittgensteinian orientation, Diamond gestures to cultural norms as the source of our moral repugnance about the idea of eating people, even those who are already dead and whose deaths we have not caused. But no such repugnance is generally associated with the eating of nonhuman animals, because eating them is woven into the way (many) people live their lives: "Animals—

these objects we are acting upon—are not given for our thought independently of such a mass of ways of thinking about and responding to them."[65] There may also be individual variations in whether we see animals (or certain kinds of animals, or particular animals) as fellow-creatures or not. Diamond acknowledges that there may be people who have no "fellow-creature response" at all.[66] By contrast, Levinas makes no reference to how our cultural inheritances or individual characters shape our sense of responsibility. The response to the other is the ground for subjectivity itself, a response "outside of history" rather than a product of it. By raising the question of what our moral obligations are, or what right we have to be, we engage in an act of saying that presupposes an openness to the other—an indeterminate other who makes a claim on us. However we answer that question, whatever norms we decide on, what Perpich calls "the moment of normativity"—the binding quality of another's demand of me—has already happened.[67]

Levinas would certainly also reject the language of "fellow-feeling," in its connotations of mutuality and in its evocation of emotion. The exposure to alterity is not something that the subject experiences as one mood or internal state among others. What he calls "compassion" has this more mundane meaning, a psychologically contingent "natural sentiment on the part of him who was hungry once, toward the other and for the hunger of the other" (GDT 173). This kind of shared identity with the other is contrasted with substitution, in which the other is "a way of signifying that is *wholly other* than manifestation, monstration, and, consequently, vision" (GDT 173, emphasis added). In Levinas's account, we may feel compassion for others (including nonhuman others), but this kind of feeling does not fundamentally disrupt the self-possession of the subject. But Diamond's discussion of woundedness in the face of normalized violence toward animals certainly resonates with that disruptive force.

In their overlapping critique of the adequacy of philosophical arguments that base moral judgments on the possession of particular properties, Diamond and Levinas confront the problem that if most people unapologetically draw the boundary around morally significant beings in a way that excludes nonhuman animals, what recourse remains for changing people's moral intuitions? If we cannot point to empirically demonstrable traits (such as the capacity to suffer) as the foundation for moral considerability, then what line of argument *will* provoke critical reflection on our current norms? Calarco notes the limitations of moral argument in provoking serious intellectual engagement or changes in behavior: "if the exigencies of the immense and ubiquitous slaughter of animals do not themselves provoke the reader to reflect critically on the justification for this sacrifice, it would seem that an extended and rigorous argument would have far less chance of succeeding."[68] Moral reasoning does not generate our exposure to the other, but more immediate experiences or knowledge of animal suffering may also not interrupt the dominant habits of consumption that frame eating meat as morally insignificant, for instance.

For Levinas, this kind of critical reflection is the difficult, oscillating work of philosophy, which both calls us to account for our beliefs and actions and cannot present a comprehensive account of how we should act. This uncertainty then calls out for what Levinas calls political judgments, in which we must weigh multiple and competing obligations. Subjectivity begins in traumatic exposure, with responsiveness to the other, but it is at this point that arguments about *how* to respond and how to evaluate the needs of others (including nonhuman others) are necessary. If we bracket Levinas's anthropocentrism, we can imagine that this would be the moment at which discussions between different subjects about *who* or *what* is morally considerable would begin. For some people, this sense of responsibility may be restricted to human beings (or to certain human groups), while others may be addressed only by the "charismatic megafauna" (dolphins, elephants, tigers, bison, owls), while still others may also feel obligated in the face of frogs, spiders, worms, blobfish,[69] rivers, trees, or whole ecosystems. All of these encounters gesture back to the basic possibility of the interruption of responsibility into an otherwise self-absorbed existence, and it is this fragile moment of normativity that most interests Levinas.

There is no way to justify—or, as Levinas often says, preach—this moral susceptibility (PM 176). It remains open to the skeptical challenge that it is perhaps simply a contingent psychological characteristic, something that some human beings experience in the face of alterity but that has no normative force. Levinas cannot entirely guard against this objection. But as Perpich argues, in even raising the question, the skeptic is engaged in saying, in reasoning, and in holding herself and others accountable: "The skeptic's question presumes a neutral, pre-social subject who has no constitutive relation to the other and thus must be provided with a reason to take the other into account. But the practices of reason-giving in which the skeptic's own question participates already belie her introduction into a socially or intersubjectively constituted world.... [Skepticism] is the *enactment* of ethical life."[70] Dialogue—and particularly dialogue in which we are called on to justify our beliefs or actions—reveals the exposure of one subject responding to another. Admittedly, Perpich frames the skeptic's question as a challenge to the normative force of *human* alterity, but her response functions more generally to demonstrate the distance between moral naturalism and Levinas's discussion of responsibility. Levinas is not claiming that we naturally feel obligated by human faces (and only impurely by nonhuman beings). Instead, the fact that we can be obligated at all indicates the possibility of a rupture in the self-interest of the *conatus*. The source of that obligation remains obscure to consciousness, in its resistance to being converted into an intentional object.

This response to the skeptic calls attention to Levinas's insistent challenge to the ideal of the sovereign subject in modern Western thought. We may be rational individuals gathering information and making judgments about our experience, but that reasoning process emerges out of a prior moment of responsibility, a moment that Levinas thinks has been generally covered over. In the case of moral reasoning about animals, Levinas himself participates in the traditional method of affirming or denying shared traits between human beings and other species, as the basis for making claims about animals. But this structure presumes a subject who is not traumatically impacted by responsibility in the encounter with nonhuman animals. The recognition of shared or disparate traits is one of the functions of the "outstretched nets of consciousness," whereas in the ethical encounter, the other slips through those nets, and consciousness can only retrospectively attempt to make sense of that encounter (OB 148). If moral reasoning is alienated from that exposure to the other, it risks becoming a calculation or indeed a rationalization of principles governed by the *conatus*.

There is no guarantee that the skeptic, who finds in herself no particular sense of exposure to the suffering of animals or the needs of the other, will be persuaded by this Levinasian account. Llewelyn argues that responsibility is beset by such uncertainty, in the sense that what he calls conscience is

> undetermined, underdetermined or overdetermined by rules and takes its guidance in the first and last place not from the universality of rules or laws but from the singularities which they are supposed to serve and which, simply because they are existents in need, make a claim upon us to be prepared to overrule those rules, to outlaw those laws, perhaps to revise our idea of what it means for something to make a claim, a claim that puts us under a direct responsibility toward it and under a responsibility to review our idea of neighborhood and responsibility.[71]

Llewelyn captures Levinas's general distrust of rules as repositories of responsibility, given the connections that he draws between the *conatus* and the tendency of reason to justify its motivations. The comprehension and application of rules leaves the self-possessed subject very much in her place in the sun. Nothing necessitates that the ego will respond to the other, not even the face. Since the vulnerability of the face can provoke either responsibility or violence, there is no method by which responsiveness can be reliably cultivated.

At its core, and despite his anthropocentric commitments, Levinas's project of unsettling the identification of subjectivity with the sovereignty of consciousness opens up how dominant notions of freedom and moral reasoning rest on a prior exposure to the other. To the extent that Levinas attempts to disrupt the ideal of self-possessed subjectivity, he also provides resources for disrupting the wider implications of that ideal, including in the realm of animal ethics.

More specifically, consciousness in Levinas's account is a form of domination—comprehension as grasping the world, in preparation for manipulating it. This conception of the subject privileges its mastery or virility in relation to its other. The gendered connotations of this kind of power are telling: self-control and domination of others have been culturally associated with the masculine subject. The Latin root *vir* refers both to a man and to a hero, one who possesses manly strength. Consciousness is a kind of hunter, if only of ideas or experiences.[72] Levinas's emphasis on the passivity of the subject in the encounter with the other interrupts this narrative—not by transforming the subject into prey, but by suspending and calling into question the whole dynamic of conquest.

The Historicality of Anthropocentrism

The most generous reading of Levinas's anthropocentrism develops the connection between being addressed by the other and dialogue. It is within human discourse that the question of our moral obligations, or our right to be, can arise, a point that Levinas and Diamond both make from different vantage points: "our *hearing* the moral appeal of an animal is our hearing it speak—as it were—the language of our fellow human beings."[73] In that specific sense, they suggest, we are rooted in an ineradicable anthropocentrism, to the extent that the demand for justification begins as a peculiarly human activity and can only be extended to animals through a kind of analogy. In Perpich's terms, the ethical significance of saying grounds Levinas's fixation on human others: "*it is only in human society that it is possible to worry about justice for others*, human and animal others alike."[74] The very interaction of questioning is a form of being called to account for oneself, to justify one's beliefs or actions. But the behavior of animals may also address us, in ways that provoke such discussions, in the open-ended but urgent theoretical work of justice.[75]

Even if human language is a principal site of saying, the political calculation of our obligations need not maintain that anthropocentrism, in which only human persons are morally considerable. In recognizing the unthematizable ground of our ethical exposure, however, we can begin to reframe the terms in which the animal ethics debate has been mainly conducted.[76] Rather than attempting to ground moral obligations in the establishment of particular shared characteristics, and thus proceeding in the certainty of our own status as subjects, we must address these questions as they emerge out of the unstable, restless domain of the ethical as Levinas describes it.

I read the work that Diamond and Derrida have done, tracing the contradictions within our ordinary and philosophical responses to animals, as revealing the repressive gesture in the disavowal of this instability. The point of this genealogical process—recognizing the contingency of the normal—is less about representing objectively the characteristics of various animals than about analyzing how we have constructed an "inextinguishable, ever-present, unforgettable, 'fixed'" idea of the human over and against that projected background.[77] Derrida challenges the idea that we could ever draw "a single, indivisible, linear, oppositional limit" between the human and the nonhuman, that we could purify ourselves of the uncanny significance of the beast or the machine.[78] Our ambivalent, contradictory fixity about the nature of animals supports a similar fixity with regard to the human. The content of that fixed idea tends to center on our sovereignty, our autonomy, and thus the minimization of our existence as embodied, vulnerable, exposed animals:

> It is *not just* a matter of asking whether one has the right to refuse the animal such and such a power (speech, reason, experience of death, mourning, culture, institution, technics, clothing, lying, pretense of pretense, covering of tracks, gift, laughter, crying, respect, etc.—the list is necessarily without limit, and the most powerful philosophical tradition in which we live has refused the "animal" *all of that*). It *also* means asking whether what calls itself human has the right rigorously to attribute to man, which means therefore to attribute to himself, what he refuses the animal, and whether he can ever possess the *pure, rigorous, indivisible* concept, as such, of that attribution.[79]

Derrida argues here that the clarity of the distinction between animals and humans must be complicated, not with the primary intent of blurring the distinction in order to assert biological and thus normative continuity, but with the idea of disrupting the uncritical identification of human beings as obviously rational or autonomous. As in Nietzsche's critique of the Stoics, our interpretations reveal more about our wishes and anxieties than they do about what is interpreted. If we are accustomed to seeing animals as sources of food or subjects of medical experimentation, we are unlikely to allow ourselves to be addressed by them. What seems morally considerable is at least in part a result of our immersion in a history of ideas about human and nonhuman animals, one which has mostly normalized the fact that "we are around the table and they are on it."[80] But philosophical discussions about the contradictions within our inherited moral intuitions can help to denormalize those assumptions that shape our perceptions.[81]

None of this directly answers the series of moral questions about how we should treat nonhuman animals. The philosophical interaction among Levinas, Diamond, and Derrida indicates the paucity of how those issues have been dominantly framed and pursued—the attempt to identify morally considerable traits in nonhuman animals, or, in other words, the observable, measurable traits that Western cultures have long identified exclusively and constitutively with human beings. These arguments ignore the idea that "the human" functions as "an ethical concept rather than a species concept," as Calarco claims, or rather an ethical concept masquerading as a species concept.[82] By challenging the claim that any particular trait provokes responsibility, Levinas radicalizes the distinction between the descriptive and the normative, and thus calls into question the pervasive ways that Western cultures have associated these two dimensions of the term "human," even if Levinas himself participates in that particular anthropocentric slippage. Agnosticism about who or what the self will find herself accused by may run counter to the need to engage in individual, cultural, and legal deliberations about what constitutes justice regarding animals. But this is the interplay that Levinas describes between ethics and politics. Without such ongoing interruptions, we risk moral catastrophe. Calarco asks in this vein, "does not a historical survey of the failures that have attended every such attempt to draw *the* line (or lines) of moral considerability provide enough evidence to persuade even common sense that this approach is inherently pernicious, both morally and politically?"[83] In this sense, the problem with the animalization of human beings is not the fluidity of the line between human and nonhuman animals, but the ease and complacency with which beings may be categorized as morally inconsiderable. The key repercussion of Levinasian responsibility is the destabilization of such normalized dismissals and the violence latent within them.

This emphasis on the moral significance of genealogical critique may seem at odds with Levinas's attempt to separate the force of moral authority from a set of ideas that can be philosophically articulated. If exposure is not a matter of understanding, how could our exposure to the other possibly be affected by critical reflection on the contingent history of our moral concepts, which might lead to a quite different understanding of the legitimacy of our habitual beliefs and practices? However, Levinas's philosophical project tries to dismantle the ways in which such trauma has been obscured or anesthetized by the conception of the autonomous subject that dominates modern Western philosophy—a subject constituted by projecting heteronomy onto animals and subpersons. In that sense he implicitly acknowledges the power of ideas to shape our attunement to alterity, and so uses his own philosophical work to counter what he sees as a deeply problematic tendency to cover over the trauma of responsibility. This complexity reflects the tensions within the discourse of philosophy—as a form of representation that gestures toward the limits of representation in order to reorient us to a vulnerability that has been historically neglected. To the extent that anthropocentrism goes unquestioned in Levinas's work, he contributes to that particular strand of disavowing responsibility toward nonhuman animals in the history of philosophy. But the genealogical study of that series of disavowals is helpfully supplemented by Levinas's more phenomenologically inflected critiques of autonomous subjectivity. In both methods, philosophical reflection cannot present us with the origin of responsibility that delineates and justifies our moral obligations, but it can unsettle our current moral intuitions—including the foundational conception of the subject as moral agent and reasoner—in order to create the space for revising them.

Llewelyn's crucial question to Levinas—who is my neighbor?—raises the problem of whether the source of moral authority undergirding Levinas's whole project, which allows him to draw a clear boundary between the faced and the faceless (or the poor in face), is an anthropocentric religious tradition that takes the sacrifices of nonhuman animals for granted.[84] That capacity to be wounded by the suffering of an animal other depends in part on the genealogy out of which our concepts of humanity, animality, suffering, and responsibility arise. How we understand and apply, but also just feel, our obligations to a dog or a snake or a snail is part of our creaturely embeddedness in a contingent history, whose authority over us should be called into question. Levinas separates creatureliness from animality, in the sense that experiencing oneself as a creature is the opening of a moral order that interrupts the Darwinian struggle for existence. But creatureliness may also be understood in historical terms—how we find our thinking and behavior shaped by a set of concepts, claims, and value judgments from which we cannot entirely detach ourselves.

In claiming that animals are morally inconsiderable, Levinas ignores the ways in which the ideal of sovereignty is entangled with anthropocentrism, or dominion over nonhuman animals, and so misses this particular dimension of our historical creatureliness. In the previous chapter, I discussed the significance of creatureliness with reference to maternity and the ways in which mothers must be disavowed by sovereign subjects. In a broader sense, animality is positioned as a second kind of origin, from which human persons must separate themselves in order to be recognized as rights-bearers, citizens, and moral agents. Given Levinas's interest in disrupting the governing ideal of the autonomous subject, his project is enriched by a genealogical analysis of how that sovereignty has been conceptually established in contrast to a highly problematic account of animality. By tracing the theoretical and normative incoherence of dominant beliefs and practices around animality, we are reminded of the incentives surrounding the disavowal of animality as it has been framed in the Western tradition. As historical creatures, we have to struggle to recognize how that trajectory has conditioned our habits of moral attunement—hence the need for ongoing philosophical questioning of our moral intuitions.

Notes

1. Nietzsche, *Beyond Good and Evil*, §9.
2. Long and Sedley (eds.), *Hellenistic Philosophers*, 1:394.
3. See Llewelyn, "Am I Obsessed by Bobby?"; Clark, "On Being the 'Last Kantian in Nazi Germany'"; Wood, "*Comment ne pas manger*"; David, "Cynesthèse"; Davy, "Other Face of Ethics in Levinas"; and Calarco, *Zoographies*.
4. See Katz, *Levinas and the Crisis of Humanism*.

5. The other two traumas are the Copernican displacement of the human from cosmic centrality and the psychoanalytic deflation of human reason (Freud, "Difficulty in the Path of Psychoanalysis," 17:140–41). See also Derrida, *Animal That Therefore I Am*, 136.

6. Llewelyn, "Am I Obsessed by Bobby?," 235.

7. Freud, *Civilization and Its Discontents*, 21:111. Hobbes and Schopenhauer also make reference to this proverb, mainly to deflate human pretensions to transcend animality (Hobbes, *On the Citizen*, 3; Schopenhauer, *World as Will and Representation*, 1:172). Giorgio Agamben makes a similar point: "The division of life into vegetal and relational, organic and animal, animal and human ... passes first of all as a mobile border within living man, and without this intimate caesura the very decision of what is human and what is not would probably not be possible. ... What is man, if he is always the place—and, at the same time, the result—of ceaseless divisions and caesurae?" (*Open*, 15).

8. This is Levinas's rendition of a proverb that has variants in many cultures: "a hungry stomach has no ears."

9. As Derrida comments, Levinas—like almost every other major figure in the history of Western philosophy—places "the animal outside of the ethical circuit" (*Animal That Therefore I Am*, 106).

10. Derrida, "'Eating Well,'" 279.

11. Ibid.

12. Llewelyn discusses the significance of the Hebrew word *ratsah* in the sixth commandment of the Decalogue, "Thou shalt not kill," which can also be translated as "Thou shalt not murder." Levinas typically uses the former language (*tuer*) but makes a moral distinction between the killing of animals and the killing of human beings, where only the latter can constitute murder ("Am I Obsessed by Bobby?," 243–44).

13. Derrida, *Animal That Therefore I Am*, 26.

14. Ibid., 25–26; see also Michael Naas, "Derrida's Flair," 241.

15. Derrida, *Animal That Therefore I Am*, 25–26.

16. Kant, *Lectures on Ethics*, 459.

17. Ibid.

18. Ibid.

19. Bentham, *Introduction to the Principles of Morals and Legislation*, 283b; Derrida, *Animal That Therefore I Am*, 27–28.

20. Derrida, *Beast and the Sovereign*, 1:111.

21. Derrida, *Animal That Therefore I Am*, 31.

22. Ibid.

23. See Benso, *Face of Things*.

24. This is the question that Llewelyn raises at the very beginning of "Am I Obsessed by Bobby?" (234).

25. Where Levinas refers positively to Marxism, he focuses on how it reorients us to the suffering of others (IFP 81, PJL 119–20).

26. For reasons that will become clear later in the chapter, I leave open the question of what sorts of beings are morally considerable, although I will focus on the issue of responsibility toward nonhuman animals, rather than plants, inanimate objects, or whole ecosystems.

27. Derrida, "'Eating Well,'" 282.

28. Heldke, "Food Politics, Political Food," 320.

29. Ibid.," 319.

30. See also VF, 179, and PT, 23.

31. We should recognize in this phrase another symptom of what Derrida calls the *animot*, the motivated construction of animality in human thought.
32. Derrida, *Animal That Therefore I Am*, 47–48.
33. Ibid., 111–13.
34. Clark, "On Being the 'Last Kantian in Nazi Germany,'" 179. Clark draws a parallel between this intermediate status that Levinas grants nonhuman animals and Heidegger's claim that animals are "poor in world" (*weltarm*) (180). Derrida argues that Levinas's anthropocentrism is a repetition of Heidegger's anthropocentrism, despite all of the ways in which Levinas reacts against Heidegger's account of *Dasein* (*Animal That Therefore I Am*, 89–91, 106).
35. Perpich, *Ethics of Emmanuel Levinas*, 154.
36. In *Totality and Infinity*, Levinas refers to the claim of Rabbi Yochanan: "To leave men without food is a fault that no circumstance attenuates; the distinction between the voluntary and the involuntary does not apply here" (TI 201). Lack of intent or even lack of knowledge does not excuse the moral transgression of allowing others to go hungry; the self stands accused by the other's hunger. Levinas's interpretation makes use of the terms in which Oedipus's guilt is articulated: "Before the hunger of men responsibility is measured only 'objectively' [despite any subjective innocence]; it is irrecusable" (TI 201).
37. Perpich, *Ethics of Emmanuel Levinas*, 169.
38. Plant, "Welcoming Dogs," 58.
39. Clark, "On Being the 'Last Kantian in Nazi Germany,'" 168.
40. On this issue, the debates around whether chimpanzees who use sign language are speaking miss the central question (which is perhaps buried in this debate) of whether even speaking nonhuman animals are allowed to *address* us: See Fouts, *Next of Kin*; and Hauser, Chomsky, and Fitch, "Faculty of Language." The Leviniasian question is whether the self is addressed or accused by the other, and how this process can fail, not whether the other is empirically capable of speech.
41. Derrida, *Animal That Therefore I Am*, 23. See also Naas, "Derrida's Flair," 228.
42. Clark, "On Being the 'Last Kantian in Nazi Germany,'" 182. See also Derrida, "'Eating Well,'" 281; and Calarco, *Zoographies*, 132–36.
43. Clark, "On Being the 'Last Kantian in Nazi Germany,'" 194.
44. Derrida, *Animal That Therefore I Am*, 109.
45. Perpich, *Ethics of Emmanuel Levinas*, 171.
46. Ibid.
47. Grossman, *Life and Fate*, 683; Levinas quotes this passage on PP, 167.
48. Davy, "Other Face of Ethics in Levinas," 50.
49. On the issue of how our underlying assumptions about animals influence our perceptions of them, thus shaping our approaches to them as either reductive or receptive, see Weston, *Back to Earth*.
50. Derrida, *Animal That Therefore I Am*, 117.
51. Atterton, "Levinas and Our Moral Responsibility toward Other Animals," 636, 641.
52. Calarco, "Faced by Animals," 113.
53. Guenther, "*Le Flair Animal*," 225.
54. Calarco, "Faced by Animals," 126.
55. Calarco argues that such complacency around these choices may truncate "the question of eating well and collaps[e] into a self-assured form of good conscience." ("Deconstruction Is Not Vegetarianism," 195). See also Wood, "*Comment ne pas manger*," 31–33.

56. See, for instance, Beauchamp and Frey (eds.), *Oxford Handbook of Animal Ethics*; Oliver, *Animal Lessons*; Sufka, Weldon, and Allen, "Case for Animal Emotions"; and McDavid, "Control and Incarceration of Human and Non-Human Beings."
57. Diamond, "Difficulty of Reality and the Difficulty of Philosophy," 74.
58. McDowell, "Comment on Stanley Cavell's 'Companionable Thinking,' " 134.
59. Diamond, "Eating Meat and Eating People," 470. A parallel line of objection could be made against arguments in favor of animal rights.
60. Ibid., 469.
61. Ibid., 470.
62. Ibid., 475.
63. Ibid., 474.
64. Ibid.
65. Ibid., 476.
66. Ibid., 477.
67. Perpich, *Ethics of Emmanuel Levinas*, 147.
68. Calarco, "Deconstruction Is Not Vegetarianism," 189.
69. This is the mascot of the Ugly Animal Preservation Society, based in the United Kingdom.
70. Perpich, *Ethics of Emmanuel Levinas*, 145.
71. Llewelyn, *Middle Voice of Ecological Consciousness*, 276–77.
72. Scholars in a variety of disciplines have investigated the cultural associations between aggression, masculinity, and carnivory (particularly the eating of red meat), and a correlative association between femininity, moral sensitivity or squeamishness, and gentleness. See Twigg, "Vegetarianism and the Meanings of Meat"; and Adams, *Sexual Politics of Meat*. See also Derrida, " 'Eating Well,' " 280–81.
73. Diamond, "Eating Meat and Eating People," 476.
74. Perpich, *Ethics of Emmanuel Levinas*, 175.
75. See Atterton, "Levinas and Our Moral Responsibility toward Other Animals."
76. See Singer, *Animal Liberation*; Singer (ed.), *Defense of Animals*; Regan, *Case for Animal Rights*; and Regan, *Defending Animal Rights*.
77. Nietzsche, *On the Genealogy of Morals and Ecce Homo*, 2:§3.
78. Derrida, " 'Eating Well,' " 116–17.
79. Derrida, *Animal That Therefore I Am*, 135.
80. Diamond, "Eating Meat and Eating People," 470.
81. Llewelyn, "Where to Cut," 178. Derrida's description approximates Agamben's notion of the "anthropological machine," the historical process by which the concept of the human is defined through its distinction from the nonhuman animal, a phrase whose traditional redundancy reveals the efficacy but not the contingency of that machine. The discourses of modernity contribute to this process of drawing boundaries around the properly human, which is "an optical machine constructed of a series of mirrors in which man, looking at himself, sees his own image always already deformed in the features of an ape. *Homo* is a constitutively 'anthropomorphous' animal (that is, 'resembling man,' according to the term that Linnaeus constantly uses until the tenth edition of the *Systema*), who must recognize himself in a non-man in order to be human" (Agamben, *Open*, 27). Human beings are those who recognize their lack of essence, their proximity to apes, their "precariousness" as humans—thus creating the anxiety that demands a clear opposition between the human and nonhuman animal. The human can only be defined through the exclusion of the nonhuman animal, from language or reason or technology, and through the identification and

management of those who stand on the borderline between human and nonhuman. This tangled history of theological, philosophical, political, medical, and legal concepts of the human helps to shape contemporary moral intuitions about what sort of being is morally considerable.
   82. Calarco, "Faced by Animals," 122.
   83. Ibid., 127.
   84. Llewelyn, "Am I Obsessed by Bobby?," 244.

Conclusion
Inheriting the Thought of Diachrony

THIS BOOK HAS focused on the array of issues around subjectivity and time that emerges out of Levinas's thought and particularly how he challenges the mastery over time that helps to define the ideal of the sovereign subject—an ideal that has prevailed in various iterations in modern Western culture. That sense of mastery and its accompanying anxieties have shaped dominant conceptions of not only responsibility, justice, and freedom, but also of gender, race, embodiment, mortality, and animality. For Levinas, this understanding of subjectivity affirms and perpetuates the basic attitude of the *conatus essendi*, the striving to persevere in one's own being. As knowers, agents, and citizens, subjects are typically framed as individuals who observe and act on the world around them, and these interactions depend upon a time whose significance can be reduced to the present. Responsibility in its diachrony challenges the exhaustiveness of those interlocking conceptions of subjectivity, in the sense that diachrony interrupts the voluntarism and detachment at the core of these characteristics. A lapse of time that resists representation exposes the subject to alterity, in which one's right to be cannot be assumed, and one finds oneself addressed by an immemorial obligation. Time in its ethical significance thus destabilizes the sovereignty of the subject and contests the practices, institutions, and norms founded on that ideal.

Levinas's late work is animated by the question of how to think diachrony as it shapes responsibility—how to articulate its significance without betraying it, or without entirely betraying it, by converting it into another idea to be digested by the synchronizing activity of consciousness. Given that our conceptual framework attunes us to beings that can be represented, he generates a philosophical discourse that reorients us to the trace that resists representation. The question that confronts his readers is how we will inherit this difficult, restless project. On those issues where Levinas is largely silent, such as how this account of responsibility should influence political activism or how disagreements in those decisions should be adjudicated, how can his thought be applied and extended? On those issues where contemporary readers may wish that Levinas had been more silent, such as his Eurocentrism, androcentrism, and anthropocentrism, how can his thought be revised without distorting what is valuable and original in it? And lastly, how can we broaden the conversation that Levinas has begun, in areas of philosophy and other disciplines that may not yet recognize their guiding questions in his vocabulary, claims, and methods? How can his work challenge the continuing dominance of the *conatus* in all of its diverse forms?

Subjectivity and Diachrony

In Levinas's account, the defining power of consciousness is its ability to conquer at least intellectually the passage of time, and thus to establish the autonomy of the knowing subject: "To begin—to ignore or suspend the undefined density of the past—is the wonder of the *present*. All contents of consciousness were received, were present and consequently are present or represented, memorable. Consciousness is the very impossibility of a past that had never been present, that is closed to memory and history" (HA 49). This passage was published in 1968, more than thirty years after "Some Thoughts on the Philosophy of Hitlerism," but it expresses the same idea, that freedom in its purity depends upon overcoming the lapse of time so that thoughts or actions can be seen as truly spontaneous, having no significant past. Levinas is by no means interested in demolishing the basis for moral or political agency, or for scientific or philosophical knowledge. But he does challenge the sufficiency of this interpretation of time and its affiliated understanding of subjectivity. Time both supports the work of consciousness and traumatically interrupts it, in an ambivalence parallel to the effect of the face, whose exposedness provokes both violence and its prohibition. The passage of time *can* function as the framework for experience, which enables the narratives through which we make sense of reality. But this formal conception of time does not exhaust its meaning and its impact on human subjects.

Time in its passing also imposes a limit on the activity of consciousness and subverts the familiar power of the sovereign subject to assimilate all that he encounters into his own comprehension. In diachrony, the subject encounters what escapes this mastery and yet imposes its significance and so experiences himself as exposed and obligated to the other. Nothing guarantees that we will attend to this ethical significance of diachrony, particularly given the synchronizing mechanisms of intentionality. Yet the (non)experiences of exposure in the encounter with the other recur, like skeptical questions that cannot quite be dismissed. In making this argument, Levinas appeals to the forms of vulnerability that would be impossible if subjectivity did not have this denucleated structure—that we would feel no compunction in refusing to offer a greeting or in visiting violence on the other. We find ourselves bound by such obligations as if these commitments arose out of a past that cannot be recalled. We may understand ourselves as autonomous, self-possessed beings, but the diachronous claim of the other interrupts this self-conception by imposing an obligation prior to any comprehension:

> My deepest thought, which carries all thought, my thought of the infinite, older than the thought of the finite, is the very diachrony of time. It is non-coincidence, dispossession itself. This is a way of "being dedicated" before any act of consciousness, and more deeply so than in consciousness, by way of the gratuity of time (in which philosophers manage to fear a vanity or privation).... This is a dia-chrony which no thematizing and inter-ested movement of consciousness—whether as memory or as hopes—can reabsorb or recuperate in the simultaneities it constitutes. (GCM xiv–xv)

Not everything significant to the subject can be represented. If time is both susceptible to synchronization and resistant to such assimilation, subjectivity comprises both the self-determining subject and the heteronomous condition of being subjected to (ethical) authority. But the "lateness" of the ethical subject is all too easily covered over, in our cultural, political, and philosophical imaginary.

This aspect of creatureliness—how the ego comes too late to make sense of or control its own responsibility—lies outside of the traditional dichotomy of free will and determinism. The lapse of time introduces exposure, in which I am neither the object controlled by another's actions nor the initiator of action (HA 53, OB 144). There is no glorification of masochism, servitude, or paralysis in Levinas's thought, particularly because those characterizations have typically functioned as the foil to an ideal of autonomous action. They thus remain within an economy familiar to the *conatus*, of active subjects and passive objects. Neither side of this polarity can account for the significance of exposure to the other. By emphasizing the ways in which the subject is subjected to responsibility, Levinas is not so much denying the reality of freedom as reshaping the ideal of autonomy, or rehabilitating heteronomy, into what he calls "difficult freedom," in which we are called to responsibility and then to live out that responsibility in the decisions that belong to the order of justice (DEL 27).

Creatureliness in Two Registers

As I suggested in the previous chapter, creatureliness can be understood in two different ways: one that refers to an immemorial origin, and the second to our immersion in a determinate history. Levinas's understanding of creatureliness makes no explicit reference to historicality but instead focuses on the subject's inability to represent his own origin in exposure. We are responsible before we are self-possessed subjects: "the passivity of a creature at the time of creation when there is no subject to assume the creative act, to, so to speak, hear the creative word" (LP 114). The diachrony that interests Levinas is the passing of time that resists representation, not the framework for a particular historical trajectory that can be reconstructed and analyzed. Creatureliness is instead the inversion of comprehension, which can gather the past, present, and future into a narrative, as Robert Gibbs emphasizes: "To be a creature and not author of oneself is not a punishment or even a sinful moral state for which the solution is to become autonomous; rather, creatureliness in its vulnerability to persecution and its incapacity to refute the accusation and to affirm one's own innocence is ... the original goodness."[1] We are accused, challenged in our right to be, not as a result of any action or intention, but nonetheless we cannot refuse the accusation. This is what Levinas means by the "original goodness of creation"—the upsurge of moral significance within a morally indifferent world (OB 121). Our inability to account for our own beginnings, for the origins of subjectivity, generates the "undeclinability" that "divest[s] the ego of its imperialism" (OB 121). In other words, creatureliness calls into question the complacent self-assertion of the autonomous ego: "*in being* the beginning is preceded but what precedes is not presented to the free gaze that would assume it" (HA 51). This is the pre-history of the ego, in responsibility. Commenting on this passage, Catherine Chalier argues that the narrative of Genesis reinforces the ineffable status of creaturely origins:

> No one knows the exact meaning of the secret from which one emerges, unless, precisely, it is that one does not stem from the steadfastness and self-assurance provided by a principle.... [The Bible's] first word—*Bereshit*—posits the inaccessible character of the beginning and invites us to separate the idea of origin from any assertion of principle. The word *Bereshit* ... begins with the second letter of the alphabet, the letter of duality. From the outset, that word brings us face to face with an enigma that has remained unsolved: the absence of the first letter, *aleph*, the letter of unity. The history of every creature stands in relation to that anteriority or that absence, it bears witness to them, in spite of itself and often unbeknownst to itself.[2]

The rejection of creatureliness is a fantasy of mastery, in which even one's own origins can be taken up and narrated. This rejection may take the form of denying the significance of materiality and temporality in the life of the subject. This fantasy attempts to overcome how I am responsible *before* being able to identify the source of that obligation or the strength of its claim on me. Levinas's project attempts to remind us of our creatureliness, to undo the hold that this fantasy of self-creation has on us, particularly those of us who are heirs of Greek thought.

But there is a second dimension of creatureliness. Alongside this immemorial, anarchic origin, we are shaped by a representable past, one that speaks to us and through us in the contingent, interlocking, and sometimes contradictory "fixed ideas" of a tradition. Acknowledging this dimension of lateness and its effects on us begins to dismantle the sedimented authority of inherited ideas. What it means to be a creature is to find oneself in a history not of one's own making. But Levinas largely ignores this historical understanding of creatureliness, at least at an explicit level—in the same way that he insists on the singularity rather than the particularity of the other. For Levinas, the historically embedded subject is still a subject defined by totality and by a vision of fulfillment within history that can be comprehended by reason. Oona Ajzenstat argues that his emphasis on the ahistorical, or the position of ethics outside of history (as a rupture in history), is a refusal to conflate world history with the divine, by which justice will be realized: "Placing one's faith or hope in the course of rooted history is equivalent to placing one's faith or hope in a spatially located and reachable God; both are signs of succumbing to the seductive grandeur of a scheme or realm that over-reaches the interpersonal, to which the inter-personal becomes secondary."[3] That is, Levinas's relative silence about how we are historical creatures stems from his suspicion about totalizing narratives, in their deafness to the ethical.

Levinas does not thereby deny that we are at least partially creatures of history or that our expectations, ideals, and moral perceptions are shaped by contingent conceptual lineages. Instead, he claims that each of us is singularly responsible for messianically reinstituting the fragile moral order. According to Levinas, the history of the twentieth century in particular should reveal to us the inherent dangers of abstracting away from the singular other and of looking for meaning in narratives or institutions that depend upon such abstractions. Therefore, as Ajzenstat claims, "while there may be meaning *in* history, there is no meaning *of* history.... 'Standing outside of history' is equivalent to standing within a history that has no overarching meaning."[4] The meaning that is possible in history is interpersonal responsibility, which resists totalization.

The two forms of creatureliness are thus in some tension with each other. In Levinas's view, the telling of history has a totalizing function, consolidating a narrative in which disparate events are invested with meaning. That constitution of meaning and the intentional subject that such a process presupposes are both called into question by the exposure to alterity, which introduces a lapse of time that cannot be recuperated and concentrates our attention on the subject's responsibility to a singular other. This is what we might call immemorial creatureliness. But insofar as subjects are embedded within a history, they cannot come to terms with how their thinking and actions are shaped by that history unless their historicality is recognized, in what I have been calling a genealogical critique. In this historical form of creatureliness, the representable past has a kind of authority built on normalization. As with the *conatus*, the ideas and practices that we inherit are likely to go unquestioned. Levinas's concern seems to be that such genealogical studies may lead to some revised narrative—some new identification of the meaning of history—without questioning the conception of subjectivity or time that underlies the very process of narration. Immemorial creatureliness "sobers us up" in this particular way, without providing any contentful narrative. It has the force of skepticism, which destabilizes our settled ideas. The historically situated form of creatureliness, belonging to a way of thought and a way of life, anchors the subject in an intelligible totality, and reflecting on that historical imbeddedness produces a new comprehension of a totality. However, analyzing the significance of both registers is necessary to the work of philosophy, as Levinas conceives of it, in its oscillating, spiraling movement of saying and unsaying.

In his downplaying of historical context, Levinas risks the appearance of making ahistorical and universal claims about human nature, subjectivity, and responsibility. I have suggested throughout this book that Levinas's discourse is more historically situated than it first appears, insofar as he focuses on the conception of subjectivity normalized in modern Western philosophy. His claims about responsibility, and particularly the characterization of responsibility as traumatic, respond specifically to that system of ideas, values, and institutions. While he may characterize the *conatus* as a universal dynamic within human and animal life, his project addresses the particular ways in which the *conatus* is affirmed in the exaltation of the sovereign subject in modern Western thought. Even his avoidance of historical narratives is an avoidance of historical narratives that are characteristic of nineteenth- and twentieth-century philosophy—namely, those of Hegel and Heidegger. The conversation that he carries on with the history of philosophy is often subterranean rather than overt, and the rhetorical style that results does not immediately lend itself to traditional philosophical analysis and evaluation. But Levinas's central series of ideas—alterity, proximity, responsibility—cannot be simply interruptive, belonging to the "outside" of the discipline of philosophy. They instead have their own genealogy in the assumptions borne along by this tradition, and therefore demand critical reflection on the background of Levinas's ideas, his interpretation of them, and the possibilities for interpreting them otherwise.

Levinas and the History of Philosophy

Levinas's thought enacts what he says philosophy should do: an awakening that is never final or certain, which invites further responses. In his published works he is participating in a dialogue with the history of philosophy, orienting his readers toward what the dominant threads of the Western philosophical tradition have diminished and ignored. But this means that he constantly engages those dominant beliefs, norms, and philosophical methods. Rolland claims that in Levinas's work "the history of philosophy is present on each page, but it is present without ever leaving the background and presents itself more in the mode of allusions than in that of analysis."[5] Most frequently, Levinas refers explicitly to Husserlian phenomenology, Plato's "Good beyond Being" (OB 95), Descartes's argument that God exceeds the idea of God in the Third Meditation, Pascal's fragment about establishing one's place in the sun, and Spinoza's *conatus essendi*. But in fact the whole tradition of Western epistemology, political philosophy, and ethics is at play in his work, given the centrality of the figure of subjectivity that he is resisting.[6] He calls on his readers to question the sedimented philosophical intuitions that have obscured the ethical significance of alterity.[7]

Levinas's project then emerges out of and in reaction to the history of Western philosophy, and the multiple, intersecting trajectories of this tradition, but this embeddedness remains largely implicit, particularly in his published writings, as opposed to interviews or lectures. His references to the *conatus* seem to describe some ahistorical human nature, as if responsibility and narcissism were engaged in a cosmic struggle within every human being. But the language of trauma introduces a highly specific reference to the entangling of the *conatus* and the history of Western thought, such that responsibility breaks in on the complacency of that ideal. Underlying much of Levinas's engagement is his claim that the history of philosophy has tended to justify the narcissism of the *conatus*, and its corollary beliefs and values—in its commitment to the assumptions that subjectivity is reducible to consciousness, that intersubjective relations are secondary to the ego's self-possession, and thus that the primary dimension of time is the present. These assumptions collectively normalize the ideal of the sovereign subject. If intersubjectivity is secondary to the sovereignty of the subject, then competition between subjects—sometimes erupting into war, sometimes lapsing into uneasy peace—is the governing political dynamic: "Being's interest takes dramatic form in egoisms struggling with one another, each against all, in the multiplicity of allergic egoisms which are at war with one another and are thus together" (OB 4). The history of philosophy has thus tended to exacerbate the effects of the *conatus*, in the war or preparation for war that political and moral calculations become when ethics as Levinas understands it is dismissed as sentimentality. That orientation continues to dominate not only philosophical discourse, but politics, law, and economics in the modern West.

That stability then is denormalized by the encounter with alterity, in which the "imperialism" of the ego is broken (OB 121). The proximity of the other would have a particularly traumatic effect on an ego who up until that point had understood itself to be autonomous. In this sense Levinas's discourse is premised on the concepts that dominate modern Western thought, and his discussion of trauma derives its significance from that intellectual context. But he uses diverse resources to challenge the sovereignty of the ego, including his particular reading of phenomenology, ideas from a wide range of Jewish thought (both ancient and modern), occasional references to literature (especially Dostoevsky, Shakespeare, and Grossman), and twentieth-century theological interpretations of Kierkegaard (as Samuel Moyn has recently argued).[8] Drawing these ideas and their implications into the mainstream of philosophical discourse is a way to recover what has otherwise been marginalized—the thought of subjectivity constituted by responsibility.

Derrida claims in "Violence and Metaphysics" that there is no final way to depart from the history of philosophy and speak in a conceptual system that is not Greek in origin.[9] What resists representation is part of the movement of philosophy itself. However, Levinas adds that this resistance is what keeps philosophy persistently incomplete.[10] Philosophical discourse must answer to "a cry of ethical revolt, a bearing witness to responsibility" and "walk among reasons that 'reason' does not know, and which have not begun in Philosophy" (GP 77). Levinas is well aware that this means that his discourse risks falling into nonsense, by attempting to reflect on what resists comprehension and the effects of that encounter on subjects. The other side of this risk is the reduction of alterity to a theme. But in writing in this way he enacts the kind of work that he thinks the discipline of philosophy is best positioned to engage in, and which the core of the Western tradition has largely ignored, to its peril: "The-one-for-the-other is the very signifyingness of signification. How can such a research be undertaken without introducing some barbarisms [*quelques barbarismes*] in the language of philosophy? Yet philosophy has, at its highest, exceptional, hours stated the beyond of being and the *one* distinct from being, but mainly remained at home in saying being, that is, inwardness to being, the being at home with oneself, of which European history itself has been the conquest and jealous defense" (OB 178). The reference to the possible barbarism of his philosophical work is deliberate: Levinas attempts to draw attention to a meaning that resists thematization, that functions as a trace rather than something intelligible. Is it then so foreign (to philosophy, or to the philosophical framework that we have inherited) as to be nonsensical? Levinas responds that the very discourse of philosophy is provoked by exposure to the other, an origin that cannot be comprehended.

A Levinasian approach to philosophy seems to negotiate restlessly between the two dimensions of creatureliness, without ever synthesizing them into a unified conception. Genealogical analyses need to be interrupted by questions about the status of the subject doing the genealogical analysis and the presumption that all that is significant in human experience can be represented. At the same time, what the infinite means and how this term has been put to use philosophically, politically, or theologically needs to be critically interrogated. Levinas's concern is that alterity will be translated unproblematically into another phenomenon, set of concepts, or moral system that would be made to function as the *telos* of history (PA 89). This reduction would once again glorify the sovereignty of the knowing subject and obscure the ethical force of the subject's exposure to alterity. He emphasizes that the reflexive nature of philosophical questioning complicates the will to knowledge:

> Philosophies: permanent revolutions, and also necessary to knowledge, concerned with reducing the naiveté of its consciousness or extending itself into epistemology, inquiring about the meaning of the results. A transcendence that cannot be reduced to an experience of transcendence, for it is a seizure prior to all *positing* of a subject and to every perceived or assimilated content. Transcendence or awakening that is the very life of the human, already troubled by the Infinite. Whence philosophy: a language of transcendence and not the tale of experience: a language in which the teller is part of the tale, thus a necessarily personal language, to be understood beyond what it says, that is, to be interpreted. (PA 89)

Knowledge is "one modality" of awakening, but Levinas calls attention to the modality that tends to be ignored in the Western philosophical tradition, which cannot be assimilated as knowledge—an "insomnia" that puts into question the knowing subject assumed by epistemological projects (PA 87). Transcendence does not introduce another phenomenon to be known. Its impact is instead traumatic, even if that trauma is then reflected on and represented in discourse. Philosophy is then both the activity of representation and an attunement to the limits of representation. At the end of this passage, Levinas claims that philosophy cannot be reduced to its propositions, the content of its arguments: it is not "the tale of experience," but instead the performance of that narrative *and its undoing*. The permanence of philosophical revolutions emerges from the fluctuating movement of thematization and its unraveling, or what Chanter calls the betrayal that philosophical discourse enacts (the reduction of the infinite to a concept) and the betrayal of that betrayal (the reflection that calls attention to the incompleteness of that reduction).[11]

Levinas's discourse reflects this unsettled movement. Even in the course of philosophical reflection, the idea of the infinite is a trace that exceeds epistemic assimilation. As soon as Levinas attempts to represent alterity, he must also "unsay" that representation in order to maintain its alterity. This is the tension between the "Greek" dynamic of representing all that is and the significance of what passes by representation:

> To speak is to speak Greek. But if it is correct that meaning is only shown in language, must we likewise argue that logical exposition does not contain a *manner of speaking* [*pour-ainsi-dire*]? Must we not ask ourselves whether the logical exposition of meaning does not call for an unsaying [*dédire*]—where the *saying* [*dire*] calls for an *unsaying* [*dédire*]—must we not ask whether speaking shows a gap between meaning and that which is manifested of it, between meaning and what, in manifesting itself, *takes on the ways of being*? (GDT 128)

Meaning cannot be reduced to what can be conceptualized in the said, in the sense that the saying, the address of the other, can "take on the ways of being," be translated into a concept, but also resists this translation. For Levinas, philosophical discourse enacts this process of saying and unsaying in a paradigmatic way, in its commitment to rendering reality intelligible but also in its capacity to reflect on the limits of intelligibility.

The oscillation between exposure to the other and the need to conceptualize the other underpins the tension between the two forms of creatureliness: one in which the ego finds itself immersed in a tradition of particular events, behaviors, and norms, and one in which the ego find itself addressed by the singular who resists reduction to the particular. But the two registers are intimately related. The assertion that what "carries all thought" is "thought of the infinite" means that conceptual representation is provoked by alterity (GCM xiv–xv). The trauma of responsibility calls out for a kind of working-through, in the sense of making sense of one's concrete obligations to others in the present and acting on those moral decisions. But in turn those calculations and concepts—the said—only ever inadequately capture the address of the saying. The said thus also calls out for the unsaying, or the interruption of the said: "justice is not a legality regulating human masses, from which a technique of social equilibrium is drawn, harmonizing antagonistic forces. . . . Justice is impossible without the one that renders it finding himself in proximity" (OB 159). Proximity addresses the self before any recognition of commonality, and it is only on this basis, Levinas claims, that justice is possible. Exposure to the singular other, and thus finding myself singularly responsible for the other, generates the need for justice, which establishes abstract moral and legal principles, recognizes the political rights of persons, and adjudicates conflicts resulting from competing interests. The restless interaction between our ethical and political obligations reflects the tension between representing the history in which we are embedded and attending to the disruptive moment of responsibility. Levinas's emphasis is always on the second stroke of that vacillation, but that is itself a historically significant element of his thought, insofar as he is reacting against a tradition in which the moral implications of representation (even genealogical representation) have gone unquestioned.

Levinas's Project and the Work That Remains

This emphasis on the immemorial dimension of creatureliness, however, raises questions around how that disruptive moment is interpreted and whether that interpretation is itself shaped by a tradition or various traditions. Levinas's unapologetic assertion that nonhuman animals have a face only in an "impure" form is an example of a contingent anthropocentric prejudice sounding like an ahistorical or self-evident boundary between who is morally considerable and what is not. His discussion of femininity similarly reinforces assumptions about what is natural or eternal. Most generously, we could read the diminishment of historicity in Levinas's discourse as a provocation to do the genealogical work of identifying how he inherits and revises the resources of Western philosophical and religious thought, and of reflecting on how to inherit his work.

This is the ongoing conversation that Levinas identifies as the core of philosophy, in which dialogue is not only the exchange of propositions but a consideration of what resists being contained in propositions. In a discussion of how meaning has been reduced to the said, Levinas proposes "think[ing] of language as a question. But is the question itself only the diminution of affirmation? In questioning, do I limit myself to doing less than affirming?" (GDT 128). Against the Greek thought that questioning is an incomplete affirmation of a proposition, a deprivation of certainty or a preparatory step toward it, Levinas suggests that questioning as an activity opens up the distance between the saying and the said, between the meaning of the address as an intersubjective event, which resists being converted into a theme, and the content of that address. This tension is not a failure of philosophy but its very activity: "This putting in question of the ontological priority is a question that is posed, philosophically, against philosophy. The question obliges us, at the same time that we seek another source of meaning, not to repudiate philosophy" (GDT 129). Despite all of Levinas's caution about the violence inherent in comprehension, philosophical reflection is part of the work of justice and the work of identifying the incompleteness of justice.

Robert Gibbs uses the term "correlation" to describe the kind of conversation that develops between Greek sources and Hebrew sources in Levinas's thought. In his reading, a correlation is not an interaction "of two fixed terms in utter autonomy, but rather of two terms that become correlates of each other, each changing in itself through its relationship to the other."[12] This relation is neither assimilation nor radical otherness, but ongoing critical reflection leading to no final, totalized representation of reality or of the Good. That model of correlation captures Levinas's general understanding of philosophical discourse, in which not only ideas but we—as knowers, moral agents, and citizens—are called to account for ourselves and to be changed through that exposure. The question that remains is how we as readers of Levinas will respond to his critical inheritance of the philosophical tradition.

Levinas acknowledges that the central historical event of his life is the Shoah, and that it casts a shadow over all of his thought (PD 126). Part of inheriting Levinas's thought well is using it to think through contemporary social and political events—including our current ecological crisis and the disparate vulnerabilities that it imposes on various communities (human and nonhuman); sexist, heterosexist, racist, xenophobic, fundamentalist, and nationalist violence; and persisting, persistently normalized forms of inequality. But this endeavor also entails allowing his work to be reinterpreted in the light of contemporary concerns. There is no simple way to apply what Levinas writes about responsibility and justice to a particular historical event or moral question, but what provokes us to think about responsibility and justice, and then act in accordance with those thoughts, is what happens in the world and to others—not just in abstraction, but those living on a distant coast or next door. In reference to the Shoah, Chanter draws out the ambivalence of Levinas's response to historical events: "To think it is to reduce it to a theme. Not to think it is to abscond responsibility."[13] What justice would look like, in any particular situation or for a whole planet, is never settled, and that is for Levinas a necessity of justice rather than a sign of its irrelevance or collapse.

Levinas offers no normative principles that might function as an ethical system or as the *telos* of a political narrative, but his work proposes a conception of subjectivity that counters the dominant ideal offered by modern Western thought, defined primarily by its autonomy, individuality, and disembodiment. This is a subject unaffected by diachrony, by a commitment older than intention or deliberation action. It is a subject impervious to the trauma of encountering the other and the question of the ego's right to be. To the extent that this kind of subject has been associated with affluent white men, and with those who have been able to claim that status in an honorific way, Levinas opens up a broader picture of what it means to be a subject. And given that this same ideal has underwritten various projects of racial, gendered, and colonial domination, the Levinasian conception of subjectivity helps to dismantle such projects and their ongoing repercussions.

Diachronous time destabilizes what seems most unquestionable: one's right to be and one's right to act according to the impulses and rationalized projects of the *conatus*. The ethical significance of time highlights the fundamental passivity of the subject—not simply his mortality or finitude, as Levinas reminds us, because the idea of finitude leaves intact the subject's powers and capabilities within certain bounds. The trauma of responsibility unsettles our complacency as moral, epistemic, and political agents, even if that trauma will be reflected on and assimilated into intelligible narratives of how we should live and what we can know. The very instability of the oscillation between the ethical and the political counters our "usurpation of the whole world" by naming it as a usurpation, a morally significant condition for which we are called to account. Despite Levinas's focus on the passivity of the subject in the face of the immemorial past, the urgent question that he poses for us is how being exposed to such a past, such intrigues of time, will inform our thinking and acting in the present and the future.

Notes

1. Gibbs, *Correlations in Rosenzweig and Levinas*, 214.
2. Chalier, *What Ought I to Do?*, 118–19. On this idea of the creature as one who comes into a world that is already formed, see Nancy, *Being Singular Plural*, 97–99.
3. Ajzenstat, *Driven Back to the Text*, 205.

4. Ibid., 217.
5. Rolland, postscript to *God, Death, and Time*, 226.
6. Michael Fagenblat claims that "Levinas accepted Heidegger's fundamental claim that thinking itself is an interpretive engagement with the intellectual heritage that constitutes the historical situation of the philosopher," and the content of that engagement attempts to interrupt the dominant assumptions that he inherits (Fagenblat, *Covenant of Creatures*, xiii).
7. See Fagenblat, *Covenant of Creatures*, 196.
8. Moyn, *Origins of the Other*, 113–63.
9. Derrida, "Violence and Metaphysics," 148–53.
10. Marrati, "Derrida and Levinas," 71.
11. Chanter, *Time, Death, and the Feminine*, 227.
12. Gibbs, *Correlations in Rosenzweig and Levinas*, 4.
13. Chanter, *Time, Death, and the Feminine*, 221.

Bibliography

For a bibliography of works by Emmanuel Levinas, see the list of abbreviations.

Adams, Carol. *The Sexual Politics of Meat: A Feminist Vegetarian Critical Theory*. New York: Continuum, 1990.
Agamben, Giorgio. *The Open: Man and Animal*. Translated by Kevin Attell. Stanford: Stanford University Press, 2004.
Ajzenstat, Oona. *Driven Back to the Text: The Premodern Sources of Levinas's Postmodernism*. Pittsburgh: Duquesne University Press, 2001.
———. "Levinas versus Levinas: Hebrew, Greek, and Linguistic Justice." *Philosophy and Rhetoric* 38, no. 2 (2005): 145–58.
Alexander, Caroline. "Faces of War." *Smithsonian* 37, no. 11 (Feb. 2007): 72–80.
Al-Saji, Alia. "The Temporality of Life: Merleau-Ponty, Bergson, and the Immemorial Past." *Southern Journal of Philosophy* 55 (2007): 177–206.
———. "'A Past Which Has Never Been Present': Bergsonian Dimensions in Merleau-Ponty's Theory of the Prepersonal." *Research in Phenomenology* 38 (2008): 41–71.
American Psychiatric Association. "Posttraumatic Stress Disorder." In *Diagnostic and Statistical Manual of Mental Disorders*, 5th ed., 271–278. Washington, DC: American Psychiatric Association, 2013.
Ansell-Pearson, Keith. *Philosophy and the Adventure of the Virtual: Bergson and the Time of Life*. London: Routledge, 2002.
Appiah, K. Anthony. "Race, Culture, Identity: Misunderstood Connections." In *Color Conscious: The Political Morality of Race*, edited by K. Anthony Appiah and Amy Gutmann, 30–105. Princeton: Princeton University Press, 1996.
Arendt, Hannah. *Eichmann in Jerusalem: A Report on the Banality of Evil*. New York: Penguin, 2006.
Aristotle. *Physics*. Translated by R. P. Hardie and R. K. Gaye. In *The Basic Works of Aristotle*, edited by Richard McKeon, 218–394. New York: Modern Library, 1941.
Atterton, Peter. "Levinas and Our Moral Responsibility toward Other Animals." *Inquiry* 54, no. 6 (Dec. 2011): 633–49.
Augustine. *Confessions*. Translated by R. S. Pine-Coffin. New York: Penguin, 1961.
Beauchamp, Tom L., and R. G. Frey, eds. *The Oxford Handbook of Animal Ethics*. Oxford: Oxford University Press, 2011.
Beauvoir, Simone de. *The Second Sex*. Translated by H. M. Parshley. New York: Bantam Books, 1952.
Benhabib, Seyla. "The Generalized Other and the Concrete Other: The Kohlberg-Gilligan Controversy and Moral Theory." In *Situating the Self: Gender, Community and Postmodernism in Contemporary Ethics*, 148–77. New York: Routledge, 1992.
Benjamin, Walter. "Theses on the Philosophy of History." In *Illuminations: Essays and Reflections*, translated by Harry Zohn, 253–64. New York: Schocken, 1968.
Benso, Silvia. *The Face of Things: A Different Side of Ethics*. Albany: State University of New York Press, 2000.

Bentham, Jeremy. *An Introduction to the Principles of Morals and Legislation*. Edited by J. H. Burns and H. L. A. Hart. Oxford: Clarendon Press, 1970.

Bergo, Bettina. *Between Ethics and Politics: For the Beauty that Adorns the Earth*. Pittsburgh: Duquesne University Press, 1999.

———. "Levinasian Responsibility and Freudian Analysis: Is the Unthinkable an Un-Conscious?" In *Addressing Levinas*, 257–95.

———. "Levinas's Weak Messianism in Time and Flesh, or the Insistence of Messiah Ben David." *Journal for Cultural Research* 13, nos. 3–4 (Jul.–Oct. 2009): 225–47.

———. "What Is Levinas Doing? Phenomenology and the Rhetoric of the Ethical Un-Conscious." *Philosophy and Rhetoric* 38, no. 2 (2005): 122–44.

Bergson, Henri. *The Creative Mind: An Introduction to Metaphysics*. Translated by Mabelle L. Andison. New York: Citadel Press, 1992.

———. *Introduction to Metaphysics*. Translated by T. E. Hulme. Indianapolis: Hackett, 1999.

———. *Time and Free Will: An Essay on the Immediate Data of Consciousness*. Translated by F. L. Pogson. New York: Harper & Row, 1960.

Bernasconi, Robert. "Different Styles of Eschatology: Derrida's Take on Levinas' Political Messianism." *Research in Phenomenology* 28, no. 1 (1998): 3–19.

———. "Levinas and the Struggle for Existence." In *Addressing Levinas*, 170–84.

———. "The Third Party: Levinas on the Intersection of the Ethical and the Political." *Journal of the British Society for Phenomenology* 30, no. 1 (Jan. 1999): 76–87.

———. "The Trace of Levinas in Derrida." In *Derrida and Difference*, edited by Robert Bernasconi and David C. Wood, 13–29. Evanston, IL: Northwestern University Press, 1988.

———. "What Are Prophets For? Negotiating the Teratological Hypocrisy of Judeo-Hellenic Europe." *Revista Portuguesa de Filosofia* 62, nos. 2/4 (Apr.–Dec. 2006): 441–55.

———. "What Is the Question to Which 'Substitution' Is the Answer?" In *The Cambridge Companion to Levinas*, 234–51.

Bernasconi, Robert, and Simon Critchley, eds. *Re-Reading Levinas*. Bloomington: Indiana University Press, 1991.

Bernet, Rudolf. "Levinas's Critique of Husserl." In *The Cambridge Companion to Levinas*, 82–99.

———. "The Traumatized Subject." *Research in Phenomenology* 30, no. 1 (2000): 160–79.

Bernstein, Richard J. "Evil and the Temptation of Theodicy." In *The Cambridge Companion to Levinas*, 252–67.

Bevis, Kathryn. "'Better than Metaphors'? Dwelling and the Maternal Body in Emmanuel Levinas." *Literature and Theology* 21, no. 3 (Sept. 2007): 317–29.

Bordo, Susan. *Unbearable Weight: Feminism, Western Culture, and the Body*. Berkeley: University of California Press, 1993.

Brenner, Athalya, ed. *Genesis: A Feminist Companion to the Bible*. Sheffield, UK: Sheffield Academic Press, 1993.

Brison, Susan. *Aftermath: Violence and the Remaking of a Self*. Princeton: Princeton University Press, 2002.

Buckingham, Will. *Levinas, Storytelling and Anti-Storytelling*. New York: Bloomsbury, 2013.

Bushnell, Rebecca. *Prophesying Tragedy: Sign and Voice in Sophocles' Theban Plays.* Ithaca: Cornell University Press, 1988.
Butler, Judith. *Bodies that Matter.* New York: Routledge, 1993.
———. *Precarious Life: The Powers of Mourning and Violence.* New York: Verso, 2006.
Calarco, Matthew. "Deconstruction Is Not Vegetarianism: Humanism, Subjectivity, and Animal Ethics." *Continental Philosophy Review* 37, no. 2 (Jun. 2004): 175–201.
———. "Faced by Animals." In *Radicalizing Levinas*, edited by Peter Atterton and Matthew Calarco, 113–33. Albany: State University of New York Press, 2012.
———. *Zoographies: The Question of the Animal from Heidegger to Derrida.* New York: Columbia University Press, 2008.
Cameron, Alister. *The Identity of Oedipus the King: Five Essays on the Oedipus Tyrannus.* New York: New York University Press, 1968.
Campbell, Sue. *Relational Remembering: Rethinking the Memory Wars.* New York: Rowman & Littlefield, 2003.
Caruth, Cathy. *Unclaimed Experience: Trauma, Narrative, and History.* Baltimore: The Johns Hopkins University Press, 1996.
Cavarero, Adriana. *In Spite of Plato: A Feminist Rewriting of Ancient Philosophy.* Translated by Serena Anderlini-D'Onofrio and Áine O'Healy. New York: Routledge, 1995.
———. *Relating Narratives: Storytelling and Selfhood.* Translated by Paul A. Kottman. London: Routledge, 2000.
Caygill, Howard. *Levinas and the Political.* London: Routledge, 2002.
Chalier, Catherine. *Figures du feminine: Lecture d'Emmanuel Lévinas.* Paris: La nuit surveillé, 1982.
———. "Levinas and the Talmud." In *The Cambridge Companion to Levinas*, 100–18.
———. "The Messianic Utopia." In *Emmanuel Levinas.* Vol. 3: *Levinas and the Question of Religion*, edited by Claire Katz, 44–58. London: Routledge, 2005.
———. *What Ought I to Do? Morality in Kant and Levinas.* Translated by Jane Marie Todd. Ithaca: Cornell University Press, 2002.
Chanter, Tina. *Time, Death, and the Feminine: Levinas with Heidegger.* Stanford: Stanford University Press, 2001.
Chanter, Tina, ed. *Feminist Interpretations of Emmanuel Levinas.* University Park: Pennsylvania State University Press, 2001.
Ciaramelli, Fabio. *Transcendence et Éthique.* Brussels: Ousia, 1989.
Clark, David. "On Being the 'Last Kantian in Nazi Germany': Dwelling with Animals after Levinas." In *Animal Acts: Configuring the Human in Western History*, edited by Jennifer Ham and Matthew Senior, 165–98. New York: Routledge, 1997.
Cohen, Richard A. *Elevations: The Height of the Good in Rosenzweig and Levinas.* Chicago: University of Chicago Press, 1994.
———. *Ethics, Exegesis, and Philosophy: Interpretation after Levinas.* Cambridge: Cambridge University Press, 2001.
———. Introduction to *Unforeseen History.* Urbana: University of Illinois Press, 2004.
———. *Levinasian Meditations: Ethics, Philosophy, and Religion.* Pittsburgh: Duquesne University Press, 2010.
Critchley, Simon. *The Ethics of Deconstruction: Derrida and Levinas.* Oxford: Blackwell, 1992.

———. *Ethics-Politics-Subjectivity: Essays on Derrida, Levinas and Contemporary French Thought*. New York: Verso, 1999.
———. *The Problem with Levinas*. Edited by Alexis Dianda. Oxford: Oxford University Press, 2015.
Critchley, Simon, and Robert Bernasconi, eds. *The Cambridge Companion to Levinas*. Cambridge: Cambridge University Press, 2002.
Darwin, Charles. *The Descent of Man*. Princeton: Princeton University Press, 1981.
———. *The Origin of Species*. New York: Collier, 1909.
David, Alain. "Cynesthèse: Autoportrait au chien." In *L'animal autobiographique: Autour de Jacques Derrida*, edited by Marie-Louise Mallet, 303–18. Paris: Galilee, 1999.
Davies, Paul. "Sincerity and the End of Theodicy: Three Remarks on Levinas and Kant." In *The Cambridge Companion to Levinas*, 161–87.
Davis, Michael. "Imaginary Cases in Ethics: A Critique." *International Journal of Applied Philosophy* 26, no. 1 (Spring 2012): 1–17.
Davy, Barbara Jane. "An Other Face of Ethics in Levinas." *Ethics and the Environment* 12, no. 1 (2007): 39–67.
Dawkins, Richard. *The Selfish Gene*. Oxford: Oxford University Press, 1989.
De Boer, Theodore. *The Rationality of Transcendence: Studies in the Philosophy of Emmanuel Levinas*. Amsterdam: J. C. Gieben, 1997.
Derrida, Jacques. *Adieu to Emmanuel Levinas*. Translated by Pascale-Anne Brault and Michael Naas. Stanford: Stanford University Press, 1999.
———. *The Animal That Therefore I Am*. Edited by Marie-Louise Mallet. Translated by David Wills. New York: Fordham University Press, 2008.
———. *Aporias: Dying-Awaiting (One Another at) the "Limits of Truth."* Translated by Thomas Dutoit. Stanford: Stanford University Press, 1993.
———. *Archive Fever: A Freudian Impression*. Translated by Eric Prenowitz. Chicago: University of Chicago Press, 1996.
———. "At This Very Moment in this Work Here I Am," translated by Ruben Berezdivin. In *Re-Reading Levinas*, 11–48.
———. *The Beast and the Sovereign*. Edited by Michel Lisse, Marie-Louise Mallet, and Ginette Michaud. Translated by Geoffrey Bennington. Chicago: University of Chicago Press, 2009.
———. "'Eating Well,' or the Calculation of the Subject," translated by Peter Connor and Avital Ronell. In *Points: Interviews 1974–1994*, edited by Elisabeth Weber, 255–87. Stanford: Stanford University Press, 1995.
———. "Violence and Metaphysics: An Essay on the Thought of Emmanuel Levinas." In *Writing and Difference*, translated by Alan Bass, 79–153. Chicago: University of Chicago Press, 1978.
Descartes, René. *Discourse on Method and Meditations on First Philosophy*. Translated by Donald A. Cress. 3rd ed. Indianapolis: Hackett, 1993.
———. Letter to Marin Mersenne. 24 December 1640. In *Descartes: Philosophical Writings*, translated by John Cottingham. Cambridge: Cambridge University Press, 1991.
Diamond, Cora. "The Difficulty of Reality and the Difficulty of Philosophy." In *Philosophy and Animal Life*, 43–90. New York: Columbia University Press, 2008.

———. "Eating Meat and Eating People." *Philosophy* 53, no. 206 (Oct. 1978): 465–79.
Drabinski, John. *Levinas and the Postcolonial: Race, Nation, Other.* Edinburgh: Edinburgh University Press, 2013.
———. *Sensibility and Singularity: The Problem of Phenomenology in Levinas.* Albany: State University of New York Press, 2001.
DuBois, Page. *Sowing the Body: Psychoanalysis and Ancient Representations of Women.* Chicago: University of Chicago Press, 1991.
Durie, Robin. "Speaking of Time . . . Husserl and Levinas on the Saying of Time." *Journal of the British Society for Phenomenology* 30, no.1 (Jan. 1999): 35–58.
Economist. Unsigned review of *Enemies of the People*, by Thet Sambath and Rob Lemkin. July 31, 2010: 31.
Enemies of the People. Directed and produced by Thet Sambath and Rob Lemkin. Mumbai: Old Street Films, 2010.
Fackenheim, Emil. *To Mend the World: Foundations of Post-Holocaust Jewish Thought.* Bloomington: Indiana University Press, 1982.
Fagenblat, Michael. *A Covenant of Creatures: Levinas's Philosophy of Judaism.* Stanford: Stanford University Press, 2010.
Fletcher, John. *Freud and the Scene of Trauma.* New York: Fordham University Press, 2013.
Fouts, Roger. *Next of Kin: My Conversations with Chimpanzees.* New York: Avon Books, 1998.
Freud, Sigmund. *Beyond the Pleasure Principle.* In *The Standard Edition of the Complete Psychological Works of Sigmund Freud*, 18:1–64.
———. *Civilization and Its Discontents.* In *The Standard Edition of the Complete Psychological Works of Sigmund Freud*, 21:57–146.
———. "A Difficulty in the Path of Psychoanalysis." In *The Standard Edition of the Complete Psychological Works of Sigmund Freud*, 17:135–44.
———. *Introductory Lectures on Psycho-Analysis.* In *The Standard Edition of the Complete Psychological Works of Sigmund Freud*, 16.
———. *Project for a Scientific Psychology.* In *The Standard Edition of the Complete Psychological Works of Sigmund Freud*, 1:283–398.
———. "Remembering, Repeating, and Working-Through." In *The Standard Edition of the Complete Psychological Works of Sigmund Freud*, 12:145–57.
———. *The Standard Edition of the Complete Psychological Works of Sigmund Freud*, translated by James Strachey. 24 vols. London: Hogarth, 1953–74.
Freud, Sigmund, and Josef Breuer, *Studies on Hysteria.* In *The Standard Edition of the Complete Psychological Works of Sigmund Freud*, 2:1–312.
Frye, Marilyn. "Some Reflections on Separatism and Power." In *The Politics of Reality*, 95–109. New York: Crossing Press, 1983.
Gibbs, Robert. *Correlations in Rosenzweig and Levinas.* Princeton: Princeton University Press, 1992.
Gordon, Peter Eli. *Rosenzweig and Heidegger: Between Judaism and German Philosophy.* Berkeley: University of California Press, 2005.
Grossman, Vasily. *Life and Fate.* Translated by Robert Chandler. New York: New York Review of Books, 2006.
Grosz, Elizabeth. *The Nick of Time: Politics, Evolution, and the Untimely.* Durham, NC: Duke University Press, 2004.

Guenther, Lisa. "*Le Flair Animal*: Levinas and the Possibility of Animal Friendship." *PhaenEx* 2, no. 2 (Fall/Winter 2007): 216–38.
———. *The Gift of the Other: Levinas and the Politics of Reproduction*. Albany: State University of New York Press, 2006.
Handelman, Susan. *Fragments of Redemption: Jewish Thought and Literary Theory in Benjamin, Scholem, and Levinas*. Bloomington: Indiana University Press, 1991.
Hauser, Marc D., Noam Chomsky, and W. Tecumseh Fitch. "The Faculty of Language: What Is It, Who Has It, and How Did It Evolve?" *Science* 298, no. 5598 (Nov. 2002): 1569–79.
Hegel, G. W. F. Introduction to *The Philosophy of History*. Translated by Leo Rauch. Indianapolis: Hackett, 1988.
———. *Phenomenology of Spirit*. Translated by A. V. Miller. Oxford: Clarendon Press, 1977.
Heidegger, Martin. *Being and Time*. Translated by Joan Stambaugh. Albany: State University of New York Press, 1996.
Heldke, Lisa. "Food Politics, Political Food." In *Cooking, Eating, Thinking: Transformative Philosophies of Food*, edited by Deane W. Curtin and Lisa Heldke, 301–27. Bloomington: Indiana University Press, 1992.
Herman, Judith. *Trauma and Recovery*. New York: Basic Books, 1997.
Hick, John. *Evil and the God of Love*. 2nd ed. New York: Palgrave Macmillan, 1966.
Hobbes, Thomas. *On the Citizen*. Edited by Richard Tuck and Michael Silverthorne. Cambridge: Cambridge University Press, 1998.
Hopkins, Burt C. "Deformalization and Phenomenon in Husserl and Heidegger." In *Heidegger, Translation, and the Task of Thinking: Essays in Honor of Parvis Emad*, edited by F. Schalow, 49–70. New York: Springer, 2011.
Horowitz, Asher. *Ethics at a Standstill: History and Subjectivity in Levinas and the Frankfurt School*. Pittsburgh: Duquesne University Press, 2008.
Horowitz, Mardi. *Stress Response Syndrome*. Northvale, NJ: Jason Aronson, 1986.
Husserl, Edmund. *Ideas: General Introduction to Pure Phenomenology*. Translated by W. R. Boyce Gibson. London: Routledge, 2012.
Irigaray, Luce. "Plato's Hystera." In *Speculum of the Other Woman*, translated by Gillian C. Gill, 243–264. Ithaca: Cornell University Press, 1985.
———. "Questions to Emmanuel Levinas: On the Divinity of Love," translated by Margaret Whitford. In *Re-Reading Levinas*, 109–18.
———. "Sorcerer Love: A Reading of Plato's *Symposium*, 'Diotima's Speech.'" *Hypatia* 3, no. 3 (Winter 1989): 32–44.
Kahn, Paul W. *Out of Eden: Adam and Eve and the Problem of Evil*. Princeton: Princeton University Press, 2007.
Kant, Immanuel. *Critique of Pure Reason*. Translated by Paul Guyer. Cambridge: Cambridge University Press, 1999.
———. *Lectures on Ethics*. Translated by Peter Heath. Edited by Peter Heath and L. B. Schneewind. Cambridge: Cambridge University Press, 1997.
Katz, Claire Elise. *Levinas and the Crisis of Humanism*. Bloomington: Indiana University Press, 2013.
———. *Levinas, Judaism, and the Feminine: The Silent Footsteps of Rebecca*. Bloomington: Indiana University Press, 2003.

Kavka, Martin. *Jewish Messianism and the History of Philosophy*. Cambridge: Cambridge University Press, 2004.

———. "Reading Messianically with Gershom Scholem." In *Rethinking the Messianic Idea in Judaism*, edited by Michael L. Morgan and Steven Weitzman, 404–18. Bloomington: Indiana University Press, 2015.

Keats, John. Letter to George and Georgiana Keats. 21 April 1819. In *Letters of John Keats to His Family and Friends*, edited by Sidney Colvin. New York: Macmillan, 1891.

Keenan, Dennis King. *Death and Responsibility: The "Work" of Levinas*. Albany: State University of New York Press, 1999.

Knox, Bernard M. W. *Oedipus at Thebes*. New Haven: Yale University Press, 1957.

Kosky, Jeffrey L. "After the Death of God: Emmanuel Levinas and the Ethical Possibility of God." *Journal of Religious Ethics* 24, no. 2 (1996): 235–59.

Kovacs, C. S. "Calcium and Bone Metabolism in Pregnancy and Lactation." *Journal of Clinical Endocrinology and Metabolism* 86, no. 6 (Jun. 2001): 2384–88.

LaCapra, Dominick. *Writing History, Writing Trauma*. Baltimore: The Johns Hopkins University Press, 2001.

Lambek, Michael. "Terror's Wake." In *The Trauma Controversy*, edited by Kristen Brown Golden and Bettina G. Bergo, 235–62. Albany: State University of New York Press, 2009.

Laplanche, Jean. "Notes on Afterwardsness." In *Essays on Otherness*, edited by John Fletcher, 260–65. New York: Routledge, 1999.

———. "Time and the Other." In *Essays on Otherness*, edited by John Fletcher, 234–59. New York: Routledge, 1999.

Laplanche, J., and J.-B. Pontalis. *The Language of Psychoanalysis*. Translated by Donald Nicholson-Smith. New York: W. W. Norton, 1973.

Laub, Dori, and Nanette C. Auerhahn. "Knowing and Not Knowing Massive Psychic Trauma: Forms of Traumatic Memory." *International Journal of Psychoanalysis* 74 (1993): 287–302.

Lawlor, Leonard. "Intuition and Duration: An Introduction to Bergson's 'Introduction to Metaphysics.'" In *Bergson and Phenomenology*, edited by Michael R. Kelly, 25–41. London: Palgrave Macmillan, 2010.

Lear, Jonathan. *Freud*. New York: Routledge, 2005.

———. "Knowingness and Abandonment: An Oedipus for Our Time." In *Open Minded: Working Out the Logic of the Soul*, 33–55. Cambridge: Harvard University Press, 1999.

Levi, Primo. *Survival in Auschwitz: The Nazi Assault on Humanity*. Translated by Stuart Woolf. New York: Collier, 1993.

Leys, Ruth. *Trauma: A Genealogy*. Chicago: University of Chicago Press, 2000.

Lin, Yael. *The Intersubjectivity of Time: Levinas and Infinite Responsibility*. Pittsburgh: Duquesne University Press, 2013.

Llewelyn, John. "Am I Obsessed by Bobby? (Humanism of the Other Animal)." In *Re-Reading Levinas*, 234–45.

———. *Emmanuel Levinas: The Genealogy of Ethics*. London: Routledge, 1995.

———. "Levinas and Language." In *The Cambridge Companion to Levinas*, 119–38.

———. *The Middle Voice of Ecological Conscience: A Chiasmic Reading of Responsibility in the Neighbourhood of Levinas, Heidegger, and Others*. Basingstoke: Macmillan, 1991.

———. "Where to Cut: *Boucherie* and *Delikatessen*." *Research in Phenomenology* 40, no. 2 (2010): 161–87.
Lloyd, Genevieve. *The Man of Reason: "Male" and "Female" in Western Philosophy*. London: Routledge, 1993.
Locke, John. *Second Treatise of Government*. Edited by C. B. Macpherson. Indianapolis: Hackett, 1980.
Long, A. A., and D. N. Sedley, eds. *The Hellenistic Philosophers*. Vol. 1. Cambridge: Cambridge University Press, 1987.
Luckhurst, Roger. *The Trauma Question*. London: Routledge, 2008.
MacAvoy, Leslie. "The Other Side of Intentionality." In *Addressing Levinas*, 109–18.
MacDonald, Michael J. "Losing Spirit: Hegel, Lévinas, and the Limits of Narrative." *Narrative* 13, no. 12 (May 2005): 182–94.
MacIntyre, Alasdair. "Danish Ethical Demands and French Common Goods: Two Moral Philosophies." *European Journal of Philosophy* 18, no. 1 (Mar. 2010): 1–16.
Marrati, Paola. "Derrida and Levinas: Ethics, Writing, Historicity." In *Levinas Studies: An Annual Review*, vol. 1, edited by Jeffrey Bloechl and Jeffrey L. Kosky, 51–71. Pittsburgh: Duquesne University Press, 2005.
McDavid, Jenna. "Control and Incarceration of Human and Non-Human Beings." In *The End of Prisons: Reflections from the Decarceration Movement*, edited by Mechthild E. Nagel and Anthony J. Nocella II, 135–46. Amsterdam: Rodopi, 2013.
McDowell, John. "Comment on Stanley Cavell's 'Companionable Thinking.'" In *Philosophy and Animal Life*, 127–38. New York: Columbia University Press, 2008.
McIntosh, Peggy. "White Privilege: Unpacking the Invisible Knapsack." *Peace and Freedom Magazine* (Jul.–Aug. 1989): 10–12.
McWhorter, Ladelle. "Sex, Race, and Biopower: A Foucauldian Genealogy." *Hypatia* 19, no. 3 (Summer 2004): 38–62.
Meir, Ephraim. "Hellenic and Jewish in Levinas's Writings." *Veritas* 51, no. 2 (Jun. 2006): 79–88.
Merleau-Ponty, Maurice. *The Visible and the Invisible*. Translated by Alphonso Lingis. Evanston, IL: Northwestern University Press, 1968.
Meskin, Jacob. "In the Flesh: Embodiment and Jewish Existence in the Thought of Levinas." *Soundings* 76, no. 1 (Spring 1993): 173–90.
Meyers, Carol L. *Discovering Eve: Ancient Israelite Women in Context*. New York: Oxford University Press, 1988.
Michaelsen, Cathrine Bjørnholt. "Tracing a Traumatic Temporality: Levinas and Derrida on Trauma and Responsibility." In *Levinas Studies: An Annual* Review, edited by Jeffrey Bloechl, vol. 10, 43–77. Pittsburgh: Duquesne University Press, 2016.
Mills, Charles. *Blackness Visible: Essays on Philosophy and Race*. Ithaca: Cornell University Press, 1998.
Morgan, Michael L. *Discovering Levinas*. Cambridge: Cambridge University Press, 2007.
———. "Levinas and Messianism." In *Rethinking the Messianic Idea in Judaism*, edited by Michael L. Morgan and Steven Weitzman, 195–228. Bloomington: Indiana University Press, 2015.
Moyn, Samuel. *Origins of the Other: Emmanuel Levinas between Revelation and Ethics*. Ithaca: Cornell University Press, 2005.

Naas, Michael. "Derrida's Flair (For the Animals to Follow . . .)." *Research in Phenomenology* 40, no. 2 (2010): 219–42.
Nagel, Thomas. "Moral Luck." In *Mortal Questions*, 24–38. Cambridge: Cambridge University Press, 1991.
Nancy, Jean-Luc. *Being Singular Plural*. Translated by Robert D. Richardson and Anne E. O'Byrne. Stanford: Stanford University Press, 2000.
Nelson, Eric Sean, Antje Kapust, and Kent Still, eds. *Addressing Levinas*. Evanston, IL: Northwestern University Press, 2005.
Nelson, Hilde Lindemann. *Damaged Identities, Narrative Repair*. Ithaca: Cornell University Press, 2001.
Nietzsche, Friedrich. *Beyond Good and Evil*. Translated by Walter Kaufmann. New York: Vintage, 1989.
———. *On the Genealogy of Morals and Ecce Homo*. Translated by Walter Kaufmann and R. J. Hollingdale. New York: Vintage, 1967.
Nolte, Eric. "Vergangenheit die nicht vergehen will." *Frankfurter Allgemeine Zeitung*, 6 June 1986.
Oliver, Kelly. *Animal Lessons: How They Teach Us to Be Human*. New York: Columbia University Press, 2009.
Omi, Michael, and Howard Winant. "Racial Formation in the United States." In *The Idea of Race*, edited by Robert Bernasconi and Tommy L. Lott, 181–211. Indianapolis: Hackett, 2000.
Oppenheim, Michael. *Speaking/Writing of God: Jewish Philosophical Reflections on the Life with Others*. Albany: State University of New York Press, 1997.
Outlaw, Lucius T., Jr. *On Race and Philosophy*. New York: Routledge, 1996.
Ovid. *Metamorphoses*. Translated by Stanley Lombardo. Indianapolis: Hackett, 2010.
Pascal, Blaise. *Pensées*. Translated by Roger Ariew. Indianapolis: Hackett, 2004.
Pecora, Vincent. "Habermas, Enlightenment, and Antisemitism." In *Probing the Limits of Representation: Nazism and the "Final Solution,"* edited by Saul Friedlander, 155–70. Cambridge: Harvard University Press, 1992.
Peperzak, Adriaan. "Levinas' Method." *Research in Phenomenology* 28, no. 1 (1998): 110–25.
Perpich, Diane. "Don't Try This at Home: Levinas and Applied Ethics." In *Totality and Infinity at 50*, edited by Scott Davidson and Diane Perpich, 127–52. Pittsburgh: Duquesne University Press, 2012.
———. *The Ethics of Emmanuel Levinas*. Stanford: Stanford University Press, 2008.
———. "Figurative Language and the 'Face' in Levinas's Philosophy." *Philosophy and Rhetoric* 38, no. 2 (2005): 103–21.
———. "Sensible Subjects: Levinas and Irigaray on Incarnation and Ethics." In *Addressing Levinas*, 296–309.
Plant, Bob. "Welcoming Dogs: Levinas and 'the Animal' Question." *Philosophy and Social Criticism* 37, no. 1 (Jan. 2011): 49–71.
Plato. *Phaedo*. Translated by Hugh Tredennick. In *Plato: The Collected Dialogues*, edited by Edith Hamilton and Huntington Cairns, 40–98. Princeton: Princeton University Press, 1989.
———. *Symposium*. Translated by Michael Joyce. In *Plato: The Collected Dialogues*, edited by Edith Hamilton and Huntington Cairns, 526–74. Princeton: Princeton University Press, 1989.

Pogge, Thomas. "Severe Poverty as a Human Rights Violation." In *Freedom from Poverty as a Human Right: Who Owes What to the Very Poor?*, edited by Thomas Pogge, 11–54. Oxford: Oxford University Press, 2007.

Raffoul, François. *The Origins of Responsibility*. Bloomington: Indiana University Press, 2010.

Regan, Tom. *The Case for Animal Rights*. Berkeley: University of California Press, 1983.

———. *Defending Animal Rights*. Urbana: University of Illinois Press, 2001.

Rich, Adrienne. *Of Woman Born: Motherhood as Experience and Institution*. New York: W. W. Norton, 1976.

Ricoeur, Paul. "Otherwise: A Reading of Emmanuel Levinas's *Otherwise than Being or Beyond Essence*." *Yale French Studies* 104 (2004): 82–99.

Robbins, Jill. Introduction to *Is It Righteous to Be? Interviews with Emmanuel Levinas*, edited by Jill Robbins, 1–19. Stanford: Stanford University Press, 2001.

Rolland, Jacques. "Death in Its Negativity." *Graduate Faculty Philosophy Journal* 20, no. 2 (1998): 461–92.

———. "Postscript: On the Other Man: Time, Death, and God." In *God, Death, and Time*, translated by Bettina Bergo, 225–39. Stanford: Stanford University Press, 2000.

Rosato, Jennifer. "Woman as Vulnerable Self: The Trope of Maternity in Levinas's *Otherwise Than Being*." *Hypatia* 27, no. 2 (Spring 2012): 359–62.

Rosen, Joseph. "From a Memory beyond Memory to a State beyond the State." In *Difficult Justice: Commentaries on Levinas and Politics*, edited by Asher Horowitz and Gad Horowitz, 285–306. Toronto: University of Toronto Press, 2006.

Rosenzweig, Franz. *The Star of Redemption*. Translated by Barbara E. Galli. Madison: University of Wisconsin Press, 2005.

Sachs, Carl. "The Acknowledgement of Transcendence: Anti-Theodicy in Adorno and Levinas." *Philosophy and Social Criticism* 37, no. 3 (Mar. 2010): 273–94.

Sandford, Stella. *The Metaphysics of Love: Gender and Transcendence in Levinas*. New Brunswick, NJ: Athlone, 2000.

Sands, Kathleen. "Tragedy, Theology, and Feminism in the Time after Time." In *Rethinking Tragedy*, edited by Rita Felski, 82–103. Baltimore: The Johns Hopkins University Press, 2008.

Santner, Eric L. "History beyond the Pleasure Principle." In *Probing the Limits of Representation: Nazism and the "Final Solution*," edited by Saul Friedlander, 143–54. Cambridge: Harvard University Press, 1992.

Scarry, Elaine. *The Body in Pain: The Making and Unmaking of the World*. Oxford: Oxford University Press, 1985.

Scheman, Naomi. "'Though This Be Method, Yet There Is Madness in It': Paranoia and Liberal Epistemology." In *Engenderings: Constructions of Knowledge, Authority, and Privilege*, 75–105. New York: Routledge, 1993.

Schopenhauer, Arthur. *The World as Will and Representation*. Translated and edited by Christopher Janaway, Judith Norman, and Alistair Welchman. Cambridge: Cambridge University Press, 2014.

Segal, Charles. *Oedipus Tyrannus: Tragic Heroism and the Limits of Knowledge*. New York: Twayne Publishers, 1993.

Severson, Eric. *Levinas's Philosophy of Time*. Pittsburgh: Duquesne University Press, 2013.

Shakespeare, William. *Four Tragedies*. Edited by David Bevington. New York: Bantam, 1980.
Sikka, Sonya. "The Delightful Other: Portraits of the Feminine in Kierkegaard, Nietzsche, and Levinas." In *Feminist Interpretations of Emmanuel Levinas*, edited by Tina Chanter, 96–118. University Park: Pennsylvania State University Press, 2001.
Singer, Peter. *Animal Liberation*. New York: Avon, 1975.
———, ed. *In Defense of Animals: The Second Wave*. Malden, MA: Blackwell, 2006.
Sophocles. *Antigone*. In *The Complete Greek Tragedies: Sophocles I*, translated by David Grene, edited by David Grene and Richmond Lattimore, 2nd ed., 159–212. Chicago: University of Chicago Press, 1991.
———. *Oedipus the King*. In *The Complete Greek Tragedies: Sophocles I*, translated by David Grene, edited by David Grene and Richmond Lattimore, 2nd ed., 9–76. Chicago: University of Chicago Press, 1991.
Spinoza, Benedict de. *Ethics*. In *Complete Works*, translated by Samuel Shirley, edited by Michael Morgan, 213–382. Indianapolis: Hackett, 2002.
Sufka, Kenneth, Morgan Weldon, and Colin Allen. "The Case for Animal Emotions: Modeling Neuropsychiatric Disorders." In *The Oxford Handbook of Philosophy and Neuroscience*, edited by John Bickle, 522–36. Oxford: Oxford University Press, 2009.
Sugarman, Richard I. "Emmanuel Levinas and the Deformalization of Time." *Analecta Husserliana* 90 (2006): 253–69.
Tennyson, Alfred. "In Memoriam A. H. H." In *Selected Poems*, edited by Christopher Ricks, 96–199. New York: Penguin, 2007.
Thomson, Judith Jarvis. "A Defense of Abortion." *Philosophy and Public Affairs* 1, no. 1 (Oct. 1971): 47–66.
Trible, Phyllis. *God and the Rhetoric of Sexuality*. Philadelphia: Fortress Press, 1986.
Twigg, Julia. "Vegetarianism and the Meanings of Meat." In *The Sociology of Food and Eating: Essays on the Sociological Significance of Food*, edited by A. Murcott, 18–30. Aldershot, UK: Gower, 1986.
Vernant, Jean-Pierre, and Pierre Vidal-Naquet. *Myth and Tragedy in Ancient Greece*. Translated by Janet Lloyd. New York: Zone Books, 1988.
Walker, Margaret Urban. "Moral Luck and the Virtues of Impure Agency." In *Moral Luck*, edited by Daniel Statman, 235–50. Albany: State University of New York Press, 1993.
Ward, Graham. "On Time and Salvation." In *Facing the Other: The Ethics of Emmanuel Levinas*, edited by Seán Hand, 153–71. London: Routledge, 2011.
Warren, Nicholas de. "Miracles of Creation: Bergson and Levinas." In *Bergson and Phenomenology*, edited by Michael R. Kelly, 174–200. New York: Palgrave Macmillan, 2010.
Weathers, F. W., B. T. Litz, T. M. Keane, P. A. Palmieri, B. P. Marx, and P. P. Schnurr. "The PTSD Checklist for DSM-5 (PCL-5)—Standard." National Center for Post-Traumatic Stress Disorder. 2013. www.ptsd.va.gov/professional/assessment/adult-sr/ptsd-checklist.asp.
Weber, Elisabeth. "Persecution in Levinas's *Otherwise than Being*." In *Ethics as First Philosophy: The Significance of Emmanuel Levinas for Philosophy, Literature and Religion*, edited by Adriaan T. Peperzak, 69–76. New York: Routledge, 1995.

West, Cornel. "A Genealogy of Modern Racism." In *Race Critical Theories*, edited by Philomena Essed and David Theo Goldberg, 90–112. Malden, MA: Blackwell, 2002.

Weston, Anthony. *Back to Earth: Tomorrow's Environmentalism*. Philadelphia: Temple University Press, 1994.

Williams, Bernard. *Shame and Necessity*. Berkeley: University of California Press, 1993.

Wollstonecraft, Mary. *A Vindication of the Rights of Woman*. Edited by Sylvana Tomaselli. Cambridge: Cambridge University Press, 1995.

Wood, David. "*Comment ne pas manger*—Deconstruction and Humanism." In *Animal Others: On Ethics, Ontology, and Animal Life*, edited by H. Peter Steeves, 15–35. Albany: State University of New York Press, 1999.

Zack, Naomi. *Race and Mixed Race*. Philadelphia: Temple University Press, 1993.

Ziarek, Ewa Plonowska. *An Ethics of Dissensus: Postmodernity, Feminism, and the Politics of Radical Democracy*. Stanford: Stanford University Press, 2001.

———. "Rethinking Dispossession: On Being in One's Skin." *Parallax* 7, no. 2 (Apr. 2001): 3–19.

Index

Abraham, 104–105
afterwardsness (*Nachträglichkeit*), 32–33
Agamben, Giorgio, 132, 135, 214n7, 216n81
agency, 65, 101–122, 157n7, 229–230; and embodiment, 138–139, 150, 181; and gender, 166–168; and time, xv, 1–2, 13; loss of, 25–27, 31–32, 52–53, 96, 114, 120–122, 126; moral, xii, 118, 122, 212–213; traditional conception of, 31–32, 93, 101–105, 110–113, 138–139, 150, 160, 167, 181, 219–220. *See also* autonomy
aging, 13, 46, 138–143, 165–166, 171
Ajzenstat, Oona, xixn4, 84, 92, 223
anarchy, xv–xvii, 52–55, 104, 120–123, 137–138, 154–156, 188, 192, 199–201, 205; as resistance to memory, 21, 29–30, 35n3, 42, 63–65, 68, 155, 182–183, 222; political, 154
Anaxagoras, 74
animals/animality, xvii, 75, 117, 132–133, 139, 149–150, 160–161, 167, 175–178, 181, 183n1, 187–217, 224, 228
anthropocentrism, xvii, 167, 187–192, 195, 199, 201–205, 210–213, 215n34, 219, 228
Antigone, 176–177, 183n11
anti-Semitism, 61, 136, 145–147
anxiety, 55–56, 83, 103, 195, 211, 216n81, 219; about embodiment, xvi–xviii, 130–136, 143–150, 156, 159–162; about time, 77, 143, 159–162, 167, 171–182; relation to trauma, 24, 61–62
Arendt, Hannah, 87
Aristotle, xiv, 2–3, 5, 9, 12, 77
Atterton, Peter, 201
Augustine, 2, 132, 142
autonomy, 101–115, 129–135, 143–150, 154–156, 165–167, 188, 211–213, 220–225, 229–230; and embodiment, 132–135, 138, 144–150, 181, 211; and masculinity, 52–53, 159–160, 163–167, 178–183, 210; link to consciousness, 2, 13–15, 22, 101–104; role of memory in, xii, 31–34, 51–55, 59, 65–67, 73–74, 79, 107–108, 131, 182; traditional ideal of, xi–xiv, xviii–xix, 1–2, 22, 46–48, 62, 83, 120–121, 165–166, 211–213; transcendence of history, 73–74, 102–103, 114, 129–131, 147–150, 154–155, 220–225. *See also* agency; heteronomy

Beauvoir, Simone de, 152, 166–167
Benhabib, Seyla, 103
Benjamin, Walter, 90–91, 99n52
Bentham, Jeremy, 192
Bergo, Bettina, 30, 43, 94
Bergson, Henri, xiv, 3–6, 8, 14, 16, 17n12, 21, 22, 46; duration, 3–5, 8, 10, 21
Bernasconi, Robert, 69n4, 83, 183n4
Bernet, Rudolf, 29, 34
Bernstein, Richard, 70n20, 88, 96
betrayal, 10–11, 40–45, 49, 73, 123, 134, 137, 155, 219, 227
Bevis, Kathryn, 58
Bloch, Ernst, 173
Blondel, Charles, 22
Brison, Susan, 26, 31, 65
Buckingham, Will, 54
Butler, Judith, 22, 157n30

Calarco, Matthew, 183n1, 201, 203, 207, 211–212, 215n55
Campbell, Sue, 52–53
Caruth, Cathy, 26, 36n29
Cavarero, Adriana, 109, 163–164
Chalier, Catherine, 17n36, 78, 94, 222
Chanter, Tina, 7, 17n24, 32, 42, 53, 62–63, 98n41, 152, 167, 177, 184n44, 227, 230
Christianity, 74, 78–79, 97n9, 131, 144
Chronos/Cronos, 4, 8, 76–77, 103
Ciaramelli, Fabio, 29
Clark, David, 196, 198–199, 215n34
Cleanthes, 187
Coetzee, J. M., 204–205
Cohen, Hermann, 93
Cohen, Richard A., 22, 47, 121
conatus essendi, xiv–xvii, 27–31, 39, 47, 104, 115–116, 125, 201–203, 208–209, 219–225, 230; and animality, 175–176, 188–198, 202–203; and anxiety, xvi–xvii, 129–130, 159–162, 169–183; and embodiment, 139–145, 175–176;

245

conatus essendi (cont.)
  and gender, xvii, 159–167, 178–183; and
  Heidegger, 184n44; and Hobbes, 104;
  interruption of, xiv–xv, 4, 28, 32, 54–55,
  94–95, 119–121, 138–145, 160–161, 172–173;
  relation to history, 91–92
consciousness, xi–xii, 47–48, 131–132, 150–151,
  206–210, 225, 227; and death, 168–172,
  176–177; and temporal representation, 1–16,
  19–20, 24–30, 40, 51–54, 58–62, 77–91, 102,
  114–116, 174, 208–209; as assimilation, 14,
  39–40, 102–105, 189–190, 199–202, 210;
  disruption by trauma, xiii, xv, 15–22, 24–30,
  51–56, 113–115, 125–126, 154, 219–221; in
  psychoanalysis, 21–22, 24–25, 33–34, 69,
  98n21; relation to embodiment, 137–138,
  140–145, 181–182. *See also* history;
  immemorial past; intentionality; memory;
  narrative; synchrony
consumption, 116–117, 125, 170, 190–196, 203,
  208
creation, 1, 11–12, 21, 95, 114, 154–155, 158n46,
  159–164, 173, 182, 221–222
creatureliness, xvii, 114–115, 132, 150–156,
  158n46, 176, 182, 187–189, 205–206, 213,
  221–228, 230n2
Critchley, Simon, 22, 44, 51, 69n4, 114, 123,
  128n60, 136

Darwin, Charles, 160, 165, 167, 170, 175,
  183nn1–2, 183n4, 184n44, 187–191, 201, 213
Davies, Paul, 83, 98n20
death, xiii–xiv, 7, 8, 10, 61, 84, 116–118, 135–36,
  153, 159–85; and animals, 190–191, 204–206,
  211, 230; anxiety about mortality, xvi–xviii,
  76–77, 159–167, 181; as sacrifice, 73, 190–191; of
  the other, 7–10, 61, 86, 90, 116–118, 153, 157n30,
  160, 169–177, 180
De Boer, Theodore, 47, 56, 126n12
denucleation, 20, 26, 28, 33–34, 46, 52, 54, 56, 59,
  116, 139–141, 150, 220. *See also* trauma
Derrida, Jacques, xvii, 41–43, 45–46, 49, 63,
  67–69, 70n35, 71n72, 127n14; on animality,
  132, 157n5, 188–204, 210–11, 214n9, 215n31,
  215n34, 216n81, 226
Descartes, René, 121, 131–132, 138, 143, 224
despair, 73–74, 76, 79–87, 94, 96–97, 122
diachrony: and creatureliness, 154–155,
  221–224; and embodiment, 139–143, 159, 167,
  171; and responsibility, xiv–xvii, 7–9, 14–16,
  28–29, 50–51, 62, 74, 97, 113–115, 121, 143–144,
  173–177, 182, 201–203, 230; and trauma,
  16, 19–21, 31, 33–34, 57–59, 62, 69, 79–80,
  197–198; opposed to synchrony, xii, 1–2, 5–8,
  10–16, 31, 39–45, 47–59, 89–93, 107, 151–152,
  174–177, 219–221. *See also* immemorial past;
  synchrony
Diamond, Cora, xvii, 188, 204–207, 210–211
Dostoevsky, Fyodor, 225
Drabinski, John, 17n18, 43, 56–59, 67–68, 139,
  151–153

embodiment, xvi–xvii, 20, 22, 49, 58–59, 103,
  129–159, 162–171, 176–183, 185n57, 187, 192,
  201–204, 211, 230
eschatology, 41, 64, 91–92, 96
Eurocentrism, xviii, 147–149, 219, 226, 230
Eve, 164
evil, 73–76, 82–88, 95, 97, 129–130, 164, 198

face, xix, 10, 47, 63, 89, 220; and
  anthropocentrism, xvii, 196–201, 206–209,
  213, 228; as trace, x–xi, 30, 40–41, 52, 57–59,
  73, 145, 151–152, 189, 201, 206; vulnerability of,
  ix–x, 30, 95, 172–173, 209
Fackenheim, Emil, 135–136
Fagenblat, Michael, 154, 161, 231n6
femininity, xvi–xvii, 53, 57, 103, 155, 159–168,
  178–185, 216n72, 228
Fletcher, John, 24, 25, 35n13
freedom, xvi, 25, 103, 124, 126n12, 127n47, 154,
  168–169, 171, 179, 219–222; as the defining
  character of subjectivity, xiii, 13–15, 29, 34,
  51–53, 74–80, 112–115, 129–137, 140–149,
  209–210; versus determinism, 1, 8, 53, 74, 114,
  120, 130, 192, 221
Freud, Sigmund, 19, 21–25, 32–34, 35n13, 36n14,
  36n29, 56, 61, 189–190, 214n5

Gadamer, Hans-Georg, 57
Gibbs, Robert, 2, 37n51, 126n6, 127n14, 221–222,
  229
God, 11–12, 66, 101–102, 160, 164, 168, 176–177,
  190, 195, 223–224; and messianism, 92–95;
  and theodicy, 75–76, 82–86; in *Oedipus*,
  101–102, 106–113, 122, 124–125
"Greek" thought, xv, xviii, 40–42, 49, 67, 73, 77,
  79, 86, 101–105, 108, 113, 121, 123–125, 126n6,
  148, 226, 227, 229
Grossman, Vasily, 96–97, 99n57, 225
Guenther, Lisa, 142, 155, 167, 179–180, 182,
  185n63, 185n65, 202

Harshav, Barbara, 85
Hegel, G. W. F., ix, xv, 11, 16, 42, 46, 53, 73–91, 96–97, 104, 131–132, 176–177, 224
Heidegger, Martin, xiv, 1, 3, 17n24, 46, 80, 115, 128n60, 184n44, 215n34, 224, 231n6; on death, 168–175; on time, 5–8, 14–16
height, 58–59, 71n58, 109. *See also* space/spatiality
Heldke, Lisa, 193–194
Herman, Judith, 26, 65–66
heteronomy, xiv, xvi–xvii, 21, 48, 53, 78, 97, 102, 140, 144–145, 149–152, 156, 159, 165, 181, 183, 187, 192, 202, 212, 221. *See also* autonomy; passivity
Hick, John, 97n9
history: and creatureliness, 103, 107, 117–119, 131, 134, 144–147, 150–156, 182, 213, 221–224; and survival, 89–91; as a discipline, xv, xvii, 10–13, 30, 40, 50–53, 61–62, 68–69, 73–80, 82–96, 98n36, 143, 202, 220; historical past, x, xiii, 41, 60–63, 66–67, 107, 134, 190–193, 210–213, 224–230. *See also* diachrony; immemorial past; memory; synchrony
Hitlerism, xvi, 60, 78–79, 129–130, 133–140, 144–147, 150, 152, 155–156, 220. *See also* anti-Semitism; race/racism
Hobbes, Thomas, 68, 103, 148, 160, 183n1, 187, 214n7
Holocaust. *See* Shoah
Homer, 105–106
Horowitz, Asher, 64
Husserl, Edmund, xiv, 1, 4–8, 12, 15–16, 43, 47–48, 56, 89, 104, 224
hyperbole, 46–47, 58

immemorial past: and responsibility, xi, xv, xviii, 1–2, 21, 29–30, 54–55, 62, 115–119, 182; resistance to representation, 13, 32, 37n46, 40, 44–45, 48, 54–55, 59, 97, 145, 154–155, 201–203, 219–223. *See also* diachrony; history; memory; synchrony
infinity: and freedom, 131–133; and responsibility, 28, 30, 41, 58, 65–66, 93, 96–97, 113–114, 123, 144, 154–155, 166; contrast with totality, ix–x, 4–5, 11–12, 14, 44, 48, 220–221, 226–228. *See also* totality
intentionality: and death, 168, 171; and time, 1–2, 5–7, 12–16, 29–32, 50–53, 73, 142–143, 174, 181, 220; as assimilation, 15, 20–21, 31–32, 43–44, 56–59, 80–81, 98n21, 102–104, 137–138, 152, 155; disruption by alterity, 6, 14, 20, 27–34, 40–44, 47–48, 63, 66, 68, 88, 208, 223. *See also* consciousness

Irenaeus, 75–76, 79
Irigaray, Luce, 164, 166–167

Judaism, xviii, 41, 61, 66, 86–87, 94–95, 126n6, 131, 161, 225
justice, 193, 210, 228–230; and the messianic, 74, 82, 87, 91–96, 223; contrast with ethics, 15, 34, 44, 53–54, 60, 63–64, 69, 119–125, 151–154, 156, 173, 179–182, 212, 221; Levinas's silence about, xv, 39, 63–69, 125

Kahn, Paul, 109
Kant, Immanuel, xiv, 1–2, 9–14, 16, 131, 149, 168, 191–192, 198
Katz, Claire, 178–180, 185n57
Kavka, Martin, 93
Keats, John, 76
Kierkegaard, Søren, 225
knowledge, 162, 180, 200, 207–208, 215n36, 220, 226–227; and trauma, 20, 25–26; as assimilation, 7, 10–11, 14–15, 20, 22, 29, 50–52, 90–91, 102–111, 123–126, 153, 190; limits of, 102–111, 168, 177; moral, xix, 148
Knox, Bernard, 106
Kojéve, Alexander, 170
Kosky, Jeffrey, 13

LaCapra, Dominick, 56, 60
Ladd, Anna Coleman, ix–xi
Laplanche, Jean, 26–27, 33
Lawlor, Leonard, 47–48
Levi, Primo, 136
Levinas, Emmanuel: "Beyond Memory," 61, 97; "Diachrony and Representation," 10–12; "Dying For . . . ," 69–175; *Existence and Existents*, 3, 5, 8, 13; *God, Death, and Time*, 8–9, 89, 168–177; "Hommage à Bergson," 4; "The Name of a Dog, or Natural Rights," 194–199; *Otherwise than Being, or Beyond Essence*, 19–22, 28, 39–44, 47–55, 58–61, 71n58, 79, 92–93, 104, 123, 137–145, 154–156, 178, 181; "The Paradox of Morality," 189–200; "Peace and Proximity," 88–89; "Some Thoughts on the Philosophy of Hitlerism," xvi, 78, 129–158, 220; "Substitution," 21–22; *Totality and Infinity*, 41–42, 45–46, 51, 54–55, 58–59, 90–92, 96, 104, 158n46, 166–167, 171, 178, 215n36; "Transcendence and Height," 58–59; "The Understanding of Spirituality in French and German Culture," 22; "Useless Suffering," 13, 60, 80–89, 96, 137
Leys, Ruth, 33, 35nn12–13, 36n14, 36n29

liberalism, xvi, 103, 114, 129–137, 139–140, 144–150, 155–156
Lin, Yael, 7–8, 29, 40, 103–104
Lingis, Alphonso, 137
Llewelyn, John, 20, 69n10, 189–190, 199, 209, 213, 214n12, 214n24
Locke, John, 52, 68, 138, 149

MacAvoy, Leslie, 48
MacDonald, Michael J., 50
MacIntyre, Alasdair, 87
Maimonides, 93
Marx, Karl, 127n46, 173, 193, 214n25
maternity, xvi–xvii, 58, 139, 155, 159–160, 163–167, 176–185, 213
McDowell, John, 205
McIntosh, Peggy, 117
memory, 2, 4, 108, 131, 140, 143, 151–152, 163, 197; and synchrony, xv, 6–7, 10–15, 50, 52–56, 80, 89, 220–221; disruptions related to trauma, 23–33, 35n13, 56, 59–69, 155. *See also* diachrony; history; immemorial past; narrative; synchrony
Merleau-Ponty, Maurice, 37n46, 152
Meskin, Jacob, 141
messianism, 11, 74, 91–97, 98n41, 99n52, 123, 166, 223
metaphor, 2, 6–7, 28–29, 57–58, 134, 138, 143, 190, 201
Mills, Charles, 149
moral considerability, 188–191, 198, 201–213, 214n26, 216n81
moral luck, 112–113
Morgan, Michael, 14
Moyn, Samuel, 66–67, 121, 225

Nagel, Thomas, 112
narrative, 11–12, 111, 119, 177, 230; and synchrony, xii–xvi, 8, 39, 50–57, 107, 131, 145–146, 152–154, 174, 220–224; and theodicy, 82–92, 97; and trauma, 2, 15, 19–20, 23–27, 39, 53–57, 65–69, 101, 107, 123–125, 158n46, 221–222, 227; historical, 61–63, 73–79, 89–92, 224. *See also* diachrony; immemorial past; memory; synchrony
Nemo, Philippe, x, 88
Nietzsche, Friedrich, 52, 55, 66; on the Stoics, 160, 187–188, 211; on suffering, 82–83; will to knowledge, 50
normativity, xi, xviii, 44, 63–64, 66–67, 87, 118–120, 188, 204–208

Odysseus, 104–105
Oedipus Tyrannos, xv–xvi, 101–117, 119–126, 147, 154, 215n36

Parmenides, 3, 12–13
Pascal, Blaise de, 27–28, 224
passivity: and embodiment, 23–25, 81–83, 210; and responsibility, 28–29, 46–47, 51–52, 58–59, 74, 114–115, 132–150, 154–156, 171–173, 176–177, 182–183, 230; and time, 2, 4–5, 12–16, 19–21, 77–78, 105–106, 168–169, 171–173, 220–222. *See also* heteronomy
paternity, 68, 103–104, 163–166, 175, 182
Pecora, Vincent, 146–147
Peperzak, Adriaan, 69n16, 151
Perpich, Diane, 46, 49, 51, 57–58, 64, 153, 179, 196–198, 200, 207–208, 210
phenomenology, xiv, 3–9, 15, 41–43, 47–49, 56–58, 70n16, 71n52, 80, 87, 113, 212, 224–225. *See also* Heidegger, Martin; Husserl, Edmund; Merleau-Ponty, Maurice
philosophy, 11, 15–16, 62–65, 73, 75–78, 98n20, 129, 170, 202–208, 211; and betrayal, x, xv, 34–35, 39–51, 57–59, 125, 219–230; as a "Greek" endeavor, 41–42, 49, 102–104, 126n6, 148, 190–191; Levinas's critique of dominant concepts in, xiii–xviii, 3, 34, 48–49, 62, 83–84, 136–137, 162–164, 167–168, 171–175, 180–181, 189–190, 192, 212–213. *See also* "Greek" thought
Plant, Bob, 198
Plato: appropriation of maternity, 180–181; on beyond being, 224; on death, 162–164, 170, 177, 183n11; on embodiment, 132; as exemplar of Greek philosophy, 10, 41–42, 89, 104
Pogge, Thomas, 118
post-traumatic stress disorder, xiii–xiv, 23, 25–27, 36n24
Providence, 74–75
proximity, 22, 27–30, 34, 40, 43–46, 49, 52–55, 58–62, 68, 84, 127n47, 138–144, 148, 151–154, 179, 191, 206, 224–228

Rabelais, François, 190
race/racism, xvi, 64, 116–117, 130, 133–136, 145–152, 156, 157n25, 159, 165, 219
Raffoul, François, 48
redemption, 1, 11–12, 66, 78–79, 82, 94–96, 131
respiration, 42, 142–143
responsibility, 44–69, 85, 87, 89–90, 92–97, 129–131, 150–156, 169–176, 178–183, 185n57,

187–189, 192–193, 195–204, 208–213; and diachrony, x–xix, 6–7, 14–16, 20–21, 50–54, 93, 97, 219–230; and intention, xv–xvi, 46–47, 90, 101–104, 109–126, 127n48, 152–153; as trauma, xii–xiv, 1–2, 15–16, 19–22, 28–35, 39–42, 50–52, 92–93, 113–115, 118–119, 137–145, 161, 179
rhetoric, xiii, xv, 20, 29, 39–51, 57–67, 70n25, 98n34, 121, 126n6, 224
Ricoeur, Paul, 46–47
Rolland, Jacques, 162–163, 167–168, 177, 224
Rosenzweig, Franz, ix, xiv, 1, 11–12, 14, 16, 17n32, 17n35, 66, 79, 93, 126n7, 162, 167–168

Sachs, Carl, 85
sacrifice, xv, 74–76, 83–87, 104, 107, 111, 144, 159–160, 166, 178–180, 191, 203–207, 213
said, the, 15, 39–45, 47, 49–54, 63, 120, 152, 227–229
Sands, Kathleen, 123–124
Santner, Eric, 61, 71n64
saying, xv, 20, 39–51, 61–63, 137, 199–201, 207–210, 224–229
Scarry, Elaine, 81
Scheman, Naomi, 147
Segal, Charles, 108
Severson, Eric, 6, 53–54
Shakespeare, William, 94, 225
Shoah, 60–62, 84–87, 146–147, 194–195, 229–230
sincerity, 134, 137–139
Singer, Peter, 205
singularity, 44, 62–67, 94–95, 144–156, 172, 198, 203–206, 209; and comprehension, ix–x, xv, 48, 63, 73–74, 79, 84, 88, 90, 102–103, 139, 148–154, 206, 222–223, 228
skepticism, 45, 84, 104, 133–135, 144, 160, 208–209, 220, 223–224
skin, 30, 49, 138–139, 140–143, 179, 201
Smith, Michael, 85
Sophocles, xv–xvi, 102–113, 121–125. See also *Antigone*; *Oedipus Tyrannos*
space/spatiality, 1, 3–4, 8–9, 21, 28–29, 58–59, 92, 142–144, 152, 223

Spinoza, Baruch, 27–28, 225
synchrony, xvii–xviii, 45, 50–53, 73, 77, 80–83, 89, 108, 121, 140, 170, 174; as assimilation, 12–13, 19–21, 50, 92, 102, 143–144, 152, 219–221; opposed to diachrony, xii, 2–16, 29–31, 40–42, 174. *See also* diachrony

Tennyson, Alfred, 160
theodicy, 73–89, 93–97, 125
time: deformalization of, xiv, 1–16, 19–21, 34–35; ethical significance of, 13–16, 27–34; formal conceptions of, 2–3, 9–11, 19
totality, xv, 2, 40–44, 53, 67, 73–74, 79–80, 86–92, 102, 126n6, 148, 151, 158n46, 162, 199, 222–224; contrast with infinity, ix–x, 4–5, 11–12, 14, 44, 48, 91–92, 220–221, 226–228; link to totalitarianism, 96–97. *See also* infinity
trace, x–xi, xiii, 24, 28, 30–32, 35, 39–49, 58–59, 117, 155, 168, 201, 206, 226–227
tragedy, xvii–xviii, 51, 54, 78, 102, 108–110, 117, 123–124
trauma, x, 41–63, 70n35, 71n61, 83–85, 93–96, 101–102, 116–126, 155, 161, 174–177, 179, 188–189, 197–203, 208–209, 224–230; as psychological disorder, xiii, 23–27, 31–37, 60–63, 65–67; Levinas's references to, xii–xvi, 15–16, 19–21, 27–35, 54–55, 60–63, 113; temporal elements, xv, 19–21, 24–25, 27–29, 50–55, 220. *See also* post-traumatic stress disorder

Vernant, Jean-Pierre, 106, 110–111

Walker, Margaret Urban, 112–113
Weber, Elisabeth, 55
Williams, Bernard, 106
Wittgenstein, Ludwig, 206–207
Wollstonecraft, Mary, 165–166
working-through, 56, 61, 65
World War I, ix–xii, 23, 60

Zeus, 4, 8, 76, 103

CYNTHIA D. COE is Professor of Philosophy at Central Washington University. She is coauthor (with Matthew C. Altman) of *The Fractured Self in Freud and German Philosophy* and the author of numerous articles on Levinas and contemporary Continental ethics.

www.ingramcontent.com/pod-product-compliance
Lightning Source LLC
Chambersburg PA
CBHW030613230426
43661CB00053B/1959